Acclaim for Sarah B~~~~

HOW TO L

"A delightful conversation across the centuries.

—PATRICIA COHEN, *New York Times*

"[Bakewell's] deceptively breezy survey of Montaigne's life, writing, and legacy is serious, engaging, and so infectiously in love with its subject . . . It is hard to imagine a better introduction—or reintroduction—to Montaigne than Bakewell's book."

—LORIN STEIN, *Harper's*

"[A] charming biography . . . [it captures] the wry, curious human spirit of one who wrote like a 'naturalist on a field trip into the human soul.'"

—*New Yorker*

"Lively and fascinating . . . *How to Live* takes its place as the most enjoyable introduction to Montaigne in the English language."

—TIMOTHY CHESTERS, *Times Literary Supplement*

"A brilliant and unconventional biography, *How to Live* captures the essence of one of history's most acute, expansive, and charming thinkers . . . [Bakewell's] book is a sophisticated mini-history of philosophy, but it reads like a late-night talk with a friend." —KATHRYN SCHULZ, *Boston Globe*

"Excellent . . . *How to Live* touches on every aspect of Montaigne's thought, life, and influence."

—MICHAEL DIRDA, *Washington Post*

"Historical biography, literary essay, witty self-help guide: Bakewell wrapped up many genres into a package to savor. Montaigne himself would have loved this radiant tribute to his happy skepticism." —*The Independent*

"An engaging introduction to the life and thought of Michel de Montaigne, and a pleasure to read . . . [Bakewell] is an excellent guide for the first-time readers of the *Essays* today."
—MARK LILLA, *The New York Review of Books*

"So artful is Bakewell's account . . . that even skeptical readers may well come to share her admiration."
—ANTHONY GOTTLIEB, *New York Times Book Review*

"Bakewell's book is so sincerely engaged with the question of how best to muddle through life that it takes a chapter or two to remember that what you're actually reading is a biography of the great French essayist Michel Eyquem de Montaigne . . . In sum, this book, like its subject, is expansive, genre-defying, and preposterously smart . . . Bakewell pulls off a kind of literary time-lapse photography, compressing a vast amount of history into a swift and enlightening narrative." —*The Los Angeles Review of Books*

"Superb . . . [*How to Live*] not only takes a long-dead Frenchman and brings him back to life. It then beautifully relates how Montaigne's philosophy can shape and affect our own lives today."
—EVAN NEWMARK, *Wall Street Journal.com*

"My book of the year is Sarah Bakewell's *How To Live*, a jewel of a book and a perfect introduction to the great Renaissance writer, whose 'essais' are a constant inspiration, source of entertainment, and practical philosophy for life." —ORLANDO FIGES, *The Telegraph*

"A charming biography of the French thinker."
—MARJORIE KEHE, *Christian Science Monitor*

"An affectionate introduction to the author . . . Bakewell is a wry and intelligent guide." —EMILY STOKES, *Daily Beast*

"Montaigne preferred biographers who tried to 'reconstruct a person's inner world from the evidence.' Bakewell honors that perspective by closely examining his writings as well as the context in which they were created, revealing one of literature's enduring figures as an idiosyncratic, humane, and surprisingly modern force." —*Publishers Weekly* (starred)

"By the end of the book, readers will have a good sense of the sweep of [Montaigne's] life and times and writing . . . A bright, genial, and generous introduction to the master's methods." —*Kirkus Reviews*

"With this splendidly conceived and exquisitely written double biography— of both Montaigne the man and "Montaigne" the book—Sarah Bakewell should persuade another generation to fall in love . . . enormously absorbing." —JAMES MCCONNACHIE, *Sunday Times* (UK)

"This is a rich book, both because of its subject and because Bakewell has a wondrous way with words." —*Library Journal* (starred)

"[*How to Live*] has the narrative pace and drive of a novel, perhaps because at its core a life is at stake. Whether it is Montaigne's or Bakewell's or the reader's is impossible to say, but that is the magnificent achievement of this beguiling book." —PATRICIA HAMPL, *Barnes & Noble Review.com*

"Suavely enlightening . . . Montaigne is, with Walt Whitman, among the most congenial of literary giants, inclined to shrug over the inevitability of human failings and the last man to accuse anyone of self-absorption. His great subject, after all, was himself . . . Bakewell, who dances from philosophy to history to biography with enviable ease, also has a gift for literary criticism." —LAURA MILLER, *Salon.com*

"Extraordinary . . . The book is a miracle of complex, revelatory organiza-tion, for as Bakewell moves along she provides a brilliant demonstration of the alchemy of historical viewpoint. She explains in her witty, genial tone exactly what Montaigne's readers found in the *Essays* and how and why that changed from age to age." —KATHERINE A. POWERS, *Boston Globe*

"Bakewell tells Montaigne's story in an admirably brisk and entertaining fashion . . . An excellent introduction to a writer whose influence is strongly felt today, and will be for some time to come."

—REBECCA HUSSEY, *The Quarterly Conversation*

"Sarah Bakewell brings Montaigne to life . . . Her vivid descriptions and deep knowledge of Montaigne and the political atmosphere of France during his time will have readers wanting to meet the man himself, and share their thoughts with him . . . *How to Live* is a great companion to Montaigne's essays, and even a great stand-alone."

—ROBYN OXBORROW, *San Francisco Book Review*

"Like recent books on Proust, Joyce, and Austen, *How to Live* skillfully plucks a life-guide from the incessant flux of Montaigne's prose . . . a superb, spirited introduction to the master." —ADAM THORPE, *The Guardian*

"Because Montaigne's capacious mirror still captivates many, this insightful life study will win high praise." —*Booklist* (starred)

"This subtle and surprising book manages the trick of conversing in a frank and friendly manner with its centuries-old literary giant, as with a con-temporary, while helpfully placing Montaigne in a historical context. The affection of the author for her subject is palpable and infectious."

—PHILLIP LOPATE, author of *The Art of the Personal Essay*

HOW TO LIVE

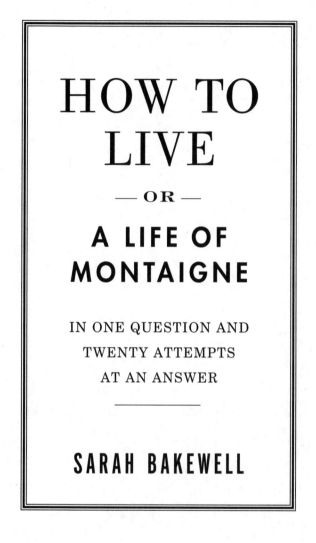

HOW TO LIVE

LIVE

— OR —

A LIFE OF MONTAIGNE

IN ONE QUESTION AND
TWENTY ATTEMPTS
AT AN ANSWER

SARAH BAKEWELL

OTHER PRESS
NEW YORK

Other Press edition 2010
First softcover printing 2011
ISBN 978-1-59051-483-2

Production Editor: Yvonne E. Cárdenas

Typeset by SX Composing DTP, Rayleigh, Essex, Great Britain

20 19

LIBRARY OF CONGRESS CATALOGING-IN-PUBLICATION DATA

Bakewell, Sarah.
How to live, or, A life of Montaigne in one question and twenty attempts
at an answer / Sarah Bakewell. — Other Press ed.
p. cm.
Originally published: London : Chatto & Windus, 2010.
Includes bibliographical references and index.
ISBN 978-1-59051-425-2 (hardcover) — ISBN 978-1-59051-426-9 (e-book)
1. Montaigne, Michel de, 1533-1592.   2. Montaigne, Michel de, 1533-1592—
Philosophy.   3. Authors, French—16th century—Biography. I. Title.   II.
Title: How to live.   III. Title: Life of Montaigne in one
question and twenty attempts at an answer.
PQ1643.B34 2010B
848.3—dc22   2010026896
[B]

For Simo

CONTENTS

Q. How to live?

THE TWENTY-FIRST CENTURY is full of people who are full of themselves. A half-hour's trawl through the online ocean of blogs, tweets, tubes, spaces, faces, pages, and pods brings up thousands of individuals fascinated by their own personalities and shouting for attention. They go on about themselves; they diarize, and chat, and upload photographs of everything they do. Uninhibitedly extrovert, they also look inward as never before. Even as bloggers and networkers delve into their private experience, they communicate with their fellow humans in a shared festival of the self.

Some optimists have tried to make this global meeting of minds the basis for a new approach to international relations. The historian Theodore Zeldin has founded a site called "The Oxford Muse," which encourages people to put together brief self-portraits in words, describing their everyday lives and the things they have learned. They upload these for other people to read and respond to. For Zeldin, shared self-revelation is the best way to develop trust and cooperation around the planet, replacing national stereotypes with real people. The great adventure of our epoch, he says, is "to discover who inhabits the world, one individual at a time." The "Oxford Muse" is thus full of personal essays or interviews with titles like:

Why an educated Russian works as a cleaner in Oxford
Why being a hairdresser satisfies the need for perfection
How writing a self-portrait shows you are not who you thought you
    were
What you can discover if you do not drink or dance
What a person adds when writing about himself to what he says in
    conversation

How to be successful and lazy at the same time
How a chef expresses his kindness

By describing what makes them different from *anyone* else, the contributors reveal what they share with *everyone* else: the experience of being human.

This idea—writing about oneself to create a mirror in which other people recognize their own humanity—has not existed forever. It had to be invented. And, unlike many cultural inventions, it can be traced to a single person: Michel Eyquem de Montaigne, a nobleman, government official, and winegrower who lived in the Périgord area of southwestern France from 1533 to 1592.

Montaigne created the idea simply by doing it. Unlike most memoirists of his day, he did not write to record his own great deeds and achievements. Nor did he lay down a straight eyewitness account of historical events, although he could have done; he lived through a religious civil war which almost destroyed his country over the decades he spent incubating and writing his book. A member of a generation robbed of the hopeful idealism enjoyed by his father's contemporaries, he adjusted to public miseries by focusing his attention on private life. He weathered the disorder, oversaw his estate, assessed court cases as a magistrate, and administered Bordeaux as the most easygoing mayor in its history. All the time, he wrote exploratory, free-floating pieces to which he gave simple titles:

Of Friendship
Of Cannibals
Of the Custom of Wearing Clothes
How we cry and laugh for the same thing
Of Names
Of Smells
Of Cruelty
Of Thumbs
How our mind hinders itself
Of Diversion
Of Coaches
Of Experience

Altogether, he wrote a hundred and seven such essays. Some occupy a page or two; others are much longer, so that most recent editions of the complete collection run to over a thousand pages. They rarely offer to explain or teach anything. Montaigne presents himself as someone who jotted down

whatever was going through his head when he picked up his pen, capturing encounters and states of mind as they happened. He used these experiences as the basis for asking himself questions, above all the big question that fascinated him as it did many of his contemporaries. Although it is not quite grammatical in English, it can be phrased in three simple words: "How to live?"

This is not the same as the ethical question, "How *should* one live?" Moral dilemmas interested Montaigne, but he was less interested in what people ought to do than in what they actually did. He wanted to know how to live a good life—meaning a correct or honorable life, but also a fully human, satisfying, flourishing one. This question drove him both to write and to read, for he was curious about all human lives, past and present. He wondered constantly about the emotions and motives behind what people did. And since he was the example closest to hand of a human going about its business, he wondered just as much about himself.

A down-to-earth question, "How to live?" splintered into a myriad other pragmatic questions. Like everyone else, Montaigne ran up against the major perplexities of existence: how to cope with the fear of death, how to get over losing a child or a beloved friend, how to reconcile yourself to failures, how to make the most of every moment so that life does not drain away unappreciated. But there were smaller puzzles, too. How do you avoid getting drawn into a pointless argument with your wife, or a servant? How can you reassure a friend who thinks a witch has cast a spell on him? How do you cheer up a weeping neighbor? How do you guard your home? What is the best strategy if you are held up by armed robbers who seem to be uncertain whether to kill you or hold you to ransom? If you overhear your daughter's governess teaching her something you think is wrong, is it wise to intervene? How do you deal with a bully? What do you say to your dog when he wants to go out and play, while you want to stay at your desk writing your book?

In place of abstract answers, Montaigne tells us what *he* did in each case, and what it felt like when he was doing it. He provides all the details we need to make it real, and sometimes more than we need. He tells us, for no particular reason, that the only fruit he likes is melon, that he prefers to have sex lying down rather than standing up, that he cannot sing, and that he loves vivacious company and often gets carried away by the spark of repartee. But he also describes sensations that are harder to capture in words, or even to be aware of: what it feels like to be lazy, or courageous, or indecisive; or to indulge a moment of vanity, or to try to shake off an obsessive fear. He even writes about the sheer feeling of being alive.

Exploring such phenomena over twenty years, Montaigne questioned himself again and again, and built up a picture of himself—a self-portrait in constant motion, so vivid that it practically gets up off the page and sits down next to you to read over your shoulder. He can say surprising things: a lot has changed since Montaigne was born, almost half a millennium ago, and neither manners nor beliefs are always still recognizable. Yet to read Montaigne is to experience a series of shocks of familiarity, which make the centuries between him and the twenty-first-century reader collapse to nothing. Readers keep seeing themselves in him, just as visitors to the "Oxford Muse" see themselves, or aspects of themselves, in the story of why an educated Russian works as a cleaner or of what it is like to prefer not to dance.

The journalist Bernard Levin, writing an article on the subject for *The*

Times in 1991, said, "I defy any reader of Montaigne not to put down the book at some point and say with incredulity: 'How did he know all that about me?'" The answer is, of course, that he knows it by knowing about himself. In turn, people understand him because they too already know "all that" about their own experience. As one of his most obsessive early readers, Blaise Pascal, wrote in the seventeenth century: "It is not in Montaigne but in myself that I find everything I see there."

The novelist Virginia Woolf imagined people walking past Montaigne's self-portrait like visitors in a gallery. As each person passes, he or she pauses in front of the picture and leans forward to peer through the patterns of reflection on the glass. "There is always a crowd before that picture, gazing into its depths, seeing their own faces reflected in it, seeing more the longer they look, never being able to say quite what it is they see." The portrait's face and their own merge into one. This, for Woolf, was the way people respond to each other in general:

> As we face each other in omnibuses and underground railways we are looking into the mirror . . . And the novelists in future will realize more and more the importance of these reflections, for of course there is not one reflection but an almost infinite number; those are the depths they will explore, those the phantoms they will pursue.

Montaigne was the first writer to create literature that deliberately worked in this way, and to do it using the plentiful material of his own life rather than either pure philosophy or pure invention. He was the most human of writers, and the most sociable. Had he lived in the era of mass networked communication, he would have been astounded at the scale on which such sociability has become possible: not dozens or hundreds in a gallery, but millions of people seeing themselves bounced back from different angles.

The effect, in Montaigne's time as in our own, can be intoxicating. A sixteenth-century admirer, Tabourot des Accords, said that anyone reading the *Essays* felt as if they themselves had written it. Over two hundred and fifty years later, the essayist Ralph Waldo Emerson said the same thing in almost the same phrase. "It seemed to me as if I had myself written the book, in some former life." "So much have I made him my own," wrote the twentieth-century novelist André Gide, "that it seems he is my very self." And Stefan Zweig, an Austrian writer on the verge of suicide after being forced into exile during the Second World War, found in Montaigne his only real friend: "Here is a 'you' in which my 'I' is reflected; here is where all distance is abolished." The printed page fades from view; a living person steps into the room instead. "Four hundred years disappear like smoke."

Enthusiastic buyers on the online bookstore Amazon.com still respond in the same way. One calls the *Essays* "not so much a book as a companion for life," and another predicts that it will be "the best friend you've ever had." A reader who keeps a copy always on the bedside table laments the fact that it is too big (in its complete version) to carry around all day too. "There's a lifetime's reading in here," says another. "For such a big fat classic of a book it reads like it was written yesterday, although if it *had* been written yesterday, he'd've been all over *Hello!* magazine by now."

All this can happen because the *Essays* has no great meaning, no point to make, no argument to advance. It does not have designs on you; you can do as you please with it. Montaigne lets his material pour out, and never worries if he has said one thing on one page and the opposite overleaf, or even in the next sentence. He could have taken as his motto Walt Whitman's lines:

> Do I contradict myself?
> Very well then I contradict myself,
> (I am large, I contain multitudes.)

Every few phrases, a new way of looking at things occurs to him, so he changes direction. Even when his thoughts are most irrational and dream-like, his writing follows them. "I cannot keep my subject still," he says. "It goes along befuddled and staggering, with a natural drunkenness." Anyone is free to go with him as far as seems desirable, and let him meander off by himself if it doesn't. Sooner or later, your paths will cross again.

Having created a new genre by writing in this way, Montaigne created *essais*: his new term for it. Today, the word *essay* falls with a dull thud. It reminds many people of the exercises imposed at school or college to test knowledge of the reading list: reworkings of other writers' arguments with a boring introduction and a facile conclusion stuck into each end like two forks in a corncob. Discourses of that sort existed in Montaigne's day, but *essais* did not. *Essayer*, in French, means simply *to try*. To essay something is to test or taste it, or give it a whirl. One seventeenth-century Montaignist defined it as firing a pistol to see if it shoots straight, or trying out a horse to see if it handles well. On the whole, Montaigne discovered that the pistol shot all over the place and the horse galloped out of control, but this did not bother him. He was delighted to see his work come out so unpredictably.

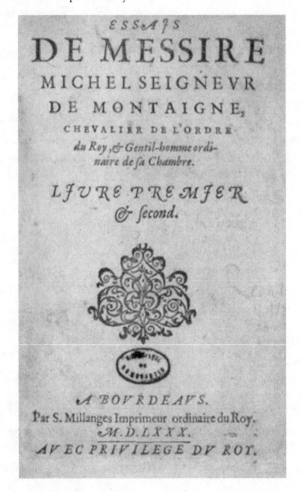

He may never have planned to create a one-man literary revolution, but in retrospect he knew what he had done. "It is the only book in the world of its kind," he wrote, "a book with a wild and eccentric plan." Or, as more often seemed the case, with no plan at all. The *Essays* was not written in neat order, from beginning to end. It grew by slow encrustation, like a coral reef, from 1572 to 1592. The only thing that eventually stopped it was Montaigne's death.

Looked at another way, it never stopped at all. It continued to grow, not through endless writing but through endless reading. From the first sixteenth-century neighbor or friend to browse through a draft from Montaigne's desk to the very last human being (or other conscious entity) to extract it from the memory banks of a future virtual library, every new reading means a new *Essays*. Readers approach him from their private perspectives, contributing their own experience of life. At the same time, these experiences are molded by broad trends, which come and go in leisurely formation. Anyone looking over four hundred and thirty years of Montaigne-reading can see these trends building up and dissolving like clouds in a sky, or crowds on a railway platform between commuter trains. Each way of reading seems natural while it is on the scene; then a new style comes in and the old one departs, sometimes becoming so outmoded that it is barely comprehensible to anyone but historians.

The *Essays* is thus much more than a book. It is a centuries-long conversation between Montaigne and all those who have got to know him: a conversation which changes through history, while starting out afresh almost every time with that cry of "How did he know all that about me?" Mostly it remains a two-person encounter between writer and reader. But sidelong chat goes on among the readers too; consciously or not, each generation approaches Montaigne with expectations derived from its contemporaries and predecessors. As the story goes on, the scene becomes more crowded. It turns from a private dinner party to a great lively banquet, with Montaigne as an unwitting master of ceremonies.

This book is about Montaigne, the man and writer. It is also about Montaigne, the long party—that accumulation of shared and private conversations over four hundred and thirty years. The ride will be a strange and bumpy one, for Montaigne's book has not slid smoothly through time like a pebble in a stream, becoming ever more streamlined and polished as it goes. It has tumbled about in no set direction, picking up debris, sometimes snagging on awkward outcrops. My story rolls with the current too. It goes "befuddled and staggering," with frequent changes of tack. At first, it sticks more closely to the man himself: Montaigne's life, personality, and literary career. Later, it diverges ever further into tales of his book and his readers, all the way up to very recent ones. Since it is a twenty-first-century book, it is inevitably pervaded by a twenty-first-century Montaigne. As one of his favorite adages had it, there is no escaping our perspective: we can walk only on our own legs, and sit only on our own bum.

Most of those who come to the *Essays* want something from it. They may be seeking entertainment, or enlightenment, or historical understanding, or something more personal. As the novelist Gustave Flaubert advised a friend who was wondering how to approach Montaigne:

Don't read him as children do, for amusement, nor as the ambitious do, to be instructed. No, read him *in order to live.*

Impressed by Flaubert's command, I am taking the Renaissance question "How to live?" as a guide-rope for finding a way through the tangle of Montaigne's life and afterlife. The question remains the same throughout, but the chapters take the form of twenty different answers—each an answer that Montaigne might be imagined as having given. In reality, he usually responded to questions with flurries of further questions and a profusion of anecdotes, often all pointing in different directions and leading to contradictory conclusions. The questions and stories *were* his answers, or further ways of trying the question out.

Similarly, each of the twenty possible answers in this book will take the form of something anecdotal: an episode or theme from Montaigne's life, or from the lives of his readers. There will be no neat solutions, but these twenty "essays" at an answer will allow us to eavesdrop on snippets of the long conversation, and to enjoy the company of Montaigne himself—most genial of interlocutors and hosts.

1. Q. How to live? A. Don't worry about death

HANGING BY THE TIP OF HIS LIPS

MONTAIGNE WAS NOT always a natural at social gatherings. From time to time, in youth, while his friends were dancing, laughing, and drinking, he would sit apart under a cloud. His companions barely recognized him on these occasions; they were more used to seeing him flirting with women, or animatedly debating a new idea that had struck him. They would wonder whether he had taken offense at something they had said. In truth, as he confided later in his *Essays*, when he was in this mood he was barely aware of his surroundings at all. Amid the festivities, he was thinking about some frightening true tale he had recently heard—perhaps one about a young man who, having left a similar feast a few days earlier complaining of a touch of mild fever, had died of that fever almost

before his fellow party-goers had got over their hangovers. If death could play such tricks, then only the flimsiest membrane separated Montaigne himself from the void at every moment. He became so afraid of losing his life that he could no longer enjoy it while he had it.

In his twenties, Montaigne suffered this morbid obsession because he had spent too much time reading classical philosophers. Death was a topic of which the ancients never tired. Cicero summed up their principle neatly: "To philosophize is to learn how to die." Montaigne himself would one day borrow this dire thought for a chapter title.

But if his problems began with a surfeit of philosophy at an impressionable age, they did not end just because he grew up. As he reached his thirties, when he might have been expected to gain a more measured perspective, Montaigne's sense of the oppressive proximity of death became stronger than ever, and more personal. Death turned from an abstraction into a reality, and began scything its way through almost everyone he cared about, getting closer to himself. When he was thirty, in 1563, his best friend Étienne de La Boétie was killed by the plague. In 1568, his father died, probably of complications following a kidney-stone attack. In the spring of the following year, Montaigne lost his younger brother Arnaud de Saint-Martin to a freak sporting accident. He himself had just got married then; the first baby of this marriage would live to the age of two months, dying in August 1570. Montaigne went on to lose four more children: of six, only one survived to become an adult. This series of bereavements made death less nebulous as a threat, but it was hardly reassuring. His fears were as strong as ever.

The most painful loss was apparently that of La Boétie; Montaigne loved him more than anyone. But the most shocking must have been that of his brother Arnaud. At just twenty-seven, Arnaud was struck on the head by a ball while playing the contemporary version of tennis, the *jeu de paume*. It cannot have been a very forceful blow, and he showed no immediate effect, but five or six hours later he lost consciousness and died, presumably from a clot or hemorrhage. No one would have expected a simple knock on the head to cut off the life of a healthy man. It made no sense, and was even more personally threatening than the story of the young man who had died of fever. "With such frequent and ordinary examples passing before our eyes," wrote Montaigne of Arnaud, "how can we possibly rid ourselves of the thought of death and of the idea that at every moment it is gripping us by the throat?"

Rid himself of this thought he could not; nor did he even want to. He was still under the sway of his philosophers. "Let us have nothing on our minds as often as death," he wrote in an early essay on the subject:

At every moment let us picture it in our imagination in all its aspects. At the stumbling of a horse, the fall of a tile, the slightest pin prick, let us promptly chew on this: Well, what if it were death itself?

If you ran through the images of your death often enough, said his favorite sages, the Stoics, it could never catch you by surprise. Knowing how well prepared you were, you should be freed to live without fear. But Montaigne found the opposite. The more intensely he imagined the accidents that might befall him and his friends, the less calm he felt. Even if he managed, fleetingly, to accept the idea in the abstract, he could never accommodate it in detail. His mind filled with visions of injuries and fevers; or of people weeping at his deathbed, and perhaps the "touch of a well-known hand" laid on his brow to bid him farewell. He imagined the world closing around the hole where he had been: his possessions being gathered up, and his clothes distributed among friends and servants. These thoughts did not free him; they imprisoned him.

Fortunately, this constriction did not last. By his forties and fifties, Montaigne was liberated into light-heartedness. He was able to write the most fluid and life-loving of his essays, and he showed almost no remaining sign of his earlier morbid state of mind. We only know that it ever existed because his book tells us about it. He now refused to worry about anything. Death is only a few bad moments at the end of life, he wrote in one of his last added notes; it is not worth wasting any anxiety over. From being the gloomiest among his acquaintances, he became the most carefree of middle-aged men, and a master of the art of living well. The cure lay in a journey to the heart of the problem: a dramatic encounter with his own death, followed by an extended midlife crisis which led him to the writing of his *Essays*.

The great meeting between Montaigne and death happened on a day some time in 1569 or early 1570—the exact period is uncertain—when he was out doing one of the things that usually dissipated his anxieties and gave him a feeling of escape: riding his horse.

He was about thirty-six at this time, and felt he had a lot to escape from. Following his father's death, he had inherited full responsibility for the family château and estate in the Dordogne. It was beautiful land, in an area covered, then as now, by vineyards, soft hills, villages, and tracts of forest. But for Montaigne it represented the burden of duty. On the estate, someone was always plucking at his sleeve, wanting something or finding fault with things he had done. He was the *seigneur*: everything came back to him.

Fortunately, it was not usually difficult to find an excuse to be somewhere else. As he had done since he was twenty-four, Montaigne worked as a magistrate in Bordeaux, the regional capital some thirty miles away—so there were always reasons to go there. Then there were the far-flung vineyards of the Montaigne property itself, scattered in separate parcels around the countryside for miles, and useful for visits if he felt so inclined. He also made occasional calls on the neighbors who lived in other châteaus of the area; it was important to stay on good terms. All these tasks formed excellent justifications for a ride through the woods on a sunny day.

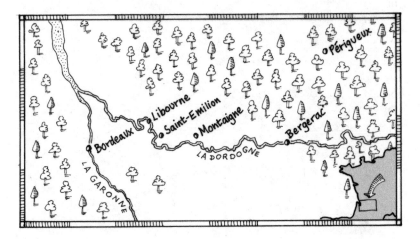

Out on the forest paths, Montaigne's thoughts could wander as widely as he wished, although even here he was invariably accompanied by servants and acquaintances. People rarely went around alone in the sixteenth century. But he could spur his horse away from boring conversations, or turn his mind aside in order to daydream, watching the light glinting in the canopy of trees over the forest path. Was it really true, he might wonder, that a man's semen came from the marrow of the spinal column, as Plato said? Could a remora fish really be so strong that it could hold back a whole ship just by fastening its lips on it and sucking? And what about the strange incident he had seen at home the other day, when his cat gazed intently into a tree until a bird fell out of it, dead, right between her paws? What power did she have? Such speculations were so absorbing that Montaigne sometimes forgot to pay full attention to the path and to what his companions were doing.

On this occasion, he was progressing calmly through the woods with a group of other mounted men, all or most of them his employees, some three or four miles from the château. It was an easy ride and he was expecting no trouble, so he had chosen a placid horse of no great strength. He was wearing ordinary clothes: breeches, a shirt, a doublet, probably a cloak. His sword was at his side—a nobleman never went anywhere without one—but he wore no armor or other special protection. Yet there were always dangers outside town or château walls: robbers were common, and France was presently suspended in a lawless state between two outbreaks of civil war. Groups of unemployed soldiers roamed the countryside, looking for any loot they could get in lieu of wages lost during the peace interlude. Despite his anxieties about death in general, Montaigne usually remained calm about such specific risks. He did not flinch from every suspicious stranger as others did, or jump out of his skin at hearing unidentified sounds in the woods. Yet the prevailing tension must have got to him too, for when a great weight slammed into him from behind, his first thought was that he had been attacked deliberately. It felt like a shot from an arquebus, the rifle-like firearm of the day.

He had no time to wonder *why* anyone should fire a weapon at him. The thing struck him "like a thunderbolt": his horse was knocked down, and Montaigne himself went flying. He hit the ground hard, meters away, and instantly lost consciousness.

There lay the horse bowled over and stunned, and I ten or twelve paces beyond, dead, stretched on my back, my face all bruised and skinned, my sword, which I had had in my hand, more than ten paces away, my belt in pieces, having no more motion or feeling than a log.

The arquebus idea came to him later; in fact, there was no weapon involved. What had happened was that one of Montaigne's servants, a muscular man riding behind him on a powerful horse, had goaded his mount into a full gallop along the path—"in order to show his daring and get ahead of his companions," as Montaigne surmised. He somehow failed to notice Montaigne in his way, or perhaps miscalculated the width of the path and thought he could pass. Instead, he "came down like a colossus on the little man and little horse."

The rest of the riders stopped in consternation. Montaigne's servants dismounted and tried to revive him; he remained unconscious. They picked him up and, with difficulty, started carrying his limp body back towards the castle. On the way, he came back to life. His first feeling was that he had been hit on the head (and his loss of consciousness suggests that this was right), yet he also started coughing, as if he had received a blow to the chest. Seeing him struggling for air, his men lifted him into a more upright position, and did their best to carry him at that awkward angle. Several times, he threw up lumps of clotted blood. This was an alarming symptom, but the coughing and vomiting helped to keep him awake.

As they approached the castle, he regained his wits more and more, yet he still felt as if he were slipping towards death, not emerging into life. His vision remained blurred; he could barely make out the light. He became aware of his body, but what he saw was hardly comforting, for his clothes were spattered with the blood he had been throwing up. He just had time to wonder about the arquebus before drifting back into semi-oblivion.

During what followed, as witnesses later told him, Montaigne thrashed about. He ripped at his doublet with his nails, as if to rid himself of a weight. "My stomach was oppressed with the clotted blood; my hands flew to it of their own accord, as they often do where we itch, against the intention of our will." It looked as if he were trying to rip his own body apart, or perhaps to pull it away from him so his spirit could depart. All this time, however, his inward feelings were tranquil:

> It seemed to me that my life was hanging only by the tip of my lips; I closed my eyes in order, it seemed to me, to help push it out, and took pleasure in growing languid and letting myself go. It was an idea that was only floating on the surface of my soul, as delicate and feeble as all the rest, but in truth not only free from distress but mingled with that sweet feeling that people have who let themselves slide into sleep.

The servants continued to carry him towards the house, in this state of inward languor and outward agitation. His family noticed the commotion and ran out to him—"with the outcries customary in such cases," as he later put it. They asked what had happened. Montaigne was able to give answers, but not coherent ones. He saw his wife picking her way awkwardly over the uneven path and considered telling his men to give her a horse to ride. You would think that all this must have come from "a wide-awake soul," he wrote. Yet, "the fact is that I was not there at all." He had traveled far away. "These were idle thoughts, in the clouds, set in motion by the sensations of the eyes and ears; they did not come from within me"—*chez moi*, a term usually meaning "at home." All his actions and words were somehow produced by the body alone. "What the soul contributed was in a dream, touched very lightly, and merely licked and sprinkled, as it were, by the soft impression of the senses." Montaigne and life, it seemed, were about to part company with neither regret nor formal farewells, like two drunken guests leaving a feast too dazed to say goodbye.

His confusion continued after he was carried indoors. He still felt as if he were borne aloft on a magic carpet instead of being heaved around by servants' hands. He suffered no pain, and no concern at the sight of those around him in emergency mode. All he felt was laziness and weakness. His servants put him to bed; he lay there, perfectly happy, not a thought in his head apart from that of how pleasurable it was to rest. "I felt infinite sweetness in this repose, for I had been villainously yanked about by those poor fellows, who had taken the pains to carry me in their arms over a long and very bad road." He refused all medicines, sure that he was destined just to slip away. It was going to be "a very happy death."

This experience went far beyond Montaigne's earlier imaginings about dying. It was a real voyage into death's territory: he slipped in close and touched it with his lips. He could *taste* it, like a person sampling an unfamiliar flavor. This was an essay of death: an exercise or *exercitation*, the word he used when he came to write about the experience. He would later spend much time going over the sensations in his mind, reconstructing them as precisely as possible so as to learn from them. Fortune had handed him the perfect opportunity to test the philosophical consensus about death. But it was hard to be sure that he had learned the right answer. The Stoics would certainly have looked askance at his results.

Parts of the lesson were correct: through his *exercitation*, he had learned not to fear his own nonexistence. Death could have a friendly face, just as the philosophers promised. Montaigne had looked into this face—but he had not stared into it lucidly, as a rational thinker should. Instead of marching forward with eyes open, bearing himself like a soldier, he had floated into death with barely a conscious thought, seduced by it. In dying, he now realized, you do not encounter death at all, for you are gone before it gets there. You die in the same way that you fall asleep: by drifting away. If other people try to pull you back, you hear their voices on "the edges of the soul." Your existence is attached by a thread; it rests only on the tip of your lips, as he put it. Dying is not an action that can be prepared for. It is an aimless reverie.

From now on, when Montaigne read about death, he would show less interest in the exemplary ends of the great philosophers, and more in those of ordinary people, especially those whose deaths took place in a state of "enfeeblement and stupor." In his most mature essays, he wrote admiringly of men such as Petronius and Tigillinus, Romans who died surrounded by jokes, music, and everyday conversation, so that death simply flowed into them amid the general good cheer. Instead of turning a party into a death scene, as Montaigne had done in his youthful imagination, they turned their death scenes into parties. He particularly liked the story of Marcellinus, who avoided a painful death from disease by a gentle method of euthanasia. After fasting for several days, Marcellinus laid himself down in a very hot bath. No doubt he was already weakened by his illness; the bath simply steamed the last breaths of life out of him. He passed out slowly, and then he passed away. As he went, he murmured languorously to his friends about the pleasure he was experiencing.

One might expect pleasure in a death like that of Marcellinus. But Montaigne had learned something more surprising: that he could enjoy the same delightful floating sensations even while his body seemed to be convulsed, thrashing around in what looked to others like torment.

This discovery of Montaigne's ran counter to his classical models; it also defied the Christian ideal which dominated his own era. For Christians, one's last thought should be the sober commending of one's soul to God, not a blissful "Aaaaah . . ." Montaigne's own experience apparently included no thoughts of God at all. Nor did it seem to occur to him that dying inebriated and surrounded by wenches might jeopardize a Christian afterlife. He was more interested in his purely secular realization that human psychology, and nature in general, were the dying man's best friends. And it now seemed to him that the only people who regularly died as bravely as philosophers should were those who knew no philosophy at all: the uneducated peasants in his local estates and villages. "I never saw one of my peasant neighbors cogitating over the countenance and assurance with which he would pass this last hour," he wrote—not that he would necessarily have known if they did. Nature took care of them. It taught them not to think about death except when they were dying, and very little even then. Philosophers find it hard to leave the world because they try to maintain control. So much for "To philosophize is to learn how to die." Philosophy looked more like a way of teaching people to *un*learn the natural skill that every peasant had by birthright.

On this occasion, despite his willingness to float away, Montaigne did not die. He recovered—and from then on, lived a bit differently. From his essay of death, he took a decidedly unphilosophical philosophy lesson, which he summed up in the following casual way:

If you don't know how to die, don't worry; Nature will tell you what to do on the spot, fully and adequately. She will do this job perfectly for you; don't bother your head about it.

"Don't worry about death" became his most fundamental, most liberating answer to the question of how to live. It made it possible to do just that: *live*.

But life is more difficult than death; instead of passive surrender, it takes attention and management. It can also be more painful. Montaigne's pleasurable drift on the currents of oblivion did not last. When he revived fully, after two or three hours, it was to find himself assailed with aches, his limbs "battered and bruised." He suffered for several nights afterwards, and there were longer-term consequences. "I still feel the effect of the shock of that collision," he wrote, at least three years later.

His memory took longer to come back than his physical sensations, although he spent several days trying to reconstruct the event by interrogating witnesses. None of it struck any spark until the whole incident came back at a blow, with a shock like being struck by lightning—a reprise of the "thunderbolt" of the initial impact. His return to life was as violent as the accident: all jostlings, impacts, flashes, and thunderclaps. Life thrust itself deeply into him, whereas death had been a light and superficial thing.

From now on, he tried to import some of death's delicacy and buoyancy into life. "Bad spots" were everywhere, he wrote in a late essay. We do better to "slide over this world a bit lightly and on the surface." Through this discovery of gliding and drifting, he lost much of his fear, and at the same time acquired a new sense that life, as it passed through his body—*his* particular life, Michel de Montaigne's—was a very interesting subject for investigation. He would go on to attend to sensations and experiences, not for what they were supposed to be, or for what philosophical lessons they might impart, but for the way they actually felt. He would go with the flow.

This was a new discipline for him, one which took over his daily routine, and—through his writing—gave him a form of immortality. Thus, around the middle of his life, Montaigne lost his bearings and found himself reborn.

2. Q. How to live? A. Pay attention

THE RIDING ACCIDENT, which so altered Montaigne's perspective, lasted only a few moments in itself, but one can unfold it into three parts and spread it over several years. First, there is Montaigne lying on the ground, clawing at his stomach while experiencing euphoria. Then comes Montaigne in the weeks and months that followed, reflecting on the experience and trying to reconcile it with his philosophical reading. Finally, there is Montaigne a few years later, sitting down to write about it—and about a multitude of other things. The first scene could have happened to anyone; the second to any sensitive, educated young man of the Renaissance. The last makes Montaigne unique.

The connection is not a simple one: he did not sit up in bed and immediately start writing about the accident. He began the *Essays* a couple of years later, around 1572, and, even then, he wrote other chapters before coming to the one about losing consciousness. When he did turn to it, however, the experience made him try a new kind of writing, barely attempted by other writers: that of re-creating a sequence of sensations as they felt from the inside, following them from instant to instant. And there does seem to be a chronological link between the accident and another turning point in his life, which opened up his path into literature: his decision to quit his job as magistrate in Bordeaux.

Montaigne had hitherto been keeping two lives going: one urban and political, the other rural and managerial. Although he had run the country estate since the death of his father in 1568, he had continued to work in Bordeaux. In early 1570, however, he put his magistracy up for sale. There were other reasons besides the accident: he had just been rejected for a post he had applied for in the court's higher chamber, probably because political enemies had blocked him. It would have been more usual to appeal against this, or fight it; instead, he bailed out. Perhaps he did so in anger, or disillusionment. Or perhaps his own encounter with death, in combination with the loss of his brother, made him think differently about how he wanted to live his life.

Montaigne had put in thirteen years of work at the Bordeaux *parlement* when he took this step. He was thirty-seven—middle-aged perhaps, by the standards of the time, but not old. Yet he thought of himself as retiring: leaving the mainstream of life in order to begin a new, reflective existence. When his thirty-eighth birthday came around, he marked the decision— almost a year after he had actually made it—by having a Latin inscription painted on the wall of a side-chamber to his library:

> In the year of Christ 1571, at the age of thirty-eight, on the last day of February, anniversary of his birth, Michel de Montaigne, long weary of the servitude of the court and of public employments, while still entire, retired to the bosom of the learned Virgins [the Muses], where in calm and freedom from all cares he will spend what little remains of his life now more than half run out. If the fates permit, he will complete this abode, this sweet ancestral retreat; and he has consecrated it to his freedom, tranquillity, and leisure.

From now on, Montaigne would live for himself rather than for duty. He may have underestimated the work involved in minding the estate, and he made no reference yet to writing essays. He spoke only of "calm and freedom." Yet he had already completed several minor literary projects. Rather reluctantly, he had translated a theological work at his father's request, and afterwards he had edited a sheaf of manuscripts left by his friend Étienne de La Boétie, adding dedications and a letter of his own describing La Boétie's last days. During those few years around the turn of 1570, his dabblings in literature coexisted with other experiences: the series of bereavements and his own near-death, the desire to get out of Bordeaux politics, and the yearning for a peaceful life— and something else too, for his wife was now pregnant with their first child. The expectation of new life met the shadow of death; together they lured him into a new way of being.

Montaigne's change of gear during his mid- to late thirties has been compared to the most famous life-changing crises in literature: those of Don Quixote, who abandoned his routine to set off in search of chivalric adventure, and of Dante, who lost himself in the woods "midway on life's path." Montaigne's steps into his own midlife forest tangle, and his discovery of the path out of it, leave a series of footprints—the marks of a man faltering, stumbling, then walking on:

June 1568—Montaigne finishes his theological translation. His father dies; he inherits the estate
Spring 1569—His brother dies in the tennis accident
1569—His career stalls in Bordeaux
1569 or early 1570—He almost dies
Autumn 1569—His wife becomes pregnant
Early 1570—He decides to retire
Summer 1570—He retires
June 1570—His first baby is born
August 1570—His first baby dies
1570—He edits La Boétie's works
February 1571—He makes his birthday inscription on the library wall
1572—He starts writing the *Essays*

Having committed himself to what he hoped would be a contemplative new life, Montaigne went to great trouble to set it up just as he wanted it. After his retirement, he chose one of two towers at the corners of his château complex to be his all-purpose retreat and center of operations; the other tower was reserved for his wife. Together with the main château building and the linking walls, these two corner-pieces enclosed a simple, square courtyard, set amid fields and forests.

The main building has gone now. It burned down in 1885, and was replaced by a new building to the same design. But, by good fortune, the fire did not touch Montaigne's tower; it remains essentially unchanged, and can still be visited. Walking around, it is not hard to see why he liked it so much. From the outside, it looks endearingly chubby for a four-story tower, having walls as thick as a sandcastle's. It was originally designed to be used for defense; Montaigne's father adapted it for more peaceful uses. He turned the ground floor into a chapel, and added an inner spiral staircase. The floor above the chapel became Montaigne's bedroom. He often slept there rather than returning to the main building. Set off the steps above this room was a niche for a toilet. Above that—just below the attic, with its

"very big bell" which rang out hours deafeningly—was Montaigne's favorite haunt: his library.

Climbing up the steps today—their stone worn into hollows by many feet—one can enter this library and walk around it in a tight circle, looking out of the windows over the courtyard and landscape just as Montaigne would have done. The view would not have been that different in his time, but the room itself would. Now stark and white, with bare stone floors, it would then have had a covering underfoot, probably of rushes. On its walls were murals, still fresh. In winter, fires would have burned in most of the rooms, though not in the main library, which had no fireplace. Cold days sent Montaigne to the cosier side-chamber next door, since that did have a fire.

The most striking feature of the main library room, when Montaigne occupied it, was his fine collection of books, housed in five rows on a beautiful curving set of shelves. The curve was necessary to fit the round tower, and must have been quite a carpentry challenge. The shelves presented all Montaigne's books to his view at a single glance: a satisfying sweep. He owned around a thousand volumes by the time he moved into

the library, many inherited from his friend La Boétie, others bought by himself. It was a substantial collection, and Montaigne actually read his books, too. Today they are dispersed; the shelves too have gone.

Also around the room were Montaigne's other collections: historical memorabilia, family heirlooms, artifacts from South America. Of his ancestors, he wrote, "I keep their handwriting, their seal, the breviary, and a peculiar sword that they used, and I have not banished from my study some long sticks that my father ordinarily carried in his hand." The South American collection was built up from travelers' gifts; it included jewelry, wooden swords, and ceremonial canes used in dancing. Montaigne's library was not just a repository or a work space. It was a chamber of marvels, and sounds like a sixteenth-century version of Sigmund Freud's last home in London's Hampstead: a treasure-house stuffed with books, papers, statuettes, pictures, vases, amulets, and ethnographic curiosities, designed to stimulate both imagination and intellect.

The library also marked Montaigne out as a man of fashion. The trend for such retreats had been spreading slowly through France, having begun in Italy in the previous century. Well-off men filled chambers with books and reading-stands, then used them as a place to escape to on the pretext of having to work. Montaigne took the escape factor further by removing his library from the house altogether. It was both a vantage point and a cave, or, to use a phrase he himself liked, an *arrière-boutique*: a "room behind the shop." He could invite visitors there if he wished—and often did—but he was never obliged to. He loved it. "Sorry the man, to my mind, who has not in his own home a place to be all by himself, to pay his court privately to himself, to hide!"

Since the library represented freedom itself, it is not surprising that Montaigne made a ritual of decorating it and setting it apart. In the side-chamber, along with the inscription celebrating his retirement, he had floor-to-ceiling murals painted. These have faded, but, from what remains visible, they depicted great battles, Venus mourning the death of Adonis, a bearded Neptune, ships in a storm, and scenes of bucolic life—all evocations of the classical world. In the main chamber, he had the roof beams painted with quotations, also mostly classical. This, too, was a fashion, though it remained a minority taste. The Italian humanist Marsilio Ficino put quotations on the walls of his villa in Tuscany, and later, in the Bordeaux area, the baron de Montesquieu would do the same in deliberate homage to Montaigne.

Over the years, Montaigne's roof beams faded too, but they were later restored to clear legibility, so that, as you walk around the room now, voices whisper from above your head:

Solum certum nihil esse certi
Et homine nihil miserius aut superbius
Only one thing is certain: that nothing is certain
And nothing is more wretched or arrogant than man. (Pliny the Elder)

ΚΡΙΝΕΙ ΤΙΣ ΑΥΤΟΝ ΠΩΠΟΤ ΑΝΘΡΩΠΟΝ ΜΕΓΑΝ ΟΝ
ΕΞΑΛΕΙΦΕΙ ΠΡΟΦΑΣΙΣ Η ΤΥΧΟΥΣ᾽ ΟΛΟΝ
How can you think yourself a great man, when the first accident that comes along can wipe you out completely? (Euripides)

ΕΝ ΤΩ ΦΡΟΝΕΙΝ ΓΑΡ ΜΗΔΕΝ ΗΔΙΣΤΟΣ ΒΙΟΣ
ΤΟ ΜΗ ΦΡΟΝΕΙΝ ΓΑΡ ΚΑΡΤ᾽ ΑΝΩΔΥΝΟΝ ΚΑΚΟΝ
There is no more beautiful life than that of a carefree man;
Lack of care is a truly painless evil. (Sophocles)

The beams form a vivid reminder of Montaigne's decision to move from public life into a meditative existence—a life to be lived, literally, under the sign of philosophy rather than that of politics. Such a shift of realms was also part of the ancients' advice. The great Stoic Seneca repeatedly urged his fellow Romans to retire in order to "find themselves," as we might put it. In the Renaissance, as in ancient Rome, it was part of the well-managed life. You had your period of civic business, then you withdrew to discover what life was really about and to begin the long process of preparing for death. Montaigne developed reservations about the second part of this, but there is no doubt about his interest in contemplating life. He wrote: "Let us cut loose from all the ties that bind us to others; let us win from ourselves the power to live really alone and to live that way at our ease."

Seneca, in advising retirement, had also warned of dangers. In a dialogue

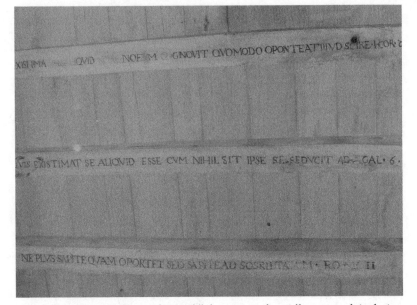

called "On Tranquillity of Mind," he wrote that idleness and isolation could bring to the fore all the consequences of having lived life in the wrong way, consequences that people usually avoided by keeping busy—that is, by continuing to live life in the wrong way. The symptoms could include dissatisfaction, self-loathing, fear, indecisiveness, lethargy, and melancholy. Giving up work brings out spiritual ills, especially if one then gets the habit of reading too many books—or, worse, laying out the books for show and gloating over the view.

In the early 1570s, during his shift of values, Montaigne seems to have suffered exactly the existential crisis Seneca warned of. He had work to do, but less of it than he was used to. The inactivity generated strange thoughts and a "melancholy humor" which was out of character for him. No sooner had he retired, he said, than his mind galloped off like a runaway horse— an apt comparison, considering what had recently happened. His head filled with nonsense, just as a fallow field fills with weeds. In another vivid image—he loved piling up effects like this—he compared his idle brain to a woman's unfertilized womb, which, as contemporary stories maintained, gives birth only to shapeless lumps of flesh instead of babies. And, in a simile borrowed from Virgil, he described his thoughts as resembling the patterns that dance across the ceiling when sunlight reflects off the surface of a water bowl. Just as the tiger-stripes of light lurch about, so an unoccupied mind gyrates unpredictably and brings forth mad, directionless whimsies. It generates *fantasies* or *reveries*—two words with less positive associations than they have today, suggesting raving delusions rather than daydreams.

His "reverie" in turn gave Montaigne another mad idea: the thought of writing. He called this a reverie too, but it was one that held out the promise of a solution. Finding his mind so filled with "chimeras and fantastic monsters, one after another, without order or purpose," he decided to write them down, not directly to overcome them, but to inspect their strangeness at his leisure. So he picked up his pen; the first of the *Essays* was born.

Seneca would have approved. If you become depressed or bored in your retirement, he advised, just look around you and interest yourself in the variety and sublimity of things. Salvation lies in paying full attention to nature. Montaigne tried to do this, but he took "nature" primarily to mean the natural phenomenon that lay closest to hand: himself. He began watching and questioning his own experience, and writing down what he observed.

At first, this mainly meant following his personal enthusiasms, especially stories from his reading: tales from Ovid, histories from Caesar and Tacitus, biographical snippets from Plutarch, and advice on how to live from Seneca and Socrates. Then he wrote down stories he heard from friends, incidents from the day-to-day life of the estate, cases that had lodged in his mind from his years in law and politics, and oddities he had seen on his (so far limited) travels. These were his modest beginnings; later, his material grew until it included almost every nuance of emotion or thought he had ever experienced, not least his strange journey in and out of unconsciousness.

The idea of publication may have crossed his mind early on, though he claimed otherwise, saying he wrote only for family and friends. Perhaps he even began with the intention of composing a commonplace book: a collection of thematically arranged quotations and stories, of a kind popular among gentlemen of the day. If so, it did not take him long to move beyond this, possibly under the influence of the one writer he liked more than Seneca: Plutarch. Plutarch had made his name in the first century AD with lively potted biographies of historical figures, and also wrote short pieces called *Moralia*, which were translated into French in the year Montaigne began writing his *Essays*. These gathered together thoughts and anecdotes on questions ranging from "Can animals be called intelligent?" to "How does one achieve peace of mind?" On the latter point, Plutarch's advice was the same as Seneca's: focus on what is present in front of you, and pay full attention to it.

As the 1570s went on and Montaigne adjusted to his new post-crisis life, paying attention became a favorite pastime. His biggest writing year was 1572: that was when he began most of the essays of Book I and some in Book II. The rest followed in 1573 and 1574. Yet it would be a long time before he felt ready to publish; perhaps only because it did not occur to him, or perhaps because it took him many years to be satisfied with what he had done. A decade would pass from his retirement in 1570 to the day after his forty-seventh birthday, March 1, 1580, when he signed and dated the preface to the first edition of the *Essays* and made himself famous overnight.

Writing had got Montaigne through his "mad reveries" crisis; it now taught him to look at the world more closely, and increasingly gave him the habit of describing inward sensations and social encounters with precision. He quoted Pliny on the idea of attending to such elusive fragments: "Each man is a good education to himself, provided he has the capacity to spy on himself from close up." As Montaigne the man went about his daily life on the estate, Montaigne the writer walked behind him, spying and taking notes.

When he came at last to write about his riding accident, therefore, he did it not only to shake out what remained of his fear of death like sand from his shoes, but also to raise his spying techniques to a level beyond anything he had tried before. Just as, in the days after the accident, he had made his servants repeatedly tell him the story of what had happened, so now he must have gone through it in his mind, reliving those floating sensations, that feeling of his breath or spirit lingering at the threshold of his body, and the pain of return. He "processed" it, as psychologists might say today, through literature. In doing so, he reconstructed the experience as it actually *was*, not as the philosophers said it should be.

There was nothing easy about this new hobby of his. Montaigne liked to pretend that he threw the *Essays* together carelessly, but occasionally he forgot the pose and admitted what hard work it was:

It is a thorny undertaking, and more so than it seems, to follow a movement so wandering as that of our mind, to penetrate the opaque depths of its innermost folds, to pick out and immobilize the innumerable flutterings that agitate it.

Montaigne may have extolled the beauty of gliding lightly over the surface of life; indeed, he did perfect that art as he got older. At the same time, as a writer, he worked at the art of plumbing the depths. "I meditate on any satisfaction," he wrote. "I do not skim over it; I sound it." He was so determined to get to the bottom even of a phenomenon that was normally lost by definition—sleep—that he had a long-suffering servant wake him regularly in the middle of the night in the hope of catching a glimpse of his own unconsciousness as it left him.

Montaigne wanted to drift away, yet he also wanted to attach himself to reality and extract every grain of experience from it. Writing made it possible to do both. Even as he lost himself in his reveries, he secretly planted his hooks in everything that happened, so that he could draw it back at will. Learning how to die was learning to let go; learning to live was learning to hang on.

STREAM OF CONSCIOUSNESS

In truth, however hard you try, you can never retrieve an experience in full. As a famous line by the ancient philosopher Heraclitus has it, you cannot step into the same river twice. Even if you return to the same spot on the bank, different water flows in upon you at every moment. Similarly, to see the world exactly as you did half an hour ago is impossible, just as it is impossible to see it from the point of view of a different person standing next to you. The mind flows on and on, in a ceaseless "stream of consciousness"—a phrase coined by the psychologist William James in 1890, though it was later made more famous by novelists.

Montaigne was among the many who quoted Heraclitus, and he mused on how we are carried along by our thoughts, "now gently, now violently, according as the water is angry or calm . . . every day a new fancy, and our

humors shift with the shifts in the weather." It is no wonder that the mind is like this, since even the apparently solid physical world exists in endless slow turmoil. Looking at the landscape around his house, Montaigne could imagine it heaving and boiling like porridge. His local river, the Dordogne, carved out its banks as a carpenter chisels grooves in wood. He had been astonished by the shifting sand dunes of Médoc, near where one of his brothers lived: they roamed the land and devoured it. If we could see the world at a different speed, he reflected, we would see everything like this, as "a perpetual multiplication and vicissitude of forms." Matter existed in an endless *branloire*: a word deriving from the sixteenth-century peasant dance *branle*, which meant something like "the shake." The world was a cosmic wobble: a shimmy.

Other sixteenth-century writers shared Montaigne's fascination with the unstable. What was unusual in him was his instinct that the observer is as unreliable as the observed. The two kinds of movement interact like variables in a complex mathematical equation, with the result that one can find no secure point from which to measure anything. To try to understand the world is like grasping a cloud of gas, or a liquid, using hands that are themselves made of gas or water, so that they dissolve as you close them.

This is why Montaigne's book flows as it does: it follows its author's stream of consciousness without attempting to pause or dam it. A typical page of the *Essays* is a sequence of meanders, bends, and divergences. You have to let yourself be carried along, hoping not to capsize each time a change of direction throws you off balance. In his chapter "Of Cripples," for example, Montaigne starts conventionally enough by repeating a rumor about lame women: they are said to be more enjoyable to have sex with. Why might this be? he wonders. Is it because their movements are irregular? Maybe, but he adds, "I have just learned that ancient philosophy, no less, has decided the question." Aristotle says that their vaginas are more muscular because they receive the nourishment of which the legs are deprived. Montaigne records this idea, but then doubles back and introduces a doubt: "What can we not reason about at this rate?" All such theories are unreliable. In fact, he eventually reveals, he has tried the experiment for himself, and has learned a quite different point: that the question means little, for your imagination can make you *believe* you are experiencing enhanced pleasure whether you "really" are or not. In the end, the oddity of the human mind is all we can be sure of—an extraordinary conclusion which seems to bear no relation to the topic he was originally aiming at.

Another essay, "That our happiness must not be judged until after our death," starts with a platitude quoted from Solon: Call no man happy till he dies. Montaigne at once swerves to a more interesting thought: perhaps our judgment about whether a man has been happy has more to do with *how* he dies. A man who dies well tends to be remembered as if he also lived well. After giving examples of this, Montaigne changes tack again. In truth, a person who has had a good life could die very badly, and vice versa. In Montaigne's own time, three of the most infamous individuals he had known died beautiful deaths, "composed to perfection." The chapter has now become a long loaf with three twists, and Montaigne seems set to finish by saying that, in any case, he hopes his own death will go well. But at the very end he remarks that by "going well" he means going "quietly and

insensibly"—hardly the usual notion of an admirable death. With this, the
piece abruptly finishes, just as the reader is beginning to wonder whether
this means Montaigne has lived well or not.

Thus, most of Montaigne's thought consists of a series of realizations
that life is not as simple as he has just made it out to be.

If my mind could gain a firm footing, I would not make essays, I
would make decisions; but it is always in apprenticeship and on trial.

The changes of direction are partly explained by this questioning attitude,
and partly by his having written the book over twenty years. A person's
ideas vary a lot in two decades, especially if the person spends that time
traveling, reading, talking to interesting people, and practicing high-level
politics and diplomacy. Revising earlier drafts of the *Essays* over and over
again, he added material as it occurred to him, and made no attempt to box
it into an artificial consistency. Within the space of a few lines, we might
meet Montaigne as a young man, then as an old man with one foot in the
grave, and then again as a middle-aged mayor bowed down by responsibilities. We listen to him complaining of impotence; a moment later, we
see him young and lusty, "impertinently genital" in his desires. He is hot-
headed and outspoken; he is discreet. He is fascinated by other people; he
is fed up with the lot of them. His thoughts lie where they fall. He makes
us *feel* the passage of time in his inner world. "I do not portray being," he
wrote, "I portray passing. Not the passing from one age to another . . . but
from day to day, from minute to minute."

Among the readers to be fascinated by Montaigne's way of depicting
the flux of his experience was one of the great pioneers of "stream of
consciousness" fiction in the early twentieth century, Virginia Woolf. Her
own purpose in her art was to immerse herself in the mental river and follow
wherever it led. Her novels delved into characters' worlds "from minute to
minute." Sometimes she left one channel to tune in elsewhere, passing the
point of view like a microphone from one individual to another, but the
flow itself never ceased until the end of each book. She identified
Montaigne as the first writer to attempt anything of this sort, albeit only
with his own single "stream." She also considered him the first to pay such

attention to the simple feeling of being alive. "Observe, observe perpetually," was his rule, she said—and what he observed was, above all, this river of life running through his existence.

Montaigne was the first to write in such a way, but not the first to attempt to *live* with full attention to the present moment. That was another of the rules recommended by the classical philosophers. Life is what happens while you're making other plans, they said; so philosophy must guide your attention repeatedly back to the place where it belongs—*here*. It plays a role like that of the mynah birds in Aldous Huxley's novel *Island*, which are trained to fly around all day calling "Attention! Attention!" and "Here and now!" As Seneca put it, life does not pause to remind you that it is running out. The only one who can keep you mindful of this is you:

> It will cause no commotion to remind you of its swiftness, but glide on quietly . . . What will be the outcome? You have been preoccupied while life hastens on. Meanwhile death will arrive, and you have no choice in making yourself available for that.

If you fail to grasp life, it will elude you. If you do grasp it, it will elude you anyway. So you must follow it—and "you must drink quickly as though from a rapid stream that will not always flow."

The trick is to maintain a kind of naive amazement at each instant of experience—but, as Montaigne learned, one of the best techniques for doing this is to write about everything. Simply describing an object on your table, or the view from your window, opens your eyes to how marvelous such ordinary things are. To look inside yourself is to open up an even more fantastical realm. The philosopher Maurice Merleau-Ponty called Montaigne a writer who put "a consciousness astonished at itself at the core of human existence." More recently, the critic Colin Burrow has remarked that astonishment, together with Montaigne's other key quality, fluidity, are what philosophy should be, but rarely has been, in the Western tradition.

As Montaigne got older, his desire to pay astounded attention to life did not decline; it intensified. By the end of the long process of writing the *Essays*, he had almost perfected the trick. Knowing that the life that remained to him could not be of great length, he said, "I try to increase it in weight, I try to arrest the speed of its flight by the speed with which I grasp it . . . The shorter my possession of life, the deeper and fuller I must make it." He discovered a sort of strolling meditation technique:

> When I walk alone in the beautiful orchard, if my thoughts have been dwelling on extraneous incidents for some part of the time, for some other part I bring them back to the walk, to the orchard, to the sweetness of this solitude, and to me.

At moments like these, he seems to have achieved an almost Zen-like discipline; an ability to just *be*.

> When I dance, I dance; when I sleep, I sleep.

It sounds so simple, put like this, but nothing is harder to do. This is why Zen masters spend a lifetime, or several lifetimes, learning it. Even then, according to traditional stories, they often manage it only after their teacher hits them with a big stick—the *keisaku*, used to remind meditators to pay full attention. Montaigne managed it after one fairly short lifetime, partly because he spent so much of that lifetime scribbling on paper with a very small stick.

In writing about his experience as if he were a river, he started a literary tradition of close inward observation that is now so familiar that it is hard to remember that it *is* a tradition. Life just seems to be like that, and observing the play of inner states is the writer's job. Yet this was not a common notion before Montaigne, and his peculiarly restless, free-form way of doing it was entirely unknown. In inventing it, and thus attempting a second answer to the question of how to live—"pay attention"—Montaigne escaped his crisis and even turned that crisis to his advantage.

Both "Don't worry about death" and "Pay attention" were answers to a midlife loss of direction: they emerged from the experience of a man who had lived long enough to make errors and false starts. Yet they also marked a beginning, bringing about the birth of his new essay-writing self.

3. Q. How to live? A. Be born

MONTAIGNE'S ORIGINAL SELF, the one that did not write essays but merely moved and breathed like everyone else, had a simpler start. He came into this world on February 28, 1533—the same year as the future Queen Elizabeth I of England. His birth took place between eleven o'clock and noon, in the family château, which would be his lifelong home. He was named Michel, but, to his father at least, he would always be known as Micheau. This nickname appears even in documents as formal as his father's will, after the boy had turned into a man.

In the *Essays*, Montaigne wrote that he had been carried in his mother's womb for eleven months. This was an odd claim, since it was well known that such a prodigy of nature was barely possible. Mischievous minds would surely have leaped to indelicate conclusions. In Rabelais's *Gargantua*, the eponymous giant also spends eleven months in his mother's womb. "Does this sound strange?" Rabelais asks, and answers himself with a series of tongue-in-cheek case studies in which lawyers were clever enough to prove the legitimacy even of a child whose supposed father had *died* eleven months before its birth. "Thanks to these learned laws, our virtuous widows may, for two months after their husbands' demise, freely indulge in games of grip-crupper with a pig in the poke, heels over head and to their hearts' content." Montaigne had read Rabelais, and must have thought of the obvious jokes, but he seemed unconcerned.

No paternity doubts emerge elsewhere in the *Essays*. Montaigne even muses on the power of inheritance in his family, describing traits that had come down to himself through his great-grandfather, grandfather, and father, including an easygoing honesty and a propensity to kidney stones. He seems to have considered himself very much his father's son.

Montaigne was happy to talk about honesty and hereditary ailments, but was more discreet about other aspects of his heritage, for he came not from ancient aristocracy but, on both sides, from several generations of upwardly mobile merchants. He even made out that the Montaigne estate was the place where "most" of his ancestors were born, a blatant fudge: his own father was the first to be born there.

The property itself had been in the family for longer, it was true. Montaigne's great-grandfather Ramon Eyquem bought it in 1477, towards the end of a long, successful money-making life dealing in wine, fish, and woad—the plant from which blue dye is extracted, an important local product. Ramon's son Grimon did little to the estate other than adding an oak- and cedar-lined path to the nearby church. But he built up the Eyquem wealth even further, and started another family tradition by getting involved in Bordeaux politics. At some point he gave up trade and began living "nobly," an important step. Being noble was not a *je ne sais quoi* of class and style; it was a technical matter, and the main rule was that you and your descendants must engage in no trade and pay no taxes for at least three generations. Grimon's son Pierre also avoided trade, so noble status fell, for the first time, on generation number three: Michel Eyquem de Montaigne himself. By that time, ironically, his father Pierre had turned the estate from a tract of land into a successful commercial concern. The château became the head office of a fairly large wine-producing business, yielding tens of thousands of liters of wine per year. It still produces wine today. This was

allowed: you could make as much money as you liked selling the products of your own land, without its being considered trade.

The Eyquem story exemplifies the degree of mobility then possible, at least towards the upper end of the social scale. New nobles sometimes found it hard to gain full respect, but this mainly applied to the so-called "nobility of the robe," who were elevated for contributions to political and civil service, not to the "nobility of the sword," who gained their status from property, as Montaigne's family did, and prided themselves on the military calling that was expected to come with it. Peasants, meanwhile, mostly stayed where they had always been: on the bottom. Their lives were still dominated by the local *seigneur*—in this case, the head of the Eyquem family. He owned their homes, employed them, and rented out the use of his wine press and bread oven. When Montaigne's turn came along, he probably remained a typical *seigneur* from their point of view, however much he praised the peasants' wisdom in the *Essays*—a book no agricultural worker on his estate was ever likely to read.

The entry on Montaigne's birth in the family book states that he was born "*in confiniis Burdigalensium et Petragorensium*": on the borders between Bordeaux and Périgord. This was significant, for Bordeaux was mostly Catholic, while Périgord was dominated by supporters of the new religion, the Reformist or Protestant one. The Eyquem family had to keep its peace with both sides of a divergence that would split Europe in two throughout Montaigne's life, and far beyond it.

The Reformation was still very recent news: its inception is generally dated to 1517, the year in which Martin Luther wrote a treatise attacking the Catholic tradition of selling fast-track earthly pardons or "indulgences," and reportedly nailed it to the church door in Wittenberg by way of a challenge. Widely circulated, the treatise set off a major rebellion against the Church. The Pope responded first by dismissing Luther as a "drunken German," then by excommunicating him. The secular powers of the Holy Roman Empire pronounced Luther an outlaw who could be killed on sight, thus making him a popular hero. Eventually most of Europe would fall into two camps: those who kept loyal to the Church, and those who backed Luther's rebellion. There was never anything geographically or ideologically neat about this division. Europe fell apart like a crumbling loaf, not like an apple halved by a knife. Almost every country was affected, but few went decisively one way or the other. In many places, especially France, the fault lines ran through villages and even families, rather than between separate territories.

Montaigne's region of Guyenne (also known as Aquitaine) did show a pattern: roughly, the countryside went one way and the capital city went the other. Tensions were heightened by the general feeling, already widespread in the area before the Reformation, that Aquitaine did not form part of France. It had its own language, and few historical connections with the north of the country. For a long time, it had been English territory. The English were driven out only in 1451, by French invaders who were seen as alien and untrustworthy raptors. People harked back to the old era with nostalgia, not because they really missed the English, but because they so hated the northern French. Rebellions were frequent. The authorities built three heavy fortresses to keep the city under watch: the Château Trompette, the Fort du Hâ, and Fort Louis. All were hated; all are gone today.

Where possible, Bordeaux formed diplomatic links with anyone other than its conquerors. In Montaigne's time the area was much influenced by the Protestant court of Navarre, based in Béarn in the Spanish border country to the south. It also kept up ties with England, which developed a taste for Bordeaux wine. An English wine fleet called there regularly to top up supplies—good news for local suppliers, not least the Eyquem family of Montaigne.

As the estate grew in importance, so "Montaigne" came to overshadow the older Eyquem name. The latter had, and has, a distinctive regional sound. One branch of the family is still remembered for its legendary wine estate: the Château d'Yquem. Despite a preference for locality and particularity in most things, Montaigne became the first to sideline this and to be known by the more generic French name of his home. Biographers have been harsh on him for this decision, but he was only extending a move his father had already made by styling himself "de Montaigne" when he signed documents. Whereas his father dropped this extra part if he wanted to be brief, Montaigne tended to leave out the "Eyquem."

If Michel Eyquem de Montaigne, product of a meteoric social rise, hastened over his father's mercantile background in the *Essays*, it could have been to ensure that his book appealed to the right sort of noble, leisured market; it could also be that he simply gave it little thought. His father probably avoided regaling him with stories about their origins; Montaigne may have grown up barely aware of them. No doubt vanity came into it too: it was one of the many petty weaknesses Montaigne cheerfully acknowledged, adding:

> If others examined themselves attentively, as I do, they would find themselves, as I do, full of inanity and nonsense. Get rid of it I cannot without getting rid of myself. We are all steeped in it, one as much as another; but those who are aware of it are a little better off—though I don't know.

That final coda—"though I don't know"—is pure Montaigne. One must imagine it appended, in spirit, to almost everything he ever wrote. His whole philosophy is captured in this paragraph. Yes, he says, we are foolish, but we cannot be any other way so we may as well relax and live with it.

If his father's background was murky, a more significant secret apparently lurked in the family of his mother, Antoinette de Louppes de Villeneuve. Her ancestors were merchants; they were also immigrants from Spain, which, in the context of the time, strongly suggests that they were Jewish refugees. Like many others, they converted to Christianity under duress, and left following the persecution of Jews on the peninsula in the late fifteenth century.

Montaigne may not have realized that he was of Jewish origin, if indeed he was. He showed no more than mild interest in the subject, mentioning Jews only occasionally in the *Essays*, usually either neutrally or with sympathy, but never in a way that suggested he felt personally involved. Traveling in Italy later in life, he visited synagogues and witnessed a circumcision, but he did all this with the same curiosity he showed for everything else he came across: Protestant church services, executions, brothels, trick fountains, rock gardens, and unusual furniture.

He also expressed a wry skepticism about the "conversions" of some recent refugees—reasonably enough, since the act was not done by choice. If, as some have speculated, this was meant as a subtle dig at his mother's family, it would not be surprising. In his political life, he suffered constant difficulties from some of her relatives in Bordeaux. He even seems to have had trouble getting on with Antoinette herself.

Montaigne's mother was undoubtedly a strong character, but convention kept her powerless and frustrated. She married young, as women usually did, and probably had little choice in the matter. Pierre Eyquem was considerably older than her: in the marriage document, of January 15, 1529, he is described as thirty-three, while she is only "of age." This could mean anything between twelve and twenty-five; since she managed to have the last of her children over thirty years after the wedding, she must have been at the young end of this range. Two babies were born before Michel, though neither survived. She was very likely still a teenager when he came along, yet by then she had been married for four years.

If there was anything childish or demure about her as a bride, that soon vanished. Legal documents surviving from various periods of her life create a picture of someone fierce, opinionated, and very able. Her husband's first will, of 1561, left the task of managing the household to her rather than to his eldest son, though he later changed this. In 1561, Pierre Eyquem either lacked faith in Micheau (nearly twenty-eight at the time) or had an exceptionally high opinion of his wife—which would be impressive in an era when women were barely considered capable of rational thought.

The second will, of September 22, 1567, showed more trust in his son, but by now Pierre seemed to feel the need to use the document to command his wife to love her children, and to tell them to respect and honor her. He apparently feared that she and her eldest son would not live together amicably, for he ordered Montaigne to find accommodation for her elsewhere if living at the family estate did not work out. Antoinette did stay with him and his family for a long time after her husband's death—until about 1587—but not very convivially. Another legal document drawn up between mother and son on August 31, 1568, asserted Antoinette's right to receive "all filial honor, respect, and service," as well as servants to attend her and a hundred *livres tournois* a year for petty cash. She, in turn, had to acknowledge his "command and mastery" of the château and estate. The contract implies that Antoinette felt poorly looked after, while Montaigne wanted to stop her meddling.

Things got worse. Antoinette's own will, written on April 19, 1597—five years after her son's death, for she outlived him—stated that she did not wish to be buried on the estate, and virtually cut Montaigne's one child Léonor out of the inheritance. She complained that her original dowry should have gone on buying more property, yet did not, and she added: "I worked for a period of forty years in the house of Montaigne with my husband in such a way that by my work, care, and management the said house has been greatly increased in value, improved, and enlarged." Her son Montaigne enjoyed the benefit of this throughout his life, as did Léonor, who thus became quite "rich and opulent" enough and needed nothing more. Finally, Antoinette remarked that she knew herself to be "of an age easy to circumvent"; she was probably around eighty. It seems that she feared a challenge to the will on grounds of senility.

Reading the frequent confessions of indolence and ineptitude that fill Montaigne's book, it is easy to see why Antoinette thought the estate was neglected during the time he was in charge of it. He found practical affairs a bore and avoided them as much as possible. It is more surprising that she should make the same complaint against her husband Pierre, for he does not come across in the *Essays* that way at all. Montaigne makes his father sound like a dynamo of a man, devoted to his duties and always at work on home improvements—restless and interventionist to a fault.

Pierre Eyquem de Montaigne was a fifteenth-century man, just—he was born on September 29, 1495. Everything about him proclaimed his remoteness from his son's world. Following noble tradition, he took up the profession of war, being the first in his family to do so. Michel did not follow him in this. As a nobleman he was obliged to carry a sword, but there is no indication in the *Essays* that he unsheathed it very often. One contemporary, Brantôme, described Montaigne as "dragging" the sword around town and suggested that he confine himself to carrying a pen. No such aspersions could have been cast on Pierre, who rushed off at the first opportunity to join France's wars in Italy.

French forces had been regularly attacking and conquering states on the peninsula since 1494, and would continue doing so until 1559, when the Peace of Câteau Cambrésis stopped France's foreign invasions and thus opened the way to its real sixteenth-century catastrophe: the civil wars. The Italian adventures were less damaging, but they were expensive and mostly pointless, as well as traumatic for those involved. Pierre plunged into battle some time around 1518. Apart from a brief interlude the year after that, he remained away from home until early 1529, when he came back to get married.

Sixteenth-century warfare was a messy business, a matter less of battle-field glamour than of hypothermia, fever, hunger, disease, and infected sword cuts and gunshot wounds for which there was little effective treatment. Above all, there were sieges, in which civilians and soldiers alike were starved into surrender. Pierre may have been involved in sieges of Milan and Pavia in 1522, and perhaps also in a disastrous siege of Pavia in 1525, which ended with French soldiers being slaughtered in large numbers and the French king being taken prisoner. In later life Pierre would regale his family with hair-raising stories of his war experiences, including accounts of whole villages of starving people committing suicide *en masse* for lack of a better way out. If Montaigne grew up to prefer dragging a pen to a sword, perhaps this was why.

The Italian wars may have been unedifying in one way, but in the literal sense of offering an education, they were highly improving for the French. Between sieges, Frenchmen encountered exciting ideas about science, politics, philosophy, pedagogy, and fashionable manners. The high Italian Renaissance had petered out by now, but Italy was still by far the most

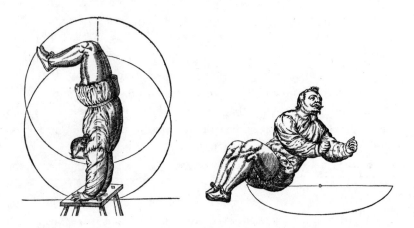

advanced civilization in Europe. French soldiers learned new ways of thinking about almost everything, and when they came home they brought their discoveries with them. Pierre was certainly one of this breed of Italianized Frenchmen, influenced by their travels and by their own charismatic, modernizing king François I. Later kings gave up on François's Renaissance ideal, and during the civil wars almost everyone lost faith in the future altogether—but in Pierre's youth that disillusionment was a long way off. The ideals were still new enough to be exciting.

Except, perhaps, for having a more soldierly bearing than his son, Pierre was physically of the same stamp. Montaigne describes him as "a small man, full of vigor, and straight and well-proportioned in stature," with "an attractive face, inclining to brown." He was fit, and kept himself that way. He liked to exercise his biceps using canes filled with lead, and he wore shoes with leaded soles to train him for running and jumping. The latter was a particular talent. "Of his vaulting, he has left some small miracles in people's memory," wrote Montaigne. "I have seen him, past sixty, put our agility to shame: leap into the saddle in his furred gown, do a turn over the table on his thumb, hardly ever go up to his room without taking three or four steps at a time."

This Father William figure had other fine qualities, all more characteristic of his generation than of Montaigne's. He was serious; he

took care over the neatness of his appearance and dress, and showed "conscientiousness and scrupulousness" in all things. His sporting talents and gallant manners made him popular with women: Montaigne describes him as "very well suited to the service of the ladies, both by nature and by art." It was probably to amuse female company that he sprang over tables. As for real sexual escapades, Pierre gave his son inconsistent messages. On the one hand, he related stories "of remarkable intimacies, especially of his own, with respectable women, free from any suspicion." On the other, "he solemnly swore that he had come to his marriage a virgin." Montaigne seemed unconvinced by the virginity claim, noting only, "and yet he had taken a very long part in the Italian wars."

After his return from Italy and his marriage, Pierre began a political career in Bordeaux. He was elected jurat and provost in 1530, then deputy mayor in 1537, and finally mayor in 1554. This period saw difficult times in the city: a new local tax on salt in 1548 inspired riots, which "France" punished by stripping Bordeaux of many legal rights. As mayor, Pierre did what he could to restore its fortunes, but the privileges came back slowly. The stress damaged his health. Just as his tales of war atrocities may have put Montaigne off the military life, so the sight of Pierre's exhaustion encouraged him to keep more distance from the job when he too became mayor of Bordeaux some thirty years later.

Pierre had some brilliant ideas, including one for a sort of sixteenth-century eBay: he proposed that each town should set up a place where anyone could advertise what they wanted: "I want to sell some pearls; I want to buy some pearls. So-and-so wants company to go to Paris; so-and-so is looking for a servant with such-and-such qualifications; so-and-so wants a master; so-and-so a workman; one man this, another man that." It sounds sensible, but for some reason nothing came of the plan.

Another good idea of Pierre's was keeping a journal in which he recorded everything that happened on the estate: the comings and goings of servants, and financial and agricultural data of all kinds. He encouraged his son to do the same. Montaigne started, in a fit of good intentions after Pierre's death, but did not keep it up: only one fragment survives. "I think I am a fool to have neglected it," he wrote in the *Essays*. He did manage to maintain another record begun by his father, using a printed calendar called the *Ephemeris*, by the German writer Michel Beuther. This survives almost in full, minus a few leaves, and is filled with notes by Montaigne and others in his family. Each date in the year has its own page, combining a printed summary of events from history with a blank area for adding remarks year by year. Montaigne used his Beuther to record births, travels, and notable visits over his lifetime. He kept it quite faithfully, but with a tendency to get dates, ages, and other such precise information wrong.

His wife's complaints notwithstanding, Pierre apparently adored hard work of all kinds, none more so than developing the estate. Perhaps what irritated her was his preference for spending on improvements rather than on buying new property, together with the habit of starting more things than he finished. Pierre's abandonment of the trading-post idea may have been more in character than it seems. On Pierre's death, Montaigne inherited a lot of half-completed jobs on the estate, which he always felt he should see through, but never did. Work left at the building-site stage is very annoying; perhaps inaction was Montaigne's way of dealing with it, just as overt exasperation was Antoinette's.

Some of the abandoned work may have been a sign that Pierre's energies were in decline, for, from the age of sixty-six, he suffered regular debilitating attacks of kidney stones. Montaigne often saw his father doubled over in agony during the last few years of his life. He never forgot the shock of witnessing the first attack, which struck Pierre without warning and knocked him unconscious from sheer pain. He fell into his son's arms as he passed out. It was probably a similar episode, or complications ensuing from one, that finally killed him. He died on June 18, 1568, at the age of seventy-four.

By this time, Pierre had replaced his first will, so implicitly critical of his son's abilities, with a new one which gave Montaigne the task of looking after his younger brothers and sisters and serving them as a replacement father. "He must take my place and represent me to them," was how he put it. Montaigne did take his father's place, and he did not always find it an easy one to occupy.

In the *Essays*, he comes across as a kind of negative image of Pierre. Praise for his father is often followed by an assertion that he himself is completely different. Having described how Pierre loved to build up the estate, Montaigne gives us an almost comically exaggerated picture of his own lack of either skill or interest in such work. Whatever he has done, "completing some old bit of wall and repairing some badly constructed building," has been in honor of Pierre's memory rather than for his own satisfaction, he says. As the nineteenth-century philosopher Friedrich Nietzsche would warn, "One should not try to surpass one's father in diligence; that makes one sick." On the whole Montaigne did *not* try, and thus he kept himself sane.

Inadequate as he felt himself to be in the practical skills of life, he knew the advantage he had when it came to literature and learning. Pierre's knowledge of books was as limited as his love of them was boundless. Typically for his generation, in Montaigne's view, he made books the object of a cult and went to great lengths to seek out their authors, "receiving them at his house like holy persons" and "collecting their sayings and discourses like oracles." Yet he showed little critical understanding. All right, so Pierre could bounce over the table on one manly thumb, Montaigne seems to say, but in matters of the intellect he was an embarrassment. He worshiped books without understanding them. His son would always try to do the opposite.

Montaigne was right in thinking this characteristic of Pierre's contemporaries. French nobles of the early 1500s loved everything clever and Italianate; they distanced themselves from their own predecessors' defiantly crass attitude to scholarship. What Montaigne neglected to observe was that he himself was just as typical of *his* era in rejecting the book-learning fetish. The fathers filled their sons with literature and history, trained them in critical thinking, and taught them to bandy around classical philosophies like juggling balls. By way of thanks, the sons dismissed it all as valueless and adopted a superior attitude. Some even tried to revive the older anti-scholarly tradition, as if it were a radical departure never thought of before.

There was a tiredness and a sourness in Montaigne's generation, along with a rebellious new form of creativity. If they were cynical, it is easy to see why: they had to watch the ideals that had guided their upbringing turn into a grim joke. The Reformation, hailed by some earlier thinkers as a blast of fresh air beneficial even to the Church itself, became a war and threatened to ruin civilized society. Renaissance principles of beauty, poise, clarity, and intelligence dissolved into violence, cruelty, and extremist theology. Montaigne's half-century was so disastrous for France that it took *another* half-century to recover from it—and in some ways recovery never came, for the turmoil of the late 1500s stopped France from building a major New World empire like those of England and Spain, and kept it inward-looking. By the time of Montaigne's death, France was economically feeble, and ravaged by disease, famine, and public disorder. No wonder young nobles of his generation ended up as exquisitely educated misanthropes.

Montaigne had some of this anti-intellectual streak in him. He grew up to feel that the only hope for humanity lay in the simplicity and ignorance of the peasantry. They were the true philosophers of the modern world, the heirs to classical sages such as Seneca and Socrates. Only they knew how to live, precisely because they knew nothing much about anything else. To this extent, he returned to the cult of ignorance: a slap in the face for Pierre.

But nothing is ever quite the same the second time around. And no one could be less like the medieval nobles than Montaigne, with his essaying and venturing, and his appending of uncertain codas to everything he wrote. His way of adding "though I don't know," implicitly or explicitly, to almost every thought he ever had sets him very far apart from the old ways. The ideals of his father survived in him after all, but in mutant form: softened, darkened, and with the certainty knocked out of them.

THE EXPERIMENT

Perhaps this willingness to question certainties and prejudices just ran in the family. Amid the religious divide, the Eyquems were well known— "famous," said Montaigne—for their freedom from sectarian disharmony. Most remained Catholics, but several converted to Protestantism, causing remarkably little upset in the process. When one young Protestant Eyquem showed signs of extremism, Montaigne's friend La Boétie advised him to desist, "out of respect for the good reputation that the family you belong to has acquired by continual concord—a family that is as dear to me as any family in the world: Lord, what a family! from which there has never come any act other than that of a worthy man."

This admirable clan was also a fairly large one. Montaigne had seven brothers and sisters, not counting the two who were born before him and who died, leaving him the eldest. The age gap between the remaining siblings was considerable; at its widest, it would have felt like a generational divide, for Montaigne was already twenty-seven when his youngest brother, Bertrand, was born.

So far as is known, none of the younger siblings received as much attention or as exceptional an education as little Micheau. The daughters probably had the normal female education, which is to say almost none at all. Even the other sons were treated more conventionally, so far as is known. The only well-documented child in the family is Michel de Montaigne—and he was not merely educated. He was made the object of an almost unprecedented pedagogic experiment.

The unusual treatment began soon after his birth, when Micheau was sent to live with a humble family in a nearby village. Having a peasant wet-nurse was normal enough, but Montaigne's father wanted his son to absorb an understanding of commoners' ways along with their breast-milk, so that he would grow up comfortable with the people who most needed a *seigneur*'s help. Instead of bringing a nurse to the baby, therefore, he sent the baby to the nurse, and left him there long enough to be weaned. Even at the christening, Pierre had "people of the lowliest class" hold the infant over the font. From the start, Montaigne had the impression at once of being a peasant among peasants, and of being very special and different. This is the mixture of feelings that would stay with him for life. He felt ordinary, but knew that the very fact of realizing his ordinariness made him extraordinary.

The village plan had one downside which Pierre is unlikely to have considered. Living with strangers, Micheau must have failed to "bond" (as we might now say) with his real parents. This would apply to some extent to any wet-nursed child, but most would have contact with their mothers the rest of the time. Montaigne apparently did not. If twentieth- and twenty-first-century ideas have any validity (and perhaps they don't: mother–child bonding might prove as transient a fad as wet-nursing), such deprivation in the crucial first months of life would have affected Montaigne's relationship with his mother for ever. According to Montaigne's own assessment, however, the scheme worked beautifully, and he advised his readers, where possible, to do the same. Let your children "be formed by fortune under the laws of the common people and of nature," he said.

However old he was when he was restored to the château—perhaps he was one or two—the break with his adoptive family must have been abrupt indeed, for the second element of his experimental education would prove totally incompatible with the first. Back in his family home, little peasant Micheau was now to be brought up as a native speaker of Latin.

Until now, the language he had heard most, in his foster home, would have been the local Périgord dialect. If he was old enough to eat his hosts' food, he was old enough for his ear to become attuned to their language, although he was too young to speak it. He now had to leap from this to Latin, bypassing the language in which he would one day write: French. This was an astounding project for anyone even to think of, let alone put into effect, and it presented a practical difficulty. Pierre himself had minimal command of Latin; his wife and the servants knew none at all. Even in the wider world, a supply of native Latin speakers could no longer be found. How did Pierre think he was going to bring Montaigne up to be fluent in the language of Cicero and Virgil?

The solution he found was a two-part one. Step one was to engage a tutor who, though no native, did have near-flawless Latin. Pierre found a German named Dr. Horst, whose greatest qualification was having good Latin but almost no French, never mind Périgordian, so that he and young Micheau could communicate in only one way. Thus, from an early age— "before the first loosening of my tongue," as Montaigne put it—Dr. Horst or (in Latin) Horstanus became the most important person in his life.

Step two was to ban everyone else in the household from speaking to Micheau in any living language. If they wanted to tell the boy to eat his breakfast, they had to do it using the Latin imperative and appropriate case-endings. They all duly set about learning a little, including Pierre himself, who worked to brush up his schoolboy knowledge. Thus, as Montaigne wrote, everyone benefited.

My father and mother learned enough Latin in this way to understand it, and acquired sufficient skill to use it when necessary, as did also the servants who were most attached to my service. Altogether, we

Latinized ourselves so much that it overflowed all the way to our villages on every side, where there still remain several Latin names for artisans and tools that have taken root by usage. As for me, I was over six before I understood any more French or Périgordian than Arabic.

Thus, "without artificial means, without a book, without grammar or precept, without the whip, and without tears," Montaigne learned a Latin as fine as that spoken by his tutor, and with a more natural flow than Horst could have managed. When he later encountered other teachers, they complimented him on a Latin that was both technically perfect and down-to-earth.

Why did Pierre do it? This is one of those moments when the half-millennium gap between ourselves and our subject suddenly yawns at our feet. Most people today would think it crazy to separate parent and child for the sake of a dead language. But in the Renaissance, the prize was considered worth the sacrifice. Command of beautiful and grammatically perfect Latin was the highest goal of a humanistic education: it unlocked the door to the ancient world—considered the locus of all human wisdom—as well as to much of modern culture, since most scholars still wrote Latin. It offered entry to a good career: Latin was essential for legal and civil service. The language bestowed an almost magical blessing on anyone who spoke it. If you spoke well, you must be able to think well. Pierre wanted to give his son the best advantage imaginable: a link both to the lost paradise of antiquity and to a successful personal future.

The *way* Pierre wanted Micheau to learn it also exemplified the ideals of the time. Most boys learned their Latin through painful effort at school, but the Romans had not done this: they spoke it as naturally as they breathed air. It was because moderns had to learn the language artificially that they were unable ever to match the ancients in wisdom or greatness of soul—or so went the theory.

It was anything but a cruel experiment, at least in obvious respects. The new theories of education emphasized that learning should be pleasurable, and that the only motivation children needed was their inborn desire for knowledge. When he was a little older, Montaigne would learn Greek in a spirit of fun too. "We volleyed our conjugations back and forth," he recalled, "like those who learn arithmetic and geometry by such games as checkers and chess." His Greek did not stick: he later admitted to having little knowledge of the language. But, in general, the hedonistic approach to education did make a difference to him. Having been guided early in life by his own curiosity alone, he grew up to be an independent-minded adult, following his own path in everything rather than deferring to duty and discipline—an outcome perhaps more far-reaching than his father had bargained for.

Other aspects of Montaigne's early life were governed by similar principles of ease. It was thought that "it troubles the tender brains of children to wake them in the morning with a start," so Pierre had his son charmed out of bed like a cobra every day by the plangent sound of a lute or other musical instrument. Corporal punishment was almost unknown to him; in his entire boyhood, he was only twice struck with a rod, and then very gently. It was an education of "wisdom and tact."

Pierre had got his ideas from his beloved scholar friends, and perhaps also from people he met in Italy, though the main ideologue to whom such an approach can be traced was a Dutchman, Erasmus of Rotterdam, who had written on education while based in Italy two decades earlier. Montaigne wrote that the scheme had been born from his father's having made "all the inquiries a man can make, among men of learning and

understanding." Typically for Pierre, it was at once a scholarly notion and a flighty one. It certainly bore the mark of Pierre, rather than Antoinette, and one would give a lot to know what she thought about the project. If Montaigne's peasant fostering had already set him apart from her, this stage of his education emphasized that separation even further. They were now living in the same house, but linguistically and culturally they were on different planets. She is unlikely to have become very proficient in Latin, although Montaigne says she learned some for his benefit. According to him, Pierre's skills remained rudimentary too. If the experiment was genuinely as rigorous as his account implies (a big if), both parents now had only a stilted and unnatural way of talking to their son. Even Horst could not speak to him in a fully spontaneous manner, however profound his knowledge. So much for "naturalness." One suspects—and hopes—that the rules were broken from time to time. Yet Montaigne mentions nothing of that. Nor does he seem to think that the experiment was anything less than a huge success.

In terms of making him a native Latinist, it did bear fruit in these early years, but the seeds of that fruit did not germinate further. Eventually, through lack of practice, he ended up on the same level as any other well-educated young nobleman. The language lurked deep within him, though. When his father fainted from a kidney-stone attack, decades later, Montaigne exclaimed in Latin as he caught him in his arms.

More lasting were the effects of Montaigne's education on his personality. As happens with much early life experience, it benefited him in exactly the areas where it also damaged him. It set him apart from his household and from his whole contemporary world. This gave him independence of mind, but may have inclined him to a certain detachment in relationships. It gave him great expectations, since he grew up in the company of the greatest writers of antiquity rather than the provincial French of his neighborhood. Yet it also cut off other, more conventional, ambitions, because it led him to question everything that other people strove for. The young Montaigne was unique. He did not need to compete; he barely needed to exert himself. He grew up constrained by some of the most bizarre limits ever imposed on a child, and at the same time had almost unlimited freedom. He was a world unto himself.

In the end he acquired good French, though never the restrained, immaculate version subsequent centuries liked to insist upon in their writers. He wrote idiosyncratically; some would accuse him of sounding like an undisciplined yokel. Still, French was his language of choice—not Latin. In the *Essays* he gives an odd reason for this. French could not be expected to last as long as the classical languages, he said; thus, his writings were doomed to ephemerality, and he could write in any way he liked without worrying about his reputation. The fact that it was not frozen in rigid perfection appealed to him on principle: if it was flawed, there was less pressure to use it impeccably.

Montaigne usually disliked idealistic schemes, but in this case he approved of his father's experiment. When he wrote about education himself, his ideas emerged as a more moderate version of Pierre's—which were too extreme ever to have much appeal to anyone else. The contemporary Montaignesque writer Tabourot des Accords did suggest that a group of gentlemen might pool resources to bring up their children in a sort of Latin commune, since it was too hard to manage alone, but there is no sign that this was actually done.

Less bizarre aspects of the sixteenth century's "child centered" education did flourish through the years, all the way to the present. In the eighteenth century, Jean-Jacques Rousseau made a cult of bringing up children in the light of nature; he borrowed some of his ideas from Montaigne, and especially from the uncharacteristically prescriptive essay Montaigne wrote about education.

He had to be prescriptive, for the essay "Of Education" was more or less commissioned from him by a neighbor, the pregnant Diane de Foix, comtesse de Gurson, who wanted Montaigne's opinion on how she should give her child (assuming it was a boy) the best start in life. Montaigne's advice shows how pleased he was with his own early experiences. First, he said, she should restrain her maternal instincts sufficiently to bring in an outsider to be her son's mentor instead; parents are too much at the mercy of their emotions. They cannot stop worrying about whether the boy might catch a cold in the rain, or be thrown from his horse, or have his skin cut in fencing practice. A tutor can be tougher. On the other hand, he must not be allowed to be cruel. Learning should be a pleasure, and children should grow up to imagine wisdom with a smiling face, not a fierce and terrifying one.

He fulminates against the brutal methods of most schools. "Away with violence and compulsion!" If you enter a school in lesson time, he says, "you hear nothing but cries, both from tortured boys and from masters drunk with rage." All this achieves is to put children off learning for life.

Often, books need not be used at all. One learns dancing by dancing; one learns to play the lute by playing the lute. The same is true of thinking, and indeed of living. Every experience can be a learning opportunity: "a page's prank, a servant's blunder, a remark at table." The child should learn to question everything: to "pass everything through a sieve and lodge nothing in his head on mere authority and trust." Traveling is useful; so is socializing, which teaches the child to be open to others and to adapt to anyone he finds around him. Eccentricities should be ironed out early, because they make it difficult to get on with others. "I have seen men flee from the smell of apples more than from harquebus fire, others take fright at a mouse, others throw up at the sight of cream, and others at the plumping of a feather bed." All this stands in the way of good relationships and of good living. It can be avoided, for young human beings are malleable.

Or at least, they are malleable up to a point. Montaigne soon changes tack. Whatever you do, he says, you cannot really change inborn disposition. You can guide it or train it, but not get rid of it. In another essay he wrote, "There is no one who, if he listens to himself, does not discover in himself a pattern all his own, a ruling pattern, which struggles against education."

Pierre, one imagines, had a less fatalistic view of human nature, for he thought that the young Micheau *could* be molded, and that the experiment was worth the trouble. With his usual can-do attitude, he set out to build and develop his son just as he set out to build and develop his estate.

Alas, as with other projects, Pierre left the job unfinished, or so Montaigne believed. At the age of about six, the boy was abruptly removed from his unconventional hothouse and sent off to school like everyone else. All his life, he remained convinced that this was his fault: that some sign of his recalcitrance—his "ruling pattern"—had made his father give up. Or perhaps Pierre had merely caved in to convention, now that his original advisers were no longer around. It seems more likely that Pierre had always intended to send Micheau to school at a certain stage. Not understanding the plan, Montaigne read in a criticism of himself that was probably not there. The whole multistage progression, from peasant family to Latin nursery to school, amounted to a recipe for producing a perfect gentleman, independent of mind yet able to mold himself to society when necessary. Thus, in 1539, Montaigne joined other boys his age at the Collège de Guyenne in Bordeaux.

He would be a pupil there for a decade, until at least 1548, and to some extent would adjust to it, but at first it was a severe shock to his system. For a start, he had to get used to a city existence after the freedom of a boy's life in the countryside. Bordeaux was some forty miles away from his home, several hours' journey even on a fast horse. The trip was slowed further by the necessity of crossing the Dordogne on the way: a ferry picked travelers

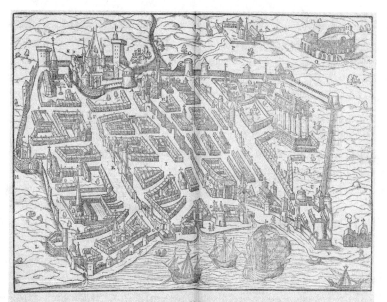

S'enfuyt les lieux notables de la ville de Bourdeaux.

ABCD, La premiere ville de Bourdeaux, quadrangle plus long que large. AH, L'Eglise Metropolitaine de saint André. D La place deuant le palais. EFGD, premiere creüe de la ville. FKG, Les Fossez. G Potte des Salinieres. I La place du Marché. K La porte ancienne de la ville. L Le Bouleuart de sainte Croix. M Le Bouleuart & porte saint Iulian. NA, Le Chasteau du Fa, du Ha, en langage du pays. O La porte Di Iau (dei Iouis) iuec son Bouleuart, autrement dicte de saint Seuerin. P Le Bourg & Eglise collegiale de saint Seuerin. Q Les restes d'vn Amphitheatre, qu'on nomme le palais Gallien. R Porte & Bouleuart de saint Germain aupres des Iacobins. S Vn ancien edifice, appellé le Palais Tutele, quadrangle, de huit colomnes de longueur, & six de largeur, desquelles y en a encores dishuict debout. TV, Le Chasteau Trom-pette. X Les Chartreux. Le port en forme de croissant, dit le Port de la Lune.

up from gentle green hills and vineyards, and dropped them in the heart of Bordeaux's commercial district—a different world.

Walled and claustrophobic, clustered tightly around the river, sixteenth-century Bordeaux was not at all like the city of today. Its old streets were ripped out in the eighteenth and nineteenth centuries, to be replaced by boulevards and big creamy buildings which now give it a slightly abstract quality. In Montaigne's day, there was nothing creamy about it. It was populous, having about twenty-five thousand residents, and very busy. Its river was full of shipping. Its banks were equipped for the unloading of cargo: mainly wine, as well as a richly aroma'd mixture of preserved fish, salt, and timber.

The mood changed once one reached the Collège de Guyenne itself, which was set in a tranquil area of the city away from the commercial center and surrounded by elms. It was an excellent school, though Montaigne spoke ill of it. Its curriculum and methods sound formidable to a modern sensibility. Everything revolved around the rote study of Latin, the one subject in which Montaigne enjoyed an advantage so great that his teachers must have marveled at him. Both teachers and pupils were expected to converse in it. Just as in Montaigne's own home, the school was full of awkward, stilted speech—but there the similarity ended. Here no gentle music was played; there was no emphasis on pleasure and, most shockingly of all, no assumption that little Micheau was the center of the universe.

Instead, he now had to fit in with everyone else. Classes began early in the morning with minute dissection of literary examples, usually from writers like Cicero who were least likely to appeal to young readers' tastes. In the afternoons, they studied grammar in the abstract, without recourse to examples. In the evenings, texts were read out together with analyses dictated by the teacher, which the boys were expected to memorize and spout back on request.

At first, Montaigne's mastery of Latin got him quickly promoted to classes beyond his age group. But the bad influence of his less privileged classmates gradually destroyed his easy command of the language, so that—according to him—he left the school knowing less of it than when he arrived.

In fact, the Collège was relatively adventurous and open minded, and some aspects of school life amused Montaigne more than he liked to admit. In the older classes, students competed in feats of oratory and debate, all in Latin of course, and with less attention to what they said than to how they said it. From these, Montaigne picked up rhetorical skills and critical habits of thought which he would use all his life. It was probably also here that he first encountered the idea of using "commonplace books": notebooks in which to write down snippets one encountered in one's reading, setting them in creative juxtaposition. In later years, as a teenager, Montaigne studied more interesting subjects, including philosophy—not, unfortunately, the kind he liked, which dealt with the question of how to live, but mostly Aristotelian logic and metaphysics. Some light relief was also allowed. A new teacher at the school, Marc-Antoine Muret, wrote and directed plays; Montaigne starred in one. He turned out to be a natural on stage, having (he wrote) an unexpected "assurance in expression and flexibility in voice and gesture."

All this occurred during a difficult period for the Collège. In 1547, the forward-thinking principal, André Gouvéa, was forced out by conservative political factions. He left for Portugal, taking his best teachers with him. The following year, upheavals broke out in Bordeaux itself: the salt-tax riots, which would cause such stress to Montaigne's father during his term as mayor. The southwest had traditionally been exempt from this tax. Now, suddenly, the new king Henri II tried to impose it, with inflammatory results.

Crowds of rebels assembled to protest, and for five days from August 17 to August 22, 1548, mobs roamed the streets setting fire to tax collectors' houses. Some attacked the homes of anyone who looked rich, until the disorder threatened to turn into a general peasant uprising. A few tax collectors were killed. Their bodies were dragged through the streets and covered in heaps of salt to underline the point. In one of the worst incidents, Tristan de Moneins, the town's lieutenant-general and governor—thus the king's official representative—was lynched. He had shut himself up in the city's massive royal citadel, the Château Trompette, but a crowd gathered outside and howled for him to come out. Perhaps thinking to earn their respect by facing up to them, he ventured forth, but it was a mistake. They beat him to death.

Then fifteen, Montaigne was out in the streets, for the Collège had suspended classes during the violence. He witnessed the killing of Moneins, a scene he never forgot. It raised in his mind, perhaps for the first time, a question that would haunt the entire *Essays* in varying guises: whether it was better to win an enemy's respect by an open display of defiance, or to throw yourself on his mercy and hope to win him over by submission or an appeal to his better self.

In this case, Montaigne thought Moneins had failed because he was not sure what he was trying to do. Having decided to brave the crowd, he then lost his confidence and behaved with deference, sending mixed messages. He also underestimated the distorted psychology of a mob. Once worked up into a frenzy, it can only be either soothed or suppressed; it cannot be expected to show ordinary human sympathy. Moneins seemed not to know this. He expected the same fellow-feeling as he would from an individual.

He was certainly brave to cast himself unarmed into a "sea of madmen." But his only hope then would have been to maintain this bold face to the end. He

> should have swallowed the whole cup and not abandoned his role; whereas what happened to him was that after having seen the danger close up, he lost his nerve and changed once again that deflated and fawning countenance that he had assumed into a frightened one, filling his voice and his eyes with astonishment and penitence. Trying to hole up and hide, he inflamed them and called them down on himself.

The shocking sight of Moneins's murder, and no doubt of other disturbing scenes during that week, taught Montaigne a great deal about the psychological complexity of conflict and the difficulty of conducting oneself well in crises. In this case, the violence was eventually calmed, mainly by Montaigne's future father-in-law, Geoffrey de La Chassaigne, who negotiated a truce. But the city would suffer a severe punishment for allowing such disobedience. Ten thousand royal troops were sent there in October under the Constable de Montmorency; the title "constable" officially meant only "chief of the royal stables," but his job was one of immense power.

The troops remained for over three months, with Montmorency conducting a reign of terror. He encouraged his men to loot and kill like an occupying force in a foreign country. Anyone directly identified as having taken part in the riots was broken on the wheel, or burned. Everything was done to humiliate Bordeaux physically, financially, and morally. It lost legal jurisdiction over its own affairs; its artillery and gunpowder were confiscated; its *parlement* was dissolved, and for a while it was governed by magistrates from other parts of France. It also had to pay the costs of its own occupation. And, when Moneins's body was exhumed for reburial in the cathedral, local officials were obliged to fall on their knees in front of Montmorency's house to beg forgiveness for the killing.

The privileges were gradually restored, thanks in part to Montaigne's father's efforts, as mayor, to make Bordeaux look good again in the king's eyes. Amazingly, in the long run, the rebellion did achieve its aim. Unnerved by the riots, Henri II decided not to enforce the salt tax. But the price had been high.

Just as this drama subsided, in 1549, plague broke out in the city. It was not a long or major outbreak, but it was enough to make everyone examine their skin uneasily and dread the sound of a cough. It also forced the Collège to close again for a while—but by this time Montaigne had probably already moved on. He left the school some time around 1548, ready to start the next phase of his young life.

There now follows a long period, until 1557, in which it is not clear what he was doing. He may have returned to the estate. He may have been sent to an academy, a sort of finishing school where young men learned the noble accomplishments of riding, dueling, hunting, heraldry, singing, and dancing. (If so, Montaigne paid no attention to anything except the riding lessons: this was the only one of these skills he later claimed to be good at.) At some stage, he must also have studied the law. He emerged into adulthood with all he needed to become a successful young *seigneur*, and, despite his dislike of the experience, with a useful set of abilities and experiences acquired from school. Foremost among these was a discovery that would have delighted his father: that of books, and of the worlds they opened up to him—worlds far beyond the vineyards of Guyenne and the tedium of a sixteenth-century schoolhouse.

4. Q. How to live? A. Read a lot, forget most of what you read, and be slow-witted

THE CLOSE GRAMMATICAL study of Cicero and Horace almost killed Montaigne's interest in literature before it was born. But some of the teachers at the school helped keep it going, mainly by not taking more entertaining books out of the boy's hands when they caught him reading them, and perhaps even by slipping a few more his way—doing this so discreetly that he could enjoy reading them without ceasing to feel like a rebel.

One unsuitable text which Montaigne discovered for himself at the age of seven or eight, and which changed his life, was Ovid's *Metamorphoses*. This tumbling cornucopia of stories about miraculous transformations among ancient gods and mortals was the closest thing the Renaissance had to a compendium of fairy tales. As full of horrors and delights as a Grimm or Andersen, and quite unlike the texts of the schoolroom, it was the sort of thing an imaginative sixteenth-century boy could read with eyes rounded and fingers white-knuckled from gripping the covers too tightly.

In Ovid, people change. They turn into trees, animals, stars, bodies of water, or disembodied voices. They alter sex; they become werewolves. A woman called Scylla enters a poisonous pool and sees each of her limbs turn into a dog-like monster from which she cannot pull away because the monsters are also *her*. The hunter Actaeon is changed into a stag, and his own hunting-dogs chase him down. Icarus flies so high that the sun burns him. A king and a queen turn into two mountains. The nymph Samacis plunges herself into the pool where the beautiful Hermaphroditus is bathing, and wraps herself around him like a squid holding fast to its prey, until her flesh melts into his and the two become one person, half male, half female. Once a taste of this sort of thing had started him off, Montaigne galloped through other books similarly full of good stories: Virgil's *Aeneid*, then Terence, Plautus, and various modern Italian comedies. He learned, in defiance of school policy, to associate reading with excitement. It was the one positive thing to come out of his time there. ("But," Montaigne adds, "for all that, it was still school.")

Many of his early discoveries remained lifelong loves. Although the initial thrill of the *Metamorphoses* wore off, he filled the *Essays* with stories from it, and emulated Ovid's style of slipping from one topic to the next without introduction or apparent order. Virgil continued to be a favorite too, though the mature Montaigne was cheeky enough to suggest that some passages in the *Aeneid* might have been "brushed up a little."

Because he liked to know what people really did, rather than what someone imagined they might do, Montaigne's preference soon shifted from poets to historians and biographers. It was in real-life stories, he said, that you encountered human nature in all its complexity. You learned the "diversity and truth" of man, as well as "the variety of the ways he is put together, and the accidents that threaten him." Among historians, he liked Tacitus best, once remarking that he had just read through his *History* from beginning to end without interruption. He loved how Tacitus treated public events from the point of view of "private behavior and inclinations," and was struck by the historian's fortune in living through a "strange and extreme" period, just as Montaigne himself did. Indeed, he wrote of Tacitus, "you would often say that it is us he is describing."

Turning to biographers, Montaigne liked those who went beyond the external events of a life and tried to reconstruct a person's inner world from the evidence. No one excelled in this more than his favorite writer of all: the Greek biographer Plutarch, who lived from around AD 46 to around 120 and whose vast *Lives* presented narratives of notable Greeks and Romans in themed pairs. Plutarch was to Montaigne what Montaigne was to many later readers: a model to follow, and a treasure chest of ideas, quotations, and anecdotes to plunder. "He is so universal and so full that on all occasions, and however eccentric the subject you have taken up, he makes his way into your work." The truth of this last part is undeniable: several sections of the *Essays* are paste-ins from Plutarch, left almost unchanged. No one thought of this as plagiarism: such imitation of great authors was then considered an excellent practice. Moreover, Montaigne subtly changed everything he stole, if only by setting it in a different context and hedging it around with uncertainties.

He loved the way Plutarch assembled his work by stuffing in fistfuls of images, conversations, people, animals, and objects of all kinds, rather than by coldly arranging abstractions and arguments. His writing is full of *things*, Montaigne pointed out. If Plutarch wants to tell us that the trick in living well is to make the best of any situation, he does it by telling the story of a man who threw a stone at his dog, missed, hit his stepmother instead, and exclaimed, "Not so bad after all!" Or, if he wants to show us how we tend to forget the good things in life and obsess only about the bad, he writes about flies landing on mirrors and sliding about on the smooth surface, unable to find a footing until they hit a rough area. Plutarch leaves no neat endings, but he sows seeds from which whole worlds of inquiry can be developed. He points where we can go if we like; he does not lead us, and it is up to us whether we obey or not.

Montaigne also loved the strong sense of Plutarch's own personality that comes across in his work: "I think I know him even into his soul." This was what Montaigne looked for in a book, just as people later looked for it in him: the feeling of meeting a real person across the centuries. Reading Plutarch, he lost awareness of the gap in time that divided them—much bigger than the gap between Montaigne and us. It does not matter, he wrote, whether a person one loves has been dead for fifteen hundred years or, like his own father at the time, eighteen years. Both are equally remote; both are equally close.

Montaigne's merging of favorite authors with his own father says a lot about how he read: he took up books as if they were people, and welcomed them into his family. The rebellious, Ovid-reading boy would one day accumulate a library of around a thousand volumes: a good size, but not an indiscriminate assemblage. Some were inherited from his friend La Boétie; others he bought himself. He collected unsystematically, without adding fine bindings or considering rarity value. Montaigne would never repeat his father's mistake of fetishizing books or their authors. One cannot imagine him kissing volumes like holy relics, as Erasmus or the poet Petrarch reportedly used to, or putting on his best clothes before reading them, like Machiavelli, who wrote: "I strip off my muddy, sweaty, workaday clothes, and put on the robes of court and palace, and in this graver dress I enter the courts of the ancients and am welcomed by them." Montaigne would have found this ridiculous. He preferred to converse with the ancients in a tone of camaraderie, sometimes even teasing them, as when he twits Cicero for his pomposity or suggests that Virgil could have made more of an effort.

Effort was just what he himself claimed never to make, either in reading or writing. "I leaf through now one book, now another," he wrote, "without order and without plan, by disconnected fragments." He could sound positively cross if he thought anyone might suspect him of careful scholarship. Once, catching himself having said that books offer consolation, he hastily added, "Actually I use them scarcely any more than those who do not know them at all." And one of his sentences starts, "We who have little contact with books . . ." His rule in reading remained the one he had learned from Ovid: pursue pleasure. "If I encounter difficulties in reading," he wrote, "I do not gnaw my nails over them; I leave them there. I do nothing without gaiety."

In truth he did work hard sometimes, but only when he thought the labor was worthwhile. Annotations in Montaigne's hand survive on a few books from his collection, notably a copy of Lucretius's *On the Nature of Things—*

clearly a text that merited close attention. This is exactly the kind of book, idiosyncratic and intellectually adventurous, that you would expect Montaigne to want to take such trouble over.

Presenting himself as a layabout, flicking through a few pages before tossing the book aside with a yawn, suited Montaigne. It accorded with the dilettantish atmosphere he wanted to evoke in his own writing. As the copy of Lucretius shows, the truth must have been more complicated. But no doubt he did abandon whatever bored him: that was how he had been brought up, after all. Pierre taught him that everything should be approached in "gentleness and freedom, without rigor and constraint." Of this, Montaigne made a whole principle of living.

MONTAIGNE THE SLOW AND FORGETFUL

Whenever Montaigne did exert himself to flick through a book, according to him, he promptly forgot almost everything he had read. "Memory is a wonderfully useful tool, and without it judgment does its work with difficulty," he wrote, before adding, "it is entirely lacking in me."

> There is no man who has less business talking about memory. For I recognize almost no trace of it in me, and I do not think there is another one in the world so monstrously deficient.

He admitted that this was a nuisance. It was annoying to lose his most interesting ideas simply because they came to him while he was out riding and had no paper on which to write them down. It would have been nice to remember more of his dreams, too. As he wrote, quoting Terence, "I'm full of cracks, and leak out on all sides."

Montaigne often sprang to the defense of the mnemonically challenged. He felt "indignation" and "personal resentment" when reading, for example, about Lyncestes, who was obliged to give a speech of defense to a whole army after being accused of conspiring against Alexander the Great. Lyncestes memorized an oration, but, when he tried to deliver it, he got only a few words out before becoming confused and forgetting the rest.

While he stammered and hedged, a nearby group of soldiers lost patience and ran him through with their pikes. They thought his inability to speak proved his guilt. "That certainly was good reasoning!" exclaimed Montaigne. It proved only that, under stress, an overburdened memory is likely to take fright at its load like a panicky horse, and dump the lot.

Even if one's life was not at stake, learning a speech by heart was not necessarily a good idea. Spontaneous talk was usually more enjoyable to listen to. When Montaigne himself had to speak in public, he tried to be nonchalant, and used "unstudied and unpremeditated gestures, as if they arose from the immediate occasion." He particularly avoided announcing a sequence of numbered points ("I will now discuss six possible approaches . . .") because it was both boring and risky: one was likely either to forget some of them or to end up with too many.

Sometimes the very significance or interest of a piece of information drove it out of his mind. Once, being lucky enough to meet a group of Tupinambá people brought over by French colonists from Brazil, he listened eagerly to their answers when they were asked what they thought of France. They replied with three remarks, all fascinating—but when Montaigne came to recount the conversation in his *Essays*, he could remember only two. Other lapses were worse. In a published letter describing the death of La Boétie—the man he loved most in his life—he confessed that he might have forgotten some of his friend's final acts and parting words.

Montaigne's admission of such failings was a direct challenge to the Renaissance ideal of oratory and rhetoric, which held that being able to think well was the same as being able to speak well, and being able to speak well depended upon remembering your flow of argument together with sparkling quotations and examples to adorn it. Devotees of the art of memory, or *ars memoriae*, learned techniques for stringing together hours' worth of rhetoric, and even developed these techniques into a whole program of philosophical self-improvement. This had no appeal for Montaigne.

From the start, some readers have refused to believe that his memory could really be as bad as he claimed. This irritated him so much that he complained about it in the *Essays*. But doubters continued to point out that, for example, he seemed to have no difficulty remembering quotations from his reading: so many appear in the *Essays*, not least the one about feeling like a leaking pot. Either he was less leaky than he claimed, or he was less lazy, for if he did not remember the quotations, he must have written them down. Some people became positively angry about this. One near-contemporary of his, the poet Dominique Baudier, said that Montaigne's lamentations about his memory drove him to "nausea and laughter"—an extreme reaction. The seventeenth-century philosopher Malebranche felt Montaigne was lying to him, a serious charge against a writer who always made much of his honesty.

It was a charge that had something to it. Montaigne surely did remember more than he let on. It is not unusual to feel let down by one's memory: this is part of the imperfect human condition. An undisciplined memory is also just what one might expect from Montaigne's easygoing upbringing and his dislike of forcing himself in anything. His apparent modesty on this subject can also be translated into a subtle claim to virtues which he thought more important. One of these, ironically, was honesty. As the old saying had it, bad memories make bad liars. If Montaigne was too forgetful to keep stories straight in his head, he had to tell the truth. Also, his lack of memory kept his speeches brief and his anecdotes concise, since he could not remember long ones, and it enabled him to exercise good judgment. People with good memories have cluttered minds, but his brain was so blissfully empty that nothing could get in the way of common sense. Finally, he easily forgot any slight inflicted on him by others, and therefore bore few resentments. In short, he presented himself as floating through the world on a blanket of benevolent vacancy.

Where Montaigne's memory did seem to work well, if he wanted it to, was in reconstructing personal experiences such as the riding accident. Instead of resolving them into neat, superficial anecdotes, he could recover feelings from the inside—not perfectly, because the Heraclitan stream kept carrying him away, but very closely. The nineteenth-century psychologist Dugald Stewart speculated that Montaigne's lack of control of his memory made him better at such tasks. Montaigne was attuned to the kind of "involuntary" memory that would one day fascinate Proust: those blasts from the past that irrupt unexpectedly into the present, perhaps in response to a long-forgotten taste or smell. Such moments seem possible only if they are surrounded by an ocean of forgetfulness, as well as a suitable mood and sufficient leisure.

Montaigne certainly did not like to strain at things. "I have to solicit it nonchalantly," he said of his memory. "It serves me at its own time, not at mine." Any effort to haul something back on demand just drove the sought item further into the shadows. Conversely, he noticed, nothing made an incident stick in the memory more than a conscious effort to forget it.

"What I do easily and naturally," he wrote, "I can no longer do if I order myself to do it by strict command." Allowing his memory to follow its own path formed part of his general policy of letting nature govern his actions. In his childhood, the result was that he often appeared to be lazy and good for nothing, and in many ways he probably was. Despite his father's constant efforts to motivate him, he wrote, he turned out to be "so sluggish, lax, and drowsy that they could not tear me from my sloth, not even to make me play."

By his own estimation, he was not only idle but slow-witted. His intelligence could not penetrate the slightest cloud: "There is no subtlety so empty that it will not stump me. Of games in which the mind has a part—chess, cards, draughts, and others—I understand nothing but the barest rudiments." He had a "tardy understanding," a "weak imagination," and a "slow mind," none of which was helped by his lack of recall. All his faculties slumbered along together, snoring gently: he makes his brain sound like a tea party at which all the guests were Dormice.

But, again, there were benefits. Once he had grasped something, he grasped it firmly. Even as a child, he says, "What I saw, I saw well." Moreover, he deliberately used his inert manner as a cover under which he could hide any number of "bold ideas" and independent opinions. His apparent modesty made it possible for him to claim something more important than quick wits: sound judgment.

Montaigne would make a good model for the modern "Slow Movement," which has spread (in a leisurely fashion) to become something of a cult since its inception in the late twentieth century. Like Montaigne, its adherents make slow speed into a moral principle. Its founding text is Sten Nadolny's novel *The Discovery of Slowness*, which relates the life of Arctic explorer John Franklin, a man whose natural pace of living and thinking is portrayed as that of an elderly sloth after a long massage and a pipe of opium. Franklin is mocked as a child, but when he reaches the far North he finds the environment perfectly suited to his nature: a place where one takes one's time, where very little happens, and where it is important to stop and think before rushing into action. Long after its publication in Germany in 1983, *The Discovery of Slowness* remained a best seller and was even marketed as an alternative management manual. Meanwhile, Italy generated the Slow Food movement, which began in protest against the Rome branch of McDonald's and grew to become an entire philosophy of good living.

Montaigne would have understood all this very well. For him, slowness opened the way to wisdom, and to a spirit of moderation which offset the excess and zealotry dominating the France of his time. He was lucky enough to be naturally immune to both, having no tendency to be carried away by the enthusiasms others seemed prone to. "I am nearly always in place, like heavy and inert bodies," he wrote. Once planted, it was easy for him to resist intimidation, for nature had made him "incapable of submitting to force and violence."

As with most things in Montaigne, this is only part of the story. As a young man he *could* fly off the handle, and he was restless: in the *Essays* he says, "I know not which of the two, my mind or my body, I have had more difficulty in keeping to one place." Perhaps he only played the sloth when it suited him.

"Forget much of what you learn" and "Be slow-witted" became two of Montaigne's best answers to the question of how to live. They freed him to think wisely rather than glibly; they allowed him to avoid the fanatical notions and foolish deceptions that ensnared other people; and they let him follow his own thoughts wherever they led—which was all he really wanted to do.

Slow wits and forgetfulness could be cultivated, but Montaigne believed he was lucky in having his by birth. His tendency to do things his own way became evident from an early age, and was accompanied by a surprising degree of confidence. "I remember that from my tenderest childhood people noticed in me some indefinable carriage of the body and certain gestures testifying to some vain and stupid pride," he wrote. The vanity was superficial: he was not deeply infused with the stuff, only lightly "sprinkled." But his inner independence kept him cool. Always prepared to speak his mind, the young Montaigne was also prepared to make other people wait for what he had to say.

THE YOUNG MONTAIGNE IN TROUBLED TIMES

Montaigne's air of nonchalant superiority was made more difficult to carry off by his having a smallish physical build: something he bemoaned constantly. It was different for women, he wrote. Other forms of good looks could compensate. In men, stature was "the only beauty," and it was just the quality he lacked.

> Where smallness dwells, neither breadth and roundness of forehead, nor clarity and softness of eyes, nor the moderate form of the nose, nor small size of ears and mouth, nor regularity and whiteness of teeth, nor the smooth thickness of a beard brown as the husk of a chestnut, nor curly hair, nor proper roundness of head, nor freshness of color, nor a pleasant facial expression, nor an odorless body, nor just proportion of limbs, can make a handsome man.

Even Montaigne's employees did not look up to him, and, when he traveled or visited the royal court with a retinue of servants, he found it most annoying to be the one asked, "Where is the master?" Yet there was little he could do, other than go on horseback wherever possible—his favorite ploy.

A visit to Montaigne's tower suggests that he was telling the truth: the doorways stand only around five foot high. People in general were shorter then, and the doors were built before Montaigne lived there, but clearly he did not bang his head often enough to go to the trouble of having them raised. Of course it is hard to know whether it was his self-proclaimed smallness or his self-proclaimed laziness that was the deciding factor.

He may have been diminutive, but he tells us that he had a strong, solid build, and that he conducted himself with flair, often strolling with a stick on which he would lean "in an affected manner." In later life, he took up his father's practice of dressing in austere black and white, but as a young man he dressed with stylish ease according to the fashion of the day, with "a cloak worn like a scarf, the hood over one shoulder, a neglected stocking."

The most vivid picture of the young Montaigne comes from a poem addressed to him by his slightly older friend Étienne de La Boétie. It shows both what was troubling about Montaigne and what made him attractive. La Boétie thought him brilliant and full of promise, but in danger of wasting his talents. He needed guidance from some calmer, wiser mentor—a role in which La Boétie cast himself—but he had a stubborn tendency to reject this guidance when it was offered. He was too susceptible to pretty young women, and too pleased with himself. "My house supplies ample riches, my age ample powers," La Boétie has Montaigne say complacently in the poem. "And indeed a sweet girl is smiling at me." La Boétie compares him to a beautiful Alcibiades, blessed by fortune, or a Hercules, capable of heroic things but hesitating too long at the moral crossroads. His greatest charms were also his greatest faults.

By the time this poem was written, Montaigne had already traveled a long way from his schoolboy days; he had entered upon his career in the Bordeaux *parlement*. Having disappeared from biographical view for some years after finishing his studies at the Collège, he reappeared in the city as a young magistrate.

To embark on such a course, he must have studied law somewhere. He is unlikely to have done this in Bordeaux; more likely cities are Paris and Toulouse. Perhaps he spent time in both. Remarks in the *Essays* show that he knew Toulouse well, and he also had a lot to say about Paris. He tells us that the city had his heart since childhood—which could mean any stage of his youth, up to around twenty-five. "I love her tenderly," he says, "even to her warts and her spots." Paris was the only place where he didn't mind feeling like a Frenchman rather than a proudly local Gascon. It was a great city in every way: "great in population, great in the felicity of her situation, but above all great and incomparable in variety and diversity of the good things of life."

Wherever Montaigne acquired his training, it fulfilled its function: it propelled him into the legal and political career that may have been envisaged for him from the start. It then kept him there for thirteen years. This period usually shrinks small in biographies, since it is patchily documented, but they were important years indeed, running from just before Montaigne's twenty-fourth birthday to just after his thirty-seventh. When he retired to his country life, growing wine and writing in his tower, he had already accumulated a wealth of experience in public service, and this was still fresh in his mind in the early essays. By the time he came to the later ones, even tougher responsibilities had taken over.

Montaigne's first post was not in Bordeaux, but in another nearby town, Périgueux, northeast of the family estate. Its court had only recently been founded, in 1554, and would almost immediately be abolished, in 1557. The main purpose of it had been to raise money, since public offices were always sold for cash. The abolition ensued because the more powerful Bordeaux *parlement* objected to Périgueux's existence, and even more strenuously to the fact that, for some reason, officials there received a higher salary than they did.

Montaigne went to Périgueux in late 1556, and the court survived just long enough to start his career. As things turned out, it even put him on a fast track into Bordeaux politics, for when Périgueux closed many officials were transferred there. Montaigne was among them: his name appears on the list. They were not exactly welcomed, but Bordeaux's magistrates had no choice in the matter. They made up for it by making life as uncomfortable for the Périgueux men as possible, allotting them a cramped working space and depriving them of the service of court ushers. The resentment is understandable: the Périgueux men were still receiving their higher salaries. These were helpfully cut in August 1561, which in turn made the Périgueux contingent unhappy. Although he was still junior, at twenty-eight, Montaigne was chosen to present their appeal to the court. His speech, reported in the Bordeaux records, marks his first appearance there. No doubt he used his newly honed public speaking tricks—all spontaneity and unrehearsed charm—but it did not work. The *parlement* ruled against the protesters, and their salaries went down after all.

Despite the unharmonious office politics, life in the Bordeaux *parlement* must have been more interesting than in Périgueux. It was one of eight key city *parlements* in France, and, even with its privileges still only partially restored, Bordeaux was among the most powerful. It had responsibility for most local laws and civic administration, and could reject royal edicts or present formal remonstrances to the king whenever he issued a law they did not like—as happened often in these troubled times.

At first, Montaigne's daily life involved the law more than politics. He worked primarily for the Chambre des Enquêtes, or court of inquiry, where his task was to assess civil cases too complex to be resolved immediately by the judges of the main court, the Grand'chambre. He would study the details, summarize them, and hand his written interpretation to the councillors. It was not up to him to pass judgment, only to sum things up intelligently and lucidly, and capture each party's point of view. Perhaps this was where he first developed his feeling for the multiplicity of perspectives on every human situation, a feeling that runs like an artery through the *Essays*.

Thinking of his job in these terms makes sixteenth-century law sound an engrossing pursuit, but it was hampered by extreme pedantry. All legal arguments had to be based on written authorities, and fitted into pre-defined categories. The facts of each case were often secondary to codes, statutes, documented customs, jurisprudential writings, and above all commentaries and glosses—volumes and volumes of them. Even simple cases required the study of seemingly infinite verbiage, usually by some long-suffering junior such as Montaigne.

It was the commentaries Montaigne hated most, as he did secondary literature of any kind:

> It is more of a job to interpret the interpretations than to interpret the things, and there are more books about books than about any other subject: we do nothing but write glosses about each other.

Rabelais had satirized the mountain of documents that piled up around every case: his character Judge Bridlegoose spent hours reading and pondering before making his final decisions by tossing dice, a method he found as reliable as any other. Many authors also attacked the widespread corruption among lawyers. In general, justice was recognized as being so unjust that, as

Montaigne complained, ordinary people avoided it rather than seeking it out. He cited a local incident in which a group of peasants found a man lying stabbed and bleeding on a path. He begged them to give him water and help him to his feet, but they ran off, not daring to touch him in case they were held responsible for the attack. Montaigne had the job of talking to them after they were tracked down. "What could I say to them?" he wrote. They were right to be afraid. In another case he mentions, a gang of killers confessed to a murder for which someone had already been tried and was about to be executed. Surely this ought to mean a stay of execution? No, decided the court: that would set a dangerous precedent for overturning judgments.

Montaigne was not the only one to call for legal reform in the sixteenth century. Many of his criticisms echoed those being put forward at the same time by France's enlightened chancellor, Michel de L'Hôpital, in a campaign which resulted in real improvements. Some of Montaigne's other arguments were more original and far-reaching. For him, the greatest problem with the law was that it did not take account of a fundamental fact about the human condition: people are fallible. A final verdict was always expected, yet by definition it was often impossible to reach one that had any certainty. Evidence was often faulty or inadequate, and, to complicate matters, judges made personal mistakes. No judge could honestly think all his decisions perfect: they followed inclinations more than evidence, and it often made a difference how well they had digested their lunch. This was natural and thus unavoidable, but at least a wise judge could become conscious of his fallibility and take it into account. He could learn to slow down: to treat his initial responses with caution and think things through more carefully. The one good thing about the law was that it made human failings so obvious: a good philosophical lesson.

If lawyers were error-prone, so too were the laws they made, since they were human products. Again, that was a fact that could only be acknowledged and accommodated rather than changed. This sideways step into self-doubt, self-awareness, and acknowledgement of imperfection became a distinctive mark of Montaigne's thought on all subjects, not just the law. It does not seem a great stretch to trace its initial spark to those early years of experience in Bordeaux.

When not in court, Montaigne's job involved another field of activity calculated to bring home to anyone how limited and unreliable human affairs are: politics. He was often sent on errands to other cities, including several to Paris, a week or so's journey away, where he had to liaise with the Paris *parlement* and sometimes with the royal court. The latter, in particular, was an education in human nature.

The first court Montaigne got to know was that of Henri II. He must have met the king in person, for he complained that Henri "could never call by his right name a gentleman from this part of Gascony"—presumably himself, this being a time when he still went under the regional name of Eyquem. Henri II was nothing like his brilliant father François I, from whom he had inherited the throne in 1547. He lacked François's political insight and relied heavily on advisers, including an aging mistress, Diane de Poitiers, and a powerful wife, Catherine de' Medici. Henri II's weakness was partly to blame for France's later problems, as rival factions sensed an opportunity and began a power struggle that would dominate the country for decades. The competition centered on three families: the Guises, the Montmorencys, and the Bourbons. Their private ambitions mixed poisonously with religious tensions already building up in France, as in much of Europe.

In matters of religion, Henri II was more repressive than François, who had cracked down on heresy only after an aggressive Protestant propaganda campaign in 1534. The French Reformist leader John Calvin fled to Geneva and made it a sort of revolutionary headquarters in exile. It was Calvinism, rather than the milder-mannered Lutheranism of the early Reformation, that now became the main form of Protestantism in France. It represented a real threat to royal and Church authority.

Calvinism is a minority religion today, but its ideology remains impressively powerful. It takes as its starting point a principle known as "total depravity," which asserts that humans have no virtues of their own and are dependent on God's grace for everything, including their salvation and even the decision to convert to Calvinism. Little personal responsibility is required, for everything is preordained, and no compromise is possible. The only possible attitude to such a God is one of perfect submission. In exchange, God grants His followers invincible strength: you give up your personal will, but receive the entire weight of God's universe behind you. This does not mean that you can sit back and do nothing. While Lutherans tend to stay aloof from worldly affairs, living according to their private conscience, Calvinists are supposed to engage with politics, and work to bring about God's will on earth. In the sixteenth century, accordingly, Calvinists were trained in Switzerland in a special academy, and sent to France armed with arguments and forbidden publications to convert the natives and destabilize the state. At some point in the 1550s, the name "Huguenot" became attached to Calvin's followers both inside and outside the country. The word probably derived from an earlier branch of exiled Reformists, the "Eidgenossen" or "confederates." It stuck: French Protestants used it of themselves, and their enemies used it of them too.

In the early days, the Catholic Church had responded to the Protestant threat by trying to reform itself. Montaigne thus grew up within a church committed to soul-searching and self-questioning, activities religious institutions do not often embrace with much fervor. But while this was going on, more militant forces gained strength. The Jesuit order, founded by Ignacio López de Loyola in 1534, set itself to fighting a battle of ideas against the enemy. A fiercer, less intellectual movement, arising in France from the 1550s, was loosely grouped under the name of the "Leagues." Their aim was not to outwit the heretics by fancy argument but to wipe them from the face of the earth by force. They and their Calvinist counterparts faced each other without a shred of compromise in their hearts, as fanatical mirror images. Leaguists opposed any French king who made feeble attempts at tolerance of Protestantism; this opposition became stronger as the decades went on.

Henri II was easily swayed by Leaguist pressure, so he introduced tough heresy laws and even a new chamber of the Paris *parlement* devoted to trying religious crimes. From July 1557, blasphemy against the saints, the publication of banned books, and illegal preaching were all punishable by death. Between such moves, however, Henri reversed gear and tried to soothe Huguenot sensibilities by allowing limited Protestant worship in certain areas, or reducing the heresy penalties again. Each time he did this, the Catholic lobby protested, so he accelerated forward into repression. He moved back and forth, satisfying no one.

During these years, other problems troubled France, including runaway inflation, which injured the poor more than anyone and benefited the landed gentry, who received higher rents and responded by buying more and more property—as happened with several generations of Montaigne's family. For less fortunate classes, the economic crisis fed extremism. Humanity had brought this misery on the world with its sins, so it must appease God by following the one true Church. But which was the true Church?

It was from this religious, economic, and political anguish that the civil wars would arise—wars which dominated France through most of the rest of the century, from 1562, when Montaigne was twenty-nine, to 1598, well after his death. Before the 1560s, military adventures in Italy and elsewhere had provided an outlet for France's tensions. But in April 1559 the treaty of Câteau Cambrésis ended several of the foreign wars at a blow. By removing distractions and filling the country with unemployed ex-soldiers amid an economic depression, this peace almost immediately brought about the outbreak of a much worse war.

The first bad omen occurred during jousting tournaments held to celebrate two dynastic marriages linked to the peace treaty. The king, who loved tournaments, took a leading role. In one encounter, an opponent accidentally knocked his visor off with the remains of a broken lance. Splinters of wood pierced the king's face just above one eye. He was carried away; after several days in bed, he seemed to recover, but a splinter had entered his brain. He developed a fever on the fourth day, and on July 10, 1559, he died.

Protestants interpreted the death as God's way of saying that Henri II had been wrong to repress their religion. But Henri's death would make things worse for them rather than better. The throne now passed successively to three of his sons: François II, Charles IX, and Henri III. The first two were minors, succeeding at fifteen and ten years old, respectively. All were weak, all were dominated by their mother Catherine de' Medici, and all were inept at handling the religious conflict. François II died of tuberculosis almost immediately, in 1560. Charles took over, and would reign until 1574. During the early years, his mother ruled as regent. She tried to achieve a balance between religious and political factions, but had little success.

The situation at the beginning of the 1560s, the decade during which Montaigne developed his career in Bordeaux, was thus marked by a weak throne, greedy rivalries, economic hardship, and rising religious tensions. In December 1560, in a speech expressing a feeling widespread at the time, the chancellor Michel de L'Hôpital said, "It is folly to hope for peace, repose, and friendship among people of different faiths." Even if desirable, it would be an impossible ideal. The only path to political unity was religious unity. As a Spanish theologian remarked, no republic could be well governed if "everyone considers his own God to be the only true God . . . and everyone else to be blind and deluded." Most Catholics would have considered this too self-evident to be worth mentioning. Even Protestants tended to impose unity whenever they got their own state to manage. *Un roi, une foi, une loi*, went the saying: one king, one faith, one law. Hatred of anyone who ventured to suggest a middle ground was practically the only thing on which everyone else could agree.

L'Hôpital and his allies did not promote tolerance or "diversity," in any modern sense. But he did think it better to lure stray sheep back by making the Catholic Church more appealing, rather than driving them back with threats. Under his influence, the heresy laws were relaxed somewhat at the beginning of the 1560s. An edict of January 1562 allowed Protestants to worship openly outside towns, and privately within town walls. As with earlier compromises, this satisfied no one. Catholics felt betrayed, while Protestants were encouraged to feel they should demand more. Some months earlier, the Venetian ambassador had written of a "great fear" spreading through the kingdom; this had now grown into a sense of imminent disaster.

The trigger came on March 1, 1562, at the town of Vassy, or Wassy, in the Champagne area of the northeast. Five hundred Protestants gathered to worship in a barn in the town, which was illegal, for such assemblies were allowed only outside the walls. The duc de Guise, a radical Catholic leader, was passing through the area with a group of his soldiers and heard about the meeting. He marched to the barn. According to survivors' accounts, he allowed his men to storm in shouting, "Kill them all!"

The Huguenot congregation fought back; they had long expected trouble and were ready to defend themselves. They forced the soldiers out and barricaded the barn door, then climbed out on scaffolding over the roof to pelt Guise's men with stones, piled there in case of need. The soldiers fired their arquebuses, and managed to reenter the barn. The Protestants now fled for their lives; many fell from the roof or were shot down as they ran. About thirty died, and over a hundred were wounded.

The consequences were dramatic. The national Protestant leader, Louis I de Bourbon, prince de Condé, urged Protestants to rise up to save themselves from further attacks. Many took up arms and, in response, Catholics did the same—both sides being driven more by fear than hatred. Catherine de' Medici, acting on behalf of the twelve-year-old Charles IX, ordered an inquiry into Vassy, but it fizzled out as public inquiries do, and by now it was too late. Leaders of both sides converged on Paris with crowds of their supporters. As the duc de Guise entered the city, he happened to pass a Protestant procession led by Condé; the two men exchanged cold salutes with the pommels of their swords.

One observer, a lawyer and friend of Montaigne's named Étienne Pasquier, remarked in a letter that all anyone could talk about after the Vassy massacre was war. "If it was permitted to me to assess these events, I would tell you that it was the beginning of a tragedy." He was right. Increasing clashes between the two sides escalated into outright battles, and these became the first of the French civil wars. It was savage but short, ending the following year when the duc de Guise was shot, leaving the Catholics temporarily without a leader and reluctantly willing to conclude a treaty. But there was no feeling of resolution, and neither side was happy. A second war would be set off on September 30, 1567, by another massacre, this time of Catholics by Protestants, at Nîmes.

The wars are generally described in the plural, but it makes at least as much sense to consider them a single long war with interludes of peace. Montaigne and his contemporaries often referred to outbreaks of fighting as "troubles." The consensus is that there were eight of these, and it may be convenient to summarize them here to get a sense of how much of Montaigne's life was conditioned by war:

First Trouble (1562–63). Started by the massacre of Protestants in Vassy, ended by the peace of Amboise.
Second Trouble (1567–68). Started by a massacre of Catholics in

Nîmes, ended by the Peace of Longjumeau.

Third Trouble (1568–70). Started by new anti-Protestant legislation, ended by the peace of Saint-Germain.

Fourth Trouble (1572–73). Started by the St. Bartholomew's Day massacres of Protestants in Paris and elsewhere, ended by the Peace of La Rochelle.

Fifth Trouble (1574–76). Started by fighting in Poitou and Saintonge, ended by the "Peace of Monsieur."

Sixth Trouble (1576–77). Started by anti-Protestant legislation at the Estates-General of Blois, ended by the Peace of Poitiers.

Seventh Trouble (1579–80). Started by Protestants seizing La Fère in Normandy, ended by the Peace of Fleix.

Eighth Trouble (1585–98). By far the longest and worst: started by Leaguist agitation, ended by the Treaty of Vervins and the Edict of Nantes.

Each followed the pattern established by the first and second wars. A period of peace would be interrupted by a sudden massacre or provocation. Battles, sieges, and general misery would ensue, until signs of weakness on one side or another led to a peace treaty. This would leave everyone dissatisfied, but would stay roughly in place until another provocation—and so the pattern cycled on. Even the last treaty did not please everyone. Nor were there always two clearly defined opponents. At least three factions were involved in most of the troubles, driven by desire for influence over the throne. These were wars of religion, like those brewing in other European countries during this period, but they were just as much wars of politics.

The end of one foreign conflict had made the civil wars possible in the first place, and the beginning of another would ultimately bring them to a close, after Henri IV declared war on Spain in 1595. The beneficial effect of this act was well understood at the time. During the final "trouble," Montaigne observed that many wished for something like this. The violence needed draining out, like pus from an infection. He had mixed feelings about the ethics of the method: "I do not believe that God would favor so unjust an enterprise as to injure and pick a quarrel with others for our own convenience." But it was what France needed, and what it got at last, from Henri IV, the first clever king it had had for years.

That was still a long way off in the 1560s, when no one dreamed that the horror could go on so long. Montaigne's years in *parlement* spanned the first three troubles; even during periods of peace, there was much political tension. By the time the third war ended, he had had enough and was on his way to retirement from public life. Until then, his position in Bordeaux placed him in the thick of it, amid a particularly complex community. Bordeaux was a Catholic city, but surrounded by Protestant territories and with a significant Protestant minority, which did not hesitate to indulge in icon-smashing and other aggressive acts.

In one especially violent confrontation, on the night of June 26, 1562—a few months after the Vassy massacre—a Protestant mob attacked the city's Château Trompette, bastion of government power. The riot was quelled, but, as with the salt-tax riots, the punishment proved worse than the crime. To teach a lesson to a city that seemed incapable of running its own affairs, the king sent in a new lieutenant-general named Blaise Monluc, and ordered him to "pacify" the troublesome area.

Monluc understood "pacification" to mean "mass slaughter." He set to work hanging Protestants in large numbers without trial, or having them broken on the wheel. After one battle at the village of Terraube, he ordered so many of its residents killed and thrown in the well that you could put your hand in from above and touch the top of the pile. Writing his memoirs years later, he reminisced about one rebel leader who begged him personally for mercy after Monluc's soldiers captured him. Monluc responded by grabbing the man's throat and throwing him against a stone cross so violently that the stone was smashed and the man died. "If I had not acted thus," wrote Monluc, "I would have been mocked." In another incident, a Protestant captain who had served under Monluc himself in Italy, many years earlier, hoped that his former comrade would spare his life for old times' sake. On the contrary, Monluc made a point of having him killed at once, and explained that he did this because he knew how brave the man was: he could never be anything other than a dangerous enemy. These were the kinds of scene that would recur frequently in Montaigne's essays: one person seeks mercy, and the other decides whether or not to grant it. Montaigne was fascinated by the moral complexity involved. What moral complexity? Monluc would have said. Killing was always the right solution: "One man hanged is more effective than a hundred killed in battle." Indeed, so many executions took place in the area that the supply of gallows equipment ran low: carpenters were commissioned to make more scaffolds, wheels for breaking limbs, and stakes for burning. When the scaffolds were full, Monluc used trees, and boasted that his travels through Guyenne could be traced in bodies swinging by the roadside. By the time he had finished, he said, nothing stirred in the whole region. All who survived kept their silence.

Montaigne knew Monluc, though mainly in later life, and took more interest in his private personality than his public deeds—especially his failings as a father and the regrets that tormented him after he lost a son,

who died in his prime. Monluc confessed to Montaigne that he realized too late that he had never treated the boy with anything other than coldness, although in reality he loved him a great deal. This was partly because he had followed an unfortunate fashion in parenting, which advocated emotional frigidity in dealings with one's children. "That poor boy saw nothing of me but a scowling and disdainful countenance," Monluc would say. "I constrained and tortured myself to maintain this vain mask." The talk of masks is apt, since, in 1571—around the time of Montaigne's retirement—Monluc was disfigured by an arquebus shot. For the rest of his life, he never went out without covering his face to conceal the scars. One can imagine the disconcerting effect of an actual mask on top of the inexpressive mask-like face of a cruel man whom few people dared to look in the eye.

Throughout the troubled 1560s, Montaigne often went to Paris on *parlement* business, and apparently remained away through much of 1562 and early 1563, though he popped back to Bordeaux almost as readily as a modern car driver or train passenger might. He was certainly in the area in August 1563 when his friend Étienne de La Boétie died. And he must have been in Bordeaux in December 1563, for a strange incident occurred then, the most noteworthy of Montaigne's few appearances in the city records.

The previous month, an extremist Catholic named François de Péruse d'Escars had launched a direct challenge to the *parlement*'s moderate president, Jacques-Benoît de Lagebâton, marching into the chambers and accusing him of having no right to govern. Lagebâton successfully faced him down, but d'Escars challenged him again the following month, and in response Lagebâton produced a list of the court members he believed to be in cahoots with d'Escars, probably working for him for pay. Surprisingly, among these names appear those of Montaigne and of the recently deceased Étienne de La Boétie. One would have expected to find both firmly on Lagebâton's side: La Boétie had been working actively for the chancellor L'Hôpital, of whom Lagebâton was a follower, and Montaigne too expressed admiration for that faction in his *Essays*. On the other hand, d'Escars was a family friend, and La Boétie had been at d'Escars's home when he came down with the illness which would kill him. This was suspicious, and perhaps Montaigne came under scrutiny by association.

All the accused had a right to defend themselves before *parlement*—a chance for Montaigne to use his rhetorical skills again. Of them all, he was the speaker who made the biggest impression. "He expressed himself with all the vivacity of his character," reads the note in the records. He finished his speech by stating "that he named the whole Court," then he flounced off. The court called him back and ordered him to explain what he meant by this. He replied that he was no enemy of Lagebâton, who was a friend of his and of everyone in his family. But—and there was clearly a "but" coming—he knew that accused persons were traditionally allowed to make counter-claims against their accuser, so he wished to take advantage of this right. Again, he left everyone puzzled, but the implication was that it was Lagebâton who was guilty of some impropriety. Montaigne made no further explanation. Pressed to withdraw the remark, he did, and there the matter ended. The accusations apparently came to nothing serious, and were quietly forgotten.

It remains an enigmatic incident, but it certainly shows us a different Montaigne from the cool, measured writer of the *Essays*, or his own portrait of his youthful self a-slumber over his books. This is a man known for "vivacity" and given to rushing in and out of rooms, making accusations which he cannot substantiate, and jabbering so wildly that no one is sure what he means to say. Montaigne does admit, in the *Essays*, that "by my nature I am subject to sudden outbursts which, though slight and brief, often harm my affairs." The last part of this makes one wonder if he damaged his career in *parlement* with his intemperate words, on other occasions if not on this one.

Even more surprising than meeting the hot-headed side of young Montaigne is seeing him bracketed with the bigots and extremists. His political allegiances were complicated; it is not always easy to guess where he will come out on any particular topic. But this case may have had more to do with personal loyalties than conviction. His own family had connections on both sides of the political divide, and he had to stay on good terms with them all. Perhaps the strain of this conflict made him volatile. The accusation was also an insult—to himself and, more seriously, to La Boétie, who was no longer around to offer any defense. Lagebâton was querying the honor of the most honorable man Montaigne had ever known:

the person he probably loved most in his entire life, and whom he had just lost. A response of helpless rage is understandable.

Slowness and forgetfulness were good responses to the question of how to live, so far as they went. They made for good camouflage, and they allowed room for thoughtful judgments to emerge. But some experiences in life brought forth a greater passion, and called for a different sort of answer.

5. Q. How to live? A. Survive love and loss

LA BOÉTIE: LOVE AND TYRANNY

MONTAIGNE WAS IN his mid-twenties when he met Étienne de La Boétie. Both were working at the Bordeaux *parlement*, and each had heard a lot about the other in advance. La Boétie would have known of Montaigne as an outspoken, precocious youngster. Montaigne had heard of La Boétie as the promising author of a controversial manuscript in local circulation, called *De la Servitude volontaire* ("On Voluntary Servitude"). He read this first in the late 1550s, and later wrote of his gratitude to it, because it brought him to its author. It started a great friendship: one "so entire and so perfect that certainly you will hardly read of the like . . . So many coincidences are needed to build up such a friendship that it is a lot if fortune can do it once in three centuries."

Although the two young men were curious about each other, they somehow did not meet for a long time. In the end the encounter happened by chance. Both were at the same feast in the city; they got talking, and found themselves "so taken with each other, so well acquainted, so bound together" that, from that moment on, they became best friends. They had only six years, about a third of which was spent apart, since both were sometimes sent to work in other cities. Yet that short period bound them to each other as tightly as a lifetime of shared experience.

Reading about Montaigne and La Boétie, you often get the impression that the latter was much older and wiser than the former. In reality La Boétie was only a couple of years Montaigne's senior. He was neither dashing nor handsome, but one has the impression that he was intelligent and warm-hearted, with an air of substance. Unlike Montaigne, he was already married when they met, and he held a higher position in the *parlement*. Colleagues knew him both as a writer and as a public official, whereas Montaigne had yet to write anything except legal reports. La Boétie attracted attention and respect. If you were to tell their Bordeaux acquaintances of the early 1560s that he is now remembered mainly for being Montaigne's friend rather than the other way around, they would probably refuse to believe you.

Some of La Boétie's air of maturity may have come from his having been orphaned at an early age. He was born on November 1, 1530, in the market town of Sarlat, about seventy-five miles from the Montaigne estate, in a fine, steep, richly ornamented building which survives today. This house had been built just five years earlier by La Boétie's father, another hyperactive parent, who then died when his son was ten years old. His mother died, too, so La Boétie was left alone. An uncle who shared the name of Étienne de La Boétie took him in and apparently gave the boy a fashionable humanist education, though a less radical one than Montaigne's.

Like Montaigne, La Boétie went on to study law. Some time around 1554, he married Marguerite de Carle, a widow who already had two children (one of whom would marry Montaigne's younger brother Thomas de Beauregard). In May of the same year—two years before Montaigne started in Périgueux—La Boétie took up office at the Bordeaux *parlement*. He was probably one of those Bordeaux officials who looked askance at the better paid Périgueux men when they arrived.

La Boétie's career in the Bordeaux *parlement* was a very good one. The strange accusations of 1563 aside, he was generally the kind of man who inspires confidence. He was given sensitive missions, and often entrusted with work as a negotiator—as Montaigne would later be. For the moment, La Boétie was probably thought the more reliable figure. He had the required air of gravity, and a better attitude to hard work and duty. The differences were significant, but the two men locked into each other like pieces in a puzzle. They shared important things: subtle thinking, a passion for literature and philosophy, and a determination to live a good life like the classical writers and military heroes they had grown up admiring. All this brought them together, and set them apart from their less adventurously educated colleagues.

La Boétie is now known mainly through Montaigne's eyes—the Montaigne of the 1570s and 1580s, who looked back with sorrow and longing for his lost friend. This created a nostalgic fog through which one can only squint to try to make out the real La Boétie. Of Montaigne as seen by La Boétie, a clearer picture is available, for La Boétie wrote a sonnet making it clear what he thought Montaigne needed by way of self-improvement. Instead of a perfect Montaigne frozen in memory, the sonnet captures a living Montaigne in the process of transition. It is by no means certain that this flawed character will ever make anything of himself, especially if he continues to waste his energies partying and flirting with pretty women.

Although La Boétie speaks to Montaigne like a fondly disapproving uncle, he adorns his poem with less familial emotions: "You have been bound to me, Montaigne, both by the power of nature and by virtue, which is the sweet allurement of love." Montaigne writes in the same way in the *Essays*, saying that the friendship seized his will and "led it to plunge and lose itself in his," just as it seized the will of La Boétie and "led it to plunge and lose itself in mine." Such talk was not unconventional. The Renaissance was a period in which, while any hint of real homosexuality was regarded with horror, men routinely wrote to each other like lovestruck teenagers. They were usually in love less with each other than with an elevated ideal of friendship, absorbed from Greek and Latin literature. Such a bond between two well-born young men was the pinnacle of philosophy: they studied together, lived under each other's gaze, and helped each other to perfect the art of living. Both Montaigne and La Boétie were fascinated by this model, and were probably on the lookout for it when they met. The shortness of their time together spared them disillusionment. In his sonnet, La Boétie expressed the hope that his and Montaigne's names would be paired for all eternity, like those of other "famous friends" throughout history; he got his wish.

They seemed to think of their relationship above all by analogy with one particular classical model: that of the philosopher Socrates and his good-looking young friend Alcibiades—to whom La Boétie overtly compared Montaigne in his sonnet. Montaigne, in return, alluded to Socratic elements in La Boétie: his wisdom, but also a more surprising quality, his ugliness. Socrates was famous for being physically unprepossessing, and Montaigne pointedly refers to La Boétie as having an "ugliness which clothed a very beautiful soul." This echoes Alcibiades' comparison, in Plato's *Symposium*, of Socrates with the little "Silenus" figures popularly used as stash boxes for jewels and other precious items. Like Socrates, they sported grotesque faces and figures on the outside but held treasures within. Montaigne and La Boétie apparently enjoyed these roles, and played them up for their amusement. At least it amused Montaigne. La Boétie's sense of his own philosophical dignity would have prevented him from showing any sign if he felt insulted.

The ugly Socrates rejected the beautiful Alcibiades's advances, according to Plato, yet their relationship was unmistakably flirtatious and sensual. Was the same true of Montaigne and La Boétie? Few today think that they had an outright sexual relationship, though the idea has had its followers. But the intensity of their language is striking, not just in La Boétie's sonnet, but in the passages where Montaigne describes their friendship as a transcendent mystery, or as a great surge of love that swept them both away. His attachment to moderation in all things fails him when it comes to La Boétie, and so does his love of independence. He writes, "Our souls mingle and blend with each other so completely that they efface the seam that joined them, and cannot find it again." Words themselves refuse to do his bidding. As he wrote in a marginal addition:

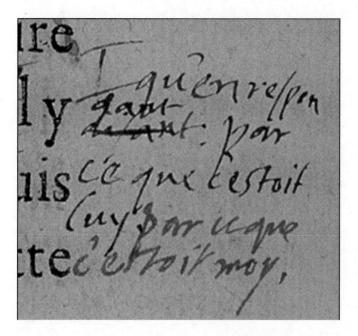

If you press me to tell why I loved him, I feel that this cannot be expressed, except by answering: Because it was he, because it was I.

Renaissance friendships, like classical ones, were supposed to be chosen in the clear, rational light of day. That was why they were of philosophical value. Montaigne's description of the love that "cannot be expressed" does not fit this pattern. Indeed, he admits: "Our friendship has no other model than itself, and can be compared only with itself." If it has a reference point at all, it again seems to be the *Symposium*, where Alcibiades finds himself equally confused by Socrates's charisma, saying, "Many a time I should be glad for him to vanish from the face of the earth, but I know that, if that were to happen, my sorrow would far outweigh my relief. In fact, I simply do not know what to do about him."

La Boétie, in his sonnet, does not go so far into perplexity as Montaigne; his emotion was not heightened by remembered grief as Montaigne's was. Similar talk of unreason and personal magnetism can be found in La Boétie, but not in the sonnet, or even in any of the mediocre love poetry he addressed to women. It appears, of all places, in his early treatise on politics—the one which was being passed so eagerly around Bordeaux when Montaigne first heard of him.

La Boétie was apparently very young when he wrote this treatise, *On Voluntary Servitude*. According to Montaigne, he was only sixteen, and produced it as a student exercise: "a common theme hashed over in a thousand places in books." Montaigne may have been deliberately underplaying the work's seriousness, for it was controversial and he did not want either to damage La Boétie's reputation or to get into trouble for mentioning it himself. Even if it was not quite so juvenile a piece as Montaigne made out, it did show early brilliance: one writer has called La Boétie the Rimbaud of political sociology.

The subject of *Voluntary Servitude* is the ease with which, throughout history, tyrants have dominated the masses, even though their power would evaporate instantly if those masses withdrew their support. There is no need for a revolution: the people need only stop cooperating, and supplying armies of slaves and sycophants to prop the tyrant up. Yet this almost never happens, even to those who maltreat their subjects monstrously. The more they starve and neglect their people, the more the people seem to love them. The Romans mourned Nero when he died, despite his abuses. The same happened on the death of Julius Caesar—whom, unusually, La Boétie does not admire. (Montaigne had similar reservations.) Here was an emperor "who abolished the laws and liberty, a personage in whom there was, it seems to me, nothing of value," yet he was adored out of all measure. The mystery of tyrannical dominance is as profound as that of love itself.

La Boétie believes that tyrants somehow hypnotize their people— though this term had not yet been invented. To put it another way, they fall in love with him. They lose their will in his. It is a terrible spectacle to see "a million men serving miserably with their necks under the yoke, not constrained by a greater force, but somehow (it seems) enchanted and charmed by the mere mention of the name of one, whose power they should not fear, since he is alone, and whose qualities they should not love, since he is savage and inhuman towards them." Yet they cannot wake from the dream. La Boétie makes it sound almost like a kind of witchcraft. If it occurred on a smaller scale, someone would probably be burned at the stake, but when bewitchment seizes a whole society, it goes unquestioned.

La Boétie's analysis of political power comes very close to Montaigne's sense of mystery about La Boétie himself: "Because it was he, because it was I." That a tyrant's charisma can work like a spell or a love potion has been made apparent by a series of autocrats in our own recent history. When one henchman of the Ugandan dictator Idi Amin was asked in an interview why he had loved his leader so loyally, he replied in a way that sounds just like Montaigne talking about La Boétie, or Alcibiades about Socrates:

> You see, love, something called love: you will find a man loving a woman who's one-eyed. If you ask that man, why do you love that ugly woman, do you think that person will tell you? The secret behind that thing is between two. What made me to love him and what also made him to love me.

Tyranny creates a drama of submission and domination, rather like the tense battle confrontation scenes often described by Montaigne. The populace willingly gives itself up, and this only encourages the tyrant to take away everything they have—even their lives, if he sends them to war to fight for him. Something in human beings drives them to a "deep forgetfulness of freedom." Everyone, from top to bottom of the system, is mesmerized by their voluntary servitude and by the power of habit, since often they have known nothing else. Yet all they need to do is to wake up and withdraw their cooperation.

Whenever a few individuals do break free, adds La Boétie, it is often because their eyes have been opened by the study of history. Learning of similar past tyrannies, they recognize the pattern in their own society. Instead of accepting what they are born into, they acquire the art of slipping out of it and seeing everything from a different angle—a trick Montaigne, in the *Essays*, would make his characteristic mode of thinking and writing. Alas, there are usually too few of these free spirits to do any good. They do not work together, but live "alone in their imaginings."

One can see why Montaigne, after reading *On Voluntary Servitude*, was so keen to meet its author. It is a bold work; whether Montaigne agreed with it all or not, it must have astounded him. Its reflections on the power of habit, a key theme of his own in the *Essays*, and its idea that freedom could come from reading historians and biographers, would have resonated with him. So would its sheer intellectual audacity and its ability to think, as it were, around corners.

La Boétie probably did not mean his treatise as a call to revolution. He circulated it in a few discreet copies, and may never have intended to publish it at all. If he did, his aim would have been to exhort the governing elite to more responsible behavior, not to make the underclass rise up and seize control. He would have been horrified, therefore, had he lived to see what was done with his work. Just over a decade after he died, *On Voluntary Servitude* reappeared as a radical Protestant tract, renamed *Contr'un* (Against One) for greater effect, and set in the context of a call to rebellion against the French monarch. A series of Protestant publications printed it, first the anonymous *Reveille-matin des François et de leurs voisins* (1574) and then various editions of Simon Goulart's *Mémoires de l'estat de France sous Charles IX* (1577). It was incendiary, and it met with an incendiary response. The Bordeaux *parlement* burned Goulart's second edition in public on May 7, 1579, just two days before Montaigne obtained his official privilege for the first edition of the *Essays*. No wonder he wanted to stress the fact that La Boétie's work was a youthful exercise, presenting no threat to anyone.

This was the beginning of a long and colorful afterlife for *On Voluntary Servitude*. Even now, it is still sometimes published as a call to arms, or at least to principled resistance. During the Second World War it appeared in America under the title *Anti-Dictator*, with marginal notes drawing attention to such themes as "Appeasement is useless" and "Why Führers make speeches." Later, anarchist and libertarian groups took it up and put out editions with radical prefaces and commentaries. La Boétie's posthumous story as a hero of anarchism is the one great exception to the rule that he is remembered only for being Montaigne's friend.

What anarchists and libertarians admire most is his Gandhi-like idea that all a society needs, in order to free itself of tyranny, is to quietly withdraw cooperation. One modern preface holds up La Boétie as the inspiration for an "anonymous, low-visibility, one-man revolution"— certainly the purest kind of revolution imaginable. "Voluntaryism" adopts La Boétie in support of its view that all political activity should be shunned, including even democratic voting, since it gives the state a false air of legitimacy. Some early Voluntaryists opposed female suffrage on the grounds that, if men should not vote, then women should not either.

The "quiet refusal" aspect of *On Voluntary Servitude*'s politics had an obvious appeal for Montaigne. He agreed that the most important thing in confronting political abuse was to maintain one's mental freedom—and that could mean opting out of public life rather than engaging with it. With its insistence on avoiding collaboration and on guarding one's integrity, the *Voluntary Servitude* could almost be one of Montaigne's own *Essays*, perhaps one written at an early stage when he was still polemical and had not yet perfected the art of sitting on every part of the fence at once. Like Ralph Waldo Emerson reading the *Essays* centuries later, Montaigne might well have exclaimed of the *Voluntary Servitude*, "It seemed to me as if I had myself written the book, so sincerely it spoke to my thought and experience."

Before its appropriation by Huguenot propagandists, he had actually intended to make it part of his own *Essays*, though duly credited to La Boétie. He was going to insert it following the chapter on friendship—the one where he writes most passionately about his feelings. The idea seems to have been to host the work as a sort of guest star or centerpiece, set off by surrounding chapters like a picture by its frame.

But by the time he delivered the book to the publisher, the situation had changed. *On Voluntary Servitude* was now thought of as a revolutionary tract: instead of standing as a tribute to his friend's brilliance, as Montaigne intended, it would look like a provocation. So he withdrew it, but left his own brief introduction as a stump marking the site of amputation. He wrote, "Because I have found that this work has since been brought to light, and with evil intent, by those who seek to disturb and change the state of our government without worrying whether they will improve it, and because they have mixed his work up with some of their own concoctions, I have changed my mind about putting it in here." It was probably now that he added his own remark about the work's junior and tentative nature.

Having done this, he had another change of mind. He did not want to make La Boétie sound insincere. So he added a note, saying that, of course, La Boétie must have believed in what he was writing; he was not the type to speak without conviction. Montaigne even said that his friend would have preferred to be born in Venice—a republic—than in the local town of Sarlat, that is, in the French state. But wait—that made La Boétie sound like a rebel again! Another reversal was needed: "But he had another maxim sovereignly imprinted in his soul, to obey and submit most religiously to the laws under which he was born." All in all, Montaigne seems to have got into quite a jumble over La Boétie's tract. One imagines him scribbling all this at the last moment in a corner of the printer's office, the removed manuscript still tucked under one arm.

Considering that *On Voluntary Servitude* was currently being burned in Bordeaux, it was daring for Montaigne to mention the work at all, let alone to make excuses for it. Contradictory as ever, he acted with prudence in withdrawing the publication, but with courage in defending it. Moreover, in discussing how La Boétie came to write the piece, Montaigne actually revealed who the author was. That was probably well known anyway, but none of the Protestant publications had gone so far.

Having decided to get rid of it, Montaigne wrote: "In exchange for this serious work, I shall substitute another, produced in that same season of his life, gayer and more lusty." This was a selection of La Boétie's verses: not the ones written to himself, but a set of twenty-nine sonnets addressed to an unidentified young woman. Some years later, however, Montaigne changed his mind again and removed these too. What was left, in the end, was only his own introduction and dedication, plus a brief note: "These verses may be seen elsewhere." One entire chapter, number 29 in Book I, became a double deletion: a ragged stub or hole which Montaigne deliberately refused to disguise. He even drew attention to its frayed edges. It is odd behavior, and has inspired a lot of speculation. Was Montaigne simply adding and subtracting material in a fluster, without bothering to tidy up the results, or was he trying to alert us to something?

One radical theory has come and gone from circulation a few times in recent years. As remarked, *On Voluntary Servitude* has features so Montaigne-like that it could almost be his own writing. It talks about habit, nature, perspective, and friendship—four themes that resound throughout the *Essays*. It emphasizes inner freedom as a path to political resistance: a Montaignean position. The work is filled with examples from classical history, just like the *Essays*. It *feels* like an *Essay*. It is persuasive, entertaining, and digression-prone. The author often goes off at some tangent—say, into a discussion of the Pléiade group of sixteenth-century poets—before coming to with a remark such as, "But to return to our purpose, which I had almost lost," or "But to return from where, I don't know how, I had lost the thread of my discussion." This playful pretense at disorganization seems unusual in a young man's literary exercise, but it fills the piece with life and spontaneity. The author talks to us as if we were sitting together over a glass of wine, or had bumped into each other on a Bordeaux street corner. The suspicion dawns: could Montaigne, rather than La Boétie, have been the author of *On Voluntary Servitude?*

But it must have been by La Boétie, comes the reply; copies of the manuscript were being passed around Bordeaux. Yet none of today's surviving copies is in La Boétie's hand—all were made by others—and the only clear source we have for the "passed around" story is Montaigne himself. It is also Montaigne who identifies the author as La Boétie, and Montaigne who talks of it as a student piece. Perhaps the teenage Rimbaud here was the hothead given to rushing in and out of *parlement* chambers, not the prematurely judicious La Boétie. Or perhaps it was not the work of a young man at all: that would explain a few anachronistic references in the text. Perhaps, as some enthusiastic conspiracy theorists suggest, Montaigne wrote the piece much later and inserted the anachronisms to tip off smart readers to the deception.

The first person to try attributing *On Voluntary Servitude* to Montaigne, in 1906, was the maverick Montaignist Arthur-Antoine Armaingaud, a man with a record of making outrageous suggestions and sitting back to watch the feathers fly. Almost no one agreed with Armaingaud at the time, and few do now, but his hypothesis has won over a new generation of mavericks, notably Daniel Martin and David Lewis Schaefer. Schaefer is keen to find a revolutionary underbelly in Montaigne on principle, as was Armaingaud, while Daniel Martin has a general penchant for approaching the book like a cryptic crossword full of clues. "Removing *On Voluntary Servitude* from the *Essays* would be like removing the flute from a symphony orchestra," he writes.

The idea of Montaigne writing a radical, proto-anarchist tract, then whipping up a dust storm of false information and hiding hints where only the sharp-eyed could spot them, appeals on several levels. Like all conspiracy theories, it offers the thrill of fitting the pieces together, and it makes Montaigne glamorous: a one-man revolutionary cell and a master of intrigue.

Occasional signs can be found in the *Essays* that Montaigne was capable of playing the slyboots when he wanted to. Once, he used an elaborate trick to help a friend who suffered from impotence and was afraid a spell had been cast on him. Instead of reasoning him out of it, Montaigne gave the friend a robe and a magical-looking coin engraved with "celestial figures." He told him to perform a series of rituals with this medallion whenever he was about to have sex, first laying it over his kidneys, then tying it around his waist, then lying down with his partner and pulling the robe over both of them. The trick worked. Montaigne felt a bit guilty, even though he had done it for his friend's benefit. Yet this shows that he could practice deception if he felt the situation called for it, or if the psychology of the case fascinated him enough.

On the whole, though, this sort of game-playing was rare for him, and he preferred to emphasize his honesty and openness in all matters, as well as his dull-wittedness at enigmas and puzzles. That could all be part of the game. But if he really was a thoroughgoing trickster, then one has to doubt almost every word he says in the book: a dizzying prospect. There are other unsettling implications. If La Boétie did not write *On Voluntary Servitude*, then he was not the man Montaigne made him out to be in the *Essays*. He existed, all right, but with no clear features: a cipher for Montaigne's own cleverness. And if he did not have exceptional capabilities—if he was not the kind of man who would write the *Servitude*—why did Montaigne love him so much? He must have had a reason for feeling so strongly, and apparently it wasn't La Boétie's good looks, unless he was lying about that too.

If one takes their love story seriously, the conspiracy theory becomes almost unthinkable. For Montaigne to ascribe the *Servitude* to La Boétie as a cover for himself would be to play fast and free with La Boétie's memory— a memory he evidently worshiped to the point of idolatry. It is surprising that he revealed La Boétie's authorship of a work currently being burned in the public square of Bordeaux, but if La Boétie was not the author, it would be more than surprising; it would be a total betrayal, an act almost of hatred. There is nothing in any of Montaigne's writings about La Boétie (including remarks made in a travel journal never meant for publication) to suggest that he felt this way.

The intensity of their affection also provides a convincing explanation for why the two men's writing styles were so similar. Montaigne and La Boétie shared everything: they blended into one another, not as a writer blends into his pseudonym, but as two writers develop their ideas in partnership—often arguing, often disagreeing, yet constantly *absorbing*. Over their few years together, Montaigne and La Boétie must have talked from morning to night: about habit, about the need to reject received ideas and to change points of view, about tyranny, and about personal freedom. At first, La Boétie's ideas would have been more clearly articulated; later, probably, Montaigne would have overtaken him, pursuing thoughts about custom and perspective in directions La Boétie would not have thought of. It all eventually found its way into the *Essays*, which became a monument to La Boétie in more ways than one. The two minds wove themselves so closely together that, with the best critical tools in the world, you could not pick them apart.

Neither man had any reason to think they could not go on like this for decades, becoming ever more successful and celebrated in their modernized Athens. But young Socrates was about to be called home from the feast.

LA BOÉTIE: DEATH AND MOURNING

It began on Monday, August 9, 1563. La Boétie had spent the day in the open air on the estate of François de Péruse d'Escars, the man who had rebelled against Lagebâton in the Bordeaux *parlement*. That evening La Boétie was supposed to dine with Montaigne, but as he was about to leave d'Escars's house he came down with stomach pains and diarrhea. He sent Montaigne a message saying that he felt ill: would Montaigne come to see him instead? Montaigne did. Our knowledge of everything that followed comes from a long narrative Montaigne later wrote in the form of a letter to his father, and which he eventually published.

Arriving at the d'Escars home, Montaigne found his friend in pain. La Boétie told him that he had caught a chill after being outside all day, but it looked worse than that. Both men may already have thought of the possibility of plague, which was then spreading in this area and in Bordeaux, as well as in Agenais, which La Boétie had recently visited for work. If La Boétie had not already caught the plague there was a danger that he might develop it now, in his weakened state. Montaigne advised him to move to a less infected region, and to stay with his own sister and brother-in-law, the Lestonnacs. But La Boétie did not feel well enough to travel. In reality, it was too late: he almost certainly already had the plague.

Montaigne left, but the next morning La Boétie's wife sent for him, saying that her husband was getting worse. Montaigne returned and, at La Boétie's request, spent the night there: "He asked me, with more affection and insistence than ever about anything else, to be with him as much as I could. This touched me considerably." He stayed the following night too. La Boétie's condition continued to worsen. On Saturday, he admitted that his illness was contagious and unpleasant—a hint that he now realized it was the plague. He again asked Montaigne to stay, but not for more than brief periods, so that he would be at less risk. Montaigne did not obey this second part. "I did not leave him again," he wrote.

On Sunday La Boétie was overcome with weakness and suffered hallucinations. When the crisis passed, he said "that he had seemed to be in some great confusion of all things and had seen nothing but a thick cloud and a dense fog in which everything was pell-mell and without order." Montaigne reassured him: "Death has nothing worse about it than that, my brother," to which La Boétie replied that, indeed, nothing could be worse than that. From this point on, he admitted to Montaigne, he lost hope of a cure.

He decided to set his affairs in order, asking Montaigne to watch his wife and uncle in case grief got the better of them. When La Boétie was ready, Montaigne summoned the family into the room. They "composed their faces as well as they could" and sat around the bed. La Boétie told them what he intended to leave in his will, specifying that most of his book collection should go to Montaigne. Afterwards he called for a priest. La Boétie had collected himself so carefully for his deathbed speeches that Montaigne felt a moment of hope, but, once the effort was over, his friend deteriorated again.

A few hours later, still at La Boétie's bedside, Montaigne told him that he "blushed for shame" to see him showing more courage in the face of his own death than he, Montaigne, was able to find in witnessing it. He promised to remember his example when his own time came. Yes, said La Boétie, that was a good thing to do. He reminded Montaigne of the many enlightening talks they had already had on such subjects. This experience was, he said, "the true object of our studies, and of philosophy."

Taking Montaigne by the hand, he assured him that he had done many things in life that had been more painful and difficult. "And when all is said," he went on, "I had been prepared for it for a very long time and had known my lesson all by heart." Like Montaigne at this stage, he had followed the ancients' advice and rehearsed his death well. After all, he went on, still echoing the wisdom of the sages, he had lived healthily and happily for long enough. There was no need for regrets. Had he not already made it to a good age? "I was soon to be thirty-three," he said. "God granted me this grace, that all my life up to now has been full of health and happiness.

In view of the inconstancy of things human, that could hardly last any longer." Old age would only have brought him pain, and might have made him miserly; it was better to have avoided this. Montaigne looked distressed; La Boétie reminded him that he must be strong. "What, my brother, do you want to put fear into me? If I felt fear, who but you should take it away from me?"

La Boétie was dying the perfect Stoic death, full of courage and rational wisdom. Montaigne was expected to do his part: to help his friend to maintain this courage, and then to act as witness, recording the details so others could learn from the story. Perhaps, in doing so, he improved on reality slightly, to make La Boétie sound nobler and braver than he was. Perhaps not; La Boétie's sense of the classical virtues went so deep that he may genuinely have been capable of emulating his philosophical heroes almost to the end. As Montaigne wrote of him, "His mind was modeled in the pattern of other ages than this."

But Montaigne himself was a different creature, and, as his account goes on, more and more of his real self comes through: his skepticism, his eye for the awkward detail, and his determination to tell things as they were. There are even moments of irreverence. Writing about La Boétie's farewell speeches later that day, he comments, "The whole room was full of wails and tears, which nevertheless did not interrupt the train of his speeches, which were a little long."

The next morning, Monday, La Boétie slipped in and out of consciousness, being revived with vinegar and wine each time. He reproached Montaigne: "Don't you see that from now on all the help you give me serves only to prolong my pain?" After one such spell, he temporarily lost his vision. The lamentations of the people around him, whom he could not see, horrified him. "My Lord, who is tormenting me so? Why do they take me out of that great pleasant rest that I am in? Leave me alone, I beg you."

A sip of wine restored his faculties, but he was now slipping away. "All his extremities, even his face, were already icy with cold, with a death sweat that ran down all along his body; and hardly any sign of a pulse could be detected any longer."

On Tuesday he received the last rites, and asked the priest, his uncle, and Montaigne to pray for him. Two or three times he called out, once saying,

"All right! All right! Let it come when it will, I'm waiting for it, strong and firm of foot."

In the evening, "having nothing left but the likeness and shadow of a man," he hallucinated again, this time with visions which he described to Montaigne as "marvelous, infinite, and ineffable." He tried to comfort his wife, saying that he had a story to tell her. "But I am going off," he said. Then, seeing her alarm, he corrected himself: "I am going off to sleep."

She left the room. La Boétie said to Montaigne, "My brother, stay close to me, please." There were still many other people around; Montaigne writes of them as "all the company." Nothing was ever done alone in the Renaissance, least of all dying. La Boétie's wife was, it seems, the only person actually sent away.

Now, the dying man became agitated. He tossed violently in the bed. He began to make strange requests. As Montaigne wrote:

> He began to entreat me again and again with extreme affection to give him a place; so that I was afraid his judgment was shaken. Even when I had remonstrated with him very gently that he was letting the illness carry him away and that these were not the words of a man in his sound mind, he did not give in at first and repeated even more strongly: "My brother, my brother, do *you* refuse me a place?" This until he forced me to convince him by reason and tell him that since he was breathing and speaking and had a body, consequently he had his place. "True, true," he answered me then, "I have one, but it is not the one I need; and then when all is said, I have no being left."

It was hard to know how to respond to these words. Montaigne tried to comfort him: "God will give you a better one very soon," he said.

"Would that I were there already," said La Boétie. "For three days now I have been straining to leave."

Over the next hours he often called out, wrote Montaigne, "simply to know whether I was near him." He always was.

From its conventional beginnings, Montaigne's account has by now become both moving and eerie. He seems to be recording what was really said and done, regardless of the philosophical meaning. La Boétie himself had moved beyond imitating models. With his talk of needing a place, he seemed to be speaking almost without awareness, as Montaigne would be when he raved and tore at his doublet a few years later.

By two in the morning he was able to rest, which seemed a good sign. Montaigne left the room to tell La Boétie's wife. Both were pleased at the improvement. But an hour or so later, when Montaigne was back in the room, La Boétie became restless again. He spoke Montaigne's name once or twice. Then he exhaled a single sigh, and stopped breathing. La Boétie was dead—"at about three o'clock on the Wednesday morning, August 18th, 1563, after living 32 years, 9 months, and 17 days," as Montaigne recorded.

This, then, was death at close quarters—probably Montaigne's first such intimate encounter with the death of someone he loved deeply. The physical reality was shocking, especially since it came from such a terrifying disease, though Montaigne says nothing of any personal fear of infection. Among the thoughts likely to have gone through his mind is the one that would later come back to him in the light of his own experience: the hope that death might be a tranquil affair for the person undergoing it, however little it looked that way from outside. He and La Boétie had discussed this question once: Montaigne thought it could be the case, but La Boétie disagreed. Now Montaigne must fervently have hoped that it was he who was right. It would be better to think that La Boétie had felt nothing but bliss while his body sweated and struggled. When Montaigne came to write about his own loss of consciousness later, one can almost see him taking up that old argument again—asking his friend, "See, you didn't suffer, did you?" and hoping that La Boétie would reply, "No."

Although he transmuted his sorrow into literature, Montaigne's grief was overwhelming, and it seemed to become greater with time. After La Boétie died, everything was "nothing but dark and dreary night." Traveling in Italy nearly eighteen years later, he wrote in his private diary: "This same morning, writing to Monsieur d'Ossat, I was overcome by such painful thoughts about Monsieur de La Boétie, and I was in this mood so long, without recovering, that it did me much harm." He also wrote in the *Essays* about how he longed for a true companion in Italy—someone whose ways harmonized with his own, and who liked to do the things he liked to do. "I have missed such a man extremely on all my travels."

No pleasure has any savor for me without communication. Not even a merry thought comes to my mind without my being vexed at having produced it alone without anyone to offer it to.

He never ruled out the possibility of finding someone to reprise La Boétie's role. Seneca had advised this: a wise man should be so good at making new friends that he can replace an old one without skipping a beat. Sometimes, in the *Essays*, Montaigne seems to issue a come-hither call to candidates: he hopes his book will please "some worthy man" who will seek him out. Yet he did not really feel that anyone could replace the original. He was forever disappointed:

> Is it not a stupid humor of mine to be out of tune with a thousand to whom I am joined by fortune, whom I cannot do without, only to cling to . . . a fantastic desire for something I cannot recapture?

Whenever Montaigne sounds cool or detached from other people, as he sometimes does, one has to remember La Boétie. People should not, he writes, be "joined and glued to us so strongly that they cannot be detached without tearing off our skin and some part of our flesh as well." These are the words of a man who knows what it feels like to be flayed in this way.

In life, Montaigne apparently rebelled against La Boétie's improving influence at times, but now no trace remained of this. With La Boétie safely dead, Montaigne could surrender to him unreservedly—and he could do what La Boétie had begged him to do: give him a place.

First he absorbed many of La Boétie's books into his library, making room for his friend among his own most treasured possessions. Then he wrote about La Boétie's death, rescuing as much as he could remember of the young philosopher's testament to posterity. He prepared a stack of La Boétie's writings for publication. Finally, when he retired, he made his friend the guiding spirit of his own new career. Alongside the main inscription about his retirement, he added another to his library wall: it is now worn and hard to decipher, but seems to consecrate all his future "studious work" to the memory of La Boétie, "the sweetest, dearest, and most intimate friend" the sixteenth century could produce. La Boétie was to watch over everything Montaigne did in his library: he would be his literary guardian angel.

By dying, La Boétie changed from being Montaigne's real-life, flawed companion to being an ideal entity under Montaigne's control. He became less a person than a sort of philosophical technique. Seneca had advised his followers to use their friends in this way. Having found some admirable man, he said, one should visualize him as an ever-present audience, in order to hold oneself to his exalted standards. If you would live for yourself, he wrote, you should live for others—above all for your chosen friend.

Montaigne was willing to try any trick of this kind, if it promised consolation. As he wrote in one of his dedications to La Boétie's posthumous books: "He is still lodged in me so entire and so alive that I cannot believe that he is so irrevocably buried or so totally removed from our communication." Letting La Boétie live on within himself was a way of fulfilling his friend's dying wish, and easing his own loneliness. Meanwhile, he used techniques of distraction and diversion to get himself through the immediate shock of loss. Best of all, he discovered the therapeutic benefits of writing. By passing on La Boétie's death narrative and farewell to the world in written form, he helped himself to relive the scene, and thus outlive it. He never fully got over La Boétie, but he learned to exist in the world without him, and, in so doing, to change his own life. Writing about La Boétie eventually led him to write the *Essays*: the best philosophical trick of all.

6. Q. How to live? A. Use little tricks

LITTLE TRICKS AND THE ART OF LIVING

ABOUT ACADEMIC PHILOSOPHERS, Montaigne was usually dismissive: he disliked their pedantries and abstractions. But he showed an endless fascination for another tradition in philosophy: that of the great pragmatic schools which explored such questions as how to cope with a friend's death, how to work up courage, how to act well in morally difficult situations, and how to make the most of life. These were the philosophies he turned to in times of grief or fear, as well as for guidance in dealing with more minor everyday irritations.

The three most famous such systems of thought were Stoicism, Epicureanism, and Skepticism: the philosophies collectively known as Hellenistic because they had their origins in the era when Greek thought and culture spread to Rome and other Mediterranean regions, from the third century BC onwards. They differed in details, but were so close in essentials as to be hard to distinguish much of the time. Like everyone else, Montaigne mixed and matched them according to his needs.

All the schools had the same aim: to achieve a way of living known in the original Greek as *eudaimonia*, often translated as "happiness," "joy," or "human flourishing." This meant living well in every sense: thriving, relishing life, being a good person. They also agreed that the best path to *eudaimonia* was *ataraxia*, which might be rendered as "imperturbability" or "freedom from anxiety." *Ataraxia* means equilibrium: the art of maintaining an even keel, so that you neither exult when things go well nor plunge into despair when they go awry. To attain it is to have control over your emotions, so that you are not battered and dragged about by them like a bone fought over by a pack of dogs.

It was on the question of how to acquire such equanimity that the philosophies began to diverge. Each had a different idea, for example, of how far one should compromise with the real world. The original Epicurean community, founded by Epicurus in the fourth century BC, required followers to leave their families and live like cult members in a private "garden." Skeptics preferred to remain amid the public hurly-burly like everyone else, but with a radically altered mental attitude. Stoics were somewhere in between. The two best known Stoic writers, Seneca and Epictetus, wrote for an elite Roman readership who were deeply involved in the affairs of their time and had no time for gardens, but who desired oases of tranquillity and self-possession wherever they could find them.

Stoics and Epicureans shared a great deal of their theory, too. They thought that the ability to enjoy life is thwarted by two big weaknesses: lack of control over emotions, and a tendency to pay too little attention to the present. If one could only get these two things right—*controlling* and *paying attention*—most other problems would take care of themselves. The catch is that both are almost impossible to do. So difficult are they that one cannot approach them head-on. It is necessary to sidle in from lateral angles, and trick oneself into achieving them.

Accordingly, Stoic and Epicurean thinkers spent much time devising techniques and thought experiments. For example: imagine that today is the last day of your life. Are you ready to face death? Imagine, even, that this very moment—*now!*—is the last moment of your existence. What are you feeling? Do you have regrets? Are there things you wish you had done differently? Are you really alive at this instant, or are you consumed with panic, denial, and remorse? This experiment opens your eyes to what is important to you, and reminds you of how time runs constantly through your fingers.

Some Stoics even acted out these "last moment" experiments with props and a supporting cast. Seneca wrote of a wealthy man named Pacuvius, who conducted a full-scale funeral ceremony for himself every day, ending with a feast after which he would have himself carried from the table to his bed on a bier while all the guests and servants intoned, "He has lived his life, he has lived his life." You could achieve the same effect more simply and cheaply just by holding the idea of your own demise in your mind and paying full attention to it. The Epicurean writer Lucretius suggested picturing yourself at the point of death, and considering two possibilities. Either you have lived well, in which case you can go your way satisfied, like a well-fed guest leaving a party. Or you have not, but then it makes no difference that you are losing your life, since you obviously did not know what to do with it anyway. This may offer scant comfort on your deathbed, but if you think about it in the midst of life it helps you to change your perspective.

Such shifts of attitude are the purpose of many of the thought experiments. If you have lost someone or something precious, you can try to value her, him, or it differently by imagining that you never knew that person, or never owned that object. How can you miss what you never had? A different angle produces a different emotion. Plutarch suggested such a ploy in a letter to his wife, after their two-year-old daughter died: he advised her to think back to before the girl was born, and pretend they were back in those days again. Whether this consoled her is not known, but at least it gave her something to focus on instead of swimming in an ocean of undifferentiated grief. Montaigne and La Boétie both knew this letter well, for La Boétie translated it into French and Montaigne edited his translation for publication. It may have come into Montaigne's mind each time one of his own children died, as well as when he lost La Boétie. The friendship had been so short that it should not have been difficult to remember a time before it and recapture his pre-La Boétie nonchalance.

Such tricks of the imagination can be used in mundane situations as well as extreme ones; they are effective even against mild feelings of boredom or depression. If you feel tired of everything you possess, suggests Plutarch, pretend that you have lost all these things and are missing them desperately. Whether the object is a favorite plate, a friend, a mistress, or the good fortune of living in a time of peace and in good health, this exercise magically makes it seem worth having after all. The principle is the same as when brooding on death: faced with the idea of losing something *now*, you realize its value.

The key is to cultivate mindfulness: *prosoche*, another key Greek term. Mindful attention is the trick that underlies many of the other tricks. It is a call to attend to the inner world—and thus also to the outer world, for uncontrolled emotion blurs reality as tears blur a view. Anyone who clears their vision and lives in full awareness of the world as it is, Seneca says, can never be bored with life.

A person who does not sleepwalk through the world, moreover, is freed to respond to situations in the right way, without hesitation—as if they were questions asked all of a sudden, as Epictetus puts it. A violent attack, a quarrel, the loss of a friend: all these are demands barked at you by life, as by a schoolteacher trying to catch you not paying attention in class. Even a moment of boredom is such a question. Whatever happens, however unforeseen it is, you should be able to respond in a precisely suitable way. This is why, for Montaigne, learning to live "appropriately" (*à propos*) is the "great and glorious masterpiece" of human life.

Stoics and Epicureans alike approached this goal mainly through rehearsal and meditation. Like tennis players practicing volleys and smashes for hours, they used rehearsal to carve grooves of habit, down which their minds would run as naturally as water down a river bed. It is a form of self-hypnotism. The great Stoic Roman emperor Marcus Aurelius kept notebooks in which he would go over the changes of perspective he wished to drill into himself:

> How good it is, when you have roast meat or suchlike foods before you, to impress on your mind that this is the dead body of a fish, this the dead body of a bird or pig; and again, that the Falernian wine is the mere juice of grapes, and your purple-edged robe simply the hair of a sheep soaked in shell-fish blood! And in sexual intercourse that it is no more than the friction of a membrane and a spurt of mucus ejected.

At other times, he imagined flying up to the heavens so that he could gaze down and see how insignificant all human concerns were from such a distance. Seneca did this too: "Place before your mind's eye the vast spread of time's abyss, and consider the universe; and then contrast our so-called human life with infinity."

Another practice of the Stoics was to visualize time circling around on itself, over eons. Thus Socrates would be born again and would teach in Athens just as he did the first time; every butterfly would flap its wings in the same way; every cloud would pass overhead at the same speed. You yourself would live again, and have all the same thoughts and emotions as before, again and again without end. This apparently terrifying idea brought comfort, because—like the other ideas—it showed one's own fleeting troubles at a reduced size. At the same time, because everything you had ever done would come back to haunt you, everything *mattered*. Nothing was flushed away; nothing could be forgotten. Meditating on this forced you to pay more attention to how you lived your everyday life. It posed a challenge, but also led to a kind of acceptance: to what the Stoics called *amor fati*, or love of fate. As the Stoic Epictetus wrote:

> Do not seek to have everything that happens happen as you wish, but wish for everything to happen as it actually does happen, and your life will be serene.

One should be able to accept everything just as it is, willingly, without giving in to the futile longing to change it. Montaigne seemed to find this trick easy: it came to him by nature. "If I had to live over again," he wrote cheerfully, "I would live as I have lived." But most people had to practice it, and this was where the mental exercises came in.

Seneca

Seneca had an extreme trick for practising *amor fati*. He was asthmatic, and attacks brought him almost to the point of suffocation. He often felt that he was about to die, but he learned to use each attack as a philosophical opportunity. While his throat closed and his lungs strained for breath, he tried to embrace what was happening to him: to say "yes" to it. I *will* this, he would think; and, if necessary, I *will* myself to die from it. When the attack receded, he emerged feeling stronger, for he had done battle with fear and defeated it.

Stoics were especially keen on pitiless mental rehearsals of all the things they dreaded most. Epicureans were more inclined to turn their vision away from terrible things, to concentrate on what was positive. A Stoic behaves like a man who tenses his stomach muscles and invites an opponent to punch them. An Epicurean prefers to invite no punches, and, when bad things happen, simply to step out of the way. If Stoics are boxers, Epicureans are closer to Oriental martial arts practitioners.

Epicurus

Montaigne found the Epicurean approach more congenial in most situations, and he took their ideas even further. He claimed to envy lunatics, because they were always mentally elsewhere—an extreme form of Epicurean deflection. What did it matter if a madman's idea of the world was skewed, so long as he was happy? Montaigne retold classical stories such as that of Lycas, who went about his daily life and successfully held down a job while believing that everything he saw was taking place on stage, as a theatrical performance. When a doctor cured him of this delusion, Lycas became so miserable that he sued the doctor for robbing him of his pleasure in life. Similarly, a man named Thrasylaus nurtured the belief that every ship that came in and out of his local port of Piraeus was carrying wonderful cargoes just for him. He was happy all the time, for he rejoiced each time a ship came safely to port, and did not seem to worry that the cargoes never materialized. Alas, his brother Crito had his delusion treated, and that was the end of it.

Not everyone can have the benefit of being insane, but anyone can make life easier for themselves by turning down the beam of their reason slightly. With grief, in particular, Montaigne learned that he could not recover simply by talking himself out of it. He did try some Stoic tricks, and he was not afraid to focus his attention on La Boétie's death long enough to write his account of it. But most of the time he found it more helpful to divert his attention to something else altogether:

> A painful notion takes hold of me; I find it quicker to change it than to subdue it. I substitute a contrary one for it, or, if I cannot, at all events a different one. Variation always solaces, dissolves, and dissipates. If I cannot combat it, I escape it; and in fleeing I dodge, I am tricky.

He used the same technique to help others. Once, trying to console a woman who was (unlike some widows, he implies) genuinely suffering grief for her dead husband, he first considered the more usual philosophical methods: reminding her that nothing can be gained from lamentation, or persuading her that she might never have met her husband anyway. But he settled on a different trick: "very gently deflecting our talk and diverting it bit by bit to subjects nearby, then a little more remote." The widow seemed to pay little attention at first, but in the end the other subjects caught her interest. Thus, without her realizing what was happening, he wrote, "I imperceptibly stole away from her this painful thought and kept her in good spirits and entirely soothed for as long as I was there." He admitted that this did not go to the root of her grief, but it got her through an immediate crisis, and presumably allowed time to begin its own natural work.

Some of this came from Montaigne's Epicurean reading; some from his own hard-won experience. "I was once afflicted with an overpowering grief," he wrote, clearly thinking of La Boétie. It could have destroyed him had he relied only on his powers of reason to rescue him. Instead, understanding that he needed "some violent diversion," he managed to develop a crush on someone. He does not say who, and it seems to have been insignificant, but it gave his emotions somewhere to go.

Similar tricks worked for another unwelcome emotion, anger: Montaigne once successfully cured a "young prince," probably Henri de Navarre (the future Henri IV), of a dangerous passion for revenge. He did not talk the prince out of it, or advise him to turn the other cheek, or remind him of the tragic consequences that could result. He did not mention the subjects of anger or revenge at all:

> I let the passion alone and applied myself to making him relish the beauty of a contrary picture, the honor, favor, and good will he would acquire by clemency and kindness. I diverted him to ambition. That is how it is done.

Later in his life, Montaigne used the trick of diversion against his own fear of getting old and dying. The years were dragging him towards death; he could not help that, but he need not look at it head-on. Instead, he faced the other way, and calmed himself by looking back with pleasure over his youth and childhood. Thus, he said, he managed to "gently sidestep and avert my gaze from this stormy and cloudy sky that I have in front of me."

He became such a connoisseur of side-stepping techniques that he even found political sleight-of-hand admirable, so long as it was not used to support tyranny. One story he relished was that of how Zaleucus, prince of the Locrians of ancient Greece, reduced excessive spending in his realm. He ordered that any woman could be attended by several maids, but only when she was drunk, and that she could wear as many gold jewels and embroidered dresses as she liked, if she was working as a prostitute. A man could sport gold rings if he was a pimp. It worked: gold jewelry and large entourages disappeared overnight, yet no one rebelled, for no one felt they had been forced into anything.

From his own experience of nearly dying, Montaigne would learn that the best antidote to fear was to rely on nature: "Don't bother your head about it." From losing La Boétie, he had already discovered that this was the best way of dealing with grief. Nature has its own rhythms. Distraction works well precisely because it accords with how humans are made: "Our thoughts are always elsewhere." It is only natural for us to lose focus, to slip away from both pains and pleasures, "barely brushing the crust" of them. All we need do is let ourselves be as we are.

Montaigne took from his Stoic and Epicurean reading what worked for him, just as his own readers would always take just what they needed from the *Essays* without worrying about the rest. For his contemporaries, this meant seizing on his most Stoic and Epicurean passages. They interpreted his book as a manual for living, and hailed him as a philosopher in the old style, great enough to stand alongside the originals. His friend Étienne Pasquier called him "another Seneca in our language." Another friend and colleague from Bordeaux, Florimond de Raemond, extolled Montaigne's courage in the face of life's torments, and advised readers to turn to him for wisdom, especially about how to come to terms with death. A sonnet by Claude Expilly, published with a 1595 edition of Montaigne's book, praised its author as a "magnanimous Stoic" and spoke warmly of his manly way of writing, his fearlessness, and his ability to give strength to the weakest of souls. Montaigne's "brave essays" will be praised for centuries to come, Expilly wrote, for—like the ancients—Montaigne teaches people to speak well, to live well, and to die well.

This provides the first inkling of the transformations Montaigne would undergo in his readers' minds over the centuries, as each generation adopted him as a source of enlightenment and wisdom. Each wave of readers found in him more or less what they expected, and, in many cases, what they themselves put there. Montaigne's first audience was a late Renaissance one, filled with neo-Stoics and neo-Epicureans fascinated by the question of how to live well, and how to achieve *eudaimonia* in the face of suffering. They embraced him as one of themselves, and made him a best seller. They thus laid the foundations for all his future fame as a pragmatic philosopher, and as a guide to the art of living.

MONTAIGNE IN SLAVERY

Montaigne's trick of absorbing La Boétie into himself, as a kind of ghost or secret sharer in all he did, might seem to run counter to his plan of distracting himself from grief. But in its way, it *was* a form of diversion: it led him away from thoughts of loss towards a new way of thinking about his present life. A split opened up between his own point of view and the one he imagined La Boétie might take, so that, at any moment, he could slip from one to the other. Perhaps this is what gave him the idea that, as he wrote elsewhere, "We are, I know not how, double within ourselves."

Montaigne himself remarked that he might not have written the *Essays* had this space not been opened in himself. Had he had "someone to talk to," he said, he might only have published letters, a more conventional literary format. Instead, he had to stage his and La Boétie's dialogue within himself. The modern critic Anthony Wilden has compared this maneuver to the master/slave dialectic in the philosophy of G. W. F. Hegel: La Boétie became Montaigne's imaginary master, commanding him to work, while Montaigne became the willing slave who sustained them both through the labor of writing. It was a form of "voluntary servitude." Out of it emerged the *Essays*, almost as a by-product of Montaigne's trick for managing sorrow and solitude.

La Boétie's death certainly did leave Montaigne with some literary slavery of a more down-to-earth kind, in the form of his stack of unpublished manuscripts. These were not particularly unusual or original, with the exception of *On Voluntary Servitude* (assuming that this was indeed La Boétie's work), but they deserved better than being left to crumble to dust. Whether because La Boétie had asked him to, or on his own initiative,

Montaigne now became his friend's posthumous editor—a demanding role, which gave a push to his own literary career.

Rather surprisingly, considering his well-ordered character, La Boétie's manuscripts seem to have been in a higgledy-piggledy state. In one of his dedications to the published work, Montaigne talks of having "assiduously collected everything complete that I found among his notebooks and papers scattered here and there." It was a formidable task, but he found many things worth publishing, including La Boétie's sonnets. There were also translations of classical texts, such as the letter of consolation from Plutarch to his wife on the death of their child, and the first ever French version of Xenophon's *Oeconomicus*, a treatise on the art of good estate and land management—a subject of relevance to Montaigne, who was just about to resign from Bordeaux.

Having sorted out the manuscripts, Montaigne saw a collected edition of them through the press. He traveled to Paris to liaise with publishers and to promote the result. For each of La Boétie's pieces he courted a suitable patron, crafting graceful and sycophantic dedications to influential people including Michel de L'Hôpital and various Bordeaux notables—as well as to his own wife, in the case of the Plutarch letter. Conventional though the "dedicatory epistle" genre was, his letters are lively and personal. He also appended an even more personal piece of writing to the book: his account of La Boétie's death. The whole undertaking confirms the sense that he was now in a literary partnership with La Boétie's memory, and that the two of them could expect a great future together. It taught Montaigne a lot about the world of publishing and about what fashionable Parisians liked to read, information that would come in useful.

The account of La Boétie's death appeared in the form of a letter to Montaigne's own father: a strange choice. Perhaps Pierre had urged him to write it. He had certainly done this once before. Around 1567, he had given his son a very challenging literary commission indeed, which had also done its part in turning him into a writer.

This early request seems to have been Pierre's attempt to shake his son out of a continuing tendency to idleness; it was another of those "tricks," inflicted for its victim's benefit. Even in his mid-thirties, Montaigne still had something of the sulky teenager about him. He was dissatisfied with his career as magistrate, disinclined to the life of a courtier, snooty about the law, and indifferent to building and property development. Moreover, despite his interest in literature, he showed no signs of writing much. Pierre may now have guessed that he himself did not have long to live, and he probably felt that Montaigne needed preparing for the responsibilities that would soon descend on him. He needed a challenge.

Micheau wanted to write: very well, let him write! Pierre handed him a 500-page folio volume, written by a Catalan theologian over a century earlier, in stilted Latin, and said, "Translate this into French for me when you get a moment, will you, son?"

This would have been a good way of putting Montaigne off literary endeavors for life; perhaps that was what Pierre was trying to do. As good luck would have it, however, the book was more than just long and boring. It also promoted a brand of theology that Montaigne found abhorrent. This woke him out of his slumbers. More than the work on La Boétie's manuscripts, and perhaps more even than the crafting of the letter describing his friend's dying moments, his father's translation task lit the spark that one day blazed up into the *Essays*.

The book was called *Theologia naturalis, sive liber creaturarum* (Natural Theology, or Book of Creatures). Its author, Raymond Sebond, had written it in 1436, though it was not published until 1484: still well before Montaigne's time, and Pierre's. It had been given to Pierre by one of the bookish friends he liked to cultivate, but the Latin was too difficult for him, so he put it away in a pile of papers. Years later, he looked through the pile. Something about the book, perhaps its dense, stubborn inscrutability, put him in mind of his errant son.

Pierre's decision to put it away when he did, and retrieve it when he did, may have been connected to the fact that it went first out of favor with the Church, then back in again. *Theologia naturalis* was placed on the *Index of Prohibited Books* in 1558, but taken off in 1564, because it promoted a distinctive style of "rational" theology about which the Church kept changing its mind. The debate centered on the claim that truths of religion could be proved through rational arguments, or by examination of evidence found in nature. Sebond thought they could be so proved: this put him at the opposite extreme both from Montaigne and, for a while, from the Church.

Montaigne inclined more towards a position known as Fideism, which placed no reliance at all on human reason or endeavor, and denied that humans could attain knowledge of religious truths except through faith. Montaigne may not have felt a great desire for faith, but he did feel a strong aversion to all human pretension—and the result was the same.

Thus Montaigne found himself with the job of translating 500 pages of theological argumentation designed to prove an assertion he deplored. "It was a very strange and a new occupation for me," he wrote. In the *Essays*, he tried to make it sound as though he had approached it in a casual way. "Being by chance at leisure at the time," he said, "and being unable to disobey any command of the best father there ever was, I got through it as best I could." But it must have been a major project, taking a year or more to complete. He probably surprised himself by how much he got out of it. It stimulated him as grit stimulates an oyster. The whole time he was writing, he must have been thinking, "But . . . but . . . ," and even "No! No!" It forced him to analyze his own ideas. Even if he didn't question the text deeply at the time, he certainly did when he was commissioned a few years later (probably by Marguerite de Valois, the king's sister and wife of the Protestant Henri de Navarre) to write an essay defending the book; that is, to defend a work he considered indefensible.

That would become his "Apology for Raymond Sebond," the twelfth chapter of Book II of the *Essays*. It is far and away the longest piece in the book, almost absurdly out of proportion to the rest. In the 1580 edition, the other ninety-three chapters average nine and a half pages each, while the "Apology" occupies 248 pages. Stylistically, though, it fits perfectly. It charms the reader and weaves complex patterns of digression just like the others, and it gives the *Essays* its weight in more than one sense. Without it, the book would have had less influence in centuries to come. It would have been less hated, by some, but also less read.

"Apology" means "defense"; and indeed the essay does begin as a defense of Sebond. It stays that way for about half a page. Then it swerves off into something very different: something much more like an attack. As the critic Louis Cons once put it, it supports Sebond "as the rope supports the hanged man."

How, then, can he call it an "apology"? Montaigne's trick is simple. He purports to defend Sebond against those who have tried to bring him down using rational arguments. He does this by showing that rational arguments, *in general*, are fallible, because human reason itself cannot be relied on. Thus he defends a rationalist against other rationalists by arguing that anything based on reason is valueless. Montaigne's defense undermines Sebond's enemies, all right, but it undermines Sebond himself even more fatally. Of this, he was obviously well aware.

Despite its length and complexity, the essay is never less than entertaining. This is because Montaigne borrows a technique from Plutarch: he constructs his argument by heaping up case studies. Stories and facts spill out in every paragraph like flowers from a cornucopia. Almost every story provides an example of how useless human reason is, how feeble human powers are, and how silly and deluded almost everyone is—not excepting Montaigne himself, as he happily admits.

Many of the examples themselves come from Plutarch as well. But the driving force behind this unapologetic "Apology" is not Plutarch's—or not his alone. It comes from the third of the great Hellenistic philosophies, the strangest of them all: Pyrrhonian Skepticism.

7. Q. How to live? A. Question everything

S ET ALONGSIDE STOICISM and Epicureanism, Skepticism looks like the
odd one out. The other two seem obvious paths to tranquillity and
"human flourishing": they teach you to prepare for life's difficulties,
to pay attention, to develop good habits of thought, and to practice
therapeutic tricks on yourself. Skepticism seems a more limited matter. A
skeptic is taken to be someone who always wants to see proof, and who
doubts things that other people take at face value. It sounds as if it concerns
only questions of knowledge, not the question of how to live. In the
Renaissance, however, and in the classical world where Skepticism was born
alongside the other pragmatic philosophies, it was seen differently.

Like the others, Skepticism amounted to a form of therapy. This, at least,
was true of Pyrrhonian Skepticism, the type originated by the Greek
philosopher Pyrrho, who died about 275 BC, and later developed more
rigorously by Sextus Empiricus in the second century AD. ("Dogmatic" or
"Academic" Skepticism, the other kind, was less far-reaching.) Some idea
of the bizarre effect Pyrrhonism had on people is apparent from the story
of how Henri Estienne, Montaigne's near-contemporary and first French
translator of Sextus Empiricus, reacted to his encounter with Sextus's
Hypotyposes. Working in his library one day, but feeling too ill and tired to
do his usual work, he found a copy while browsing through an old box of
manuscripts. As soon as he started reading, he found himself laughing so
heartily that his weariness left him and his intellectual energy returned.
Another scholar of the period, Gentian Hervet, had a similar experience. He
too came across Sextus by chance in his employer's library, and felt that a
world of lightness and pleasure had opened up before him. The work did
not so much instruct or convince its readers as give them the giggles.

A modern reader perusing the *Hypotyposes* might wonder what was so
funny. It does contain some sprightly examples, as philosophy books often

do, but it does not seem wildly comic. It is not obvious why it cured both Estienne and Hervet of their ennui—or why it had such an impact on Montaigne, who would find in it the perfect antidote to Raymond Sebond and his solemn, inflated ideas of human importance.

The key to the trick is the revelation that nothing in life need be taken seriously. Pyrrhonism does not even take itself seriously. Ordinary dogmatic Skepticism asserts the impossibility of knowledge: it is summed up in Socrates's remark: "All I know is that I know nothing." Pyrrhonian Skepticism starts from this point, but then adds, in effect, "and I'm not even sure about that." Having stated its one philosophical principle, it turns in a circle and gobbles itself up, leaving only a puff of absurdity.

Pyrrhonians accordingly deal with all the problems life can throw at them by means of a single word which acts as shorthand for this maneuver: in Greek, *epekho*. It means "I suspend judgment." Or, in a different rendition given in French by Montaigne himself, *je soutiens*: "I hold back." This phrase conquers all enemies; it undoes them, so that they disintegrate into atoms before your eyes.

This sounds about as uplifting as the Stoic or Epicurean notion of "indifference." But, like the other Hellenistic ideas, it works, and that is all that matters. *Epekho* functions almost like one of those puzzling koans in Zen Buddhism: brief, enigmatic notions or unanswerable questions such as "What is the sound of one hand clapping?" At first, these utterances cause nothing but perplexity. Later, they open a path to all-encompassing wisdom. This family resemblance between Pyrrhonism and Zen may be no accident: Pyrrho traveled to Persia and India with Alexander the Great, and dabbled in Eastern philosophy—not Zen Buddhism, which did not yet exist, but some of its precursors.

The *epekho* trick makes you laugh and feel better because it frees you from the need to find a definite answer to anything. To borrow an example from Alan Bailey, a historian of Skepticism, if someone declares that the number of grains of sand in the Sahara is an even number and demands to know your opinion, your natural response might be, "I don't have one," or "How should I know?" Or, if you want to sound more philosophical, "I suspend judgment"—*epekho*. If a second person says, "What rubbish! There is obviously an *odd* number of grains of sand in the Sahara," you would still say *epekho*, in the same unflappable tone. In effect, you respond with the deadpan statement Sextus himself cited as a definition of *epekho*:

> I cannot say which of the things proposed I should find convincing and which I should not find convincing.

Or:

> I now feel in such a way as neither to posit dogmatically nor to reject any of the things falling under this investigation.

Or:

> To every account I have scrutinized which purports to establish something in dogmatic fashion, there appears to me to be opposed another account, purporting to establish something in dogmatic fashion, equal to it in convincingness or lack of convincingness.

This last formulation in particular might be memorized as a useful way of shutting up anyone making outlandish claims about the Sahara or anything else. In reciting it, one feels a kind of mental calm descending. One cannot know the answer and feels it doesn't matter, so one's nonengagement causes no distress.

For a Pyrrhonian, this remains true even when the questions get more difficult. Is it all right to lie to someone to make them feel better? *Epekho*. Is my cat better-looking than your cat? Am I kinder than you? Does love make one happy? Is there such a thing as a just war? *Epekho*. And it goes further. A real Pyrrhonian will suspend judgment even in response to questions that ordinary folk might think had an obvious answer. Do hens lay eggs? Do other people really exist? Am I looking at a cup of coffee at this moment? It is *epekho* all the way.

The Pyrrhonians did this, not to unsettle themselves profoundly and throw themselves into a paranoid vortex of doubt, but to attain a condition of relaxation about everything. It was their path to *ataraxia*—a goal they shared with the Stoics and Epicureans—and thus to joy and human flourishing. The most obvious advantage is that Pyrrhonians need never worry about getting anything wrong. If they win their arguments, they show that they are right. If they lose, that just proves that they were right to doubt their own knowledge. This makes them simultaneously very peaceful and very contrary. They are fond of arguing for unpopular points of view, for the fun of it. As Montaigne wrote:

> If you postulate that snow is black, they argue on the contrary that it is white. If you say that it is neither one nor the other, it is up to them to maintain that it is both. If you maintain with certain judgment that you know nothing about it, they will maintain that you do. Yes, and if by an affirmative axiom you assure them that you are in doubt about it, they will go and argue that you are not, or that you cannot judge and prove that you are in doubt.

By this time they will probably have been silenced by a punch on the nose, but even that does not bother them, since they are undisturbed by the idea of someone being angry with them, and they are not unduly bothered by physical pain. Who is to say that pain is worse than pleasure? And if a shard of bone penetrates their brain and kills them, so what? Is it better to live than to die?

"Hail, skeptic ease!" wrote the Irish poet Thomas Moore, long after Montaigne:

> When error's waves are past
> How sweet to reach thy tranquil port at last,
> And gently rocked in undulating doubt,
> Smile at the sturdy winds which war without!

So immense was this ease that it could separate Skeptics entirely from ordinary people—even though, unlike the Epicureans in their Garden, they preferred to remain immersed in the real world. Some extraordinary stories were told about Pyrrho himself. He was supposed to be so aloof and so tranquil that he would not react to things at all. When walking somewhere, he would not change his course even for precipices or oncoming carts, so his friends had to keep intervening to save him. And, as Montaigne recorded, "If he had begun to say something, he never failed to finish it, even though the man he was speaking to had gone away"—because he did not want to be diverted from his inner reality by external changes.

Meanwhile, other stories suggested that even Pyrrho could not maintain perfect indifference all the time. A friend caught him "quarreling very sharply" with his sister, and accused him of betraying his principles. "What, must this silly woman also serve as testimony to my rules?" replied Pyrrho. Another time, having been caught defending himself against a frenzied dog, he admitted, "It is very difficult entirely to strip off the man."

Montaigne loved both kinds of story: the ones that showed Pyrrho departing radically from normal behavior, as well as the ones that showed him to be merely human. And, like a true Skeptic, he tried to suspend judgment about them all. He felt it more likely, however, that Pyrrho was an ordinary man like himself, striving only to be clear-sighted and to take nothing for granted.

He did not want to make himself a stump or a stone; he wanted to make himself a living, thinking, reasoning man, enjoying all natural pleasures and comforts, employing and using all his bodily and spiritual faculties.

All Pyrrho renounced, according to Montaigne, was the pretension most people fall prey to: that of "regimenting, arranging, and fixing truth." This was what really interested Montaigne in the Skeptical tradition: not so much the Skeptics' extreme approach to warding off pains and sorrows (for that, he preferred the Stoics and Epicureans, who seemed more closely attuned to real life), but their desire to take everything provisionally and questioningly. This was just what he always tried to do himself. To keep this goal in the forefront of his mind, he had a series of medals struck in 1576, featuring Sextus's magic word *epekho*, together with his own arms and an emblem of weighing scales. The scales are another Pyrrhonian symbol, designed to remind himself both to maintain balance, and to weigh things up rather than merely accepting them.

The imagery he used was unusual, but the idea of inscribing such

personal statements on medals or *jetons* was not: it was a fashion of the time, and functioned both as an *aide-mémoire* and as a token of belonging or identity. Had Montaigne been a young man of the early twenty-first century instead of the sixteenth, he would probably have had it done as a tattoo.

If the medal was indeed designed to remind him of his principles, it worked: Skepticism guided him at work, in his home life, and in his writing. The *Essays* are suffused with it: he filled his pages with words such as "perhaps," "to some extent," "I think," "It seems to me," and so on— words which, as Montaigne said himself, "soften and moderate the rashness of our propositions," and which embody what the critic Hugo Friedrich has called his philosophy of "unassumingness." They are not extra flourishes; they *are* Montaigne's thought, at its purest. He never tired of such thinking, or of boggling his own mind by contemplating the millions of lives that had been lived through history and the impossibility of knowing the truth about them. "Even if all that has come down to us by report from the past should be true and known by someone, it would be less than nothing compared with what is unknown." How puny is the knowledge of even the most curious person, he reflected, and how astounding the world by comparison. To quote Hugo Friedrich again, Montaigne had a "deep need to be surprised by what is unique, what cannot be categorized, what is mysterious."

And of all that was mysterious, nothing amazed him more than himself, the most unfathomable phenomenon of all. Countless times, he noticed himself changing an opinion from one extreme to the other, or shifting from emotion to emotion within seconds.

> My footing is so unsteady and so insecure, I find it so vacillating and ready to slip, and my sight is so unreliable, that on an empty stomach I feel myself another man than after a meal. If my health smiles upon me, and the brightness of a beautiful day, I am a fine fellow; if I have a corn bothering my toe, I am surly, unpleasant, and unapproachable.

Even his simplest perceptions cannot be relied upon. If he has a fever or has taken medicine, everything tastes different or appears with different colors. A mild cold befuddles the mind; dementia would knock it out entirely. Socrates himself could be rendered a vacant idiot by a stroke or brain damage, and if a rabid dog bit him, he would talk nonsense. The dog's saliva could make "all philosophy, if it were incarnate, raving mad." And this is just the point: for Montaigne, philosophy *is* incarnate. It lives in individual, fallible humans; therefore, it is riddled with uncertainty. "The philosophers, it seems to me, have hardly touched this chord."

And what of the perceptions of different species? Montaigne correctly guesses (as Sextus did before him) that other animals see colors differently from humans. Perhaps it is we, not they, who see them "wrongly." We have no way of knowing what the colors really are. Animals have faculties that are weak or lacking in us, and maybe some of these are essential to a full understanding of the world. "We have formed a truth by the consultation and concurrence of our five senses; but perhaps we needed the agreement of eight or ten senses, and their contribution, to perceive it certainly and in its essence."

This seemingly casual remark proposes a shocking idea: that we may be cut off by our very nature from seeing things as they are. A human being's perspective may not merely be prone to occasional error, but limited by definition, in exactly the way we normally (and arrogantly) presume a dog's intelligence to be. Only someone with an exceptional ability to escape his immediate point of view could entertain such an idea, and this was precisely Montaigne's talent: being able to slip out from behind his eyes so as to gaze back upon himself with Pyrrhonian suspension of judgment. Even the original Skeptics never went so far. They doubted everything around them, but they did not usually consider how implicated their innermost souls were in the general uncertainty. Montaigne did, all the time:

We, and our judgment, and all mortal things go on flowing and rolling unceasingly. Thus nothing certain can be established about one thing by another, both the judging and the judged being in continual change and motion.

This might seem a dead end, closing off all possibility of knowing anything, since nothing can be measured against anything else, but it can also open up a new way of living. It makes everything more complicated and more interesting: the world becomes a vast multidimensional landscape in which every point of view must be taken into account. All we need to do is to remember this fact, so as to "become wise at our own expense," as Montaigne put it.

Even for him, the discipline of attention required constant effort: "We must really strain our soul to be aware of our own fallibility." The *Essays* helped. By writing them, he set himself up like a lab rat and stood over himself with notebook in hand. Each observed oddity made him rejoice. He even took pleasure in his memory lapses, for they reminded him of his failings and saved him from the error of insisting that he was always right. There was only one exception to his "question everything" rule: he was careful to state that he considered his religious faith beyond doubt. He adhered to the received dogma of the Catholic Church, and that was that.

This can come as a surprise to modern readers. Today, Skepticism and organized religion are usually thought to occupy opposite sides of a divide, with the latter representing faith and authority while the former allies itself with science and reason. In Montaigne's day, the lines were drawn differently. Science in the modern sense did not yet exist, and human reason was only rarely considered something that could stand alone, unsupported by God. The idea that the human mind could find things out for itself was the very thing Skeptics were likely to be most skeptical about. And the Church currently favored faith over "rational theology," so it naturally saw Pyrrhonism as an ally. Attacking human arrogance as it did, Pyrrhonian Skepticism was especially useful against the "innovation" of Protestantism, which prioritized private reasoning and conscience rather than dogma.

Thus, for several decades, Catholicism embraced Pyrrhonism, and held up books such as Henri Estienne's Sextus translation and Montaigne's

Essays as valuable antidotes to heresy. Montaigne helped them with his attack on rational hubris, as well as with the many overt statements of Fideism scattered through his work. Religion, he wrote, must come to us from God by means of "an extraordinary infusion," not by our own efforts. God provides the tea bag; we provide the water and cup. And if we do not receive the infusion directly, it is enough to trust in the Church, which is a sort of authorized mass samovar, filled with pre-brewed faith. Montaigne made it clear that he recognized the Church's right to govern him in religious matters, even to the extent of policing his thoughts. At a time when people were rushing to novelty, he wrote, the principle of unquestioning obedience had saved him many a time:

> Otherwise I could not keep myself from rolling about incessantly. Thus I have, by the grace of God, kept myself intact, without agitation or disturbance of conscience, in the ancient beliefs of our religion, in the midst of so many sects and divisions that our century has produced.

It is hard to tell whether the disturbance he had in mind was a spiritual one, or whether he was thinking more of the inconvenience of being called a heretic and having his books burned. Fideism could be a handy pretext for secret unbelievers. Having paid God His due and immunized oneself against accusations of irreligion, one could in theory go on to be as secular as one wished. What possible accusation could you bring against someone who advocated submission to God and to Church doctrine in every detail? Indeed, the Church eventually noticed this danger, and by the following century had cast Fideism into disrepute. For the moment, however, anyone who wanted to take this path could do so with impunity. Did Montaigne fall into this category?

It is true that he showed little sign of real interest in religion. The *Essays* has nothing to say about most Christian ideas: he seems unmoved by themes of sacrifice, repentance, and salvation, and shows neither fear of Hell nor desire for Heaven. The idea that witches and demons are active in the world gets shorter shrift than does the idea of cats hypnotizing birds out of trees. When Montaigne broods on death, he apparently forgets that he is supposed to believe in an afterlife. He says things like, "I plunge head down, stupidly, into death . . . as into a silent and dark abyss which swallows me up at one leap and overwhelms me in an instant with a heavy sleep free from feeling and pain." Theologians of the following century were horrified by this godless description. Another topic Montaigne shows no interest in is Jesus Christ. He writes about the noble deaths of Socrates and Cato, but does not think to mention the crucifixion alongside them. The sacred mystery of redemption leaves him cold. He cares much more about secular morality—about questions of mercy and cruelty. As the modern critic David Quint has summed it up, Montaigne would probably interpret the message for humanity in Christ's crucifixion as being "Don't crucify people."

On the other hand, it is unlikely that Montaigne was an out-and-out atheist; in the sixteenth century almost no one was. And it would be no surprise to find him genuinely drawn to Fideism. It accorded well both with his Skeptical philosophy and his personal temperament—for, despite his love of independence, he often preferred giving up control, especially of things that did not interest him much. Besides, whatever he really thought about Fideism's high-altitude God, the attraction of what remains down *here* exerted a much stronger pull on him.

The result, in any case, was that he lived his life without ever encountering serious problems with the Church: quite an achievement for a man who wrote so freely, who lived on a border between Catholic and Protestant lands, and who occupied public office in a time of religious war. When he was traveling in Italy in the 1580s, Inquisition officials did inspect the *Essays* and produced a list of mild objections. One was that he used the word *Fortune* instead of the officially approved *Providence*. (Providence comes from God and allows room for free will; Fortune is just the way the cookie crumbles.) Others were that he quoted heretical poets, that he made excuses for the apostate emperor Julian, that he thought anything beyond simple execution cruel, and that he recommended bringing children up naturally and freely. But the Inquisition did not mind his views on death, his reservations about witchcraft trials, or—least of all—his Skepticism.

It was, in fact, the *Essays'* Skepticism that made it such a success on first publication, alongside its Stoicism and Epicureanism. It managed to appeal to thoughtful, independent-minded readers, but also to the most orthodox of churchmen. It pleased people like Montaigne's Bordeaux colleague Florimond de Raemond, a zealous Catholic whose favorite subject, in his own writings, was the imminent arrival of the Antichrist and the coming Apocalypse. Raemond advised people to read Montaigne to fortify themselves against heresy, and particularly praised the "beautiful Apology" because of its abundance of stories demonstrating how little we know about the world. He borrowed several such stories for a chapter of his own work *L'Antichrist*, entitled "Strange things of which we do not know the reason." Why does an angry elephant become calm on seeing a sheep? he asked. Why does a wild bull become docile if he is tethered to a fig tree? And how exactly does the remora fish apply its little hooks to a ship's hull to hold it back at sea? Raemond sounds so amiable and shows such a bright amazement about natural wonders that one has to pinch oneself to remember that he believed the end of the world was nigh. Fideism produced odd bedfellows indeed; extremists and secular moderates were brought together by a shared desire to marvel at their own ignorance.

Thus, the early Montaigne was embraced by the orthodox as a pious Skeptical sage, a new Pyrrho as well as a new Seneca: the author of a book at once consoling and morally improving. It comes as a surprise, therefore, to discover that by the end of the following century he was shunned with horror and that the *Essays* was consigned to the *Index of Prohibited Books*, there to stay for almost a hundred and eighty years.

The problem began with discussion of a topic which one might think of little importance: animals.

ANIMALS AND DEMONS

Montaigne's favorite trick for undermining human vanity was the telling of animal stories like those that so intrigued Florimond de Raemond—many of them liberated from Plutarch. He liked them because they were entertaining, yet had a serious purpose. Tales of animal cleverness and sensitivity demonstrated that human abilities were far from exceptional, and indeed that animals do many things better than we do.

Animals can be good, for example, at working cooperatively. Oxen, hogs, and other creatures will gather in groups for self-defense. If a parrotfish is hooked by a fisherman, his fellow parrotfish rush to chew through the line and free him. Or, if one is netted, others thrust their tails through the net so he can grab one with his teeth, and be pulled out. Even different species can work together in this way, as with the pilot fish that guides the whale, or the bird that picks the crocodile's teeth.

Tuna fish demonstrate a sophisticated understanding of astronomy: when the winter solstice arrives, the whole school stops precisely where it is in the water, and stays there until the following spring equinox. They know geometry and arithmetic too, for they have been observed to form themselves into a perfect cube of which all six sides are equal.

Morally, animals prove themselves at least as noble as humans. For repentance, who can surpass the elephant who was so grief-stricken about having killed his keeper in a fit of temper that he deliberately starved himself to death? And what of the female halcyon, or kingfisher, who loyally carries a wounded mate around on her shoulders, for the rest of her life if need be? These loving kingfishers also show a flair for technology: they use fishbones to build a structure that acts as both nest and boat, cleverly testing it for leaks near a shore first before launching it into open sea.

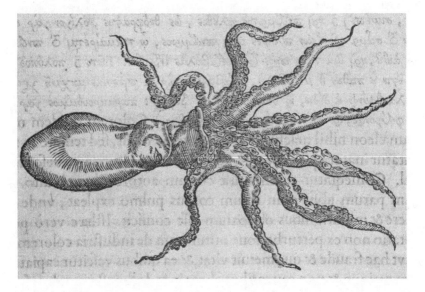

Animals surpass us in miscellaneous abilities of all kinds. Humans change color, but in an uncontrolled way: we blush when we are embarrassed, and go pale when we are frightened. This places us on the same level as chameleons, who also change at the mercy of chance conditions, but far below the octopus, who can blend his colors however and whenever he pleases. We and the chameleons can only gaze up in admiration at the mighty octopus—a shock for human vanity.

Yet still we humans persist in thinking of ourselves as separate from all other creatures, closer to gods than to chameleons or parrotfish. It never occurs to us to rank ourselves among animals, or to put ourselves in their minds. We barely stop to wonder whether they have minds at all. Yet, for Montaigne, it is enough to watch a dog dreaming to see that it must have an inner world just like ours. A person who dreams about Rome or Paris conjures up an insubstantial Rome or Paris within. Likewise, a dog dreaming about a hare surely sees a disembodied hare running through his dream. We sense this from the twitching of his paws as he runs after it: a hare is there for him somewhere, albeit "a hare without fur or bones." Animals populate their internal world with ghosts of their own invention, just as we do.

Montaigne's animal stories seemed both delightful and innocuous to his first readers. If anything, they were morally useful, pointing out that humans are modest beings who cannot expect to master or understand much on God's earth. But as the sixteenth century receded into history and the seventeenth rolled on, people became increasingly disturbed by this picture of themselves as less refined or capable than an octopus. It seemed degrading rather than merely humbling. By the 1660s, the "Apology," where most of the animal stories are found, no longer looked like a treasure chest of uplifting wisdom. It looked like a case study in everything that had gone wrong with the morals of the previous century. Montaigne's easy acceptance of human fallibility and of our animalistic side was now something to be fought against—almost a trick of the Devil himself.

Typical of the new attitude was a denunciation from the pulpit by the bishop Jacques-Bénigne Bossuet in 1668. Montaigne, he said,

> prefers animals to men, their instinct to our reason, their simple, innocent, and plain nature . . . to our refinements and malices. But tell

me, subtle philosopher, who laughs so cleverly at man for imagining himself to be something [more than an animal], do you reckon it as nothing to know God?

The challenging tone was new, and so was the feeling that human dignity needed defending against a "subtle" enemy. The seventeenth century would cease to accept Montaigne as a sage; it would begin to see him as a trickster and a subversive. Montaigne's animal stories and his debunking of human pretensions would prove particularly irksome to two of the greatest writers of the new era: René Descartes and Blaise Pascal. They had no sympathy for each other; this makes it all the more noteworthy that they came together in disapproval of Montaigne.

René Descartes, the greatest philosopher of the early modern era, was interested in animals mainly as a contrast to human beings. Humans have a conscious, immaterial mind; they can reflect on their own experience, and say "I think." Animals cannot. For Descartes, they therefore lack souls and are no more than machines. They are programmed to walk, run, sleep, yawn, sneeze, hunt, roar, scratch themselves, build nests, raise young, eat, and defecate, but they do this in the same way as a clockwork automaton might whirr its gears and trundle across the floor. A dog, for Descartes, has no perspective, no true experience. It does not create a hare in its inner world and chase it across the fields. It can snuffle and twitch its paws all it likes; Descartes will never see anything but contracting muscles and firing nerves, triggered by equally mechanical operations in the brain.

Descartes cannot truly exchange a glance with an animal. Montaigne can, and does. In one famous passage, he mused: "When I play with my cat, who knows if I am not a pastime to her more than she is to me?" And he added in another version of the text: "We entertain each other with reciprocal monkey tricks. If I have my time to begin or to refuse, so has she hers." He borrows his cat's point of view in relation to him just as readily as he occupies his own in relation to her.

Montaigne's little interaction with his cat is one of the most charming moments in the *Essays*, and an important one too. It captures his belief that all beings share a common world, but that each creature has its own way of perceiving this world. "All of Montaigne lies in that casual sentence," one critic has commented. Montaigne's cat is so celebrated that she has inspired a full scholarly article, and an entry to herself in Philippe Desan's *Dictionnaire de Montaigne*.

All Montaigne's skills at jumping between perspectives come to the fore when he writes about animals. We find it hard to understand them, he says, but they must find it just as hard to understand us. "This defect that hinders communication between them and us, why is it not just as much ours as theirs?"

We have some mediocre understanding of their meaning; so do they of ours, in about the same degree. They flatter us, threaten us, and implore us, and we them.

Montaigne cannot look at his cat without seeing her looking back at him, and imagining himself as he looks to her. This is the kind of interaction between flawed, mutually aware individuals of different species that can never happen for Descartes, who was disturbed by it, as were others in his century.

In Descartes's case, the problem was that his whole philosophical structure required a point of absolute certainty, which he found in the notion of a clear, undiluted consciousness. There could be no room in this for Montaigne's boundary-blurring ambiguities: his reflections on a deranged or rabid Socrates or on the superior senses of a dog. The complications which gave Montaigne pleasure alarmed Descartes. Yet, ironically, his desire for such a point of pure certainty had arisen largely in response to his understanding of Pyrrhonian doubt, as transmitted primarily by Montaigne—leading Pyrrhonian of the modern world.

Descartes's solution came to him in November 1619 when, after a period of traveling and observing the diversity of human customs, he shut himself up in a German room heated by a wood stove and devoted one whole uninterrupted day to thinking. He started with the Skeptical assumption that nothing was real, and that all his previous beliefs had been false. Then he advanced slowly, with careful steps, "like a man who walks alone, and in the dark," replacing these false beliefs with logically justified ones. It was a purely mental progress; as he moved from step to step, his body remained by the fire, where one imagines him staring into the embers for hours. The image of Descartes in front of his stove, perhaps in the hunched position of Rodin's *Thinker*, provides a neat contrast to the image of Montaigne pacing up and down, pulling books off the shelves, getting distracted, mentioning odd thoughts to his servants to help himself remember them, and arriving at his best ideas in heated dinner-party discussions with neighbors or while riding in the woods. Even in "retirement," Montaigne did his thinking in a richly populated environment, full of objects, books, animals, and people. Descartes needed motionless withdrawal.

By his stove, Descartes gradually wound out a chain of reasoning, each link of which he considered to be riveted firmly to the previous one. His first discovery was that he himself existed:

> I think, therefore I am.

From this secure point he proceeded to establish, using nothing but deduction, that God must exist, that his own "clear and distinct" idea of God's existence must have come from God himself, and thus that anything else he had a clear and distinct idea about must be true as well. He put this last point even more boldly in a work called the *Meditations*, where he wrote, "Everything I perceive clearly and distinctly cannot fail to be true"—surely one of the most astonishing statements in the whole of philosophy, and one as far removed from Montaigne's way of doing things as can be imagined. Yet it all grew out of Montaigne's favorite brand of Skepticism—the one that threw everything into doubt, even itself, and thus raised a huge question mark at the heart of European philosophy.

Descartes's supposedly infallible chain of reasoning can seem absurd, but it makes more sense in the context of the previous century's ideas—ideas he wanted to escape. These were, above all, the two great traditions transmitted to his generation by Montaigne: Skepticism, which took everything apart, and Fideism, which put it all together again on the basis of faith. Descartes did not want to end up at this point. He was anything but a Fideist. But in a way, that is just what happened; it was a hard tradition to get away from.

Descartes's real innovation was the strength of his desire for certainty. Also new was his general spirit of extremism. Trying to get away from Skepticism, he stretched it to a hitherto unimaginable length, as one might pull a strand of gum stuck to one's shoe. There could be no question of floating in doubt indefinitely, as on a "sea of speculation." Uncertainty was not a way of life, as it was for Montaigne and the original Pyrrhonians. For Descartes, it was a crisis stage. One can feel his disorientation when he writes, in the *Meditations*:

> The Meditation of yesterday has filled my mind with so many doubts that it is no longer in my power to forget them . . . I can neither put

my feet firmly down on the bottom nor swim to keep myself on the surface.

This was where the seventeenth century really separated itself from Montaigne's world: in its discovery of the nightmare side of Skepticism. In that "Meditation of yesterday," Descartes—always good at using vivid metaphors to make his points—had even personified his uncertainties in a figure of real horror:

> I shall suppose, therefore, that there is, not a true God, who is the sovereign source of truth, but some evil demon, no less cunning and deceiving than powerful, who has used all his artifice to deceive me. I will suppose that the heavens, the air, the earth, color, shapes, sounds, and all external things that we see are only illusions and deceptions which he uses to take me in. I will consider myself as having no hands, eyes, flesh, blood, or senses, but as believing wrongly that I have all these things.

Demons still seemed real and frightening in Descartes's day, just as they had in Montaigne's. Some thought they filled the world in clouds, like microorganisms in pollution; they and their master, Satan, could weave illusions out of air, or tie up rays of light or the very threads of your brain in order to make you see beasts and monsters. The thought that such a spirit might be systematically fooling us as to the nature of the entire physical world— and of ourselves—was enough to send anyone mad. The only thing worse was the possibility that God Himself might be such a deceiver, something Descartes hinted at fleetingly, then withdrew from.

Perhaps strangely for someone who advocated pure reason and swore enmity to tricks of the imagination, Descartes used every novelistic device in his power to play on the reader's emotions. But, like most horror writers, his impulse was essentially conservative. The demon threatens the order of things, but he is then defeated and normality is restored on a more secure foundation—except that it isn't. In horror fiction, the monster often threatens a comeback in a coda at the end: not truly defeated at all but only waiting for the sequel. Descartes did not want sequels. He thought he had covered up the abyss forever, but he had not; his reassuring ending fell to pieces almost at once.

A practical way out of the mess was found at last, not through Descartes's extremist challenge, but through a pragmatic compromise that has far more in common with the Montaignean spirit. Instead of seeking total certainty, modern science allows for an element of doubt, in theory, while in practice everyone gets on with the business of learning about the world, comparing observations to hypotheses according to agreed codes of practice. We live as though there were no abyss. Like Montaigne accommodating himself to his own fallibility, we accept the world as it appears to be, with just a formal nod to the possibility that nothing is solid at all. The demon waits in the wings, yet life goes on.

Descartes's horror story was what ensued when Montaigne's Pyrrhonism reached a more anxious, self-divided mind than the sixteenth century could generate. Montaigne was not without his moments of existential anxiety: he could write lines such as, "We are, I know not how, double within ourselves," and "We have no communication with being." Still, Descartes's feeling of drowning in doubt would have left him puzzled.

Today, many people might find Descartes's terror easier to understand than the peculiar comfort that Montaigne and the original Pyrrhonians derived from their Skepticism. The idea that a void underlies everything we experience no longer seems an obvious source of consolation.

Our sense of this void has been inherited largely from Descartes's very contrary reading of Montaigne. Some of it has also been passed down to us from Montaigne's other great disciple and antagonist in the seventeenth century, a man who was even more unsettled by the implications of Pyrrhonism. This was Blaise Pascal: philosopher, mystic, and another great horror writer.

A PRODIGIOUS SEDUCTION MACHINE

The work for which Pascal is best remembered, the *Pensées* ("Thoughts"), was never meant to terrify anyone except himself: it was a collection of disorderly notes for a more systematic theological treatise which he never managed to write. Had he completed this work, it would probably have become less interesting. Instead, he left us one of the most mysterious texts in literature, a passionate outpouring largely written to try to ward off what he saw as the dangerous power of Montaigne's *Essays*.

Blaise Pascal was born in Clermont-Ferrand in 1623. As a boy he showed precocious talents for mathematics and invention, and even designed an early calculating machine. At the age of thirty-one, while staying at the abbey of Port-Royal-des-Champs, he had a visionary experience which he tried to describe on a piece of paper headed FIRE:

> Certainty. Certainty. Feeling, Joy, Peace.
> God of Jesus Christ.
> *Deum meum et Deum vostrum.*
> Oblivion of the world and of everything excepting God.
> He is found solely by the ways taught in the Gospel.
> Grandeur of the human soul.
> Just Father, the world does not know You, but I know You.
> Joy, Joy, Joy, tears of joy.

This epiphany changed his life. He sewed the piece of paper into his clothes so that he could carry it everywhere, and from then on devoted his time to theological writing and to the notes that became the *Pensées*. He did not have long for this work. At thirty-nine, he died from a brain hemorrhage.

Pascal had almost nothing in common with Descartes except for an obsession with Skepticism. Rapturously mystical, he disliked Descartes's trust in reason, and deplored what he called the "spirit of geometry" taking over philosophy. If anything, his aversion from rationality should have led him towards Montaigne instead—and it did, for he read the *Essays* constantly. But he also found the Pyrrhonian tradition, as transmitted through Montaigne, so disturbing that he could hardly get through a page of the "Apology" without racing to his notebook to pour out violent thoughts about it. Pascal cast Montaigne as "the great adversary," to borrow a phrase used by the poet T. S. Eliot to describe their relationship. Such language is normally reserved for Satan himself,

but the allusion is apt, for Montaigne was Pascal's tormentor, his seducer, and his tempter.

Pascal feared Pyrrhonian Skepticism because, unlike the readers of the sixteenth century, he felt sure it did threaten religious belief. By now, doubt was no longer thought a friend of the Church; it belonged to the Devil, and must be fought against. And here lay the problem, for, as everyone had always seen, Pyrrhonian Skepticism was almost impossible to fight. Any attempt to quarrel with it only strengthened its claim that everything was open to dispute, while if you remained neutral this confirmed the view that it was good to suspend judgment.

In a short piece usually included with the *Pensées*, recounting a conversation with Isaac Le Maître de Sacy, director of the Port-Royal abbey, Pascal sums up Montaigne's Pyrrhonian argument, or lack of it:

He puts everything into a universal doubt, and this doubt is so widespread that it becomes carried away by its very self; that is to say, he doubts whether he doubts, and doubting even this last proposition, his uncertainty goes around in an endless and restless circle. He contradicts both those who maintain that all is uncertainty, and those who maintain it is not, because he does not want to maintain anything at all.

Montaigne is "so advantageously positioned in this universal doubt that he is equally strengthened both in success and defeat." You can feel the frustration: how can anyone fight such an opponent? Yet one must. It is a moral duty, for otherwise doubt will carry everything away like a great flood: the world as we know it, human dignity, our sanity, and our sense of God. As T. S. Eliot also remarked:

> Of all authors Montaigne is one of the least destructible. You could as well dissipate a fog by flinging hand-grenades into it. For Montaigne is a fog, a gas, a fluid, insidious element. He does not reason, he insinuates, charms, and influences, or if he reasons, you must be prepared for his having some other design upon you than to convince you by his argument.

Because Pascal could not fight against Montaigne, he could not stop reading him—or writing about him. He struggled against the *Essays* from such close quarters that he could get no angle for a blow. If La Boétie hovered over Montaigne's page as his invisible friend, Montaigne hovered over Pascal's writing as his ever-present enemy and coauthor. At the same time, Pascal knew that the real drama was taking place in his own soul. He admitted: "It is not in Montaigne but in myself that I find everything I see there."

He could just as well have looked at his own notebook and said, "It is not from myself but from Montaigne that I have taken everything I see here"—for he was in the habit of transcribing quantities of material almost word for word.

Montaigne: How we cry and laugh for the same thing.
Pascal: Hence we cry and laugh at the same thing.

Montaigne: They want to get out of themselves and escape from the man. That is madness: instead of changing into angels, they change into beasts.

Pascal: Man is neither angel nor beast, and unhappily whoever wants to act the angel, acts the beast.

Montaigne: Put a philosopher in a cage of thin iron wire in large meshes, and hang it from the top of the towers of Notre Dame of Paris; he will see by evident reason that it is impossible for him to fall, and yet (unless he is used to the trade of the steeplejacks) he cannot keep the sight of this extreme height from terrifying and paralyzing him . . . Lay a beam between these two towers of such width as we need to walk on: there is no philosophical wisdom of such great firmness that it can give us courage to walk on it as we should if it were on the ground.

Pascal: If you put the world's greatest philosopher on a plank wider than he needs, but with a precipice beneath, however strongly his reason may convince him of his safety, his imagination will prevail.

Harold Bloom in *The Western Canon* calls the *Pensées* "a bad case of indigestion" in regard to Montaigne. But, in copying Montaigne, Pascal also changed him. Even where he used Montaigne's words, he set them in a different light. Like Jorge Luis Borges's twentieth-century character Pierre Menard, who writes a novel which happens to be identical to *Don Quixote*, Pascal wrote the same words in a different era and with a different temperament, and thus created something new.

It is the emotional difference that counts. Montaigne and Pascal had similar insights into the less flattering sides of human nature—into the realm of the "human, all too human," where selfishness, laziness, pettiness, vanity, and countless other such failings lurk. But Montaigne gazed upon them with indulgence and humor; in Pascal, they inspired a horror greater even than anything Descartes managed to muster.

For Pascal, fallibility is unbearable in itself: "We have such a high idea of man's soul that we cannot bear to think that this idea is wrong and therefore to be without this esteem for it. The whole of man's happiness lies in this esteem." For Montaigne, human failings are not merely bearable;

they are almost a cause for celebration. Pascal thought limitations should not be accepted; Montaigne's whole philosophy revolves around the opposite view. Even when Montaigne writes, "It seems to me that we can never be despised as much as we deserve"—the sort of thing Pascal says all the time—he writes it in a cheerful mood, and adds that mostly we are just silly rather than wicked.

Pascal must always be at one extreme or another. He is either sunk in despair or transported by euphoria. His writing can be as thrilling as a high-speed chase: he whizzes us through vast spaces and scales of disproportion. He contemplates the emptiness of the universe, or the insignificance of his own body, saying, "Whoever looks at himself in this way will be terrified by himself." Just as Descartes lifted the Pyrrhonians' mental comfort blanket—universal doubt—and found monsters beneath it, so Pascal does the same with one of the Stoics' and Epicureans' favorite tricks: the imaginary space voyage and the idea of human tininess. He follows this thought into a place of terror:

> On contemplating our blindness and wretchedness, and on observing the whole of the silent universe, and humanity with no light abandoned to itself, lost in this nook of the universe not knowing who put us there, what we have come to achieve, what will become of us when we die, incapable of all knowledge, I become frightened, like someone taken in his sleep to a terrifying, deserted island who wakes up with no knowledge of what has happened, nor means of escape.

It makes for exciting reading, but after a few pages one craves a dose of Montaigne's easygoing humanism. Pascal wants people to remain aware of ultimate things: the huge empty spaces, God, death. Yet few of us find it possible to maintain such thoughts for long. We get distracted; the mind drifts back to concrete and personal matters. Pascal found this infuriating: "What does the world think about? Never about that! But about dancing, playing the lute, singing, writing verse, tilting at the ring..." Montaigne liked asking big questions too, but he preferred to explore life through his reading, the animals in his household, incidents he had witnessed on his travels, or a neighbor's problems with his children. Pascal wrote: "Human sensitivity to little things and insensitivity to the greatest things: sign of a strange disorder." Montaigne would have put it exactly the other way around.

A century or so later, Voltaire, who thoroughly disliked Pascal, wrote: "I venture to champion humanity against this sublime misanthropist." He ran through fifty-seven quotations from the *Pensées*, dismantling each in turn. "As for me," he remarked,

> when I look at Paris or London I see no reason for falling into this despair Pascal talks about. I see a city not looking in the least like a desert island, but populous, wealthy, policed, where men are as happy as human nature permits. What man of sense will be prepared to hang himself because he doesn't know how one looks upon God face to face? . . . Why make us feel disgusted with our being? Our existence is not so wretched as we are led to believe. To look on the world as a prison cell and all men as criminals is the idea of a fanatic.

This led Voltaire to rush to the defense of Pascal's "great adversary":

> What a delightful design Montaigne had to portray himself without artifice as he did! For he has portrayed human nature itself. And what a paltry project of . . . Pascal, to belittle Montaigne!

Voltaire was much more at home with a credo like Montaigne's, as it appears in the final chapter of the *Essays*:

> I accept with all my heart and with gratitude what nature has done for me, and I am pleased with myself and proud of myself that I do. We wrong that great and all-powerful Giver by refusing his gift, nullifying it, and disfiguring it.

This comfortable acceptance of life as it is, and of one's own self as *it* is, drove Pascal to a greater fury than Pyrrhonian Skepticism itself. The two go together. Montaigne places everything in doubt, but then he deliberately reaffirms everything that is familiar, uncertain, and ordinary—for that is all we have. His Skepticism makes him celebrate imperfection: the very thing

Pascal, as much as Descartes, wanted to escape but never could. To Montaigne, it would be obvious why such escape is impossible. No one can rise above humanity: however high we ascend, we take that humanity with us. At the end of his final volume, in its final version, he wrote:

> It is an absolute perfection and virtually divine to know how to enjoy our being rightfully. We seek other conditions because we do not understand the use of our own, and go outside of ourselves because we do not know what it is like inside. Yet there is no use our mounting on stilts, for on stilts we must still walk on our own legs. And on the loftiest throne in the world we are still sitting only on our own rump.

Like Pyrrhonism, the "rump" argument is impossible to argue against, yet it also seemed to Pascal to *require* refutation, because it represented a moral danger. Montaigne's overriding principle of "convenience and calm," as Pascal described it, was pernicious. It worried Pascal and sent him into a helpless rage, as if Montaigne were enjoying some advantage that he could not have.

A similar level of anger is visible in the reaction of another reader of the same period, the philosopher Nicolas Malebranche. He was a rationalist, closer to Descartes than to Pascal, but, like Pascal, he deplored Montaigne as much for his general attitude of nonchalance as for his acceptance of doubt.

Malebranche recognized that Montaigne's book was a perennial best seller—but of course it would be, he writes bitterly. Montaigne tells good stories and appeals to the reader's imagination: people enjoy that. "His ideas are false but beautiful; his expressions irregular or bold but agreeable." But to read Montaigne for pleasure is especially dangerous. As you float in your bath of sensuous ease, Montaigne is lulling your reason to sleep and filling you with his poison. "The mind cannot be pleased by reading an author without adopting his opinions, or at least without receiving some coloring from them which, mixed with its own ideas, makes them confused and obscure." That is, reading pleasure corrupts Descartes's "clear and distinct ideas." Montaigne neither argues nor persuades; he does not need to, for he *seduces*. Malebranche conjures up an almost diabolical figure. Montaigne fools you, like Descartes's demon; he lures you into doubt and spiritual laxity.

These sinister images would prove long-lived. In 1866, the literary scholar Guillaume Guizot was still calling Montaigne the great "seducer" among French writers. T. S. Eliot saw him the same way. And the modern critic Gisèle Mathieu-Castellani describes the *Essays* as "a prodigious seduction machine." Montaigne works his spell through his nonchalance, his meandering and casual tone, and his pretense of not caring about the reader—all tricks designed to draw you in and take possession.

Subjected to such a machine, modern readers are often happy to lie back like Barbarella and enjoy it. Seventeenth-century readers felt more threatened, for serious matters of reason and religion were at stake.

Even during this period, however, other readers loved Montaigne for the pleasure he gave them. Several came overtly to his defense. In his *Caractères*, the aphorist Jean de La Bruyère suggested that Malebranche had missed the point of Montaigne because he was too intellectual and could not "appreciate thoughts which come naturally." This easygoing naturalness, together with Skeptical doubt, would make Montaigne a hero to a new breed of thinker: the vague confederacy of wits and rebels known as the *libertins*.

In English, "libertine" brings to mind a disreputable Casanova-like figure, but there was more to them than that (as indeed there was to Casanova). Although some *libertins* did seek sexual freedom, they also wanted philosophical freedom: the right to think as they liked, politically, religiously, and in every other way. Skepticism was a natural route to this inner and outer liberty.

They were a varied group, ranging from the major philosopher Pierre Gassendi to more lightweight scholars like François La Mothe le Vayer and imaginative writers like Cyrano de Bergerac, then best known for his science-fiction novel about a voyage to the moon. (His role in a more famous story based on his protuberant nose came later.) Montaigne's first editor, Marie de Gournay, may have been a secret *libertine*, along with many of her friends. Another was Jean de La Fontaine, author of Plutarch-style fables about animals' cleverness and stupidity. He got away with these by keeping them gentle in tone, yet they still constituted a challenge to human dignity. Their premise was the same as Montaigne's: that animals and humans are made of the same material.

Libertinism remained a minority pursuit, but a disproportionately influential one, because out of the *libertins* would evolve the Enlightenment philosophers of the following century. They gave Montaigne a dangerous yet positive new image, which would stick. They also spawned a less radical breed of salon socialites: aphorists such as La Bruyère, and La Rochefoucauld whose *Maximes* gathered together brief, Montaignean observations on human nature:

> At times we are as different from ourselves as we are from others.

> The surest way to be taken in is to think oneself craftier than other people.

> Chance and caprice rule the world.

And, as it happens, one La Rochefoucauld maxim provided a neat comment on Montaigne's own seventeenth-century predicament:

> We often irritate others when we think we could not possibly do so.

As with Montaigne himself, much of what the *libertins* and aphorists said revolved around the question of how to live well. *Libertins* prized qualities such as *bel esprit*, which might be translated as "good spirits," but was better defined by one writer of the time as being "gay, lively, full of fire like that displayed in the *Essays* of Montaigne." They also aspired to *honnêteté*, "honesty," which meant a life of good morals, but also of "good conversation" and "good company," according to the French Académie's dictionary of 1694.

Someone like Pascal did not even want to live like this; it would entail being distracted by the affairs of this world rather than keeping his eyes fixed on ultimate things. One imagines Pascal staring upwards into the open spaces of the universe, in mystical terror and bliss, just as Descartes stared with equal intensity into the blazing stove. In both cases, there is silence, and there is a fixed gaze: eyes rounded with awe, deep cogitation, alarm, or horror.

Libertins, and all those of the company of the *bel esprit*, did not stare. My dears! They would not dream of fixing anything, high or low in the universe, with gawping owl-eyes. Instead, they watched human beings slyly, from under half-closed lids, seeing them as they were—beginning with themselves. Those sleepy eyes perceived more about life than Descartes with his "clear and distinct ideas," or Pascal with his spiritual ecstasies. As Friedrich Nietzsche would remark centuries later, most of the genuinely valuable observations about human behavior and psychology—and thus also about philosophy—"were first detected and stated in those social circles which would make every sort of sacrifice not for scientific knowledge, but for a witty coquetry."

Nietzsche relished the irony of this because he abhorred professional philosophers as a class. For him, abstract systems were of no use; what counted was critical self-awareness: the ability to pry into one's own motivations and yet to accept oneself as one was. This is why he loved the aphorists La Rochefoucauld and La Bruyère, as well as their forefather Montaigne. He called Montaigne "this freest and mightiest of souls," and added: "That such a man wrote has truly augmented the joy of living on this earth." Montaigne apparently managed the trick of living as Nietzsche longed to do: without petty resentments or regrets, embracing everything that happened without the desire to change it. The essayist's casual remark, "If I had to live over again, I would live as I have lived," embodied everything Nietzsche spent his life trying to attain. Not only did Montaigne achieve it, but he even wrote about it in a throwaway tone, as if it were nothing special.

Like Montaigne, Nietzsche simultaneously questioned everything and tried to accept everything. The very things that most repelled Pascal about Montaigne—his bottomless doubt, his "skeptical ease," his poise, his readiness to accept imperfection—were the things that would always appeal to this other, very different tradition, running from the *libertins* through to Nietzsche and beyond, to many of his biggest fans today.

Unfortunately, in the seventeenth century, the resenters of Montaigne proved stronger than the devotees, especially once the former organized themselves and launched a direct campaign for suppression. In 1662, the year after Pascal's death, his former colleagues Pierre Nicole and Antoine Arnauld unleashed an assault on Montaigne in their best-selling book *Logique du Port-Royal*. Their second edition, in 1666, openly called for the *Essays* to be put on the Catholic Church's *Index of Prohibited Books*, as an irreligious and dangerous text. The call was heeded ten years later: the *Essays* appeared on the *Index* on January 28, 1676. Montaigne stood condemned, as much by association as anything else—for by now he was the favorite reading of a disreputable crew of fops, wits, atheists, skeptics, and rakes.

This marked the beginning of a dramatic decline in Montaigne's fortunes in France. From their first publication in 1580 to 1669, new editions of the *Essays* had appeared every two or three years, together with popular reworkings by editors who often drew attention to the most Pyrrhonian passages. After the ban, this changed. The work in its full form could no longer be published or sold in full in Catholic countries; no French publisher would touch it. For years, it was available only in bowdlerized or foreign editions, the latter often in French and designed to be smuggled home for a nonconformist readership.

Montaigne once remarked that certain books "become all the more marketable and public by being suppressed." To some extent, this happened to him: the suppression of his book in France gave it an irresistible aura. In the century to come, it enhanced his appeal to rebellious Enlightenment philosophers and even to full-blown revolutionaries.

But, on the whole, censorship did his posthumous sales more harm than good. It confined him to a limited audience in France, while in some other countries he continued to appeal to a wider range of taste—rebels and pillars of the community alike. Astonishingly, the *Essays* would stay on the *Index* for almost two hundred years, until May 27, 1854. It was a long exile, and one that outlived the genuine *frisson* of alarm he provoked in the late seventeenth century.

Pascal's remark, "It is not in Montaigne but in myself that I find everything I see there," could be intoned like a mantra through the whole of the story to come. The centuries go on; each new reader finds his or her own self in the *Essays* and thus adds to the accumulation of its possible meanings. In Descartes's case, what he found were two nightmare figures from his own psyche: a demon resistant to logic, and an animal that could think. He shrank from both. Pascal and Malebranche saw the prospect of their own seduction on a bed of Skeptic ease, and they too fled in horror.

The *libertins*, seeing the same things, responded with an amused smile and a raised eyebrow. They too recognized themselves in Montaigne. Their much later descendant, Nietzsche, would do the same, and would also return Montaigne to his philosophical homeland: to the heart of the three great Hellenistic philosophies, with their investigation of the question of how to live.

8. Q. How to live? A. Keep a private room behind the shop

GOING TO IT WITH ONLY ONE BUTTOCK

THE FLESH-AND-BLOOD Montaigne, back in the 1560s, was still getting on with that very question. He used all three of the Hellenistic philosophical traditions to manage his life and to help himself recover from the loss of La Boétie. He successfully merged his Skepticism with loyalty to Catholic dogma—a combination no one yet questioned. He finished his first major literary project, the translation of Raymond Sebond, and he worked on the dedications for La Boétie's books and his own published letter describing his friend's death. Another change occurred during this period too: he got married, and became the head of a family.

Montaigne seems, in general, to have been attractive to women. At least some of the appeal must have been physical: he makes ironic remarks about women who claim to love men only for their minds. "I have never yet seen that for the sake of our beauty of mind, however wise and mature that mind may be, they were willing to grant favors to a body that was slipping the least little bit into decline." Yet his intelligence, his humor, his amiable personality, and even his tendency to get swept away by ideas and talk too loudly, probably all contributed to his charm. So, perhaps, did the air of emotional inaccessibility hanging over him after La Boétie's death. It presented a challenge. In reality, when he liked someone, the aloofness soon disappeared: "I make advances and I throw myself at them so avidly, that I hardly fail to attach myself and to make an impression wherever I land."

Montaigne liked sex, and indulged in a lot of it throughout his life. It was only in late middle age that both his performance and his desire declined, as well as his attractiveness—all facts he bemoaned in his final *Essays*. It is depressing to be rejected, he said, but even worse to be accepted out of pity. And he hated to be troublesome to someone who did not want him. "I abhor the idea of a body void of affection being mine." This would be like making love to a corpse, as in the story of the "frantic Egyptian hot after the carcass of a dead woman he was embalming and shrouding." A sexual relationship must be reciprocal. "In truth, in this delight the pleasure I give tickles my imagination more sweetly than that which I feel."

He was realistic about the extent to which he made the earth move for his lovers, however. Sometimes a woman's heart is not really in it: "Sometimes they go to it with only one buttock." Or perhaps she is fantasizing about someone else: "What if she eats your bread with the sauce of a more agreeable imagination?"

Montaigne understood that women know more about sex than men usually think, and indeed that their imagination leads them to expect better than they get. "In place of the real parts, through desire and hope, they substitute others three times life-size." He tutted over irresponsible graffiti: "What mischief is not done by those enormous pictures that boys spread about the passages and staircases of palaces! From these, women acquire a cruel contempt for our natural capacity." Does one conclude that Montaigne had a smallish penis? Yes, indeed, because he confessed later in the same essay that nature had treated him "unfairly and unkindly," and he added a classical quotation:

> "Even the matrons—all too well they know—
> Look dimly on a man whose member's small."

He showed no shame about revealing such things: "Our life is part folly, part wisdom. Whoever writes about it only reverently and according to the rules leaves out more than half of it." It also seemed unfair to him that poets had more license simply because they wrote in verse. He quoted two examples from contemporaries:

> "May I die if your crack is more than a faint line." —Théodore de Bèze

> "A friendly tool contents and treats her well." —Saint-Gelais

Amid the varied adventures of his friendly tool, nevertheless, Montaigne also did what all dutiful noblemen must do, particularly heirs to great estates: he got himself a wife.

Her name was Françoise de La Chassaigne, and she came from a family greatly respected in Bordeaux. The marriage, which took place on September 23, 1565, would have been arranged in collaboration between the two families. This was traditional, and even the spouses' ages were more or less what custom decreed. Montaigne noted that his own age (thirty-three, he says, though he was thirty-two), was close to the ideal recommended by Aristotle, which Montaigne thought was thirty-five (actually it was thirty-seven). If he was slightly too young, his wife was a little older than usual: she was born on December 13, 1544, which made her just under twenty-one on her wedding day. At that age she could still expect to have many childbearing years ahead of her. Unfortunately, children were to bring the couple mostly disappointment and sorrow. And, despite his being over a decade older than his wife, Montaigne very decidedly seems to have done what many men do: he married his mother. The choice would not make him particularly happy.

He does not mention Françoise often in the *Essays;* when he does, he makes her sound like Antoinette, only louder. "Wives always have a proclivity for disagreeing with their husbands," he wrote. "They seize with both hands every pretext to go contrary to them." He was probably thinking of Françoise both here and in another passage, where he wrote that there was no point in raging uselessly at servants:

> I admonish . . . my family not to get angry in the air, and to see to it that their reprimand reaches the person they are complaining about: for ordinarily they are yelling before he is in their presence and continue yelling for ages after he has left . . . No one is punished or affected by it, except someone who has to put up with the racket of their voice.

One can imagine Montaigne putting his hands over his ears, and heading off to his tower.

Among the many things for which he admired the philosopher Socrates was his having perfected the art of living with an aggressive wife. Montaigne presented this as a tribulation almost as great as the one Socrates suffered at the hands of the Athenian parliament, when it condemned him to death by hemlock. He hoped to emulate Socrates's policy of forbearance and humor, and liked the reply he gave when Alcibiades asked him how he stood the nagging. One gets used to it, said Socrates, as those who live close to a mill do to the sound of the water-wheel turning. Montaigne also liked the way Socrates adapted the experience as a philosophical "trick" for his own spiritual improvement, using his wife's bad temper for practice in the art of enduring adversity.

As well as forcefulness, Françoise had staying power. She would outlive Montaigne by nearly thirty-five years, dying on March 7, 1627, at the age of eighty-two. She also survived all her children, including the only one to make it beyond infancy into adulthood. Montaigne's mother survived him too. One almost gets the impression that, between them, they drove him into an early grave.

Some of the best information about Françoise's character dates from her old age, long after Montaigne's time. By then, she had become very pious. Her daughter's second husband, Charles de Gamaches, described her as observing fasts every Friday and for half of Lent, even at seventy-seven years old. She kept up an intense correspondence with a spiritual adviser, Dom Marc-Antoine de Saint-Bernard; several letters survive. He sent her gifts of oranges and lemons; she sent him quince marmalade and hay. She often wrote to him about her money worries and legal affairs. Her last letter shows relief over some business deal: "By this God has given me a means of supporting this house of my late husband and my children." The tone is sometimes passionate: "Truly I do not know whether I would not rather choose to die than to know that you are going away." On the other hand, she feared for her adviser's safety if he traveled to visit her: "I would rather die than have you take the road in this miserable weather." As a young woman, she was probably less fretful, but her preoccupation with matters of money and law may have been a constant. At the very least, one can venture to state that she was more alert to practical concerns than Montaigne. This was not difficult: so was almost everyone, if his own account is to be believed.

Françoise and her husband usually spent their days in separate parts of the château complex. Montaigne went to his tower and she went to hers, at the other end of the boundary wall: the "Tour de Madame." (After being converted into a pigeon loft in the early nineteenth century, the tower collapsed, and does not survive today.) This left the main building as the domain of Montaigne's mother, who remained there through most of her son's marriage, until about 1587. It looks as if the towers were adapted as retreats partly so the young couple could get away both from each other and from her. In his writing, Montaigne remains silent about his mother's presence in their lives; when he mentions playing card games with his family in the evenings, he gives no indication that Granny was playing too.

This image of a family dispersed around the property is a sad one. But there must have been days when spirits were lighter, and in any case, nowhere on the estate would have felt solitary or empty. People were always around: servants, employees, guests and their entourages, sometimes children. Montaigne himself did not brood in his tower like a Gormenghast earl: he liked to be out walking. "My thoughts fall asleep if I make them sit down. My mind will not budge unless my legs move it." And separation of male and female lifestyles was normal. Husband and wife were expected to have different realms; new or modernized properties were often designed with this in mind. In 1452, Leon Battista Alberti recommended in his *De re aedificatoria* (On Building), "The husband and wife must have separate bedrooms, not only to ensure that the husband be not disturbed by his wife, when she is about to give birth or is ill, but also to allow them, even in summer, an uninterrupted night's sleep." The only differences in the Montaigne household were that an entire outdoor gallery divided their "rooms," and that his tower was also his workplace.

Was it a good marriage, by the standards of the time? Some commentators have seen it as disastrous; others as typical of its era and even good. On balance, it does not seem to have been a terrible relationship, merely a mildly unsatisfactory one. It is probably best summed up, as Montaigne's biographer Donald Frame suggested, by the remark in the *Essays*: "Whoever supposes, to see me look sometimes coldly, sometimes lovingly, on my wife, that either look is feigned, is a fool."

Genuine affection is implied in Montaigne's decision to dedicate one of his earliest publications to Françoise: La Boétie's translation of the letter written by Plutarch to his own wife following the death of their child. Uxorious dedications were not fashionable; they could be seen as quaint and rustic. Montaigne remarks defiantly, "Let us let them talk . . . You and me, my wife, let us live in the old French way." His dedication has a warm tone, and he even says, "I have, so I believe, none more intimate than you," which puts her on a level close to La Boétie's.

Whatever affection he felt for Françoise probably built up after marriage rather than before. He had entered into wedlock like an unresisting prisoner being put into handcuffs. "Of my own choice, I would have avoided marrying Wisdom herself, if she had wanted me. But say what we will, the custom and practice of ordinary life bears us along." He did not really mind having such business arranged for him: he often felt that other people had better sense than he did anyway. But he still needed persuasion, being in an "ill-prepared and contrary" state of mind. Had he been free to choose, he would not have been the marrying kind at all. "Men with unruly humors like me, who hate any sort of bond or obligation, are not so fit for it." Later, he made the best of things, and even attempted to remain faithful—with, he said, more success than he had expected. He became contented, in a way, as he discovered was often the case with developments one would rather have avoided. "For not only inconvenient things, but anything at all, however ugly and vicious and repulsive, can become acceptable through some condition or circumstance."

Fortunately, Françoise herself was by no means ugly or repulsive. Montaigne seems to have found her attractive enough—or so his friend Florimond de Raemond asserted in a marginal note on a copy of the *Essays*. The problem lay more in the *principle* of being obliged to have regular sex with someone, for Montaigne never liked feeling boxed in. He fulfilled his conjugal duties reluctantly, "with only one buttock" as he would have said, doing what was necessary to beget children. This, too, comes from Florimond de Raemond's marginal note, which, in full, reads:

> I have often heard the author say that although he, full of love, ardor, and youth, had married his very beautiful and very lovable wife, yet the fact is that he had never played with her except with respect for the honor that the marriage bed requires, without ever having seen anything but her hands and face uncovered, and not even her breast, although among other women he was extremely playful and debauched.

This sounds appalling to a modern reader, but it was conventional enough. For a husband to behave as an impassioned lover to his wife was thought morally wrong, because it might turn her into a nymphomaniac. Minimal, joyless intercourse was the proper sort for marriage. In an essay almost entirely about sex, Montaigne cites the wisdom of Aristotle: "A man . . . should touch his wife prudently and soberly, lest if he caresses her too lasciviously the pleasure should transport her outside the bounds of reason." The physicians warned, too, that excessive pleasure could make sperm curdle inside the woman's body, rendering her unable to conceive. It was better for the husband to bestow ecstasy elsewhere, where it did not matter what damage it caused. "The kings of Persia," relates Montaigne, "used to invite their wives to join them at their feasts; but when the wine began to heat them in good earnest and they had to give completely free rein to sensuality, they sent them back to their private rooms." They then brought on a more suitable set of women.

The Church was with Aristotle, the doctors, and the kings of Persia in this. Confessors' manuals of the time show that a husband who engaged in sinful practices with his wife deserved a heavier penance than if he had done the same things with someone else. By corrupting his wife's senses, he risked ruining her eternal soul—a betrayal of his responsibility to her. If a married woman *must* pick up licentious habits, it was better to get them from someone who had no such duty. As Montaigne observed, most women seemed to prefer that option anyway.

Montaigne is amusingly wry on the subject of women, but he can also sound conventional. Unlike some contemporaries, however, he does not seem to have considered wives mere breeding cows. His ideal marriage would be a true meeting of minds as well as bodies; it would be even more complete than an ideal friendship. The difficulty was that, unlike friendship, marriage was not freely chosen, so it remained in the realm of constraint and obligation. Also, it was hard to find a woman capable of an exalted relationship, because most of them lacked intellectual capacity and a quality he called "firmness."

Montaigne's opinion on women's spiritual flaccidity can be disheartening enough to make one come over quite floppy oneself. George Sand confessed that she was "wounded to the heart" by it—the more so because she found Montaigne an inspiration in other respects. Yet one has to remember what most women were like in the sixteenth century. They were woefully uneducated, often illiterate, and they had little experience of the world. A few noble families hired private tutors for daughters, but most taught vapid accomplishments, as in Victorian times: Italian, music, and some arithmetic for household management. Classical education, the only kind considered worth having, was almost always absent. The few truly learned women of the sixteenth century were vanishingly rare exceptions, like Marguerite de Navarre, author of the collection of stories known as the *Heptameron*, or the poet Louise Labé, who (assuming she really existed, and was not a pseudonym for a group of male poets as one recent hypothesis suggests) urged other women to "lift their minds a little above their distaffs and spindles."

France did have a feminist movement in the sixteenth century. It formed one side of the *"querelle des femmes,"* a fashionable quarrel among intellectual men who formulated arguments for and against women: were they, in general, a good thing? Those in favor seemed to have more success than those against, but such arch debate made little difference to women's lives.

Montaigne is often dismissed as anti-feminist, but had he taken part in this *querelle*, he would probably have been on the pro-woman side. He did write, "Women are not wrong at all when they reject the rules of life that have been introduced into the world, inasmuch as it is the men who have made these without them." And he believed that, by nature, "males and females are cast in the same mold." He was very conscious of the double standard used to judge male and female sexual behavior. Aristotle notwithstanding, Montaigne suspected that women had the same passions and needs as men, yet they were condemned far more when they indulged them. His usual perspective-shifting habits also made it apparent to him that his view of women must be as partial and unreliable as women's views of men. His feelings on the whole subject are encapsulated in his observation: "We are in almost all things unjust judges of their actions, as they are of ours."

Given such injustice, it is not surprising that he decided his own best policy at home was to absent himself from the female realm as much as possible. He let them enjoy their kind of domesticity, while he enjoyed his. In an essay on solitude, he wrote:

> We should have wife, children, goods, and above all health, if we can; but we must not bind ourselves to them so strongly that our happiness depends on them. We must reserve a back shop all our own, entirely free, in which to establish our real liberty and our principal retreat and solitude. Here our ordinary conversation must be between us and ourselves, and so private that no outside association or communication can find a place; here we must talk and laugh as if without wife, without children, without possessions, without retinue and servants, so that, when the time comes to lose them, it will be nothing new to us to do without them.

The phrase about the "back shop," or "room behind the shop" as it is sometimes translated—the *arrière boutique*—appears again and again in books about Montaigne, but it is rarely kept within its context. He is not writing about a selfish, introverted withdrawal from family life so much as about the need to protect yourself from the pain that would come if you lost that family. Montaigne sought detachment and retreat so that he could not be too badly hurt, but in doing so he also discovered that having such a retreat helped him establish his "real liberty," the space he needed to think and look inward.

He certainly had reason to work at Stoic detachment. Having lost his friend, his father, and his brother in short order, Montaigne was now to lose almost all of his children—all daughters. He noted the sad sequence of births and deaths in his diary, the Beuther *Ephemeris*:

> June 28, 1570: Thoinette. Montaigne wrote, "This is the first child of my marriage," but later added, "And died two months later."
> September 9, 1571: Léonor was born—the only survivor.
> July 5, 1573: Unnamed daughter. "She lived only seven weeks."
> December 27, 1574: Unnamed daughter. "Died about three months later, and was hastily baptized under pressure of necessity."
> May 16, 1577: Unnamed daughter; died after a month.

February 21, 1583: "We had another daughter who was named Marie, baptised by the sieur de Jaurillac councillor of *parlement,* her uncle, and my daughter Léonor. She died a few days later."

Montaigne wrote that he had lost most of the children "without grief, or at least without repining," because they were so young. People generally did try not to get too attached to children while they were in early infancy, because the likelihood of their dying was great, but Montaigne seemed exceptionally good at staying aloof. It was an affliction he did not feel deeply, he admitted. He even wrote, in the mid-1570s, of having lost "two or three" children, as if uncertain of the figure, though this could just be his usual habit of vagueness about numbers. It is very much like his way of dating his riding accident, which he said happened "during our third civil war, or the second (I do not quite remember which)." In his dedication to his wife in the Plutarch translation, he gets the details even more startlingly wrong, writing that their first daughter had died "in the second year of her life," although she died at two months. This was probably a slip of the pen rather than of the mind. Or was it? One has the feeling, with Montaigne, that anything is possible.

There were other disasters in life that he knew would not bother him as much as they should:

> I see enough other common occasions for affliction which I should scarcely feel if they happened to me, and I have disdained some, when they came to me, to which the world has given such an atrocious appearance that I wouldn't dare boast of my indifference to them to most people without blushing.

One wonders if he was contemplating the possible death of his wife, here, or perhaps of his mother. If so, he had no such luck in either case. Or perhaps he was thinking back to the death of his father, or wondering what it would be like if his castle were sacked in the wars, or his lands burned. He seems to have found almost anything manageable other than the death of La Boétie: that was the one thing that knocked him off balance and made him unwilling to become so attached again.

In reality, his detachment is likely to have been less extreme than he pretended. His written notes of his children's deaths are plain but poignant. And he could be eloquent about fatherly grief in the *Essays*—just not his own. His essay on sadness, written in the mid-1570s when he had already lost several children, dwells on stories of paternal bereavement in literature. He also wrote feelingly about the ancient story of Niobe, who, after losing seven sons and then seven daughters, wept so much that she changed into a waterfall of stone—"to represent that bleak, dumb, and deaf stupor that benumbs us when accidents surpassing our endurance overwhelm us." Whether or not it was losing his children that gave Montaigne this sensation, he surely knew what it felt like.

Montaigne failed in the main responsibility of a nobleman, which was to have a male heir to ensure the succession. But he did have one healthy child, Léonor, and he became fond of her as she grew beyond infancy. Born in 1571, she must have been conceived not long after his ceremonial retirement in 1570. This made her the child of his midlife crisis and of his spiritual rebirth; perhaps it gave her that extra shot of life force. The sole survivor, she lived until 1616, marrying twice and having two daughters of her own.

While she was growing up, her father gave her over mostly to the female domain, as he was supposed to. "The government of women has a mysterious way of proceeding; we must leave it to them," he wrote, in a tone that suggests someone tiptoeing away from a place where he was not wanted. Indeed, when he once overheard something he thought was bad for Léonor, he did not intervene because he knew he would be waved aside with derision. She was reading a book aloud to her governess; the word *fouteau* came up in the text—meaning beech, but reminiscent of *foutre*, meaning fuck. The innocent child thought nothing of it, but her flustered governess shushed her. Montaigne felt that this was a mistake: "The company of twenty lackeys could not have imprinted in her imagination in six months the understanding and use and all the consequences of those wicked syllables as did this good old woman by her reprimand and interdict." But he kept silent.

He described Léonor as seeming younger than she was, even once she was of an age to marry. She was "of a backward constitution, slight and soft." He thought this was his wife's doing: she had sequestered the girl too much. But Montaigne also agreed to give Léonor an easy, pleasant upbringing like his own; he wrote that they had both decided she should be punished by nothing more than stern words, and even then, "very gentle ones."

Despite his assertion that he had little to do with nursery life, other passages in the *Essays* do give us a charming picture of Montaigne *en famille*. He describes playing games together, including games of chance played for small amounts: "I handle the cards and keep score for a couple of pennies just as for double doubloons." And they amused themselves with word puzzles. "We have just now at my house been playing a game to see who could find the most things that meet at their two extremes," such as the term "sire" as a title for the king and as a way of addressing lowly tradesmen, or "dames" for women of the highest quality and those of the lowest. This is not a cold, detached Montaigne, despiser of females and ignorer of children, but a family man, trying his best to play the genial patriarch in a home full of women who regard him most of the time with little more than exasperation.

PRACTICAL RESPONSIBILITIES

Montaigne deserved some of this: he was, as he admitted, useless around the house. He preferred to leave its management to his wife, who, like his mother, was skilled in such affairs. He liked Françoise's willingness to take on such responsibility when he went away on his travels or for work; he would probably have been happy to have her do the same when he was there as well. Not being able to do this was one of the main reasons he was generally so glad to leave. "It is pitiful to be in a place where everything you see involves and concerns you," he wrote.

Looking after the estate must have had its onerous side. "There is always something that goes wrong," he complained. The main business to be managed was the production of wine, of which the estate could produce tens of thousands of liters in a good year. Not all years were good. Severe weather ruined the harvests in 1572, 1573, and 1574—the years in which Montaigne wrote his first essays. Another bad patch occurred in 1586, when soldiers roamed the nearby countryside, causing havoc. Montaigne managed to recoup some of the losses by using his influence with *parlement* in Bordeaux to sell what little remained of his wine, which shows that he could tackle difficulties when he needed to. His overall grasp of the business may be gauged, however, by his admission that he did not know, until a late stage in life, what was meant by "fermenting wine."

Montaigne did what he had to, but he confessed that he did not enjoy it, and that therefore he kept it to a minimum. This was why he made no attempt to expand or build on the estate. Pierre had undertaken such projects for the pleasure and challenge of the job—but that was Pierre. He was the sort of man who would today keep himself busy with DIY work, and probably leave half of it unfinished. If his type seems familiar, so too does the Montaigne type, whose two mottoes would surely be "Anything for a quiet life" and "If it ain't broke, don't fix it."

When he did get an urge to do something, he could apply himself to it with energy. "I stand up well under hard work; but I do so only if I go to it of my own will, and as much as my desire leads me to it." He hated exerting himself doing things that bored him. In eighteen years of running the estate, he wrote, he had never managed to study a title deed or scrutinize a contract properly. He was a mass of inabilities and reluctances:

> I cannot reckon, either with counters or with a pen; most of our coins I do not know; nor do I know the difference between one grain and another, either in the ground or in the barn, unless it is too obvious, and I can scarcely distinguish the difference between the cabbages and lettuces in my garden. I do not even understand the names of the chief household implements or the roughest principles of agriculture, which children know. I know still less of the mechanical arts, of trade and merchandise, of the diversity and nature of fruits, wines, and foods, and of how to train a bird, or doctor a horse or dog. And since I must make my shame complete, not a month ago I was caught ignorant that leaven was used to make bread.

Montaigne runs through his negative catechism of failings in the same way as he later ran through the list of things absent from the lives of the "cannibals" of Brazil: servants, magistrates, contracts, and private property, but, by the same token, also lying, poverty, treachery, envy, and greed. It could be a blessing to lack such things.

It was not that Montaigne did not want to learn. In principle he approved of practical know-how, admiring all that was concrete and specific. But he could not help his own lack of interest, and any feeling of compulsion only made him more resistant. Some of this went back to the gentle lutes of his childhood: "Having had neither governor nor master forced on me to this day, I have gone just so far as I pleased, and at my own pace. This has made me soft and useless for serving others, and no good to anyone but myself." This passage reveals some of his true motivation: it was *his* life he wanted to live. Being impractical made him free. "Extremely idle, extremely independent, both by nature and by art," was the way he summed up his character. He was ruled by "freedom and laziness."

He knew that there was a price to be paid, apart from that of being berated by his wife. People often took advantage of his ignorance. Yet it seemed to him better to lose money occasionally than to waste time tracking every penny and watching his servants' tiniest movements. In any case, other people were swindled too, however much they tried to prevent it. His favorite example of foolishness was a neighbor, the powerful Germain-Gaston de Foix, marquis de Trans, who became a miser and domestic tyrant in old age. His family and servants let him rant, and put up with his tightly rationed issues of food, while all the time helping themselves behind his back. "Everybody is living it up in various corners of his house, gaming, spending, and exchanging stories about his vain anger and foresight." Still, added Montaigne on second thought, it did not matter, since the old man was convinced that he wielded absolute power in the house, and was therefore as happy as such a person could ever be.

"Nothing costs me dear except care and trouble," wrote Montaigne. "I seek only to grow indifferent and relaxed." One can imagine Pascal's blood pressure going up on reading this line. What Montaigne claimed to want most for his old age was a son-in-law who would take all his responsibilities away. In reality, had he been patronized and pandered to by an outsider, his love of independence would probably have surged up in protest—and he does follow this remark about the son-in-law with a flurry of contrary statements:

> I avoid subjecting myself to any sort of obligation.

> I try to have no express need of anyone . . . It is very pitiful and hazardous to be dependent on another.

> I have conceived a mortal hatred of being obliged either to another or by another than myself.

He was not thinking of household management when he wrote this: the subject is his commitments later in life to France's new king, Henri IV, who seemed to want Montaigne at his beck and call. Montaigne would resist this with a determination verging on insolence—which was very much his attitude to more homely demands. Laziness was only half of his self-description; freedom was the other half. He even fantasized about becoming like Hippias of Elis, a Greek Sophist philosopher of the fifth century BC, who learned to be self-sufficient, teaching himself to cook, shave, make his own clothes and shoes—everything he needed. It was a fine idea. Still: a self-sufficient Montaigne, mending his doublet with needle and thread, digging his garden, baking bread, tanning leather for his boots? Even Montaigne himself must have found this hard to picture.

As usual, he let the whole topic lie amid contradiction and a spirit of compromise. If his protestations of incompetence failed to save him from a particular responsibility, he would knuckle down and do the job anyway, and probably more conscientiously than he liked to admit.

Nietzsche wrote of certain "free-spirited people" who are perfectly satisfied "with a minor position or a fortune that just meets their needs; for they will set themselves up to live in such a way that a great change in economic conditions, even a revolution in political structures, will not overturn their life with it." He adds that such a person will tend to have "cautious and somewhat shortwinded" relationships with those around him. This sounds so much like Montaigne's home arrangement that you almost wonder if Nietzsche was thinking of him, especially when he adds that this person "must trust that the genius of justice will say something on behalf of its disciple and protégé, should accusatory voices call him poor in love."

In Montaigne's case, his own voice was the first to pronounce this awful accusation. Others have taken this as encouragement to repeat it ever since, in a harsh tone, and without either Montaigne's or Nietzsche's sense of irony. But nothing in Montaigne's writing, or his character, was ever so straightforward. However much he tries to persuade us that he is cold and detached, other images rise up before the mind's eye: Montaigne springing to his feet in *parlement* to plunge into hot debate, Montaigne deep in passionate conversation with La Boétie, even Montaigne playing games for pennies with his wife and daughter by the fireside. Some of his answers to the question of how to live are indeed chilly: mind your own business, preserve your sense of self, stay out of trouble, and keep your room behind the shop. But there is another which is almost the exact opposite. It is . . .

9. Q. How to live? A. Be convivial: live with others

"THERE ARE PRIVATE, retiring, and inward natures," writes Montaigne. His is not one of them.

> My essential pattern is suited to communication and revelation. I am all in the open and in full view, born for company and friendship.

He loves to mingle. Conversation is something he enjoys more than any other pleasure. He depends on it so much that he would rather lose his sight than his hearing or speech, for talk is better than books. There is no need for it to be of a serious nature: what he likes best is "the sharp, abrupt repartee which good spirits and familiarity introduce among friends, bantering and joking wittily and keenly with one another." Any conversation is good, so long as it is kind-spirited and friendly. Social grace of this kind should be encouraged in children from an early age, to bring them out of their private worlds. "Wonderful brilliance may be gained for human judgment by getting to know men. We are all huddled and concentrated in ourselves, and our vision is reduced to the length of our nose."

Montaigne loved open debate. "No propositions astonish me, no belief offends me, whatever contrast it offers with my own." He liked being contradicted, as it opened up more interesting conversations and helped him to think—something he preferred to do through interaction rather than staring into the fire like Descartes. His friend Florimond de Raemond described his conversation as "the sweetest and most enriched with graces." Yet when Montaigne was not feeling sweet, or when he was carried away by the topic of a discussion, he could be vociferous. His passion led him to say things that were indiscreet, and he encouraged others to do the same. Freedom of expression was the law of his house. At the Montaigne estate, he said, there was never any "waiting on people and escorting them here and away, and other such troublesome prescriptions of our code of manners (oh, what a servile and bothersome practice!)." Guests behaved as they pleased, and those who craved solitude could also go and do their own thing for as long as they liked, without causing offense.

As well as banishing formal etiquette, Montaigne discouraged tedious small talk. Self-conscious solo performances bored him too. Some of his friends could keep a group rapt for hours with anecdotes, but Montaigne preferred a natural give and take. At official dinners away from home, where the talk was merely conventional, his attention would wander; if someone suddenly addressed him, he would often make inappropriate replies, "unworthy of a child." He regretted this, for easy conversation in trivial situations was valuable: it opened the path to deeper relationships, and to the more pleasant evenings where one could joke and laugh at ease.

For Montaigne, "relaxation and affability" were not merely useful talents; they were essential to living well. He tried to cultivate what he called a "gay and sociable wisdom"—a phrase that calls to mind a famous definition of philosophy, by Nietzsche, as the "gay" or "joyful" science. Nietzsche, like the *libertins*, agreed with Montaigne that a humane, sociable understanding was what mattered, although Nietzsche himself found it difficult. His relationships were often traumatic. Yet, in a touching passage of his early book *Human All Too Human*, he wrote:

> Among the small but endlessly abundant and therefore very effective things that science ought to heed more than the great, rare things, is goodwill [*Wohlwollen*]. I mean those expressions of a friendly disposition in interactions, that smile of the eye, those handclasps, the ease which usually envelops nearly all human actions. Every teacher, every official brings this ingredient to what he considers his duty. It is the continual manifestation of our humanity, its rays of light, so to speak, in which everything grows . . . Good nature, friendliness, and courtesy of heart . . . have made much greater contributions to culture than those much more famous expressions of this drive, called pity, charity, and self-sacrifice.

To Montaigne, most of the time, friendly goodwill came easily. This was fortunate, for he had much need of it both at home and in his professional life. He had to get on well with colleagues in Bordeaux; later, his work required him to charm diplomats, kings, and fearsome warlords further afield. He often had to establish a rapport with opponents blinded by religious fanaticism. Around the estate, too, it was important to socialize with the neighbors—not always easy. They appear from time to time in the *Essays*, often with colorful stories attached: the miserly marquis de Trans, whose family the Foix were very powerful in the region; a Jean de Lusignan, who tired himself by organizing too many parties for his grown-up children; François de La Rochefoucauld, who believed that blowing one's nose into a handkerchief was a disgusting practice and that it was nicer to use just fingers. Some noblewomen of the area became dedicatees of individual chapters: Diane de Foix, comtesse de Gurson; Marguerite de Gramond; and Mme d'Estissac, whose son later accompanied Montaigne to Italy. Above all, Montaigne befriended the woman who became the mistress of Henri de Navarre (later to be Henri IV): Diane d'Andouins, comtesse de Guiche et de Gramont, usually known as "Corisande" after a character in one of her favorite chivalric novels.

To keep up with such friends, Montaigne had to take part in many fashionable entertainments which he privately disliked. When he had guests, he might start a deer in his forests for them, much as he recoiled from hunting. He had more success in avoiding jousting, which he thought lethal and futile. He also tried to wriggle out of the indoor amusements of the period, including poetry games, cards, and rebus-like puzzles—perhaps because, by his own admission, he was not good at them.

His home was often visited by itinerant performers: acrobats, dancers, trainers of performing dogs, and human "monsters," all desperately trying to make a living by touring the country. Montaigne tolerated them, but remained unimpressed by clever-clogs displays such as that of a man who tossed grains of millet through the eye of a needle from a distance. He was more interested in novelties that meant something, such as the group of Tupinambá whom he met in Rouen. And he would travel considerable distances to investigate reports of anomalous births, like that of a child who was born with a headless portion of another child attached to his torso. He visited a hermaphroditic shepherd in Médoc, and met a man without arms who could use his feet to load and fire a pistol, thread a needle, sew, write, comb his hair, and play cards. Like the millet-tosser, he survived by exhibiting himself, but Montaigne found him much more interesting. People spoke of "monsters," he wrote, but such individuals were not contrary to nature, only to habit. Where real oddity was concerned, there was no doubt where Montaigne thought the prize should go:

> I have seen no more evident monstrosity and miracle in the world than myself. We become habituated to anything strange by use and time; but the more I frequent myself and know myself, the more my deformity astonishes me, and the less I understand myself.

Thus the estate was a busy crossroads, traversed by streams of people in all directions. The atmosphere was more like that of a village than of a private home. Even when Montaigne went off to his tower to write, he rarely worked alone or in silence. People talked and worked around him; outside his window horses would have been led back and forth from the stables, while hens clucked and dogs barked. In the wine-making season, the air would be filled with the sound of clanking presses. Even at the height of the wars, Montaigne kept his property more open to the world than others did—a rare decision in such dangerous times.

In some ways, Montaigne's world became a private universe unto itself, with its own values and an atmosphere of freedom. Yet he never made it a fortress. He insisted on welcoming anyone who arrived at the gate, though he knew the risks and admitted that sometimes it meant going to bed not knowing whether he would be murdered in his sleep by some itinerant soldier or vagrant. But the principle was too important. When Montaigne wrote, "I am all in the open and in full view," he was not alluding only to social chitchat. He meant that he wanted to remain in free, honest communication with other human beings—even those who seemed bent on killing him.

OPENNESS, MERCY, AND CRUELTY

According to Giovanni Botero, an Italian political writer living in France in the 1580s, the French countryside of that decade was so rife with thieves and murderers that every house was obliged to keep "watchmen of the vineyards and orchards; gates, locks, bolts, and mastiffs." Apparently Botero had not visited the Montaigne estate. There the only defender was a person whom Montaigne described as "a porter of ancient custom and ceremony, who serves not so much to defend my door as to offer it with more decorum and grace."

Montaigne lived this way because he was determined to resist intimidation, and did not want to become his own jailer. But he also believed that, paradoxically, his openness made him safer. Heavily guarded houses in the area suffered far more attacks than his did. He quoted Seneca for the explanation: "Locked places invite the thief. The burglar passes by what is open." Locks made a place look valuable, and there could be no sense of glory in robbing a household where one was welcomed by an elderly doorkeeper. Also, the usual rules of fortification hardly apply in a civil war: "Your valet may be of the party that you fear." You cannot barricade the gates against a threat that is already inside; far better to win the enemy over by behaving with generosity and honor.

Events seemed to prove Montaigne right. Once, he invited a troop of soldiers in, only to realize that they were plotting to take advantage of his hospitality by seizing the place. They abandoned the plan, however, and the leader told Montaigne why: he had been "disarmed" by the sight of his host's "face and frankness."

In the outer world, too, Montaigne's openness protected him from violence. Once, traveling through a forest in a dangerous rural area, he was attacked by fifteen to twenty masked men, followed by a wave of mounted archers—a huge assault, apparently planned in advance. They took him to a thick part of the forest, rifled through his possessions, seized his traveling cases and money box, and discussed how to divide his horses and other equipment among themselves. Worse, they then got the idea of holding him as a hostage for further gain, but could not decide how much ransom to ask. Montaigne overheard them debating the matter and realized they were likely to set the sum excessively high, which would mean his death if no one could afford to pay. He could stand it no more, and called out to interrupt them. They already had everything they were going to get, he declared. However high they set the ransom, it made no difference: they would see none of it. It was a risky way to speak, but after this the bandits underwent a dramatic change. They huddled for a moment in fresh discussion, then the leader walked over to Montaigne with an air almost of friendliness. He removed his mask—a significant gesture, since the two men could now confront each other face to face, like human beings—and said that they had decided to let him go. They even gave back some of his possessions, including the money box. The leader explained it by saying that, as Montaigne wrote later, "I owed my deliverance to my face and the freedom and firmness of my speech." He was saved by his natural, honest appearance, combined with his bravery in facing up to aggression.

This was the kind of confrontation that could happen at any time, to any person, and Montaigne often wondered about the best way of dealing with it. Is it wiser to face up squarely to your enemy and challenge him, or should you curry favor by showing submission? Should you throw yourself on the aggressor's mercy and hope that his sense of humanity will make him spare you? Or is that foolhardy?

The problem is that each response brings its own dangers. Defiance might impress the other, but it might also infuriate him. Submission might inspire pity, but it is just as likely to draw your enemy's contempt, so that he wipes you out with no more thought than he would give to stamping on an insect. As for appealing to his sense of humanity, how can you be sure that he has one?

These questions were no easier to decide in the violent sixteenth century than on an ancient Mediterranean battlefield, or in an alleyway in a modern city, facing up to a mugger. They are perennial, and Montaigne did not see any one good answer. Yet he never tired of exploring the question. Again and again in the *Essays*, he sets up scenes featuring two individuals in confrontation, one defeated and obliged either to beg for his life or show defiance, the other required either to show mercy or deny it.

In one such incident, described in the first essay in the book, the fifteenth-century Albanian military hero Skanderbeg was on the point of killing one of his own soldiers in a rage. The man appealed for pity, but Skanderbeg remained unmoved. In desperation, the soldier grabbed his sword and fought back—which so impressed Skanderbeg that his anger evaporated and he let the man go. Another story tells of Edward, Prince of Wales, who strode through a defeated French town ordering mass killings of citizens to left and right. He stopped only when he came to three men, cornered but still fighting. Admiring them, he spared their lives, and added as an afterthought that everyone else in the town might be spared as well.

These stories imply that defiance is a better policy. But the same essay looks at incidents that turned out differently. When Alexander the Great attacked the city of Gaza, he found the enemy leader Betis "alone, abandoned by his men, his armor cut to pieces, all covered with blood and wounds, still fighting on." Like Edward, Alexander admired this, but only for a moment. As Betis continued to defy him, staring him insolently in the face, Alexander lost patience. He had Betis pierced through the heels and dragged behind a cart until he was dead. The defeated leader had gone too far, and with the wrong opponent.

Other stories show, just as clearly, the dangers of submission. Montaigne vividly remembered the case of Tristan de Moneins, the lieutenant-general who was lynched in a Bordeaux street after he presented himself too humbly to the salt-tax rioters in 1548. Once one has shown weakness and triggered a sort of hunting instinct in the other, all is lost. And there is rarely any hope if one really is facing a hunter. Montaigne was haunted by the image of a stag at bay after hours of pursuit, exhausted and trapped, having no option but to give himself up to the hunters—"asking for our mercy by his tears." Such mercy will never be granted.

However many confrontations Montaigne restaged in his mind's eye, they all seemed to suggest different interpretations and different answers. This is why they fascinated him. In each case the defeated party must make a decision, but so must the victor, for things can go badly wrong for him if he misjudges the situation. If he spares someone who interprets his generosity as weakness, he may be killed in turn. If he is too harsh, he will attract rebellion and revenge.

Christianity seems to offer a simple answer: the victor should always show mercy, and the victim should always turn the other cheek. But the real world cannot be relied upon to work that way—and neither could most Christians in this era of violent religious war. Montaigne paid little attention to theology: he was immersed in his classical reading and, as usual, seemed to forget the Christian angle. For him, in any case, the true difficulties were psychological rather than moral. Or if they were moral, it was in the broader sense of that term used in classical philosophy, where it did not mean following precepts but knowing how to make just and intelligent decisions in real life.

Montaigne's view, on balance, was that both victim and victor should take the path that entailed placing maximum trust in the other—that is, like good Christians, the defeated party should seek mercy and the victor should grant it. But both must do this boldly, with an "open countenance," free of cringing and submissiveness. A "pure and clean confidence" should characterize the situation on both sides. Montaigne would have found his ideal encounter in the scene that took place in Beijing's Tiananmen Square in 1989, when tanks moved in to suppress a demonstration. One man, incongruously carrying an ordinary shopping bag, stood calm and still in front of them; in response, the first tank's driver stopped. Had the man been cowering or trying to escape, or, conversely, had he been yelling and waving his fists, it would have been easier for the driver to kill him. Instead, the man's "pure and clean confidence" brought out a similar resolution in his opponent.

This would not work for a stag, where fellow-feeling is blocked by the hunting relationship; perhaps it would not work between an accused witch and a torturer, where fanaticism and obedience to roles would get in the way. War disrupts normal psychology too, just as mob hysteria does. Although the Tiananmen Square scene was violent, it occurred in what was technically peacetime, whereas battle creates an altered state of mind. In the classical world, and to some extent in Montaigne's time, it was considered only right that a soldier in battle should be incapable of restraint. He should be in a *furor*: a fearless, ecstatic frenzy in which no moderation or mercy could or should be expected.

Montaigne found *furor* appalling, as he did most extreme states. He disliked the way Julius Caesar reportedly whipped up his soldiers to savagery before a battle with speeches like this:

When weapons flash, no pious sentiments,
Though you confront your fathers, you must feel;
No, slash their venerable faces with the steel.

Of all famous warriors, Montaigne most admired the Theban general
Epaminondas, who was known for his ability to keep *furor* in check: once,
in mid-battle and "terrible with blood and iron," Epaminondas found
himself face to face with an acquaintance in whose house he had stayed. He
turned aside and did not kill him. That might seem unremarkable, but in
theory a soldier should no more be capable of such conscious restraint than
would a shark in a feeding frenzy. Epaminondas proved himself "in
command of war itself," as Montaigne wrote; he made the battle "endure
the curb of benignity" at the very height of the ecstasy.

Montaigne suspected that the *furor* tradition was often used merely as an
excuse. "Let us take away from wicked, bloody, and treacherous natures this
pretext of reason." Brutality was bad enough in itself; brutality on the
excuse of an elevated mental state was worse. Above all, he deplored the
holy zeal of religious fanatics, who believed that God demanded such
extreme, unreasoning violence as proof of devotion.

Cruelty nauseated Montaigne: he could not help himself. He hated it
cruelly, as he wrote, making a point of the paradox. His revulsion was
instinctive, as much a part of him as the openness written all over his face.
This was why he could not stand hunting. Even seeing a chicken having its
neck wrung, or a hare caught by dogs, horrified him. The same perspective-
leaping tendency that enabled him to borrow his cat's point of view made
it impossible for him to see a hare being ripped apart without feeling it in
his own guts.

If he could not watch a hare in pain, still less could he stomach the human
tortures and judicial killings that were common in his day. "Even the
executions of the law, however reasonable they may be, I cannot witness with
a steady gaze." In his own career, he was expected to order such
punishments, but he refused to do so. "I am so squeamish about hurting that
for the service of reason itself I cannot do it. And when occasions have
summoned me to sentencing criminals, I have tended to fall short of justice."

He was not the only writer of his time to oppose either hunting or torture. What is unusual in Montaigne is his reason for it: his visceral rapport with others. When speaking to the Brazilian Indians in Rouen, he was struck by how they spoke of men as halves of one another, wondering at the sight of rich Frenchmen gorging themselves while their "other halves" starved on their doorstep. For Montaigne, all humans share an element of their being, and so do all other living things. "It is one and the same nature that rolls its course." Even if animals were less similar to us than they are, we would still owe them a duty of fellow-feeling, simply because they are alive.

> There is a certain respect, and a general duty of humanity, that attaches us not only to animals, who have life and feeling, but even to trees and plants. We owe justice to men, and mercy and kindness to other creatures that may be capable of receiving it. There is some relationship between them and us, and some mutual obligation.

This obligation applies in trivial encounters as well as life-or-death ones. We owe other beings the countless small acts of kindness and empathy that Nietzsche would describe as "goodwill." After the passage just quoted, Montaigne added this remark about his dog:

> I am not afraid to admit that my nature is so tender, so childish, that I cannot well refuse my dog the play he offers me or asks of me outside the proper time.

He indulges his dog because he can imaginatively share the animal's point of view: he can *feel* how desperate the dog is to banish boredom and get his human friend's attention. Pascal mocked Montaigne for this, saying that Montaigne rides his horse as one who does not believe it to be his right to do so, and who wonders whether "the animal, on the contrary, ought really to be making use of him." This is exactly right—and, as much as it annoyed Pascal, it would have pleased Nietzsche, whose final mental breakdown is (unreliably) reported to have begun with his flinging his arms around a horse's neck on a Turin street and bursting into tears.

Among less emotionally wrought readers, one much affected by

Montaigne's remarks on cruelty was Virginia Woolf's husband, Leonard Woolf. In his memoirs, he held up Montaigne's "On Cruelty" as a much more significant essay than people had realized. Montaigne, he wrote, was "the first person in the world to express this intense, personal horror of cruelty. He was, too, the first completely modern man." The two were linked: Montaigne's modernity resided precisely in his "intense awareness of and passionate interest in the individuality of himself and of all other human beings"—and nonhuman beings, too.

Even a pig or a mouse has, as Woolf put it, a feeling of being an "I" to itself. This was the very claim that Descartes had denied so strenuously, but Woolf arrived at it through personal experience rather than Cartesian reasoning. He recalled being asked, as a young boy, to drown some unwanted day-old puppies—an astonishing task to give to a child, one might think. He did what he was told, but was more upset by it than he had expected. Years later, he wrote:

> Looked at casually, day-old puppies are little, blind, squirming, undifferentiated objects or things. I put one of them in the bucket of water, and instantly an extraordinary, a terrible thing happened. This blind, amorphous thing began to fight desperately for its life, struggling, beating the water with its paws. I suddenly saw that it was an individual, that like me it was an "I," that in its bucket of water it was experiencing what I would experience and fighting death, as I would fight death if I were drowning in the multitudinous seas. It was I felt and feel a horrible, an uncivilized thing to drown that "I" in a bucket of water.

What brought this incident back to Woolf, as an adult, was reading Montaigne. He went on to apply the insight to politics, reflecting especially on his memory of the 1930s, when the world seemed about to sink into a barbarism that made no room for this small individual self. On a global scale, no single creature can be of much importance, he wrote, yet in another way these I's are the *only* things of importance. And only a politics that recognizes them can offer hope for the future.

Writing about consciousness, the psychologist William James had a similar instinct. We understand nothing of a dog's experience: of "the rapture of bones under hedges, or smells of trees and lamp-posts." They understand nothing of ours, when for example they watch us stare interminably at the pages of a book. Yet both states of consciousness share a certain quality: the "zest" or "tingle" which comes when one is completely absorbed in what one is doing. This tingle should enable us to recognize each other's similarity even when the objects of our interest are different. Recognition, in turn, should lead to kindness. Forgetting this similarity is the worst political error, as well as the worst personal and moral one.

In the view of William James, as of Leonard Woolf and Montaigne, we do not live immured in our separate perspectives, like Descartes in his room. We live porously and sociably. We can glide out of our own minds, if only for a few moments, in order to occupy another being's point of view. This ability is the real meaning of "Be convivial," this chapter's answer to the question of how to live, and the best hope for civilization.

10. Q. How to live? A. Wake from the sleep of habit

THE ART OF seeing things from the perspective of another person or animal may come instinctively to some, but it can also be cultivated. Novelists do it all the time. While Leonard Woolf was thinking through his political philosophy, his wife Virginia was writing in her diary:

> I remember lying on the side of a hollow, waiting for L[eonard] to come & mushroom, & seeing a red hare loping up the side & thinking suddenly "This is Earth life." I seemed to see how earthy it all was, & I myself an evolved kind of hare; as if a moon-visitor saw me.

This eerie, almost hallucinatory moment gave Woolf a sense of how both she and the hare would look to someone who did not view them through eyes dulled by habit. It enabled her to de-familiarize the familiar—a mental trick, rather like those used by the Hellenistic philosophers when they imagined looking down on human life from the stars. Like many such tricks, it works by helping one pay proper attention. Habit makes everything look bland; it is sleep-inducing. Jumping to a different perspective is a way of waking oneself up again. Montaigne loved this trick, and used it constantly in his writing.

His favorite device was simply to run through lists of wildly divergent customs from all over the world, marveling at their randomness and strangeness. His two essays "Of Custom" and "Of Ancient Customs" describe countries where women piss standing and men squatting, where children are nursed for up to twelve years, where it is considered fatal to nurse a baby on its first day, where hair grows on the right side of the body but is shaved completely off the left side, where one is supposed to kill one's father at a certain age, where people wipe their rears with a sponge on a stick, and where hair is worn long in front and short behind instead of the other way around. Similar lists in the "Apology" run from Peruvians who elongate their ears to Orientals who blacken their teeth because they consider white ones inelegant.

Each culture, in doing these things, takes itself as the standard. If you live in a country where teeth are blackened, it seems obvious that ebony ivories are the only beautiful ones. Reciting diversities helps us to break free of this, if only for brief moments of enlightenment. "This great world," writes Montaigne, "is the mirror in which we must look at ourselves to recognize ourselves from the proper angle." After running through such a list, we look back upon our own existence differently. Our eyes are opened to the truth that our customs are no less weird than anyone else's.

Some of Montaigne's initial interest in such leaps of perspective went back to his observation of the Tupinambá visitors' amazement in Rouen. Watching them watching the French was an awakening, like Virginia Woolf's on the hillside. The encounter stimulated in Montaigne what became a lifelong interest in the New World—an entire hemisphere unknown to Europeans until a few decades before his own birth, and still so surprising that it hardly seemed real.

By the time Montaigne was born, most Europeans had come around to the acceptance that America really did exist and was not a fantasy. Some people had taken up eating hot peppers and chocolate, and a few smoked tobacco. The cultivation of potatoes was under way, although their vaguely testicular shape still made people think they were good only as an aphrodisiac. Returning travelers passed on tales of cannibalism and human sacrifice, or of fabulous fortunes in gold and silver. As life in Europe became more difficult, many considered emigrating, and colonies sprouted like mold spores along the eastern coasts. Most were Spanish, but the French also tried their luck. In Montaigne's youth, France looked well placed to prosper in the new colonial adventure. It had a strong fleet, and well-equipped international ports from which to sail—Bordeaux foremost among them.

Several French expeditions were launched in the middle of the century, but they ran into difficulties one by one. French colonists had a particular tendency to undo their enterprises through religious conflict, which they imported with them. The first French settlement in Brazil, founded by

Nicolas Durand de Villegaignon near the present site of Rio de Janeiro in the 1550s, was so weakened by its Catholic–Protestant divisions that it succumbed to invasion by the Portuguese. In the 1560s, a mainly Protestant French colony in Florida fell victim to the Spanish. By this time, full civil war had broken out in the French homeland, and the money and organization for major voyages were hard to find. France missed its place in the first great bonanza overseas, the one that made the fortunes of England and Spain. By the time it recovered and tried again later, it was too late to recover the advantage in full.

Like many of his generation, Montaigne had a fascination with all things American combined with cynicism about colonial conquest. He treasured what he remembered of his conversation with the Tupinambá—who had traveled to France in one of Villegaignon's returning ships—and collected South American memorabilia for his cabinet of curiosities in the tower: "specimens of their beds, of their ropes, of their wooden swords, and the bracelets with which they cover their wrists in combats, and of the big canes, open at one end, by whose sound they keep time in their dances." Much of this probably came from a household servant who had lived for a time in the Villegaignon colony. The same man introduced Montaigne to sailors and merchants who could further feed his curiosity. He was himself "a simple, crude fellow," but Montaigne believed this made him an excellent witness, for he was not tempted to embroider or overinterpret what he reported.

Besides conversation, Montaigne also read everything he could get hold of on the subject. His library included French translations of López de Gómara's *Historia de las Indias* and Bartolomé de Las Casas's *Brevísima relación de la destrucción de las Indias*, as well as more recent French originals, notably two great rival accounts of the Villegaignon colony by the Protestant Jean de Léry and the Catholic André Thevet. Of the two, he much preferred Léry's *Histoire d'un voyage fait en la terre du Brésil* (1578), which observed Tupinambá society with sympathy and precision. As befitted a Protestant puritan, Léry admired the Tupinambá preference for going naked rather than adorning themselves with ruffs and furbelows as the French did. He observed that very few of their elderly people had white hair, and suspected it was because they did not wear themselves out with "mistrust, avarice, litigation, and squabbles." And he thought highly of their courage in war. The Tupinambá fought bloody battles with magnificent swords, but only for honor, never for conquest or greed. Such encounters usually ended with a feast at which the main course was prisoners of war. Léry himself attended one such event; that night he woke in his hammock to see a man looming over him brandishing a roasted human foot in what seemed to be a threatening manner. He leaped up in fright, to the merriment of the crowd. Later, it was explained to him that the man was only being a generous host and offering him a taste. Léry's faith in his friends was restored. He felt safer among them, he said, than he did at home "among disloyal and degenerate Frenchmen." Indeed, he was destined to witness equally gruesome scenes in the French civil wars, when he became stranded in the hilltop town of Sancerre during a winter siege at the end of 1572 and saw townspeople eating human flesh to survive.

Montaigne read Léry avidly, and, in writing up his own Tupinambá encounter in "Of Cannibals," followed Léry's practice of drawing out the

contrast with France and the implications for European assumptions of superiority. A later chapter, "Of Coaches," also noted how the gilded gardens and palaces of the Incas and Aztecs put European equivalents to shame. But the simple Tupinambá appealed to Montaigne far more. He described them with a list of desirable negatives:

> This is a nation . . . in which there is no sort of traffic, no knowledge of letters, no science of numbers, no name for a magistrate or for political superiority, no custom of servitude, no riches or poverty, no contracts, no successions, no partitions, no occupations but leisure ones, no care for any but common kinship, no clothes, no agriculture, no metal, no use of wine or wheat. The very words that signify lying, treachery, dissimulation, avarice, envy, belittling, pardon—unheard of.

Such "negative enumeration" was a well-established rhetorical device in classical literature, long predating the New World encounter. It even turns up in four-thousand-year-old Sumerian cuneiform texts:

> Once upon a time, there was no snake, there was no scorpion,
> There was no hyena, there was no lion,
> There was no wild dog, no wolf,
> There was no fear, no terror,
> Man had no rival.

It was only natural that it should recur in Renaissance writing about the New World. The tradition would continue: in the nineteenth century Herman Melville described the happy valley of Typee in the Marquesas as a place where there were "no foreclosures of mortgages, no protested notes, no bills payable, no debts of honor . . . no poor relations . . . no destitute widows . . . no beggars; no debtors' prisons; no proud and hard-hearted nabobs in Typee; or to sum up all in one word—no money!" The idea was that people were happier when they lived uncluttered lives close to nature, like Adam and Eve in the Garden of Eden. Stoics had made much of this "Golden Age" fantasy: Seneca fantasized about a world in which property was not hoarded, weapons were not used for violence, and no sewage pipes polluted the streams. Without houses, people even slept better, for there were no creaking timbers to wake them with a start in the middle of the night.

Montaigne understood the appeal of the fantasy, and shared it. Like wild fruit, he wrote, wild people retain their full natural flavor. This was why they were capable of such bravery, for their behavior in war was untainted by greed. Even the Tupinambá cannibal rituals, far from being degrading, showed primitive people at their best. The victims displayed astonishing courage as they awaited their fate; they even defied their captors with taunts of their own. Montaigne was impressed by a song in which a doomed prisoner challenges his enemies to go ahead and eat their fill. As you do, sings the prisoner, remember that you are eating your own fathers and grandfathers. I have eaten them in the past, so it will be *your* flesh you will savor! This is another of those archetypal confrontation scenes: the defeated man is doomed, yet he shows Stoic firmness in the face of his enemy. This, it is implied, is what humans would always be capable of if they only followed their true nature.

The prisoner's song is one of two "cannibal songs" to appear in Montaigne's *Essays*. The other, also from the Tupinambá, is a love lyric which he may have heard performed in Rouen in 1562, for he praises the sound of it: he describes Tupinambá as "a soft language, with an agreeable

sound, somewhat like Greek in its endings." In his prose translation, the song goes:

> Adder, stay; stay, adder, that from the pattern of your coloring my sister may draw the fashion and the workmanship of a rich girdle that I may give to my love; so may your beauty and your pattern be forever preferred to all other serpents.

Montaigne liked the simple elegance of this, by contrast with the over-refined European versifying of his day. In another essay, he wrote that such "purely natural poetry"—among which he counted the traditional villanelles of his own Guyenne as well as the songs brought back from the New World—rivaled the finest found in books. Even the classical poets could not compete.

Montaigne's "cannibal love song" went on to have an impressive little afterlife of its own, independent of the rest of the *Essays*. Chateaubriand borrowed it for his *Mémoires d'outre-tombe*, where he had an attractive North American girl sing something similar. It then migrated to Germany, where it flourished as a *Lied* throughout the eighteenth century—this in a country which otherwise took little early interest in Montaigne. The two cannibal songs, together with some complimentary remarks about German stoves, were the only fragments of Montaignalia to make much impact at all in that part of the world until Nietzsche's time. "Adder, Stay" was translated by some of the best German Romantic poets: Ewald Christian von Kleist, Johann Gottfried Herder, and the great Johann Wolfgang von Goethe himself—who produced both a *Liebeslied eines Amerikanischen Wilden* ("Love Song of an American Savage") and a *Todeslied eines Gefangenen* ("Death Song of a Prisoner"). German Romantics especially favored songs about love and death, so it is not surprising that they took so eagerly to Montaigne's transcriptions. What is striking is that they seized them from the text while ignoring almost everything else—but this is what all readers do, to a greater or lesser extent.

Montaigne, like Léry, could be accused of romanticizing the peoples of the New World. But he understood too much about the complexity of human psychology to really want to wipe half of it out in order to live like wild fruit. He also recognized that American cultures could be just as stupid and cruel as European ones. Since cruelty was the vice he deplored most, it is significant that he made no attempt to gloss over its role in New World religions, some of which were bloodthirsty indeed. "They burn the victims alive, and take them out of the brazier half roasted to tear their entrails out. Others, even women, are flayed alive, and with their bloody skins they dress and disguise others."

He described such atrocities, but then pointed out that they seemed excessive mainly because Europeans were unfamiliar with them. Equally terrible practices were accepted nearer home, because of the power of habit. "I am not sorry that we notice the barbarous horror of such acts," he wrote of the New World sacrifices, "but I am heartily sorry that, judging their faults rightly, we should be so blind to our own." Montaigne wanted his readers to open their eyes and *see*. The peoples of South America were not just fascinating for their own sake. They made an ideal mirror, in which Montaigne and his countrymen could "recognize themselves from the proper angle," and which woke them out of their self-satisfied dream.

NOBLE SAVAGES

Eighteenth-century German readers may have found little of interest in Montaigne other than his *Volkslieder*, but a new generation of French readers rediscovering him in the same period made more of his cannibals and mirrors than even Montaigne himself could have anticipated.

They were encouraged in this by a sleek modern edition which appeared in 1724. The *Essays* were still outlawed in France—it had been fifty years since the ban—but now the country began receiving a stream of smuggled Montaigne texts from England, where the French Protestant exile Pierre Coste had put together an edition for the new century. Coste deliberately brought out Montaigne's subversive side, not by interfering with the text but by adding extra paraphernalia, most dramatically La Boétie's *On Voluntary Servitude*, which he included in full with the edition of 1727. This was the first time the *Voluntary Servitude* had been published at all since the Protestant tracts of the sixteenth century, and certainly the first time it had appeared joined to the *Essays*. It altered Montaigne by association, and gave him the aura of a political and personal rebel, the sort of writer whose calm philosophy might conceal more turbulent meanings. Coste helped to create a version of Montaigne still popular today: a secret radical, who conceals himself under a veil of discretion. In particular, Coste's edition made Montaigne look like a free-thinking Enlightenment *philosophe* born two centuries too early. Eighteenth-century readers recognized themselves in him, as so many do, and they felt amazed that he had needed to wait so long before meeting the generation truly capable of understanding him.

This new breed of "enlightened" reader responded passionately to his portrayal of the courageous Tupinambá. Montaigne's cannibal Stoics aligned themselves with a new fantasy figure: that of the noble savage, an impossibly perfect being who united primitive simplicity with classical heroism, and who now became the object of a cult. Adherents of the cult kept hold of Montaigne's sense that cannibals had their own sense of honor, and that they held up a mirror to European civilization. What they lost was Montaigne's understanding that "savages" were also as flawed, cruel, and barbarous as anyone else.

Among the writers to fall upon Montaigne's Tupinambá with delight was Denis Diderot, a philosopher who became famous for his contributions to the era's monumental compilation of knowledge, the *Encyclopédie*, as well as for countless philosophical novels and dialogues. Diderot read Montaigne early in his career, loved him, and paid him the compliment of quoting the *Essays* in his own writings—usually, but not always, with due credit. In his short *Supplément au voyage de Bougainville*, of 1796, Diderot wrote excitedly about the peoples of the South Pacific, recently encountered by Europeans, and thus his century's equivalent to native Americans in Montaigne's time. Like the Tupinambá, Pacific islanders seemed to lead a simple life, almost in a state of grace. Less palatable aspects of their culture were easy to ignore, because Europe knew little about them. This left plenty of room to make things up, notably the idea that the islanders enjoyed hedonistic sex with anyone they liked at any time. In the *Supplément*, Diderot had one of his Tahitian characters advise Europeans that they need only follow nature to be happy, for no other law applied. This was what his compatriots wanted to hear.

The noble savage was raised to a more exalted level by Jean-Jacques Rousseau, another writer influenced by Montaigne—his annotated copy of the *Essays* survives. Unlike Diderot, Rousseau took primitive society to be something so perfect that it could not actually exist in any real part of the world, not even the Pacific. It functioned only as an ideal contrast to the mess that real societies had become. By definition, all existing civilization was corrupt.

In his *Discourse on the Origin of Inequality*, Rousseau imagines what man might have been like without the chains of civilization. "I see an animal . . . eating his fill under an oak tree, quenching his thirst at the first stream, making his bed at the base of the same tree that supplied his meal." The earth gives this natural man everything he needs. It does not pamper him, but he needs no pampering. Harsh conditions from infancy have made him resistant to illness, and he is strong enough to fight off wild beasts unarmed. He has no axes, but he uses his muscles to break thick branches unaided. He has no slingshots or guns, but he can throw a stone powerfully enough to bring down any prey. He needs no horses, for he can run as fast as one. Only when civilization makes man "sociable and a slave" does he lose his manliness, learning to be weak and to fear everything around him. He also learns despair: no one ever heard of a "free savage" killing himself, says Rousseau. He even loses his natural tendency to be compassionate. If someone slits a person's throat under a philosopher's window, the philosopher is likely to put his hands over his ears and pretend not to hear; a savage would never do this. A natural man could not fail to heed the voice within that makes him identify with his fellows—a voice that sounds very much like the one which calls Montaigne to feel sympathy for all suffering fellow beings.

If one reverses chronology and imagines Montaigne settling down in his armchair to read Rousseau, it is intriguing to wonder how far he would have followed this before tossing the book from him. In the early stages of this passage, he might have felt enchanted; here was a writer with whom he was in perfect harmony. A few paragraphs later, one imagines him faltering and frowning. "Though I don't know . . ." he might murmur, as the wave of Rousseau's rhetoric keeps swelling. Montaigne would want to pause and examine it all from alternative angles. Does society really make us callous? he would ask. Are we not better in company? Is man really born free; is he not filled with weaknesses and imperfections from the start? Do sociability and slavery go together? And by the way, could anyone really throw a stone powerfully enough to kill something at a distance without a slingshot?

Rousseau never stops or reverses direction. He sweeps along, and sweeps many readers with him too: he became the most popular author of his day. Reading a few pages of Rousseau makes one realize just how different he is from Montaigne, even when the latter seems to have been a source for his ideas. Montaigne is saved from flights of primitivist fantasy by his tendency to step aside from whatever he says even as he is saying it. His "though I don't know" always intervenes. Moreover, his overall purpose is different from Rousseau's. He does not want to show that modern civilization is corrupt, but that all human *perspectives* on the world are corrupt and partial by nature. This applies to the Tupinambá visitors, gazing at the French in Rouen, just as much as to Léry or Thevet in Brazil. The only hope of emerging from the fog of misinterpretation is to remain alert to its existence: that is, to become wise at one's own expense. But even this only provides an imperfect solution. We can never escape our limitations altogether.

Writers like Diderot and Rousseau were drawn not only to the "cannibal" Montaigne, but to all the passages in which he wrote of simple and natural ways of life. The book in which Rousseau seems to have borrowed most from the *Essays* is *Émile*, a hugely successful pedagogical novel which changed the lives of a whole generation of fashionably educated children by promoting a "natural" upbringing. Parents and tutors should bring up children gently, he suggested, letting them learn about the world by following their own curiosity while surrounding them with opportunities for travel, conversation, and experience. At the same time, like little Stoics, they should also be inured to tough physical conditions. This is clearly traceable to Montaigne's essay on education, although Rousseau mentions Montaigne only occasionally in the book, usually to attack him.

He insults Montaigne again at the outset of his autobiography, the *Confessions*—a work which might be thought to owe something to Montaigne's project of self-portraiture. In his original preface (often omitted in later editions), Rousseau wards off such accusations by writing, "I place Montaigne foremost among those dissemblers who mean to deceive by telling the truth. He portrays himself with defects, but he gives himself only lovable ones." If Montaigne misleads the reader, then it is not he but Rousseau who is the first person in history to write an honest and full account of himself. This frees Rousseau to say, of his own book, "This is the only portrait of a man, painted exactly according to nature and in all its truth, that exists and will probably ever exist."

The works do differ, and not just because the *Confessions* is a narrative, tracing a life from childhood on rather than capturing everything at once as the *Essays* does. There is also a difference of purpose. Rousseau wrote the book because he considered himself so exceptional, both in brilliance and sometimes in wickedness, that he wanted to capture himself before this unique combination of features was lost to the world.

> I know men. I am not made like any that I have seen; I venture to believe that I was not made like any that exist . . . As to whether Nature did well or ill to break the mold in which I was cast, that is something no one can judge until after they have read me.

Montaigne, by contrast, saw himself as a thoroughly ordinary man in every respect, except for his unusual habit of writing things down. He "bears the entire form of the human condition," as everyone does, and is therefore happy to cast himself as a mirror for others—the same role he bestows on the Tupinambá. That is the whole point of the *Essays*. If no one could recognize themselves in him, why would anyone read him?

Some contemporaries noticed suspicious similarities between Rousseau and Montaigne. Rousseau was overtly accused of theft: a tract by Dom Joseph Cajot, bluntly called *Rousseau's Plagiarisms on Education*, opined that the only difference was that Montaigne gushed less than Rousseau and was more concise—surely the only time the latter quality has ever been attributed to Montaigne. Another critic, Nicolas Bricaire de la Dixmerie, invented a dialogue in which Rousseau admits to having copied ideas from Montaigne, but argues that they have nothing in common because he writes "in inspiration" while Montaigne writes "coldly."

Rousseau lived in an era when gushing, inspiration, and heat were admired. They meant, precisely, that you were in touch with "Nature," rather than being a slave to the frigid requirements of civilization. You were savage and sincere; you had cannibal chic.

Eighteenth-century readers who embraced Montaigne for his praise of the Tupinambá, and for all his writings on nature, were gradually blossoming into full Romantics—a breed who would dominate the late years of that century and the early years of the following one. And Montaigne would never be quite the same again once the Romantics had finished with him.

From its beginning in the form of a mildly rebellious, open-minded answer to the question of living well, "Wake from the sleep of habit" gradually metamorphosed into something much more rabble-rousing and even revolutionary. After Romanticism, it would no longer be easy to see Montaigne as a cool, gracious source of Hellenistic wisdom. From now on, readers would persist in trying to warm him up. He would, for evermore, have a wild side.

11. Q. How to live? A. Live temperately

RAISING AND LOWERING THE TEMPERATURE

IN MANY WAYS, readers of the late eighteenth and early nineteenth centuries found it easy to like the Montaigne they constructed for themselves. As well as appreciating his praise for the Americans, they responded to his openness about himself, his willingness to explore the contradictions of his character, his disregard for convention, and his desire to break out of fossilized habits. They liked his interest in psychology, especially his sense of the way different impulses could coexist in a single mind. Also—and they were the first generation of readers to feel this way in great numbers—they enjoyed his writing style, with all its exuberant disorder. They liked the way he seemed to blurt out whatever was on his mind at any moment, without pausing to set it into neat array.

Romantic readers were particularly taken by Montaigne's intense feeling

for La Boétie, because it was the only place where he showed strong emotion. The tragic ending of the love story, with La Boétie's death, made it more beautiful. Montaigne's simple answer to the question of why they loved each other—"Because it was he, because it was I"—became a catchphrase, denoting the transcendent mystery in all human attraction.

In her autobiography, the Romantic writer George Sand related how she became obsessed with Montaigne and La Boétie in her youth, as the prototype of spiritual friendship she herself longed to find—and did, in later life, with writer friends such as Flaubert and Balzac. The poet Alphonse de Lamartine felt similarly. In a letter, he wrote of Montaigne: "All that I admire in him is his friendship for La Boétie." He had already borrowed Montaigne's formula to describe his own feelings in an earlier letter to the same friend: "Because it is you, because it is I." He embraced Montaigne himself as such a companion, writing of "friend Montaigne, yes: friend."

The new highly charged or heated quality of such responses to Montaigne can be measured in the increase, during this era, in pilgrimages to his tower. Visitors called on the Montaigne estate, drawn by curiosity, but once there they lost their heads; they stood rapt in meditation, feeling Montaigne's spirit all around them like a living presence. Often, they felt almost as though they had *become* him, for a few moments.

There had been little of this in previous centuries. Montaigne's descendants lived at the estate until 1811, and for most of this time no one interfered with them while they converted the ground floor of the tower into a potato store and the first-floor bedroom sometimes to a dog kennel, sometimes to a chicken coop. This changed only after a trickle of early Romantic visitors turned into a regular flow, until eventually the potatoes and chickens gave way to an organized re-creation of his working environment.

This all seemed self-explanatory to the Romantics. Naturally, if you responded to Montaigne's writing, you must want to be there in person: to gaze out of his window at the view he would have seen every day, or to hover behind the place where he might have sat to write, so you could look down and almost see his ghostly words appear before your eyes. Taking no account of the hubbub that would really have been going on in the courtyard below, and probably in his room too, you were free to imagine the tower as a monastic cell, which Montaigne inhabited like a hermit. "Let us hasten to cross the threshold," wrote one early visitor, Charles Compan, of the tower library:

> If your heart beats like mine with an indescribable emotion; if the memory of a great man inspires in you this deep veneration which one cannot refuse to the benefactors of humanity—enter.

The pilgrimage tradition outlived the Romantic era proper. When the marquis de Gaillon wrote of his visit to the tower in 1862, he summoned up the pain of departure in lover's language:

> But at last one must leave this library, this room, this dear tower. Farewell, Montaigne! for to leave this place is to be separated from you.

The problem with all such passionate swooning into Montaigne's arms has always been Montaigne himself. To fantasize about him in this way is to set oneself at odds with his own way of doing things. Blocking out parts of the *Essays* that interfere with one's chosen interpretation is a timeless activity, but the hot-blooded Romantics had a harder task than most. They were constantly brought up against things like this:

> I have no great experience of these vehement agitations, being of an indolent and sluggish disposition.

> I like temperate and moderate natures.

> My excesses do not carry me very far away. There is nothing extreme or strange about them.

> The most beautiful lives, to my mind, are those that conform to the common human pattern, with order, but without miracle and without eccentricity.

The poet Alphonse de Lamartine was one such frustrated reader. When he first came across Montaigne he hero-worshiped him, and kept a volume of the *Essays* always in his pocket or on his table so he could seize it whenever he had the urge. But later he turned against his idol with equal vehemence: Montaigne, he now decided, knew nothing of the real miseries of life. He explained to a correspondent that he had only been able to love the *Essays* when he was young—that is, about nine months earlier, when he first began to enthuse about the book in his letters. Now, at twenty-one, he had been weathered by pain, and found Montaigne too cool and measured. Perhaps, he wondered, he might return to Montaigne many years later, in old age, when even more suffering had dried his heart. For now, the essayist's sense of moderation made him feel positively ill.

George Sand also wrote that she was "not Montaigne's disciple" when it came to his Stoical or Skeptical "indifference"—his equilibrium or *ataraxia*, a goal that had now gone out of fashion. She had loved his friendship with La Boétie, as the one sign of warmth, but it was not enough and she tired of him.

The worst sticking-point for Romantic readers was a passage in which Montaigne described visiting the famous poet Torquato Tasso in Ferrara, on his Italian travels in 1580. Tasso's most celebrated work, the epic *Gerusalemme liberata*, enjoyed immense success on its publication that same year, but the poet himself had lost his mind and was confined to a madhouse, where he lived in atrocious conditions surrounded by distressed lunatics. Passing through Ferrara, Montaigne called on him, and was horrified by the encounter. He felt sympathy, but suspected that Tasso had driven himself into this condition by spending too long in states of poetic ecstasy. The radiance of his inspiration had brought him to unreason: he had let himself be "blinded by the light." Seeing genius reduced to idiocy saddened Montaigne. Worse, it irritated him. What a waste, to destroy oneself in this way! He was aware that writing poetry required a certain "frenzy," but what was the point of becoming so frenzied that one could never write again? "The archer who overshoots the target misses as much as the one who does not reach it."

Looking back at two such different writers as Montaigne and Tasso, and admiring both, Romantics were prepared to go along with Montaigne's

belief that Tasso had blown his own mind with poetry. They could understand Montaigne's sadness about it. What they could neither understand nor forgive was his irritation. Romantics did blinding brilliance; they did melancholy; they did intense imaginative identification. They did not do irritation.

Montaigne is obviously "no poet," spat one such reader, Philarète Chasles. Jules Lefèvre-Deumier deplored what he saw as Montaigne's "stoic indifference" to another man's sufferings—which seems a misreading of Montaigne's passage about Tasso. The real problem was that Romantics took sides. They identified with Tasso in this encounter, not with Montaigne, who represented the uncomprehending world they felt was always opposing them, too. As Nietzsche could have warned Montaigne:

> Moderation sees itself as beautiful; it is unaware that in the eye of the immoderate it appears black and sober, and consequently ugly-looking.

Actually, in this situation, it was Montaigne who was playing the rebel. By singing the praises of moderation and equanimity, and doubting the value of poetic excess, Montaigne was bucking the trend of his own time as much as that of the Romantics. Renaissance readers fetishized extreme states: ecstasy was the only state in which to write poetry, just as it was the only way to fight a battle and the only way to fall in love. In all three pursuits, Montaigne seems to have had an inner thermostat which switched him off as soon as the temperature rose beyond a certain point. This was why he so admired Epaminondas, the one classical warrior who kept his head when the sound of clashing swords rang out, and why he valued friendship more than passion. "Transcendental humors frighten me," he said. The qualities he valued were curiosity, sociability, kindness, fellow-feeling, adaptability, intelligent reflection, the ability to see things from another's point of view, and "goodwill"—none of which is compatible with the fiery furnace of inspiration.

Montaigne even went so far as to claim that true greatness of the soul is to be found "in mediocrity"—a shocking remark and even, paradoxically, an extreme one. Most moderns have been so trained to regard mediocrity as a poor, limited condition that it is hard to know what to think when he says this. Is he playing games with the reader again, as some suspect he does when he writes of having a bad memory and a slow intellect? Perhaps he is, to some extent, yet he seems to mean it too. Montaigne distrusts godlike ambitions. For him, people who try to rise above the human manage only to sink to the subhuman. Like Tasso, they seek to transcend the limits, and instead lose their ordinary human faculties. Being truly human means behaving in a way that is not merely ordinary, but *ordinate*, a word the *Oxford English Dictionary* defines as "ordered, regulated; orderly, regular, moderate." It means living appropriately, or *à propos*, so that one estimates things at their right value and behaves in the way correctly suited to each occasion. This is why, as Montaigne puts it, living appropriately is "our great and glorious masterpiece"—grandiose language, but used to describe a quality that is anything but grandiose. Mediocrity, for Montaigne, does not mean the dullness that comes from not bothering to think things through, or from lacking the imagination to see beyond one's own viewpoint. It means accepting that one is like everyone else, and that one carries the entire form of the human condition. This could not be further removed from Rousseau and his feeling that he is set apart from all humanity. For Montaigne:

There is nothing so beautiful and legitimate as to play the man well and properly, no knowledge so hard to acquire as the knowledge of how to live this life well and naturally; and the most barbarous of our maladies is to despise our being.

He knew, all the same, that human nature does not always conform to this wisdom. Alongside the wish to be happy, emotionally at peace and in full command of one's faculties, something else drives people periodically to smash their achievements to pieces. It is what Freud called the *thanatos* principle: the drive towards death and chaos. The twentieth-century author Rebecca West described it thus:

Only part of us is sane: only part of us loves pleasure and the longer day of happiness, wants to live to our nineties and die in peace, in a house that we built, that shall shelter those who come after us. The other half of us is nearly mad. It prefers the disagreeable to the agreeable, loves pain and its darker night despair, and wants to die in a catastrophe that will set back life to its beginnings and leave nothing of our house save its blackened foundations.

West and Freud both had experience of war, and so did Montaigne: he could hardly fail to notice this side of humanity. His passages about moderation and mediocrity must be read with one eye always to the French civil wars, in which transcendental extremism brought about subhuman cruelties on an overwhelming scale. The third "trouble" ended in August 1570, and a two-year peace ensued during the period when Montaigne lived on his estate and began work on the *Essays*. But, long before he had finished that work, the peace came to an abrupt and shocking end, with an event that could leave no one in doubt about the dark side of human nature.

12. Q. How to live? A. Guard your humanity

L IKE EARLIER PEACE agreements, 1570's Treaty of Saint-Germain displeased everyone. Protestants, always wanting more, thought its terms did not go far enough, as it granted them limited freedom of worship. Catholics thought it went too far; they were anxious that Protestants would take any concessions at all as encouragement. They feared that Protestants would press for an all-out revolution against the legitimate Catholic monarch, and start another war. They were right about there being another war, but wrong about who would be responsible.

Tensions kept rising, and reached a peak during celebrations held in Paris in August 1572 to mark a dynastic wedding between the Catholic Marguerite de Valois and the Protestant Henri de Navarre. The leaders of three main factions came to the ceremony in a grim mood: the moderate Catholic king Charles IX, the radical Protestant leader Admiral Gaspard de Coligny, and the extremist Catholic duc de Guise. Each faction was haunted by fear of the others. Inflammatory preachers raised the emotional temperature further among ordinary Parisians, urging them to rise up to prevent the wedding and wipe out the heretic leaders while they had the chance.

The marriage went ahead, on August 18, and four days of official festivities followed. No doubt many breathed a sigh of relief when they ended. But late on the final night, August 22, 1572, someone fired an arquebus at the Protestant leader Coligny as he walked back to his house from the Louvre palace, not killing him outright but breaking his arm.

News of the incident spread around town. The next morning, streams of Huguenots came to see Coligny, vowing revenge. Many of them believed (as most historians still do) that the king himself was behind the assassination attempt, together with his mother Catherine de' Medici—the idea being to nip any potential Protestant rebellion in the bud by removing its leader. If true, this was a miscalculation on Charles's part. The attack on

Coligny made Protestants angry. More dangerously still, it made Catholics fearful. Expecting Protestants to rise up in response to what had happened, they gathered around the city and prepared to defend themselves. The king was probably unnerved too, and may have reasoned that a dead rebel leader was less dangerous than a wounded one. Apparently on his orders, a royal guard broke into Coligny's house and finished the botched job by killing the injured man in his bed. This was early on the morning of Sunday, August 24: St. Bartholomew's Day.

The killers cut off Coligny's head and dispatched it to the royal palace; it would eventually be embalmed and sent to Rome for the Pope to admire. Meanwhile the rest of the body was thrown out of the window to the street, where a Catholic crowd set fire to it and dragged it around the district. The body fell to pieces as it smoldered, but segments were paraded about and further mutilated for days.

The commotion at Coligny's house caused further panic among Parisian Catholics as well as Protestants. Catholic gangs rushed onto the streets; they seized and killed any recognizable Protestants, and burst into houses where Protestants were known to live—and where many were sleeping peacefully, having no idea what was going on in the city. The mobs dragged them

outside, slit their throats or tore them to pieces, then set fire to their bodies or threw them in the river. The mayhem attracted larger and larger crowds, and fueled further atrocities. To pick just one reported incident, a man named Mathurin Lussault was killed when he made the mistake of answering his door; his son came down to investigate the noise and was stabbed too. Lussault's wife, Françoise, tried to escape by leaping from her upstairs window into a neighbor's courtyard. She broke both her legs. The neighbor helped her, but the attackers burst in and dragged her into the street by her hair. They cut off her hands to get her gold bracelets, then impaled her on a spit; later they dumped her body in the river. The hands, chewed by dogs, were still to be seen outside the building several days later. Similar scenes took place all over the city, and so many bodies were thrown into the Seine that it was said to run red with blood.

Whatever Charles had intended by the original assassination—if indeed he was responsible—he can hardly have intended this. He now ordered his soldiers to suppress the violence, but it was too late. The killing went on for nearly a week through the districts of Paris, then spread around the rest of the country. In Paris alone, the massacres, which were known for ever more by the name of St. Bartholomew, left up to five thousand dead. By the end some ten thousand had been killed in France. Cities were sucked into the violence like fishing-boats into a tornado: Orléans, Lyon, Rouen, Toulouse, Bordeaux, and countless smaller towns.

It was a *furor* of the kind Montaigne detested even on a traditional battlefield, but here the victims were civilians. On the whole, so were the killers; only in a few places were soldiers or officials involved. Bordeaux was one of these few. Nothing happened there until October 3, but when it did, it was apparently organized and approved by the fanatical Catholic mayor of the time, Charles de Montferrand, who produced a formal list of targets to be attacked. In most places, the bloodshed was done more chaotically and by people who would have been reasonable folk the rest of the time. In Orléans, the mob stopped at taverns between killings to celebrate, "accompanied by singing, lutes and guitars," according to one historian. Some groups were composed mainly of women or children. Catholics interpreted the presence of the latter as a sign that God Himself was in favor of the massacres, for He had caused even innocents to take part. In general, many thought that, since the killings were on no ordinary human scale, they must have been divinely sanctioned. They were not the result of human decisions; they were messages from God *to* humanity, portents of cosmic mayhem just as much as a blighted harvest or a comet in the sky. A medal made in Rome to commemorate the massacres showed the Huguenots struck down, not by fellow mortals, but by an armed angel shining with holy wrath. In general, the new Pope, Gregory XIII, seems to have been pleased with events in France. Apart from the medal, he commissioned Giorgio Vasari to paint celebratory frescos in the Sala Regia of the Vatican. The French king likewise took part in processions of thanksgiving, and had two medals struck, one portraying himself as Hercules doing battle with the Hydra, the other depicting him on his throne surrounded by naked corpses and holding a palm frond to represent victory.

Once the Huguenots had collected themselves and gathered armies to fight back, all-out war broke out again. It would continue through the 1570s, with only occasional pauses. The St. Bartholomew's events formed a dividing line. After this, the wars were more anarchic, and more driven by fanaticism. Besides ordinary battles, much misery was now caused by uncontrolled gangs of soldiers on the rampage, even during supposed peace interludes, when they had no masters and no pay. Peasants sometimes fled and lived wild in the forests rather than wait in town to be attacked and sometimes tortured for the fun of it. This was the state of nature with a

vengeance. In 1579, one provincial lawyer, Jean La Rouvière, wrote to the king to beg help for the rustic poor in his area—"miserable, martyrized, and abandoned men" who lived off the land as best they could, having lost all they had. Among the horrors he had seen or heard of were tales of people

> buried alive in heaps of manure, thrown into wells and ditches and left to die, howling like dogs; they had been nailed in boxes without air, walled up in towers without food, and garroted upon trees in the depths of the mountains and forests; they had been stretched in front of fires, their feet fricasseed in grease; their women had been raped and those who were pregnant had been aborted; their children had been kidnapped and ransomed, or even roasted alive before the parents.

The wars were fed by religious ardor, but the sufferings of war in turn generated further apocalyptic imaginings. Both Catholics and Protestants thought that events were approaching a point beyond which there could be no more normal history, for all that remained was the final confrontation between God and the Devil. This is why Catholics celebrated the St. Bartholomew's massacres so joyfully: they saw them as a genuine victory over evil, and as a way of driving countless misled individuals back to the true Church before it was too late for them to save their souls.

It all mattered a great deal, because time was short. In the Last Days, Christ would return, the world would be obliterated, and everyone would have to justify his or her actions to God. There could be no compromise in such a situation, no seeing the other person's point of view, and certainly no mutual understanding between rival faiths. Montaigne, with his praise of ordinary life and of mediocrity, was selling something that could have no market in a doomed world.

Signs of the imminence of this Apocalypse were plentiful. A series of famines, ruined harvests, and freezing winters in the 1570s and 1580s indicated that God Himself was withdrawing His warmth from the earth. Smallpox, typhus, and whooping cough swept through the country, as well as the worst disease of all: the plague. All four Horsemen of the Apocalypse seemed to have been unleashed: pestilence, war, famine, and death. A werewolf roamed the country, conjoined twins were born in Paris, and a

IVSTORVM ANIMAE IN MANV DEI SVNT, NEC ATTINGET ILLOS CRVCIATVS; INSIPIENTIVM VERO
IVDITIO MORI VIDENTVR. CALMITOSVS EXISTIMATVR EXITVS EORV, CVM ILLI FRVATVR FELICITATE.

new star—a nova—exploded in the sky. Even those not given to religious extremism had a feeling that everything was speeding towards some indefinable end. Montaigne's editor, Marie de Gournay, later remembered the France of her youth as a place so abandoned to chaos "that one was led to expect a final ruin, rather than a restoration, of the state." Some thought the end was very nigh indeed: the linguist and theologian Guillaume Postel wrote in a letter of 1573 that "within eight days the people will perish."

The Devil, too, knew that his time of influence on earth was drawing to a close, so he sent armies of demons to win the last few vulnerable souls. They were armies indeed. Jean Wier, in his *De praestigis daemonum* (1564), had calculated that at least 7,409,127 demons were working for Lucifer, under the middle-management of seventy-nine demon-princes. Alongside them were witches: a dramatic rise in witchcraft cases after the 1560s provided more proof that the Apocalypse was coming. As fast as they were detected, the courts burned them, but the Devil replaced them even faster.

Contemporary demonologist Jean Bodin argued that, in crisis conditions such as these, standards of evidence must be lowered. Witchcraft was so serious, and so hard to detect using normal methods of proof, that society could not afford to adhere too much to "legal tidiness and normal procedures." Public rumor could be considered "almost infallible": if everyone in a village said that a particular woman was a witch, that was sufficient to justify putting her to the torture. Medieval techniques were revived specifically for such cases, including "swimming" suspects to see if they floated, and searing them with red-hot irons. The numbers of convicted witches kept rising as standards of evidence went down, and the increase amounted to further proof that the crisis was real and that further adjustment of the law was necessary. As history has repeatedly suggested, nothing is more effective for demolishing traditional legal protections than the combined claims that a crime is uniquely dangerous, and that those behind it have exceptional powers of resistance. It was all accepted with hardly a murmur, except by a few writers such as Montaigne, who pointed out that torture was useless for getting at the truth since people will say anything to stop the pain—and that, besides, it was "putting a very high price on one's conjectures" to have someone roasted alive on their account.

A major development warned of by the theologians was the imminent arrival of the Antichrist. Signs would abound in coming years: in 1583 an old woman in an African country gave birth to an infant with cat's teeth who announced, in an adult voice, that it was the Messiah. Simultaneously, in Babylon, a mountain burst open to reveal a buried column on which was written in Hebrew: "The hour of my nativity is come." The leading French expert on such Antichrist tales was Montaigne's successor in the Bordeaux *parlement*, Florimond de Raemond, also an enthusiastic witch-burner. Raemond's work *L'Antichrist* analyzed portents in the sky, the withering of vegetation and harvests, population movements, and cases of atrocity and cannibalism in the wars, showing how all proved that the Devil was on his way.

To join in mass violence, in such circumstances, was to let God know that you stood with Him. Both Protestant and Catholic extremists made a cult of holy zeal, which amounted to a total gift of yourself to God and a rejection of the things of this world. Anyone who still paid attention to everyday affairs at such a time might be suspected of moral weakness, at best, and allegiance to the Devil at worst.

In reality, many people did carry on with their lives and keep out of trouble as best they could, remaining faithful to the ordinariness which Montaigne thought was the essence of wisdom. Even if they believed in it, the coming confrontation between Satan and God interested them no more than the scandals and diplomacy of the royal court. Many Protestants quietly renounced their faith after 1572, or at least concealed it, an implicit admission that they considered the life of this world more important than their belief in the next. But a minority went to the opposite extreme. Radicalized beyond measure, they called for total war against Catholicism and the death of the king—the "tyrant" responsible for the deaths of Coligny and all the other victims. It was in this context that La Boétie's *On Voluntary Servitude* was suddenly taken up and published by Huguenot radicals, who reinvented it as propaganda for a cause La Boétie himself would never have favored.

As it turned out, regicide was unnecessary. Charles IX died of natural causes a year and a half later, on May 30, 1574. The throne passed to another of Catherine de' Medici's sons, Henri III, who proved even more unpopular. He was not even liked by many Catholics. Support grew throughout the 1570s for the Catholic extremists known as *Ligueurs* or Leaguists, who would cause the monarchy at least as much trouble as the Huguenots in coming years, under the leadership of the powerful and ambitious duc de Guise. From now on, the wars in France would be a three-way affair, with the monarchy often caught in the weakest position. Henri tried occasionally to take over leadership of the Leagues himself, to neutralize their threat, but they rejected him, and often portrayed him as a Satanic agent in disguise.

He may have been too moderate for the Leagues, but Henri III was extremist in other ways, showing no understanding of Montaigne's sense of moderation. Montaigne, who met him several times, did not like him much. On the one hand, Henri filled his court with fops, and turned it into a realm of corruption, luxury, and absurd points of etiquette. He went out dancing every night and, in youth, wore robes and doublets of mulberry satin, with coral bracelets and cloaks slashed to ribbons. He started a fashion for shirts with four sleeves, two for use and two trailing behind like wings. Some of his other affectations were considered even stranger: he used forks at table

instead of knives and fingers, he wore nightclothes to bed, and he washed his hair from time to time. On the other hand, Henri also put on exaggerated displays of mysticism and penitence. The more perplexed he became by the problems facing the kingdom, the more frequently he took part in processions of flagellants, trudging with them barefoot over cobbled streets, chanting psalms and scourging himself.

To Montaigne, the notion that the solution to the political crisis could lie in prayer and extreme spiritual exercises made no sense. He recoiled from these processions, and put no credence in comets, freak hailstorms, monstrous births, or any of the other signs of doom. He observed that those who made predictions from such phenomena usually kept them vague, so that later they could claim success whatever happened. Most reports of witchcraft seemed to Montaigne to be the effects of human imagination, not of Satanic activity. In general, he preferred to stick to his motto: "I suspend judgment."

His Skepticism drew some mild criticism; two contemporaries in Bordeaux, Martin-Antoine del Rio and Pierre de Lancre, warned him that it

was theologically dangerous to explain apocalyptic events in terms of the human imagination, because it distracted attention from the real threat. On the whole, he managed to avoid serious suspicions, but Montaigne did risk his reputation by speaking out against torture and witch trials. He was already associated in many people's minds with a category of thinkers known to their enemies as *politiques*, who were distinguished by their belief that the kingdom's problems had nothing to do with the Antichrist or the End Times, but were merely political. They deduced that the solution should be political too—hence the nickname. In theory, they supported the king, believing that the one hope for France was unity under a legitimate monarch, though most of them secretly hoped that a more inspiring, more *unifying* king than Henri III might one day come along. While remaining loyal, they worked to find points of common ground between the other parties, in the hope of halting the wars and laying a foundation for France's future.

Unfortunately, the one piece of common ground that really brought extreme Catholics close to extreme Protestants was hatred of *politiques*. The word itself was an accusation of godlessness. These were people who paid attention only to political solutions, not to the state of their souls. They were men of masks: deceivers, like Satan himself. "He wears the skin of a lamb," wrote one contemporary of a typical *politique*, "but nevertheless is a raging wolf." Unlike real Protestants, they tried to pass as something they were not, and, since they were so clever and intellectual, they did not have the excuse of being innocent victims of the Devil's deception. Montaigne's association with the *politiques* gave him a good reason to emphasize his openness and honesty, as well as his Catholic orthodoxy (though, of course, claiming to be honest is exactly what a wolf in sheep's clothing would do).

Leaguists accused *politiques* of untrustworthiness, but *politiques*, in turn, accused Leaguists of abandoning themselves to their passions and losing their judgment. How strange, reflected Montaigne, that Christianity should lead so often to violent excess, and thence to destruction and pain:

Our zeal does wonders when it is seconding our leaning towards hatred, cruelty, ambition, avarice, detraction, rebellion. Against the grain, toward goodness, benignity, moderation, unless as by a miracle some rare nature bears it, it will neither walk nor fly.

"There is no hostility that exceeds Christian hostility," he even wrote at one point. In place of the figure of the burning-eyed Christian zealot, he preferred to contemplate that of the Stoic sage: a person who behaves morally, moderates his emotions, exercises good judgment, and knows how to live.

There was indeed much of Stoic philosophy in the *politiques*. They did not urge revolution or regicide, but recommended acceptance of life as it is, on the Stoic principle of *amor fati*, or love of fate. They also promoted the Stoic sense of continuity: the belief that the world would probably continue to cycle through episodes of decay and rejuvenation, rather than accelerating into a one-directional rush towards the End. While the religious parties imagined the armies of Armageddon assembling in the sky, *politiques* suspected that sooner or later everything would calm down and people would come back to their senses. In millenarian times, they were the only people systematically to shift their perspective and think ahead to a time when the "troubles" would have become history—and to plan exactly how to build this future world.

Montaigne's Stoic side led him to downplay the wars to an astonishing extent in his writing. Biographers have invariably made much of his experience of war, and with good reason: it did affect his life profoundly. Some critics have based whole readings of Montaigne on the wars. But, after studying any such book, it can come as a surprise to turn back to the *Essays* and find Montaigne saying things like, "I am amazed to see our wars so gentle and mild," and "It will be a lot if a hundred years from now people remember in a general way that in our time there were civil wars in France." Those living through the present assume that things are worse than they are, he says, because they cannot escape their local perspective:

> Whoever considers as in a painting the great picture of our mother Nature in her full majesty; whoever reads such universal and constant variety in her face; whoever finds himself there, and not merely himself, but a whole kingdom, as a dot made with a very fine brush; that man alone estimates things according to their true proportions.

Montaigne reminded his contemporaries of the old Stoic lesson: to avoid feeling swamped by a difficult situation, try imagining your world from different angles or at different scales of significance. This is what the ancients did when they looked down on their troubles from above, as upon a commotion in an ant colony. Astrologers now warn of "great and imminent alterations and mutations," writes Montaigne, but they forget the simple fact that, however bad things are, most of life goes on undisturbed. "I do not despair about it," he added lightly.

Admittedly, Montaigne was lucky. The wars ruined his harvests, made him fear being murdered in bed, and forced him to take part in political activities he would have preferred to avoid. They would land him in even greater troubles in the 1580s, when the war entered its last and most desperate phase. But no one could claim that he was badly scarred by these experiences, and, if he ever took up arms himself, he says nothing about it in the *Essays*. In short, he had a good war. Yet that would not have stopped most people from indulging in lamentation.

And Montaigne was right. Life did go on. The St. Bartholomew's massacres, terrible as they were, gave way to years of inconclusive individual suffering rather than heralding the end of the world. The Antichrist did not come. Generation followed generation until a time came when, as Montaigne predicted, many people had only the vaguest idea that his century's wars ever took place. This happened partly because of the work he and his fellow *politiques* did to restore sanity. Montaigne, affecting ease and comfort, contributed more to saving his country than his zealous contemporaries. Some of his work was directly political, but his greatest contribution was simply to stay out of it and write the *Essays*. This, in the eyes of many, makes him a hero.

HERO

Those who have adopted Montaigne in this role usually cast him as a hero of an unusual sort: the kind that resists all claim to heroism. Few revere him for doing great public deeds, though he did accomplish some noteworthy things in his later life. More often, he is admired for his stubborn insistence on maintaining normality in extraordinary circumstances, and his refusal to compromise his independence.

Many contemporaries saw him in this light; the great Stoic political thinker Justus Lipsius told him to keep writing because people needed his example to follow. Long after the sixteenth-century Stoic Montaigne was forgotten, readers in troubled times continued to think of him as a role model. His *Essays* offered practical wisdom on questions such as how to face up to intimidation, and how to reconcile the conflicting demands of openness and security. He also provided something more nebulous: a sense of how one could survive public catastrophe without losing one's self-respect. Just as you could seek mercy from an enemy forthrightly, without compromising yourself, or defend your property by electing to leave it undefended, so you could get through an inhumane war by remaining human. This message in Montaigne would have a particular appeal to twentieth-century readers who lived through wars, or through Fascist or Communist dictatorships. In such times, it could seem that the structure of civilized society had collapsed and that nothing would ever be the same again. Montaigne was at his most reassuring when he provided the least sympathy for this feeling—when he reminded the reader that, in the end, normality comes back and perspectives shift again.

Among the many readers who have responded to this aspect of the *Essays*, one can stand for all: the Austrian Jewish writer Stefan Zweig, who, living in enforced exile in South America during the Second World War, calmed and distracted himself by writing a long personal essay on Montaigne—his nonheroic hero.

When Zweig first came across the *Essays* as a young man in turn-of-the-century Vienna, he admitted, the book made little impression. Like Lamartine and Sand before him, he found it too dispassionate. It lacked "the leap of electricity from soul to soul"; he could see no relevance to his own life. "What appeal could there be to a 20-year-old youth in the rambling excursus of a Sieur de Montaigne on the 'Ceremony of interview of kings' or his 'Considerations on Cicero'?" Even when Montaigne turned to topics that ought to have been more appealing, such as sex and politics, his "mild, temperate wisdom" and his feeling that it was wiser not to involve oneself too much in the world repelled Zweig. "It is in the nature of youth that it does not want to be advised to be mild or skeptical. Every doubt seems to it to be a limitation." Young people crave beliefs; they want to be roused.

Moreover, in 1900, the freedom of the individual hardly seemed to require defense. "Had not all that long ago become a self-evident matter, guaranteed by law and custom to a humanity long since liberated from tyranny and serfdom?" Zweig's generation—he was born in 1881—assumed that prosperity and personal freedom would just keep growing. Why should things go backwards? No one felt that civilization was in danger; no one had to retreat into their private selves to preserve their spiritual freedom. "Montaigne seemed pointlessly to rattle chains that we considered broken long ago."

Of course, history proved Zweig's generation wrong. Just as Montaigne himself had grown up into a world full of hope only to see it degenerate, so Zweig was born into the luckiest of countries and centuries, and had it all fall apart around him. The chains were reforged, stronger and heavier than ever.

Zweig survived the First World War, but this was followed by the rise of Hitler. He fled Austria and was forced to wander for years as a refugee, first to Britain, then to the United States, and finally to Brazil. His exile made him "defenseless as a fly, helpless as a snail," as he put it in his autobiography. He felt himself to be a condemned man, waiting in his cell for execution, and ever less able to engage with his hosts' world around him. He kept sane by throwing himself into work. In his exile, he produced a biography of Balzac, a series of novellas and short stories, an autobiography, and, finally, the essay on Montaigne—all without proper sources or notes, since he was cut off from his possessions. He never achieved Montaigne's attitude of nonchalance, but then, his situation was far worse than Montaigne's:

> I belong nowhere, and everywhere am a stranger, a guest at best. Europe, the homeland of my heart's choice, is lost to me, since it has torn itself apart suicidally a second time in a war of brother against brother. Against my will I have witnessed the most terrible defeat of reason and the wildest triumph of brutality in the chronicle of the ages.

By the time he reached Brazil in 1941, he was at several removes from any sense of home, and, although he was grateful to the country for taking him in, he found it hard to maintain hope. Finding a volume of the *Essays* in the house where he was staying, he reread it and discovered that it had transformed itself out of all recognition. The book that had once seemed stuffy and irrelevant now spoke to him with directness and intimacy, as if it were written for him alone, or perhaps for his whole generation. He at once thought of writing about Montaigne. In a letter to a friend, he wrote: "The similarity of his epoch and situation to ours is astonishing. I am not writing a biography; I propose simply to present as an example his fight for interior freedom." In the essay itself, he admitted: "In this brothership of fate, for me Montaigne has become the indispensable helper, confidant, and friend."

His Montaigne essay did turn out to be a biography of sorts, but a highly personal one, unapologetically bringing out the similarities between Montaigne's experience and his own. In a time such as that of the Second World War, or in civil-war France, Zweig writes, ordinary people's lives are sacrificed to the obsessions of fanatics, so the question for any person of integrity becomes not so much "How do I survive?" as "How do I remain fully human?" The question comes in many variants: How do I preserve my true self? How do I ensure that I go no further in my speech or actions than I think is right? How do I avoid losing my soul? Above all: How do I remain free? Montaigne was no freedom fighter in the usual sense, Zweig admits. "He has none of the rolling tirades and the beautiful verve of a Schiller or Lord Byron, none of the aggression of a Voltaire." His constant assertions that he is lazy, feckless, and irresponsible make him sound a poor hero, yet these are not really failings at all. They are essential to his battle to preserve his particular self as it is.

Zweig knew that Montaigne disliked preaching, yet he managed to extract a series of general rules from the *Essays*. He did not list them as such, but paraphrased them in such a way as to resolve them into eight separate commandments—which could also be called the eight freedoms:

Be free from vanity and pride.
Be free from belief, disbelief, convictions, and parties.
Be free from habit.
Be free from ambition and greed.
Be free from family and surroundings.
Be free from fanaticism.
Be free from fate; be master of your own life.
Be free from death; life depends on the will of others, but death on
  our own will.

Zweig was selecting a very Stoic Montaigne, thus returning to a sixteenth-century way of reading him. And, in the end, the freedom Zweig took most to heart was the last one on the list, which comes straight from Seneca. Having fallen into depression, Zweig chose the ultimate form of internal emigration. He killed himself, with the drug Vironal, on February 23, 1942; his wife chose to die with him. In his farewell message, Zweig expressed his gratitude to Brazil, "this wonderful land" which had taken him in so hospitably, and concluded, "I salute all my friends! May it be granted them yet to see the dawn after the long night! I, all too impatient, go on before."

It seemed—and this was how Zweig himself saw it—that the real value of Montaigne could be seen only when one had been pushed close to this extreme point. One must reach a state where one had nothing left to defend but one's naked "I": one's simple existence.

> Only a person who has lived through a time that threatens his life and that valuable substance, his individual freedom, with war, power, and tyrannical ideologies—only he knows how much courage, how much honesty and determination are needed to maintain the inner self in such a time of herd insanity.

He would have agreed with Leonard Woolf, when Woolf said that Montaigne's vision of interlinked I's was the essence of civilization. It was the basis on which a future could be built once the terror had passed and the war was over—though Zweig could not wait that long.

Does Montaigne's vision of private integrity and political hope have the same moral authority today? Some certainly think so. Books have been written promoting Montaigne as a hero for the twenty-first century; French journalist Joseph Macé-Scaron specifically argues that Montaigne should be adopted as an antidote to the new wars of religion. Others might feel that the last thing needed today is someone who encourages us to relax and withdraw into our private realms. People spend enough time in isolation as it is, at the expense of civil responsibilities.

Those who take Montaigne as a hero, or as a supportive companion, would argue that he did not advocate a "do-as-thou-wilt" approach to social duty. Instead, he thought that the solution to a world out of joint was for each person to get themselves back in joint: to learn "how to live," beginning with the art of keeping your feet on the ground. You can indeed find a message of inactivity, laziness, and disengagement in Montaigne, and probably also a justification for doing nothing when tyranny takes over, rather than resisting it. But many passages in the *Essays* seem rather to suggest that you should engage with the future; specifically, you should not turn your back on the real historical world in order to dream of paradise and religious transcendence. Montaigne provides all the encouragement anyone could need to respect others, to refrain from murder on the pretense of pleasing God, and to resist the urge that periodically makes humans destroy everything around them and "set back life to its beginnings." As Flaubert told his friends, "Read Montaigne . . . He will calm you." But, as he also added: "Read him in order to live."

13. Q. How to live? A. Do something no one has done before

T HROUGH THE 1570s, with their alternating episodes of peace and war, Montaigne got on with life, and with his book. He spent much of the decade writing and tinkering with his first crop of essays, then published them in 1580 at the press of local Bordeaux publisher Simon Millanges.

Millanges was an interesting choice. He had only been established in the city for a few years—for about as long as Montaigne had been writing. Montaigne would have had little difficulty finding a Parisian publisher; he had dealt with them before, and the value of a work like the *Essays* would not have escaped them. Even in its first edition, it was unique, yet it slotted neatly into the established marketing genres of classical miscellanies and commonplace books. It had that perfect commercial combination: startling originality and easy classification. Yet Montaigne insisted on staying with a local man, either because of a personal connection or as a matter of Gascon principle.

This first version of Montaigne's book was quite different from the one usually read now. It filled only two fairly small volumes and, although the "Apology" was already outsized, most chapters remained relatively simple. They often oscillated between rival points of view, but they did not wash around like vast turbulent rivers or fan out into deltas, as later essays did. Some of them even kept to their supposed point. Yet they were already suffused with Montaigne's curious, questioning, restless personality, and they often opened up puzzles or quirks in human behavior. Contemporary readers had an eye for quality; the work at once found an enthusiastic audience.

Millanges's first edition was probably small, perhaps around five or six hundred copies, and it soon sold out. Two years later he issued another edition with a few changes. Five years later, in 1587, this edition was revised again and republished in Paris by Jean Richer. By now it had become *the* fashionable reading for the French nobility of the early 1580s. In 1584, the bibliographer La Croix du Maine held up Montaigne as the one contemporary author worth classing with the ancients—just four years after his publication by a modest press in Bordeaux. Montaigne himself wrote that the *Essays* did better than he had expected, and that it became a sort of coffee-table book, popular with ladies: "a public article of furniture, an article for the parlor."

Among its admirers was Henri III himself. When Montaigne traveled through Paris later in 1580, he presented the king with a copy, as was conventional. Henri told him that he liked the book, to which Montaigne is said to have replied, "Sir, then Your Majesty must like me"—because, as he always maintained, he and his book were the same.

This, in fact, should have been an obstacle to its success. By writing so openly about his everyday observations and inner life, Montaigne was breaking a taboo. You were not supposed to record yourself in a book, only your great deeds, if you had any. The few Renaissance autobiographies so far written, such as Benvenuto Cellini's *Vita sua* and Girolamo Cardano's *De vita propria*, had been left unpublished largely for this reason. St. Augustine had written about himself, but as a spiritual exercise and to document his search for God, not to celebrate the wonders of being Augustine.

Montaigne did celebrate being Montaigne. This disturbed some readers. The classical scholar Joseph Justus Scaliger was especially annoyed about Montaigne's revelation, in his later edition of 1588, that he preferred white wine to red. (Actually Scaliger was oversimplifying. Montaigne tells us that he changed his tastes from red to white, then back to red, then to white again.) Pierre Dupuy, another scholar, asked, "Who the hell wants to know what he liked?" Naturally it annoyed Pascal and Malebranche too; Malebranche called it "effrontery," and Pascal thought Montaigne should have been told to stop.

Only with the coming of Romanticism was Montaigne's openness about himself not merely appreciated, but loved. It especially charmed readers on the other side of the Channel. The English critic Mark Pattison wrote in 1856 that Montaigne's supposed egotism made him come as vividly to life on the page as a character in a novel. And Bayle St. John observed that all true "relishers of Montaigne" loved his inconsequential "twaddling," because it made his character real and enabled readers to find themselves in him. The Scottish critic John Sterling contrasted Montaigne's way of writing about himself with the more socially acceptable tradition of memoirs by public figures attending only to the boring "din and whirl" of external events. Montaigne gave us "the very man": the "kernel" of himself. In the *Essays*, "the inward is that which is clearest."

Even in his 1580 version, Montaigne was fascinated by his inner world. It was not in some adventurous late chapter, but in his first edition that he wrote:

> I turn my gaze inward, I fix it there and keep it busy. Everyone looks in front of him; as for me, I look inside of me; I have no business but with myself; I continually observe myself, I take stock of myself, I taste myself . . . I roll about in myself.

The image is intensely physical. One sees Montaigne rolling about in himself like a puppy in long grass. When he is not rolling, he *folds*. "I refold my gaze inward" would be a more literal translation of the first sentence of this passage: *je replie ma veue au dedans*. He seems constantly to turn back on himself, thickening and deepening, fold upon fold. The result is a sort of baroque drapery, all billowing and turbulence. No wonder Montaigne has sometimes been described as the first writer of the Baroque period, although he predated it; less anachronistically, he has been called a Mannerist writer. Mannerist art, flourishing just before Baroque, was even more elaborate and anarchic, featuring optical illusions, misshapes, clutter, and odd angles of all kinds, in a violent rejection of the classical ideals of poise and proportion which had dominated the Renaissance. Montaigne, who described his *Essays* as "grotesques" and as "monstrous bodies . . . without definite shape, having no order, sequence, or proportion other than accidental," sounds the very type of the Mannerist. According to the classical principles put forward by Horace, one should not even mention monsters in one's art, because they are so ill-made, yet Montaigne compares his entire book to one.

Montaigne, the political conservative, proved himself a literary revolutionary from the start, writing like no one else and letting his pen

follow the natural rhythms of conversation instead of formal lines of construction. He omitted connections, skipped steps of reasoning, and left his material lying in solid chunks, *coupé* or "cut" like freshly chopped steaks. "I do not see the whole of anything," he wrote.

> Of a hundred members and faces that each thing has, I take one, sometimes only to lick it, sometimes to brush the surface, sometimes to pinch it to the bone. I give it a stab, not as wide but as deep as I know how. And most often I like to take them from some unaccustomed point of view.

This last part is unquestionably true. Already he skates into his early chapters from oblique directions, and the tendency becomes even more extreme with the essays of the 1580s. "Of Coaches" begins by talking about authors, goes on to a bit about sneezing, and arrives at its supposed subject of coaches two pages later—only to race off again almost immediately and spend the rest of its time discussing the New World. "Of Physiognomy" comes to the subject of physiognomy in the form of a sudden observation about the ugliness of Socrates twenty-two pages into an essay that (in Donald Frame's English translation) runs only to twenty-eight pages in total. The English writer Thackeray joked that Montaigne could have given every one of his essays the title of another, or could have called one "Of the Moon" and another "Of Fresh Cheese": it would have made little difference. Montaigne admitted that his titles had little obvious connection with the contents—"often they only denote it by some sign." Yet he also said that, if the title seems random or the thread of his logic seems lost, "some words about it will always be found off in a corner, which will not fail to be sufficient." The "words in the corner" often hide his most interesting themes. He tucks them into exactly those parts of the text that seem most destructively to be breaking up the flow, muddying the waters and making his arguments impossible to follow.

Montaigne's *Essays* initially presented itself as a fairly conventional work: a bunch of blossoms plucked from the garden of the great classical authors, together with fresh considerations on diplomacy and battlefield ethics. Yet, once its pages were opened, they metamorphosed like one of Ovid's creatures into a freak held together by just one thing: the figure of Montaigne. One could hardly defy convention more comprehensively than this. Not only was the book monstrous, but its only point of unity was the thing that should have been vanishing modestly into the background. Montaigne is the book's massive gravitational core; and this core becomes stronger as the book goes on through its subsequent variants, even as it becomes ever more heavily laden with extra limbs, ornaments, baggage, and jumbled body parts.

The 1570s were Montaigne's first great writing decade, but the 1580s would be his big decade as an author. The coming ten years doubled the size of the *Essays*, and took Montaigne from being a nonentity to being a star. At the same time, the 1580s removed him from his quiet position in rural Guyenne, sent him on a long trip around Switzerland, Germany, and Italy as a feted celebrity, and made him mayor of Bordeaux. They enhanced Montaigne's stature as a public figure as well as a literary one. They ruined his health, exhausted him, and made him a man who would be remembered.

14. Q. How to live? A. See the world

THE SUCCESS OF Montaigne's first edition of the *Essays* in 1580 must have changed his way of thinking about life. The acclaim knocked him out of his routine, and perhaps gave him the feeling that it was time to engage with the world again. Although he says little about this in the *Essays*, it may now have occurred to him that an interesting diplomatic career beckoned, and that the best way into it was a bout of international networking. He was also keen to get away from the domestic constraints of the estate, which could be left in his wife's capable hands. Montaigne had always wanted to travel, so as to discover the "perpetual variety of the forms of our nature." Even as a boy, he had felt a great "honest curiosity" about the world—about "a building, a fountain, a man, the field of an ancient battle, the place where Caesar or Charlemagne passed"—everything. Now he imagined walking in the footsteps of his classical heroes, while at the same time exploring the variety of the present world, where he could "rub and polish" his brains by contact with strangers.

Another, less glamorous, reason for traveling existed too. From his father, Montaigne had inherited a propensity to attacks of kidney stones. Having seen Pierre literally pass out from the pain, he was more terrified of this illness than any other. Now, in his mid-forties, he found out for himself what this particular form of torture was like.

Kidney stones form when calcium or other minerals build up in the system and create lumps and crystals which block the flow of urine. They often splinter, creating jagged shards. Whole or split, they must pass through, and, as they do, they produce a sensation that feels like being sliced open from the inside. They also cause general discomfort around the kidneys, stabbing pains in the abdomen and back, and sometimes nausea and fever. Even once they are passed, that is not the end, for they often recur throughout life. In Montaigne's day, they carried a real danger of death each time, either from simple blockage or from infection.

Today, stones can be broken up using sound waves to make the passage easier, but in Montaigne's time one could only hope that the spheres, spikes, needles and burrs would find their own way to the exit. He would try to sluice them out by refraining from urinating for as long as he could, to build up pressure; this was painful and dangerous in itself, but sometimes it worked. He tried other remedies, though he usually distrusted all forms of medicine. Once, he took "Venetian turpentine, which they say comes from the mountains of Tyrol, two large doses done up in a wafer on a silver spoon, sprinkled with one or two drops of some good-tasting syrup." The only effect was to make his urine smell like March violets. The blood of a billy-goat fed on special herbs and wine was supposed to be efficacious. Montaigne tried this, rearing the goat at his estate, but he abandoned the idea on noticing calculi very similar to his own in the goat's organs after it was killed. He did not see how one faulty urinary system could cure another.

The most common remedy for kidney stones was the use of spa waters and thermal baths. Montaigne went along with this too; at least it was a natural method, unlikely to do harm. The spas were often set in attractive environments, and the company was interesting. He tried a couple in France in the late 1570s; the illness returned after each visit, but he was willing to try more. This therefore became another reason to travel, for the resorts of Switzerland and Italy were famous. It had the virtue of being the kind of reason he could easily quote to his wife and friends.

And so, in the summer of 1580, the renowned forty-seven-year-old author left his vines and set off to cure his ailment and see the world, or at least selected areas of the European world. The trip would keep him away until November 1581: seventeen months. He began with trips around parts of France, apparently on business and perhaps collecting instructions for political errands on the journey. It was now that he had his audience with Henri III, and presented him with his *Essays*. After this he turned east and crossed over into German lands, then towards the Alps and Switzerland, and finally to Italy. Had he had his way, the trip might have been longer and he might have ended up anywhere. At one point, he fancied going to

Poland. Instead, he contented himself with the more common goal of
Rome—great pilgrimage site for every good Catholic and every
Renaissance intellectual.

Montaigne did not have the luxury of traveling solo, following personal
whim alone. He was a nobleman of substance, and was expected to support
an unwieldy entourage of servants, acquaintances, and hangers-on, from
whom he tried to escape as often as possible. The group included four
youngsters who came for the educational experience. One was his own
youngest brother, Bertrand de Mattecoulon, still only twenty; the others
were the young husband of one of his sisters and a neighbor's teenage son
with a friend. As the voyage went on, each of these would peel away to take
up various pursuits. The most ill-fated was Mattecoulon, who stayed in
Rome to study fencing and there killed a man in a duel; Montaigne had to
get him rescued from prison.

Traveling was itself something of an extreme sport at the time, not much
less dangerous than dueling. Roads on established pilgrim routes could be
good, but others were rough. You always had to be ready to change your
plans on hearing reports of plague ahead, or of gangs of highwaymen.

Montaigne once altered his route to Rome because of a warning about armed robberies on the road he had intended to take. Some people hired escorts, or traveled in convoy. Montaigne was already in a large group, which helped, but that could attract unwelcome attention too.

There were other irritations. Officials had to be bribed, especially in Italy, which was known for corruption and bureaucratic excess. Throughout Europe, the gates to cities were heavily guarded; you had to arrive with the correct passports, travel and baggage permits, plus properly attested letters stating that you had not recently been through a plague area. City checkpoints often issued a pass to stay at a particular hotel, the proprietor of which had to countersign it. It must have been like traveling in the Communist world at the height of the Cold War, but with greater lawlessness and danger.

Then there were the discomforts of the journey itself. Most traveling was done on horseback. You could go by carriage, but the seats were usually harder on the buttocks than saddles. Montaigne certainly preferred to ride. He would buy and sell horses on the way, or hire them for short stretches. River transport was another option, but Montaigne suffered from seasickness and avoided it. In general, riding gave him the freedom he craved; surprisingly, he also found a saddle the most comfortable place to be during a kidney-stone attack.

What he loved above all about his travels was the feeling of going with the flow. He avoided all fixed plans. "If it looks ugly on the right, I take the left; if I find myself unfit to ride my horse, I stop." He traveled as he read and wrote: by following the promptings of pleasure. Leonard Woolf, roaming Europe with his wife over three centuries later, would describe how she too cruised along like a whale sieving the ocean for plankton, cultivating a "passive alertness" which brought her a strange mingling of "exhilaration and relaxation." Montaigne was the same. It was an extension of his everyday pleasure in letting himself "roll relaxedly with the rolling of the heavens," as he luxuriously put it, but with the added delight that came from seeing everything afresh and with full attention, like a child.

He did not like to plan, but he did not like to miss things either. His secretary, accompanying him and (for a while) keeping his journal for him, remarked that people in the party complained about Montaigne's habit of

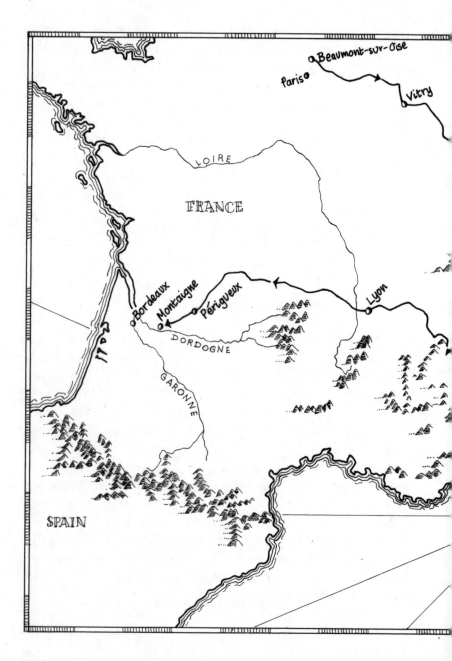

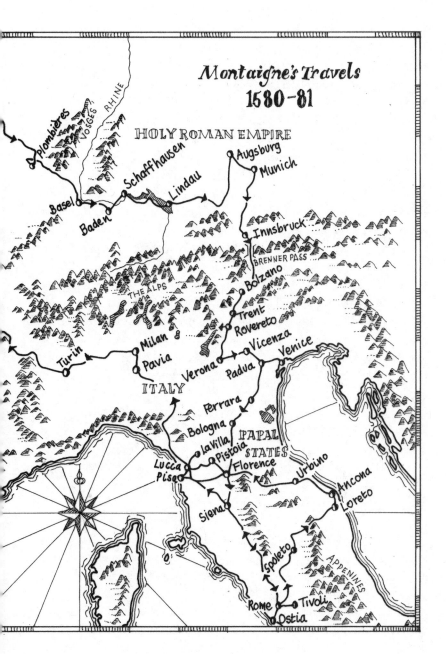

Montaigne's Travels
1580-81

straying from the path whenever he heard of extra things he wanted to see. But Montaigne would say it was impossible to stray from the path: there *was* no path. The only plan he had ever committed himself to was that of traveling in unknown places. So long as he did not repeat a route, he was following this plan to the letter.

The one limit to his energy was that he never liked to start out too early. "My laziness in getting up gives my attendants time to dine at their ease before starting." This accorded with his usual habit, for he always had trouble getting under way in the mornings. On the whole, however, he made a point of shaking up his habits while traveling. Unlike other travelers, he ate only local food and had himself served in the local style. At one point in the trip he regretted that he had not brought his cook with him—not because he missed home cooking, but because he wanted the cook to learn new foreign recipes.

He blushed to see other Frenchmen overcome with joy whenever they met a compatriot abroad. They would fall on each other, cluster in a raucous group, and pass whole evenings complaining about the barbarity of the locals. These were the few who actually noticed that locals did things differently. Others managed to travel so "covered and wrapped in a taciturn and incommunicative prudence, defending themselves from the contagion of an unknown atmosphere" that they noticed nothing at all. In the journal, the secretary observed how far Montaigne himself would err in the other direction, showering exaggerated praise on whichever country they were in while having nary a good word to say for his own. "In truth there entered into his judgment a bit of passion, a certain scorn for his country," wrote the secretary, and added his own speculation that Montaigne's aversion from all things French came from "other considerations"—perhaps a reference to the wars.

His adaptability extended to language. In Italy, he spoke in Italian and even kept his journal in that language, taking over from the secretary. He imitated the chameleon, or octopus, and tried to pass incognito wherever possible—or what he thought was incognito. In Augsburg, wrote the secretary, "Monsieur de Montaigne, for some reason, wanted our party to dissemble and not tell their ranks; and he walked unattended all day long through the town." It did not work. Sitting on a pew in freezing air in

Augsburg's church, Montaigne found his nose running and unthinkingly took out a handkerchief. But handkerchiefs were not used in this area, so he blew his cover along with his nose. Was there a bad smell around? the local people wondered. Or was he afraid of catching something? In any case, they had already guessed he was a stranger: his style of dressing gave him away. Montaigne found this irksome. For once, "he had fallen into the fault that he most avoided, that of making himself noticeable by some mannerism at variance with the taste of those who saw him."

Churches played an important part in Montaigne's tour, not because he was addicted to prayer, but because he was so curious about their practices. He observed the Protestant churches of Germany with as much interest as the Catholic ones of Italy. In Augsburg, he witnessed the christening of a child. On the way out (having already been unmasked as a stranger) he asked many questions about the process. In Italy, he visited synagogues, and "had quite a talk with them about their ceremonies." He also observed a Jewish circumcision, in a private house.

Odd events and human narratives of all kinds appealed to him. In the early stages of the trip, in Plombières-les-Bains in Lorraine, he met a soldier who had a half-white beard and one white eyebrow. The man told Montaigne that both had changed color in a single day when his brother died, because he wept for hours with a hand covering one side of his face. Nearby, in Vitry-le-François, he was regaled with stories about seven or eight girls in the area who had "plotted together" to dress and live as men. One married a woman and lived with her for several months—"to her satisfaction, so they say"—until someone reported the case to the authorities and she was hanged. Another story in the same region concerned a man named Germain who had been a girl until the age of twenty-two, when a set of "virile instruments" popped out one day as he leaped over an obstacle. A folk song arose in the town, warning girls not to open their legs too wide when they jumped in case the same thing happened to them.

Montaigne was fascinated by differences in eating habits—always an obvious point of cultural comparison for any traveler. In Switzerland, goblets were refilled with wine from a distance using a long-beaked vessel, and, after the meat course, everyone tossed their plates into a basket in the middle of the table. People ate with knives, "hardly ever put their hands into the dish," and had minuscule napkins only six inches square, despite their liking for messy sauces and soups. More strangeness awaited in Swiss bedrooms: "Their beds are raised so high that commonly you climb into them by steps; and almost everywhere they have little beds under the big ones."

Everything engaged Montaigne's attention, or that of his secretary, who was writing at his direction. At an inn in Lindau, a cage full of birds ran along one entire wall of the dining room, with alleyways and brass wires so that the birds could hop from one end of the room to the other. In Augsburg, they met a group taking two ostriches on leashes as presents to the duke of Saxony. Montaigne also noticed, in that city, that "they dust their glassware with a hair-duster attached to the end of a stick." And he was intrigued by the city's multiple remote-controlled gates, which closed off chambers in turn like locks in a canal, so that aggressors could not force their way through.

Everywhere they went, they visited fashionable fountains and water gardens, good for hours of sadistic entertainment. In the gardens of the Fugger family in Germany, a wooden walkway leading between two fishponds concealed brass jets primed to spray unsuspecting ladies and gentlemen as they passed. Elsewhere in the same garden, you could press a button to shoot a spout of water into the face of anyone who looked at a particular fountain. A Latin sign in the garden read, "You were looking for trifling amusements; here they are; enjoy them." Apparently Montaigne's party did.

Great art seemed to impress Montaigne less, or at least he says little about it, only occasionally commenting on such works as the "very beautiful and excellent statues by Michelangelo" in Florence. The *Essays* also contain little about visual art. He filled his tower with frescos, so must have had some taste for pictures, yet he seems to have had little desire to write about them—although the paint was barely dry on so much Renaissance art throughout Italy.

This omission was held against him by some later readers of the journal, especially the Romantics, who became its first audience, for the manuscript turned up in a trunk at the château only in 1772. Readers fell on the discovery with excitement, but emerged disappointed with what they found there. Along with a better appreciation of art, eighteenth-century readers would have liked sublime gushings about the beauty of the Alps, and melancholy meditations on the ruins of Rome. Instead, they got a record of Montaigne's urinary blockages interspersed with closely observed, piquant, but non-sublime details about the inns, food, technology, manners, and social practices at each stop. People were less than enthralled to learn, from the secretary, that "the water that Monsieur de Montaigne drank on Tuesday caused him three stools," and that two days later another dose of spa water was effective "both in front and behind." They were no happier when Montaigne himself took over the diary-writing and told them that he had voided a stone "as big and long as a pine nut, but as thick as a bean at one end, and having, to tell the truth, exactly the shape of a prick." The only thing which Swiss and German readers, at least, could enjoy was the fact that the journal was also full of compliments about their lands, especially the well-designed stoves of the Swiss.

The muted response to the work by its first audience seems to have set the tone for its reception ever since; it has always been regarded as a poor cousin to the *Essays*. Yet it makes for a better read than any number of overblown Romantic travelogues, precisely because it remains so tied to detail. It has little beds under big beds, messy Swiss sauces, room-sized birdcages, circumcisions, sex changes, and ostriches: what's not to like?

Another appealing feature of the journal is that it allows the secretary to give us a portrait of Montaigne from the outside—a portrait which turns out to be remarkably consistent with the self-reflective Montaigne of the *Essays*. The reader sees Montaigne exerting himself to shake off all national prejudices, just as one might expect him to. He seems enthusiastic and full of curiosity, but sometimes also selfish, dragging his grumbling entourage off to places they could see no point in visiting. There is even the odd hint that he waffled too much in formal orations, despite (or perhaps because of) his lack of interest in them. In Basel, after Montaigne was subjected to "a long welcoming speech" at dinner, the secretary writes that he gave an equally "long reply." And in Schaffhausen, Montaigne was presented with a gift of wine—"not without several ceremonious speeches on both sides."

There were fewer demands on Montaigne's oratorical powers once they reached Italy, which they did on October 28, 1580. Yet, the closer they came to it, the more he questioned how much he really wanted to go there. This was *the* great destination, the center of European culture; Venice and Rome had called to him all his life. But he now discovered that he preferred less well known places. Had Montaigne had his way, remarked the secretary as they reached the Alps, he might have turned towards Poland or Greece instead, perhaps just to prolong the whole trip. But he met with opposition, and so agreed to follow the Italy route like everyone else. He soon recovered. "I never saw him less tired or complaining less of his pains," wrote the secretary now, "for his mind was so intent on what he encountered, both on the road and at his lodgings, and he was so eager on all occasions to talk to strangers, that I think this took his mind off his ailment."

Venice, one of their first major Italian stops, confirmed his fears about overpopular tourist destinations. As the secretary put it, he found it slightly less wonderful than people said it would be. Still, he explored it with no lack of zest, hiring a gondola and meeting all the interesting people he could find, and he was won over by Venice's bizarre geography, its cosmopolitan population, and its government as an independent republic. It seemed to have some special political magic that other places lacked, engaging in conflicts only when it had something to gain, and maintaining a just government within its own boundaries. Montaigne was also impressed by the way the city's courtesans lived in dignity and luxury, openly maintained by noblemen and respected by all. He met one of the most famous, Veronica Franco, who had recently survived trial at the hands of the Inquisition and had published a book of correspondence, the *Lettere familiari e diversi*, which she personally presented to Montaigne.

After Venice, they traveled through Ferrara, where Montaigne met Tasso, then Bologna, where they watched a fencing demonstration, and Florence, where they visited trick gardens with seats that squirted water at your bottom when you sat down. In another garden, the party "had the very amusing experience" of being squirted with water from "an infinite number of tiny holes," so as to form a shower so fine it was almost a mist.

They carried on, getting ever closer to Rome. On the last day before reaching the city, November 3, 1580, Montaigne was so excited that, for once, he made everyone get up three hours before dawn to travel the last few miles. The road through the outskirts was not promising, all humps and clefts and potholes, but as they went on they glimpsed the first few ruins, and, at last, the great city itself.

The thrill palled a little as they waited to get through the bureaucracy at the gate; their baggage was searched "down to the smallest articles." The officials spent an inordinate amount of time examining Montaigne's books. Rome was the domain of the Pope himself: thought crimes were taken seriously here. They confiscated a book of hours, simply because it was published in Paris rather than Rome, and some Catholic theological works which Montaigne had picked up in Germany. He considered himself lucky that he was not carrying anything more incriminating. Having been unprepared for such a rigorous inspection, he could easily have had truly heretical books on him, since, as the secretary remarked, he was of such an "inquiring nature."

Also taken away for examination was a copy of his own *Essays*. This was not returned to him until March, four months later, and it came back with suggested amendments marked in it. The word "fortune" was flagged up in several places, with other odds and ends. But a Church official later told him that the objections were not serious, and that the French friar who had made them was not even particularly competent. "It seemed to me that I left them well pleased with me," wrote Montaigne in the journal. He duly ignored all the suggestions. Some writers have made much of Montaigne's defiance of the Inquisition, but he did not have to be a Galileo to stand his ground.

Still, these encounters got Montaigne off to a bad start with Rome; he felt its atmosphere was intolerant. Yet it was also cosmopolitan. To be a Roman was to be a citizen of the world, which was what Montaigne wanted to be. He accordingly sought Roman citizenship, an honor which was granted towards the end of his four-and-a-half-month stay. This pleased him so much that he transcribed the document in its entirety in a chapter about vanity in the *Essays*. He realized that "vanity" was the right category, but he did not care. "At all events I received much pleasure in having obtained it."

Rome was so vast and varied that there seemed no limit to the things you could do there. Montaigne could hear sermons or theological disputations. He could visit the Vatican library and, being granted access to areas that had been closed even to the French ambassador, see precious manuscript copies of works by his heroes Seneca and Plutarch. He could watch a circumcision, visit gardens and vineyards, and talk to prostitutes. He tried to learn all the latter's trade secrets, but learned only that they charged a great deal even for conversation, which presumably *was* one of their secrets.

Besides the prostitutes, Montaigne also had an audience with the current octogenarian Pope, Gregory XIII. The secretary described the ritual in detail. First Montaigne and one of his young traveling companions entered the room where the Pope was seated, and knelt to receive a benediction. They sidled along the wall, then cut across towards him; halfway there, they stopped for another benediction. Then they knelt on a velvet carpet at the Pope's feet, beside the French ambassador, who was presenting them. The ambassador knelt too, and pulled back the Pope's robe to expose his right foot, shod in a red slipper with a white cross. The visitors each bent towards this foot and kissed it; Montaigne noted that the Pope lifted his toes a little to make the kiss easier. After this almost erotic performance, the ambassador covered the papal foot again, and rose to deliver a speech about the visitors. The Pope blessed them and said a few words, urging Montaigne to continue in his devotion to the Church. Then he rose to signal their dismissal; they retraced their route across the room in reverse, never turning their backs, and stopping twice to kneel for more benedictions. At last they backed out of the door, and the performance was over. Montaigne had his secretary note, later, that the Pope had spoken with a Bologna accent— "the worst idiom in Italy." He was "a very handsome old man, of middle height, erect, his face full of majesty, a long white beard, more than eighty years old, as healthy and vigorous for his age as anyone can wish, without gout, without colic, without stomach trouble"—quite different from poor suffering Montaigne, and having a sort of family resemblance to God himself. He seemed "of a gentle nature, not very passionate about the affairs of the world," which is either very like or very unlike God, depending on your point of view. Gentle or not, this was the same Pope who had once struck medals and commissioned paintings to celebrate the St. Bartholomew's massacre.

There was no forgetting that Rome was the Pope's city. Montaigne often saw him conducting ceremonies and taking part in processions. In Holy Week, he watched thousands of people pouring towards St. Peter's, carrying torches and scourging themselves with ropes, some as young as twelve or thirteen years old. They were accompanied by men carrying wine, which they sipped and blew over the ends of the scourges to wet the cords and separate them when they became clotted with blood. "This is an enigma that I do not yet well understand," wrote Montaigne. The penitents were cruelly wounded, yet they seemed neither to feel pain nor to be entirely serious about what they were doing. They drank plenty of wine themselves and performed the rite "with such nonchalance that you see them talk with one another about other matters, laugh, yell in the street, run, and jump." As he deduced, most of them were doing it for money: the pious rich had paid them to go through the penance process for them. This mystified him even more: "What do those who hire them do it for, if it is only a counterfeit?"

Montaigne also witnessed an exorcism. The possessed man, who seemed almost comatose, was held down at the altar while the priest beat him with his fists, spat in his face, and shouted at him. Another day, he saw a man hanged: a famous robber and bandit named Catena, whose victims had included two Capuchin monks. Apparently he had promised to spare their lives if they denied God; they did so, risking the loss of their eternal souls, but Catena killed them anyway. Of all the twists Montaigne had yet encountered on the kind of scene that so fascinated him—the vanquished individual who begs for mercy, the victor who decides whether to grant it— this was probably the most unpleasant. At least Catena himself had the courage to die bravely. He made not a sound as he was seized and strangled; then his body was cut into quarters with swords. The crowd were more agitated by the violence done to the dead body, howling at every blow of the sword, than by the execution itself: another phenomenon which puzzled Montaigne, who thought living cruelty more disturbing than anything that could be done to a corpse.

All these were the marvels of modern Rome, but that was not why most sixteenth-century tourists of a humanistic disposition came to the city. They came to absorb the aura of the ancients, and none was more susceptible to this aura than Montaigne, who was almost a native himself. Latin was, after all, his first language; Rome was his home country.

The classical city was very much in evidence all around them, though, for the most part, Montaigne and his secretary did not so much walk *in* the

Romans' footsteps as far above them. So much earth and rubble had built up over the centuries that the ground level had risen by several meters. What remained of the ancient buildings was buried like boots in mud. Montaigne marveled at the realization that he was often on the tops of old walls, something that became obvious only in spots where rain erosion or the wheel ruts uncovered glimpses of them. "It has often happened," he wrote with a shiver of glee, "that after digging deep down into the ground people would come merely down to the head of a very high column which was still standing down below."

This is much less the case today. Excavation has since freed most of the ruins down to their ankles again, and some have been reassembled. Today, the Arch of Severus soars into the air; in Montaigne's day, only the upper part of it emerged. The Colosseum was then a jumble of stone overgrown by weeds. Medieval and early modern buildings had also grown over everything; people built on top of ruins or recycled old materials for new constructions. Slabs of stone kept being repositioned at higher levels, to patch up walls or to form shanties. Some areas had been cleared completely to make way for triumphalist projects such as the brand-new church of St. Peter's. Roman history did not lie in neat strata; it had been repeatedly churned up and rearranged as if by earthquakes.

The result was atmospheric, but it created an impression of ancient Rome to about the extent that a scrambled egg puts one in mind of a freshly laid whole one. In fact, modern Rome had been formed by a similar process to the one Montaigne used to write his *Essays*. Ceaselessly adding quotations and allusions, he recycled his classical reading as the Romans recycled their stone. The similarity seems to have occurred to him, and he once called his book a building assembled from the spoils of Seneca and Plutarch. In the city, as with his book, he thought creative bricolage and imperfection preferable to a sterile orderliness, and took pleasure in contemplating the result. It also required a certain mental effort, which brought further satisfaction. The experience of Rome that resulted was mainly the product of one's own imagination. One might almost as well have stayed at home— *almost*, for there was still something unique about being there.

Such a feeling of hallucinatory strangeness frequently strikes visitors to Rome, partly because everything there is already so familiar to the

imagination long before you see it. Two hundred years later, Goethe would find it at once exhilarating and disorienting. "All the dreams of my youth have come to life," he wrote on his arrival. "The first engravings I remember—my father hung views of Rome in the hall—I now see in reality, and everything I have known for so long through paintings, drawings, etchings, woodcuts, plaster casts, and cork models is now assembled before me." Something similar happened to Freud in Athens when he saw the Acropolis. "So all this really does exist, just as we learned at school!" he exclaimed, and almost immediately thereafter felt the conviction: "What I see here is not real." Montaigne found this meeting between inner and outer versions strange, too, writing of "the Rome and Paris that I have in my soul," which were "without size and without place, without stone, without plaster, and without wood." They were dream-images which he compared to the dream-hare chased by his dog.

Rome would bring Goethe an almost mystical peace: "I am now in a state of clarity and calm such as I had not known for a long time." Montaigne felt this too; despite its touristic frustrations, Italy in general had this effect on him. "I enjoyed a tranquil mind," he wrote a little later, in Lucca. But he

added: "I felt only one lack, that of company that I liked, being forced to enjoy these good things alone and without communication."

Eventually leaving Rome on April 19, 1581, Montaigne crossed the Apennines and headed for the great pilgrimage site of Loreto, joining the crowd pouring in procession behind banners and crucifixes. He left votive figures in the church there, for himself and for his wife and daughter. Then he continued up the Adriatic coast and back across the mountains to a spa at La Villa, where he stayed for over a month to try the waters. As was expected of a visiting nobleman, he hosted parties for locals and fellow guests, including a dance "for the peasant girls" in which he participated himself "so as not to appear too reserved." He returned to La Villa after a detour to Florence and Lucca, and stayed through the height of the summer, from August 14 to September 12, 1581. His pain from the stone was bad, and he came down with toothache, a heaviness in the head, and aching eyes. He suspected that these were the fault of the waters, which ravaged his upper half even as they helped the bottom half, assuming that they even did that. "I began to find these baths unpleasant."

Then, unexpectedly, he was called away. Montaigne, who claimed to want only a quiet life and the chance to pursue his "honest curiosity" around Europe, was issued with a long-distance invitation which he could not refuse.

15. Q. How to live? A. Do a good job, but not too good a job

MAYOR

THE LETTER ARRIVED for Montaigne at the La Villa baths, bearing the full weight of remote authority. Signed by all the jurats of Bordeaux—the six men who governed it alongside its mayor—it informed him that he had been elected, in his absence, to be the next mayor of the city. He must return immediately to fulfill his duties.

This was flattering, but, according to Montaigne, it was the last thing he wanted to hear. The responsibilities would be more onerous than those of a magistrate. Demands would be made on his time. There would be speeches and ceremonies—all the things he had least enjoyed about his progress through Italy. He would need his diplomatic skills, for the mayor's job would mean managing the different religious and political factions in town, and liaising between Bordeaux and an unpopular king. It also meant he had to cut his trip short.

Disillusioned though he was with the spa life, he felt no desire to go home. By now, he had been away for fifteen months—a long time, but not long enough to satisfy him. He seems now to have tried to eke out as many remaining weeks as he could. He did not refuse the jurats' request, but neither did he hurry back to see them. First, he traveled back down to Rome, at a leisurely pace, stopping in Lucca for a while and trying some other baths on the way. One wonders why he went to Rome at all, since it meant going over two hundred miles in the wrong direction. Perhaps he was hoping to get advice on whether he could extricate himself from the task. If so, the answer was discouraging. Arriving in Rome on October 1, he found a second letter from the Bordeaux jurats, this time more peremptory. He was now "urgently requested" to return.

In the next edition of the *Essays*, he emphasized how little he had sought such an appointment, and how strenuously he had tried to avoid it. "I excused myself," he wrote—but the reply came back that this made no difference, since the "king's command" figured in the matter. The king even wrote him a personal letter, obviously intended to be forwarded to him abroad, though Montaigne received it only when he got back to his estate:

> Monsieur de Montaigne, because I hold in great esteem your fidelity and zealous devotion to my service, it was a pleasure to me to understand that you were elected mayor of my city of Bordeaux; and I have found this election very agreeable and confirmed it, the more willingly because it was made without intrigue and in your remote absence. On the occasion of which my intention is, and I order and enjoin you very expressly, that without delay or excuse you return as soon as this is delivered to you and take up the duties and services of the responsibility to which you have been so legitimately called. And you will be doing a thing that will be very agreeable to me, and the contrary would greatly displease me.

It seemed almost a punishment for being so little given to political ambition —assuming that Montaigne's protestations of reluctance were true.

His lack of haste in getting home certainly does not suggest a greed for power. Still taking his time, he meandered towards France via Lucca, Siena, Piacenza, Pavia, Milan, and Turin, taking around six weeks to make the journey. As he crossed into French territory, he switched back from Italian to French in the journal, and when at last he reached his estate he recorded his arrival together with a note that his travels had lasted "seventeen months and eight days"—a rare case of his getting a precise figure correct. In his Beuther diary, he also wrote a note under the date November 30: "I arrived in my house." He then presented himself to the officials of Bordeaux, obedient and ready for duty.

Montaigne would be the city's mayor for four years, from 1581 to 1585. It was a demanding job, but not an entirely thankless one. It came with honors and trappings of all kinds: he had his own offices, a special guard, mayoral robes and chain, and pride of place at public functions. The only thing he lacked was a salary. Yet he was more than a figurehead. Together with the jurats, he had to select and appoint other town officials, decide civic laws, and judge court cases—a task Montaigne found especially difficult to fulfill to his own high standards of evidence. Above all, he had to play the politics game, with care. He had to speak for Bordeaux before the royal authorities, while conveying royal policy downwards to the jurats and other notables of the city, many of whom were set on resistance.

The previous mayor, Arnaud de Gontault, baron de Biron, had upset many people, so another of Montaigne's early tasks was to smooth over the damage. Biron had governed strictly but irresponsibly; he had allowed resentment to develop between various factions, and had alienated Henri of Navarre, the powerful prince of nearby Béarn—a person with whom it was important to maintain good relations. Even Henri III himself had taken offense at Biron's obvious sympathy for the Catholic Leaguists, who were still rebelling against royal authority. Contemplating Biron makes it apparent why the city chose Montaigne to succeed him: they now had a new mayor known for his moderation and diplomatic skills, the very qualities Biron lacked. In particular, although Montaigne was affiliated with the despised *politiques*, he knew how to get on with everyone. He was known as a man who would listen thoughtfully to all sides, whose Pyrrhonian principle was to lend his ears to everyone and his mind to no one, while maintaining his own integrity through it all.

It helped that the years of Montaigne's mayoralty were also technically years of peace. The wars halted from 1580 to 1585, a period spanning Montaigne's traveling years as well as his time in office. But this peace was not easy either, and, as usual, everyone was unhappy with the limited degree of tolerance extended to Protestant worship. Bordeaux was a divided city: its own Protestant minority numbered about one seventh of the population, and it was surrounded by Protestant lands, but it had a powerful Leaguist faction too. It was hard to manage the place at the best of times. These were not the best of times, though they were by no means the worst either, as Montaigne would have been quick to point out.

He shared responsibility for maintaining peace and loyalty with the king's lieutenant-general in the area, a man named Jacques de Goyon, comte de Matignon. An experienced diplomat, eight years older than Montaigne, Matignon may have reminded him somewhat of La Boétie. They did not become intimate friends, but they got on well. Both had a talent for dealing delicately with extremists, and they were men of principle. During the St.

Bartholomew's massacres, Matignon had distinguished himself by being one of the few officials to protect Huguenots in his areas of responsibility, Saint-Lô and Alençon. Calm and firm, he was the right personality for the situation in Guyenne at the moment. So was Montaigne, though he lacked two crucial things: experience and enthusiasm.

Montaigne was anxious to forestall any expectation that he might be a copy of his own father, ruining his health with work. He remembered seeing Pierre worn out by business trips, "his soul cruelly agitated by this public turmoil, forgetting the sweet air of his home." Montaigne's own enthusiasm for traveling declined now that, like his father, he was supposed to do it out of duty. But he could not avoid it, and he did make several trips to Paris, notably in August 1582, when he went to obtain confirmation of the privileges at last fully restored to Bordeaux following the long-ago salt-tax riots. Towards the end of his second term, he became even more peripatetic. Documents show him at Mont-de-Marsan, at Pau, at Bergerac, at Fleix, and at Nérac. He also commuted regularly between Bordeaux and his own château, where, happily, much of his work could be done. While there, he could carry on with his own projects too, and his second, corrected edition of the *Essays* came out in 1582, the year after he took office.

Even if he did not exactly treat it as a full-time job, Montaigne must have performed well in his first term, for he was reelected on August 1, 1583. He could not help feeling pride in this, for it was unusual to be voted in for two terms. "This was done in my case, and had been done only twice before." It did meet opposition, especially from a rival who wanted to be mayor himself: Jacques d'Escars, sieur de Merville, governor of the city's Fort du Hâ. Montaigne did not give in to him, which suggests that he felt more commitment to the job than he had initially professed.

Perhaps he had a change of heart because he had discovered how much of an aptitude he had for political work. With Matignon, he was now responsible for keeping communication going between the officials of the king, the Leaguist rebels in Bordeaux, and the Protestant Henri of Navarre, who wielded more power than ever in the region. Increasingly, through his second term, Montaigne played the role of go-between. He built up particularly good relations with the king's officials and with the Navarre camp. The Leaguists became more difficult, since they rejected compromise with anyone and still seemed determined to maneuver Montaigne out of his job and take over Bordeaux themselves.

The most dramatic rebellion came from the baron de Vaillac, Leaguist governor of the city's Château Trompette. In April 1585, Matignon and Montaigne heard that he was planning a full-scale political coup in the city. They must have debated how to deal with the threat: whether to face up to it aggressively, or make overtures and try to win Vaillac over. It was one of those loggerhead scenes, again. In this case, they decided that bold opposition combined with a willingness to offer mercy was the best response. Presumably with the active collaboration of Montaigne, Matignon invited Vaillac and his men into the *parlement,* then had the exit blocked as soon as the conspirators were inside. Matignon offered the trapped Vaillac a choice between arrest, with a probable death sentence, or giving up his rights even to the Trompette fortress and leaving Bordeaux for good. Vaillac chose the latter. He went into exile, but from just outside the city walls he set about building up League forces as if preparing to attack. That was always the risk of showing your enemies mercy.

Several anxious days followed. On May 22, 1585, Montaigne wrote to Matignon saying that he and other officials in the city were watching the gates, knowing that men were assembled outside. Five days later he wrote that Vaillac was still in the area. Every day brought fifty urgent alarms, he said.

> I have spent every night either around the town in arms or outside of town at the port, and before your warning I had already kept watch there one night on the news of a boat loaded with armed men which was due to pass. We saw nothing.

In the end, there was no attack. Perhaps, seeing the preparations for defense, Vaillac slunk away, proving that Montaigne and Matignon's blend of aggression and sympathy could prevail after all. In any case, the crisis passed. Yet the build-up to war in the region continued, as it did throughout France, and the League continued to resist Montaigne's efforts to establish a middle ground.

Many who knew Montaigne during this period admired his work. The magistrate and historian Jacques-Auguste de Thou wrote that he had "learned many things from Michel de Montaigne, a man free in spirit and foreign to factions, who . . . had great and certain knowledge of our affairs, and especially of those of his own Guienne." The politician Philippe Duplessis-Mornay praised Montaigne's calmness and wrote of him as a person who neither stirred up trouble nor was readily stirred himself.

As generally happened when contemporaries recorded impressions of Montaigne, this fits remarkably well with his assessment of himself. He wrote that his terms in office were characterized most of the time by "order" and by "gentle and mute tranquillity." He had enemies, but he had good friends too. And the solution to the Vaillac crisis suggests that he was capable of decisive action when it was necessary, unless this decisiveness all came from Matignon.

Some did apparently feel that Montaigne was too lax and disengaged, for a certain defensiveness on this point comes across in the *Essays*, in which Montaigne admits that he was accused of showing "a languishing zeal." He looked to some like a typical *politique*, a person who refused to commit himself in any direction. This was clearly true, and Montaigne owned up to it; the difference is that his opponents considered it a bad thing. For modern Stoics and Skeptics such as himself, it was not bad at all. Stoicism encouraged wise detachment, while Skeptics held themselves back on principle. Montaigne's politics flowed from his philosophy. People complain that his terms as mayor passed without much trace, he wrote. "That's a good one! They accuse me of inactivity in a time when almost everyone was convicted of doing too much." With "innovation" (that is, Protestantism) having caused such mayhem, surely it was commendable to have kept a city in a mostly uneventful state for so long. And Montaigne had long since learned that much of what passed for passionate public commitment was just showing off. People involve themselves because they want to have an air of consequence, or to advance their private interests, or simply to keep busy so that they don't have to think about life.

One of Montaigne's problems was that he was so honest about his choices. Other people, far less conscientious than he, were praised because they pretended to be committed and energetic. Montaigne warned his employers that this would not happen with him: he would give Bordeaux what duty commanded, no more and no less, and there would be no play-acting.

Montaigne here sounds remarkably like another great truth-teller in Renaissance literature: Cordelia, the daughter in Shakespeare's *King Lear* who refuses to wax on insincerely about her love for her father as her greedy sisters do to win his favor. Like her, Montaigne remains honest and thus comes across as gruff and indifferent. Cordelia might well have said of herself, as Montaigne did:

> I mortally hate to seem a flatterer, and so I naturally drop into a dry, plain, blunt way of speaking . . . I honor most those to whom I show least honor . . . I offer myself meagerly and proudly to those to whom I belong. And I tender myself least to those to whom I have given myself most; it seems to me that they should read my feelings in my heart, and see that what my words express does an injustice to my thought.

It seems a rebellious position, but Montaigne and Cordelia were not really at odds with their late Renaissance world in this. The virtues of sincerity and naturalness were much admired. Also, by emphasizing his plain-speaking, Montaigne was usefully distancing himself from the accusation constantly made against *politiques*: that they were men of masks and silver tongues who could not be trusted. At times, in the *Essays*, Montaigne can sound like the nightmare vision of a *politique*, equivocal, oversophisticated, secular, and elusive. It did him no harm to be blunt once in a while.

And, by the same kind of twist that made the lack of door locks a good security feature, Montaigne's rough honesty proved a formidable diplomatic talent. It opened more doors than the labyrinthine deceptions of his colleagues ever could. Even when dealing with the most powerful princes in the land—perhaps especially then—he looked them straight in the face. "I frankly tell them my limits." His openness made other people open up as well; it drew them out, he said, like wine and love.

As to the political difficulties of being caught between sides, Montaigne typically belittled these. It is not really difficult to get on when caught between two hostile parties, he wrote; all you have to do is to behave with a temperate affection towards both, so that neither thinks he owns you. Don't expect too much of them, and don't offer too much either. One could sum up Montaigne's policy by saying that one should do a good job, but not *too* good a job. By following this rule, he kept himself out of trouble and remained fully human. He did only what was his duty; and so, unlike almost everyone else, he did do his duty.

He realized that not everyone understood his way of conducting himself. Where his attitude really caused problems was not with his contemporaries but with posterity. Cordelia's choice is vindicated within the play: there is no doubt about her genuine love for her father. Montaigne, on the other hand, has suffered image problems connected with his mayoralty ever since. He knew the dangers of writing too unassumingly about his actions in the *Essays*: "When all is said and done, you never speak about yourself without loss. Your self-condemnation is always accredited, your self-praise discredited." Perhaps the old rule against writing about yourself had something going for it after all.

MORAL OBJECTIONS

Montaigne's circumscribed sense of where his duty lay became most apparent in June 1585, when Bordeaux suffered a heat wave rapidly followed by an outbreak of plague: a particularly destructive combination. The epidemic lasted until December, and during those few months more than 14,000 people died in the city, almost a third of its population. More people were killed than in the St. Bartholomew's massacres across the whole country, yet, as often happens with epidemics occurring in time of war, it left little trace on historical memory. In any case, plague was common. So frequent were outbreaks in the sixteenth century that it is easy to forget how catastrophic they were, each time, for those unfortunate enough to be caught up in them.

As usual, when the first rumors of plague began in Bordeaux that year, anyone who could flee the city did so. Almost no one stayed out of choice, though a few officials remained at their posts. Most of those connected with the *parlement* left, including four out of the six jurats. Matignon wrote to the king on June 30: "The plague is spreading so in this city that there is no one having the means to live elsewhere who has not abandoned it." That was still in the early stages. A month later, Matignon told Montaigne that "every one of the inhabitants has abandoned the city, I mean those who can bring some remedy to it; for as for the little people who have stayed, they are dying like flies."

Matignon apparently did stay, but Montaigne had not been in the city to begin with. He was at home when the plague began, getting ready to travel in for a handover ceremony; his mayoralty was now over, and he was about to be succeeded by Matignon himself. The first of August 1585 was his last official date, so, when Matignon's letter was written on July 30, Montaigne had two days to go. His only task during those two days was apparently to attend the ceremony to mark the election of Matignon. Under present conditions, however, that event would be almost entirely unattended, if it took place at all.

Montaigne now had to decide whether he should go to Bordeaux for the handover or not. His own estate was unaffected by the disease; if he went to Bordeaux now, he would be entering a plague zone purely for the sake of form. What, really, did duty require? Unsure what to do, he traveled as far as Libourne, nearer to the city but outside the danger area. From there, he wrote to the few remaining jurats in town, asking for their advice. "I will spare neither my life nor anything else," he wrote. But he added: "I will leave you to judge whether the service I can render you by my presence at the coming election is worth my risking going into the city in view of the bad condition it is in." Meanwhile, he would wait in the château of Feuillas, just across the river from the city. From Feuillas, he wrote again the following day, repeating his question: what did they recommend?

The jurats' reply, if there was one—if indeed any of them were still there—does not survive. The only certain thing is the outcome, which is that Montaigne did not go to Bordeaux. It seems that they either told him to stay away, or did not answer. Someone must have been at work in the *parlement*, for about this time a new order came into force: it stated that no one who was not already in the city should enter it. Had Montaigne insisted on going in, he would have been contravening this order. Evidently he cleared the matter with his conscience, and returned to his estate. By now, those two days had passed, so his mayoralty was officially over. Instead of ending with a gratifying ceremonial and speeches of thanks, it had petered out in confusion.

No one in Montaigne's own century seems to have commented harshly on his decision. The trouble began two hundred and seventy years later, when nineteenth-century antiquarians discovered the relevant letters in the Bordeaux City Archives, published them, and exposed Montaigne to the judgment of a very different world—a world of stark new ideas about heroism and self-sacrifice.

The researcher responsible for the find, Arnaud Detcheverry, commented that Montaigne's letters displayed his well-known tendency to "nonchalant Epicureanism," and this set the tone for other critics' comments. The early biographer Alphonse Grün thought Montaigne showed a lack of courage in remaining on the safe side of the river. In a lecture course on Grün's book, Léon Feugère said that Montaigne "had the misfortune to forget his duty in the most serious situation." For him, the story discredited Montaigne's entire *Essays*. If the book's author failed at such a moment, how could one trust what he said about how to live? The incident exposed the *Essays'* deepest philosophical failing: their "absolute absence of decision." Other writers agreed. The chronicler Jules Lecomte dismissed Montaigne and his entire philosophy with one word: "coward!"

What they all seemed to find intolerable was not just a lack of personal courage—after all, Montaigne had stayed for over a week by the bed of a man dying from the plague—but his failure to fulfill his *public* duties. Montaigne's cool calculations and written inquiries seemed odious to a generation whose new moral strictness still preserved the lingering whiff of Romanticism. The latter made them feel that one should be prepared to make any sacrifice, however pointless. The former made them long for Montaigne to sacrifice himself in the name of work.

The source of the problem, just as in the seventeenth century, was a distaste for his Skepticism. Nineteenth-century readers were disturbed by it in a way few had been since Pascal. They did not mind Montaigne doubting facts, but they did not like him applying Skepticism to everyday life and showing emotional detachment from agreed standards. The Skeptic *epekho*, or "I hold back," seemed to show an untrustworthiness in his nature. It sounded very much like the greatest bugbear of the new era: nihilism.

Nihilism, for the late nineteenth century, meant godlessness, pointlessness, and meaninglessness. It could be used as code for atheism, but it suggested something even worse: the abandonment of all moral standards. In the end, "nihilist" became almost synonymous with "terrorist." Nihilists were people who, having no God, threw bombs and advocated the destruction of the existing social order. They were a kind of revolutionary wing to the Skeptics' party, or Skeptics turned bad. If they took charge, nothing would be preserved and nothing could be taken for granted.

In the face of this, it suddenly became an urgent task for his remaining defenders to prove, not just that Montaigne had acted reasonably during the plague outbreak, but that he was not a great Skeptic after all. He was, rather, a conservative moralist and a good Christian. One influential critic, Émile Faguet, devoted a series of articles to showing how negligible a role Skepticism played in the *Essays*. Another, Edme Champion, thought Skeptical elements could be detected, but not the kind of destructive Skepticism that "denied" or "annihilated" everything.

The debate took on more significance because, as it happened, the *Essays* had just come off the *Index* in France. It was removed in 1854, just a year or two after the discovery of the first plague letter, though certainly not as a consequence of it. It was a long overdue decision. Despite Church condemnation, Montaigne was now canonical in France and had become the object of a new industry of literary and biographical research. The lifting of the ban raised his profile and opened the way for a larger readership, while intensifying the question of his moral acceptability.

And for many, he became once again what he had been for Pascal and Malebranche: a trickster who was bad for the soul. Guillaume Guizot, who in 1866 called Montaigne a great "seducer," did his best to arm readers against such seduction. Having once fallen under Montaigne's spell himself, he now wrote to guide victims out of the web, like a deprogrammed former cultist who devotes his life to helping others escape.

He listed the dangers in Montaigne, each of which matched up to a specific character defect. Montaigne was weak-willed. He was egotistical. He was not as much of a Christian as he claimed to be. He withdrew from public life for purely selfish reasons, in order to spend more time in contemplation—and not even religious contemplation, which might have been forgivable. When this introspection turned up faults, he did not try to correct them; he accepted himself as he was. He was godless and irresponsible. He is not the kind of writer we need: "He will not make us into the kind of men our times require."

The historian Jules Michelet, one of the toughest critics Montaigne ever had, thought that all this could be blamed on Montaigne's having received too free an education, one designed to produce a merely "feeble and negative" idea of a human being, rather than a hero or a good citizen. Those plangent musical awakenings in his childhood had a lot to answer for. Michelet pictured the adult Montaigne as an invalid who isolated himself in his tower to "watch himself dream"—the inevitable consequence of a decadent, undisciplined upbringing. Over in England, the theologian Richard William Church concluded an otherwise admiring study by opining that Montaigne had too overwhelming a sense of "the nothingness of man, of the smallness of his greatest plans and the emptiness of his greatest achievements"—all a clear indication of nihilism. This made it impossible for him to believe in "the idea of duty, the wish for good, the thought of immortality." In general, he showed "indolence and want of moral tone."

A less serious moral problem also troubled Montaigne's nineteenth-century readers: his openness about sex. (At least, it seems less serious to many of us today.) This was not completely new, but it now became central to the question of his authority as a writer. Even among earlier generations, his talk of buttocks, cracks, and tools had occasionally bothered people. Lord Halifax, the dedicatee of an English translation in the seventeenth century, remarked: "I cannot abide that, after having discoursed of the exemplary life of a holy man, he should immediately talk as he does of cuckoldom and privy-parts, and other things of this nature . . . I wish he had left out these things, that ladies might not be put to the blush, when his *Essays* are found in their libraries." This last part seems ironic, since Montaigne had joked that the risqué parts of his final volume would get his book out of the libraries and into ladies' boudoirs, where he would rather be.

One solution to feminine blushes was the creation of bowdlerized editions, a popular pursuit in the nineteenth century. Abridged versions of the *Essays* had existed for a long time, but the usual aim had been to reorganize the material so that nuggets of wisdom could be more easily located. Now, the feeling was that Montaigne needed intervention on grounds of taste and morals too.

A typical sanitized *Essays* appeared in England in 1800, recast for a female audience by an editor who called herself "Honoria." Her *Essays, Selected from Montaigne with a Sketch of the Life of the Author* took the standard English translation of the day, that of Charles Cotton, and cut it down to produce the perfect Montaigne for the coming century, purged of anything distressing or confusing.

"If, by separating the pure ore from the dross, these Essays are rendered proper for the perusal of my own sex," writes Honoria, "I shall feel amply gratified." The fact that, to do this, she must have pored over the "gross and indelicate allusions" herself passes unacknowledged. She also helps Montaigne with basic writing techniques. "He is also so often unconnected in his subjects, and so variable in his opinions, that his meaning cannot always be developed." Honoria enables him to make himself clearer, and adds footnotes, sometimes to rebuke him (for not mentioning the massacres of St. Bartholomew's Day, for example), and sometimes to warn readers not to try his more dangerous ideas at home. In particular, waking children gently by music is an "eccentric mode of education" which is "by no means here recited, as a method to be recommended."

Her preface creates a Montaigne who sounds intolerably earnest and worthy. "He was desirous that his philosophy should be more than speculation, as he wished to regulate not only his old age, but his whole life, according to its precepts." She emphasizes his political conformism, and draws attention to the "many excellent religious sentiments interspersed in his Essays." Today, this sort of thing would hardly inspire a rush to the bookshops. But Honoria was attuned to the market of the coming nineteenth century, and helped to create for it a frowning, pensive new Montaigne in a starched collar.

Of course, a lot of nineteenth-century readers continued to love the subversive, individualistic, free-as-the-wind version of Montaigne. But the efforts of Honoria and others would increasingly make him acceptable to readers of varied kinds, all chasing Montaignes of their own invention. It made it possible to read Montaigne, not only in the boudoir, or on a Romantic mountaintop, or in the library of a man of the world, but also in a garden, on a summer's day, where you might see a young lady of moral delicacy and innocence perusing Montaigne in bowdlerized octavo. And if she wanted to catch up on the naughty bits, she could always sneak into her father's library later.

MISSIONS AND ASSASSINATIONS

Montaigne is indeed often shocking, but not always in the places where a shock might be expected. He can unsettle the reader most when he seems to be at his mildest, as when he cheerfully says, "I doubt if I can decently admit at what little cost to the repose and tranquillity of my life I have passed more than half of it amid the ruin of my country." It takes a few moments' thought to realize just how unusual it is for anyone to write about life in such terms, in any period of history. One might dismiss such remarks if, indeed, he had always remained passive and tranquil. But in the 1580s Montaigne would be increasingly weighed down by war-related responsibilities, which—however he downplays them in his book—surely took a toll on his peace of mind.

The country had stayed technically at peace through his time as mayor, but by the time he retired again to his estate the Catholic Leagues were doing all they could to provoke another war. By now, the conflict was at least as much political as religious. The biggest political question was who would succeed to the French throne after Henri III. No obvious line of inheritance existed, for he had no son or suitable close relative. The monarchy was up for grabs at a moment of extreme national instability: not a good combination.

Most Protestants, as well as a few Catholics, favored Henri of Navarre, the Protestant prince from Béarn who had so much influence in the Bordeaux area and who was technically first in the royal line—but whom many thought should be disqualified by his religion. His main rival was his uncle,

Charles, cardinal de Bourbon, whose claim was supported by the Leaguists and their powerful leader Henri, duc de Guise. Meanwhile, the king himself was still very much alive, and seemingly uncertain about which successor to endorse. The next stage of the war would become known as the War of the Three Henris, because it revolved around the three-cornered, crazily spinning pinwheel of Henri III, Henri of Navarre, and Henri of Guise.

Politiques, including Montaigne, were committed on principle to supporting the present king whatever he did. But, as a successor, most preferred Navarre, a choice which earned them extra hatred from the Leagues. Catholic extremists thought you might as well put the Devil himself on the throne as have a Protestant king.

As mayor, Montaigne had made attempts to broker an understanding between the two parties. Both politically, as mayor of a Catholic city near Navarre's territory, and personally, as a good diplomat, he was well placed to do this. He met and entertained Navarre from time to time, and made friends with his influential mistress Diane d'Andouins, or "Corisande." In December 1584, Navarre stayed for a few days on Montaigne's estate, at a moment when the king himself was trying to persuade him to abjure Protestantism so as to inherit the throne. Navarre refused. It thus seemed

that one of the few avenues of hope for France might be to persuade Navarre to reconsider this refusal—so Montaigne tried to do just that.

On a personal level, the visit was successful. Navarre trusted his host enough to rely on Montaigne's servants rather than his own, and to eat without having the food tested for poison in the usual way. Montaigne recorded all this in his Beuther diary:

> December 19, 1584. The king of Navarre came to see me at Montaigne, where he had never been, and was here for two days, served by my men without any of his officers. He would have neither tasting nor covered dishes, and slept in my bed.

It was a great responsibility, and guests of this caliber expected to be royally entertained, too. Montaigne organized a hunting trip: "I had a stag started in the forest, which led him a chase for two days." The entertainments went well (though probably not from the stag's point of view), but the diplomatic project did not. A letter from Montaigne to Matignon a month later shows that he was still working on the same task. Meanwhile, Henri III came under pressure from the Leaguists—now very powerful, especially in Paris—to introduce anti-Protestant legislation that would cut Navarre off from the throne altogether. Feeling he had no support in his own city, Henri III gave in to them, and, in October 1585, issued an edict giving Huguenots three months to abjure their faith or go into exile.

If this was an attempt to avoid war, it had the opposite effect. Navarre called on his followers to rise up and resist this new oppression. Henri III passed further anti-Protestant laws the following spring, alienating Navarre further. The king's mother Catherine de' Medici traveled around the country trying, like Montaigne, to engineer a last-minute agreement with Navarre, but she failed too. At last, open war broke out.

This would be the last of the wars, but also by far the longest and worst of them. It lasted until 1598, which meant that Montaigne would never see peace again, since he lived only to 1592. More than ever, in this "trouble," the worst suffering was caused on a local, chaotic level, by lawless bands of soldiers and gangs of starving refugees roaming the countryside, as well as by famine and plague.

Montaigne was in a dangerous position, threatened not only by the anarchy in the countryside but by his old Bordeaux enemies. He seemed to have too many Protestant friends for a good Catholic; he was known for having entertained Navarre, and he had a brother fighting in Navarre's forces. As he put it, he was a Guelph to the Ghibellines and a Ghibelline to the Guelphs—an allusion to the two factions that had divided Italy for centuries. "There were no formal accusations, for there was nothing they could sink their teeth into," he wrote, but "mute suspicions" always hung in the air. Yet he continued to leave his property undefended, sticking to his principle of openness. In July 1586, a Leaguist army of twenty thousand men laid siege to Castillon on the Dordogne, about five miles away; the fighting spread over the borders of Montaigne's estate. Some of the army camped on his land. The soldiers pillaged his crops and robbed his tenants.

At this time, Montaigne had been trying to get back to work on his book, beginning a third volume and inserting additions into existing chapters. It was right in the midst of this that, as he wrote, "a mighty load of our disturbances settled down for several months with all its weight right on me. I had on the one hand the enemy at my door, on the other hand the free-booters, worse enemies . . . and I was sampling every kind of military mischief all at once." In late August, plague broke out among the besieging army. It spread to the local population, and infected Montaigne's estate.

Yet again, he found himself having to decide what to do about the threat of plague. A facile conception of heroic behavior might dictate that he should remain with his tenants in order to suffer and, if necessary, die along-side them, together with his family. But, as before, the reality of the situation was more complicated. Anyone who could avoid remaining in a plague zone would certainly do so. Very few peasants had this option, but Montaigne did, and so he left. He interrupted work on the essay he was writing at the time, "On Physiognomy," and took to the road with his family.

One could say that he was deserting his tenants in doing this. Their predicament must already have been dire before he left, for he wrote in the *Essays* of having seen people dig their own graves and lie down in them to wait for death. Once they had reached this stage, they were beyond rescue. No doubt Montaigne took his valets and personal servants with him, but he could not have taken the whole community of agricultural workers.

When they saw his family packing up and leaving, they must have felt that they were being left to die: probably about what they would expect from their supposed noble protectors. Strangely, by contrast with the savage judgments on his desertion of Bordeaux, there has been almost no criticism of Montaigne on this count. Yet, here too, it is hard to see how he could have done otherwise, and he had a responsibility to his family.

Now converted into homeless wanderers, they would be obliged to stay away for six months, until they heard that the plague had subsided in March 1587. It was not easy to find six months' worth of hospitality. Montaigne knew former colleagues from his years of public life, and both he and his wife had family connections. They were obliged to use all of these. Few people had room for his whole party, though, and of those who did, most looked with horror on plague refugees. Montaigne wrote: "I, who am so hospitable, had a great deal of trouble finding a retreat for my family: a family astray, a source of fear to their friends and themselves, and of horror wherever they sought to settle, having to shift their abode as soon as one of the group began to feel pain in the end of his finger."

During these wandering months, Montaigne also resumed his political activity. Perhaps, in some cases, it was the price he had to pay for accommodation. He played an increasingly major role in attempts by *politiques* and others to defuse the crisis and secure a future for France. Leaving public office in 1570 had allowed him some space to meditate on life; this time was different. His post-mayoral years drew him ever higher into the pyramid of power, towards a realm where the air was thin and the fall could be dangerous. He liaised with some of the most eminent players of the era: first with Henri de Navarre, and now with Catherine de' Medici, mother of the troubled king.

Catherine de' Medici was always a believer in the idea that if everyone could just sit down and talk, problems would go away. She, more than anyone else, did her best to make this happen, and she found Montaigne a natural ally for such a plan. She summoned him to at least one in a series of meetings she held with Navarre at the château of Saint-Brice, near Cognac, between December 1586 and early March 1587. Montaigne brought his wife, and the couple were rewarded with a special allowance for travel expenses and clothes while there. It gave them somewhere to stay, but the pressure must have been intense. Catherine hoped to get a treaty out of these meetings; unfortunately, as so often before, talk proved not to be enough.

The Périgord plague receded during this period, so Montaigne returned with his family to find the château intact but the fields and vines devastated. He resumed work on the essay he had abandoned when he went away, picking up the pen and carrying on with the remark about the mighty load of disturbances. But his political commitments did not abate. That autumn, he met with Corisande, and then, separately, with Navarre, who called on the château in October. Montaigne apparently urged him again to seek compromise with the king. When Navarre went on to see Corisande, she tried to talk him into the same thing. She and Montaigne seem to have cooked up this strategy together: a two-pronged attack. Navarre began to show signs of giving in.

Early in 1588, Montaigne met Navarre again; shortly afterwards, Navarre sent him on a top-secret mission to the king in Paris. Suddenly, everyone in the capital seemed to be talking about this mission and its mysterious hero, so it must have been an important one. The Protestant writer Philippe Duplessis-Mornay discussed it in a letter to his wife. Sir Edward Stafford, English ambassador to France, talked about "Montigny" in his reports, describing him as "a very wise gentleman of the king of Navarre" and later adding that "all the king of Navarre's servants here are jealous of his

coming." Navarre's usual entourage must have felt out of the loop: here was Montaigne on an errand from their leader, yet no one would tell them what was going on. The Spanish ambassador, Don Bernardino de Mendoza, wrote to his king, Philip II, that Navarre's men in Paris "do not know the reason why he has come," and "suspect that he is on some secret mission." A few days later, on February 28, he also alluded to Montaigne's rumored influence over Corisande, adding that Montaigne was "considered to be a man of understanding, though somewhat addle-pated." Stafford mentioned the Corisande connection too. Montaigne, he said, was her "great favorite"; he was also "a very sufficient man," which in the language of the day meant a very capable one. It seems that Montaigne and Corisande had succeeded in maneuvering Navarre into some sort of a compromise, perhaps a preliminary agreement to renounce Protestantism if necessary, and that Montaigne was there to convey this message to the king.

The sensitivity of the affair meant that both the Leaguists and Navarre's Protestant followers had every reason to want to stop Montaigne ever reaching Paris. Indeed, almost everyone seemed to dislike this mission of reconciliation and moderation. Even the English ambassador feared it, for England wished to remain influential over Navarre and did not want him reconverting to Catholicism. The only people who could have felt happy were the king, Catherine de' Medici, and a scattering of *politiques*, ever hopeful for the future of a united France.

It is no wonder, then, that Montaigne's trip did not go smoothly. Shortly after leaving home, while traveling through the forest of Villebois just southeast of Angoulême, his party was ambushed and held up by armed robbers. This was not the incident in which he was freed because of his honest face: that had evidently been a more random attack. This time the motive was political—or such, at least, was his belief. Writing to Matignon about it afterwards, Montaigne said that he suspected the perpetrators were Leaguists wanting to thwart any agreement between their two enemies. Under threat of violence, in the middle of the forest, he was forced to hand over his money, the fine clothes in his coffers (presumably intended for his appearance at the royal court), and his papers, which no doubt included secret documents from the Navarre camp. It was fortunate that they did not finish the job by killing him. Instead he survived and, one presumes, delivered his message safely. Yet, once again, despite all that Montaigne had risked, and despite all the excitement about him, nothing came out of the deal. And things were about to get worse.

The trouble began when the duc de Guise, still the most dangerous of the king's enemies, arrived in the capital in May 1588, shortly after Montaigne. Henri III had banned Guise from the city, so this was an open challenge to royal authority, but Guise knew he had the backing of Paris's rebellious parliamentarians. The king should have responded by having Guise arrested. Instead he did nothing even when Guise called on him in person. The new Pope, Sixtus V, reportedly later commented of this meeting, "Guise was a reckless fool to put himself in the hands of a King whom he was insulting; the King was a coward to let him go untouched." It was another of those delicate balances: here, a stronger party had to decide how far to push a challenge, while the weaker had to decide whether to bow his head or offer resistance.

Henri III proceeded to make the wrong decision three times over. First he did nothing when he should have done something. Then, to compensate, he overreacted. On the night of May 11, he posted royal troops all over the city as if getting ready for all-out battle, possibly even a massacre of Guise's supporters. In alarm and fury, crowds of Leaguists poured out and blocked off streets, ready to defend themselves. What followed became known as the "Day of the Barricades."

Henri III now made his third mistake. He retreated in a panic, showing the very combination of weakness and excess that Montaigne considered disastrous, especially when dealing with a mob. The king pleaded with Guise to calm his supporters; Guise rode through the streets, supposedly to comply with the request but actually stirring up the crowds further. Riots ensued. "I have never seen such a furious debauch of the people," Montaigne's friend Étienne Pasquier wrote in a letter afterwards. It looked like another St. Bartholomew, but there was less killing and, this time, there was a specific goal, which was achieved quickly. By the end of the next day, Pasquier said, "everything had become so quiet again that you would have said it had been a dream." It was not a dream: Paris awoke to a changed reality. The king had fled his city. Slipping out so quietly that hardly anyone noticed, he had gone to Chartres and left Paris to Guise.

Having abandoned his city without a fight, Henri III was now a king in exile. He had virtually abdicated, though his supporters still recognized him as their monarch. Guise ordered him to accept the cardinal de Bourbon as his successor; Henri had no choice but to agree. There was no shortage of people ready to point out to him how this disaster had occurred. He had missed his one chance to take Guise out of the picture, either by arresting him or, more conclusively, by having him killed. Montaigne, still a loyal monarchist, joined the king in Charters. When Henri later moved on to Rouen, Montaigne went too. It is not surprising; the alternative would have been to remain with the Leaguists in Paris, or to back out entirely and go home. He did neither, but eventually he did part company with the king and returned to Paris in July 1588. He was ill at the time, being stricken by gout or rheumatism: an attack so bad that he was bedridden during part of his stay.

He would have expected to be left unmolested there, having probably gone for nothing more seditious than a meeting with his publishers—he had recently finished work on his final volume. But Paris was not the right place for anyone associated with the king. While Montaigne was resting in bed one afternoon, still very unwell, armed men burst in and seized him on League orders. The motive may have been revenge for a recent incident in Rouen, when Henri III had ordered the arrest of a Leaguist in similar circumstances: that at least was Montaigne's theory, as he recorded it in his Beuther diary. They took him, mounted on his own horse, to the Bastille, and locked him up.

In the *Essays*, Montaigne had written of his horror of captivity:

> No prison has received me, not even for a visit. Imagination makes the sight of one, even from the outside, unpleasant to me. I am so sick for freedom, that if anyone should forbid me access to some corner of the Indies, I should live distinctly less comfortably.

To be thrown into the Bastille, especially while ill, was a shock. Yet Montaigne had reason to hope that he would not be there for too long—and he wasn't. After five hours, Catherine de' Medici came to the rescue. She too was now in Paris, hoping as usual to sort out the crisis by getting everyone talking, beginning with Guise, with whom she was in conversation when the news of Montaigne's arrest arrived. She immediately asked Guise to arrange for Montaigne's release. With evident reluctance, he complied.

Guise's orders went off to the commander of the Bastille, but even this did not suffice at first. The commander insisted on having confirmation from the *prévôt des marchands*, Michel Marteau, sieur de La Chapelle, who in turn sent his message of consent via another powerful man, Nicolas de Neufville, seigneur de Villeroy. Thus, in the end, it took four powerful people to get Montaigne freed. His own understanding of it was that he was "released by an unheard-of favor" and only after "much insistence" from Catherine de' Medici. She must have liked him; the duc de Guise probably didn't, but even he could see that Montaigne deserved special consideration.

Montaigne stayed in Paris for just a short while after this. The pain in his joints receded, but another illness struck him soon after. It was probably an attack of kidney stones, a condition from which he still suffered with little respite, and which he had so often feared might kill him. On this occasion, it nearly did. His friend Pierre de Brach described the episode some years later, in a highly Stoic-flavored letter to Justus Lipsius:

> When we were together in Paris a few years ago, and the doctors despairing of his life and he hoping only for death, I saw him, when death stared him in the face from close up, push her well away by his disdain for the fear she brings. What fine arguments to content the ear, what fine teachings to make the soul wise, what resolute firmness of courage to make the most fearful secure, did that man then display! I never heard a man speak better, or better resolved to do what the philosophers have said on this point, without the weakness of his body having beaten down any of the vigor of his soul.

Brach's account is conventional, but it does suggest that Montaigne had, to some extent, come to terms with his mortality since the days of his riding accident. He had been through a great deal since then, and his kidney-stone attacks had forced him into close encounters with death on a regular basis. These, too, were confrontations on a battlefield. Death was bound to prove the stronger party in the end, but Montaigne stood up to it for the moment.

While recuperating, Montaigne went to see a new friend he had met in Paris the previous year: Marie de Gournay, an enthusiastic reader of his work who invited him to stay with her family at her château in Picardy. This provided a welcome resting place. In the meantime, the new edition of the *Essays* had come out, and already he was thinking of new additions he would like to make to it, perhaps in the light of his recent experiences. He began adding notes to the freshly printed copy, sometimes alone, sometimes with secretarial help from Gournay and others.

Once he was fully recovered, around November of that year, Montaigne moved on to Blois, where the king was attending a meeting of the national legislative assembly known as the Estates-General, together with Guise. The aim was supposed to be further negotiation, but Henri III had gone beyond that. A king without a kingdom, he was feeling desperate. And he had spent six months listening to advisers remind him that it could all have been different had he wiped Guise out when he had the chance.

Now, with Guise in the Blois castle with him, the opportunity arose again and Henri decided to correct his mistake. On December 23, he invited Guise to his private chamber for a talk. Guise agreed, although his advisers warned him that it was dangerous. As he entered the private room beside Henri III's bedchamber, several royal guardsmen leaped out from hiding places, slammed the door behind him, and stabbed him to death. Once again, to the shock even of his own supporters this time, the king had gone

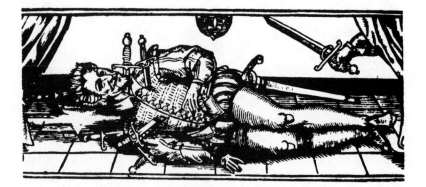

from one extreme to another, bypassing Montaigne's zone of judicious moderation in the middle.

Although Montaigne had come to Blois to join the king's entourage, there is no suggestion that he knew anything about the murder plot. In the days before the incident, he had been rather enjoying himself, catching up with old friends such as Jacques-Auguste de Thou and Étienne Pasquier— although the latter had the irritating habit of dragging Montaigne off to his room to point out all the stylistic errors in the latest edition of the *Essays*. Montaigne listened politely, and ignored everything Pasquier said, just as he had done with the officials of the Inquisition.

Pasquier, more emotionally volatile than Montaigne, fell into a black depression when he heard about the killing of Guise. "Oh, miserable spectacle!" he wrote to a friend. "I have long been nurturing a melancholic humor within me, which I must now vomit into your lap. I fear, I believe, that I am witnessing the end of our republic . . . the king will lose his crown, or will see his kingdom turned completely upside down." Montaigne was not given to such dramatic talk, but he too must have felt shocked. The worst of it, for a *politique*, was that this cold-blooded and mistimed killing threw serious doubt on the moral status of the king, whom the *politiques* considered the focus for all hopes of stability.

Henri III had apparently thought a surgical strike would end his troubles, rather like Charles IX in the run-up to the St. Bartholomew's massacres. Instead, the death of Guise radicalized Leaguists further, and a new revolutionary body in Paris, the Council of Forty, pronounced Henri III tyrannical. The Sorbonne inquired of the Pope whether it were theologically permissible to kill a king who had sacrificed his legitimacy. The Pope said not, but Leaguist preachers and lawyers argued that any private person who felt suffused with zeal and called to the task by God could do the deed anyway. "Tyrant" was the word always in the air, but, unlike La Boétie in *On Voluntary Servitude*, the preachers did not call for passive resistance and peaceful withdrawal of consent. They unleashed a fatwa. If Henri was the Devil's agent on earth, as a flood of propaganda publications now proclaimed, killing him was a holy duty.

The agitation in Paris in 1589 overflowed into every aspect of life. Protestant chronicler Pierre L'Estoile wrote of a city gone mad:

For today, to mug one's neighbor, massacre one's nearest relatives, rob the altars, profane the churches, rape women and young girls, ransack everybody, is the ordinary practice of a Leaguer and the infallible mark of a zealous Catholic; always to have religion and the mass on one's lips, but atheism and robbery in one's heart, and murder and blood on one's hands.

Signs and portents sprang forth everywhere; even Montaigne's usually level-headed friend Jacques Auguste de Thou saw a snake with two heads emerge from a woodpile, and read omens into it. Just when the situation looked as if it could get no worse, Catherine de' Medici died, on January 5, 1589. With his mother gone, Henri III was alone, protected from the hatred around him only by his underpaid troops and those *politiques* who felt obliged to stay on his side as a matter of principle.

As always, it was the *politiques* who attracted everyone else's distrust. It did not help matters for someone like Montaigne to point out, in cool and measured tones, that the League and the radical Huguenots had now become virtually indistinguishable from each other:

> This proposition, so solemn, whether it is lawful for a subject to rebel and take arms against his prince in defense of religion—remember in whose mouths, this year just past, the affirmative was the buttress of one party, the negative was the buttress of what other party; and hear now from what quarter comes the voice and the instruction of both sides, and whether the weapons make less din for this cause than for that.

As for the idea of holy assassination, how could anyone think that killing a king would get one to heaven? How could salvation come from "the most express ways that we have of very certain damnation"? At some point during this period, Montaigne lost what remained of his taste for politics. He left Blois around the beginning of 1589. By the end of January, he was back in his estate and his library. There, he remained active, liaising with Matignon—still lieutenant-general of the area as well as the new mayor of Bordeaux—but he appears to have sworn off diplomatic traveling from now on. Ironically, just after he gave up, Henri III and Navarre did at last come to the long-awaited *rapprochement*. They joined forces and prepared to besiege the capital in the summer of 1589.

But this was yet another of the king's mistakes. The Leaguists in the city realized that, with the armies assembling in camps outside their gates, Henri III was within their reach. A young Dominican friar named Jacques Clément received God's command to act. Pretending to carry a message from secret supporters in the city, he came to the camp on August 1 and was admitted to see the king, who was sitting on the toilet at the time—a common way for royals to receive visitors. Clément pulled out a dagger and just had time to stab the seated king in the abdomen before he himself was killed by the guards. Slowly, over several hours, Henri bled to death. One of his last acts was to confirm Navarre as his heir, though he repeated the condition that Navarre return to the Catholic Church.

News of the king's death was greeted with jubilation in Paris. In Rome, even Pope Sixtus V praised Clément's action. Navarre agreed, at last, to revert to Catholicism. At first, some Catholics still refused to recognize him, especially members of the Paris *parlement*, who insisted that Bourbon was their king. For a while, there were two different realities, depending on which side you were on. But slowly, patiently, Navarre won out. He became the undisputed king of France as Henri IV: the monarch who would eventually find a way of ending the civil wars and imposing unity, mostly through sheer power of personality. He was the king the *politiques* had always hoped for.

Having always had a friendly relationship with Navarre, Montaigne would now find himself drawn again into a semi-official role as adviser to Henri IV—an astonishingly outspoken adviser, as it turned out. Montaigne wrote to Henri to offer his services, as etiquette demanded; Henri responded on November 30, 1589, by summoning Montaigne to Tours, the temporary location of his court. The letter either traveled very slowly, or Montaigne let it sit on the mantelpiece for a long while, for his answer is dated January 18, 1590—too late to obey the command. Allegiance was all right in theory, but Montaigne was determined not to travel, especially as his health was now worse than ever. He explained to the king that, alas, the letter had been delayed; he repeated his congratulations, and said that he looked forward to seeing the king win further support.

This part of the letter was conventional enough, but then Montaigne added some tougher advice. Still speaking with formal deference, he told the new king that he should have been less indulgent recently to the soldiers in his army. He should impose his authority but, at the same time, make conquests through "clemency and magnanimity," since these are better lures for winning people over than threats. The king must be strong, but he must also show trust in people, and be loved rather than feared.

He wrote another letter on September 2, after Henri had again asked Montaigne to travel, this time to go to see Matignon. He offered to pay Montaigne's expenses. But, again, Montaigne waited for a leisurely six weeks before replying, then claimed to have only just received the letter. He had in fact written to Matignon three times already, proposing to visit him, he said, but Matignon had not sent an answer. Perhaps, suggested Montaigne, Matignon wished to spare him the dangers and length of the journey, considering "the length and hazard of the roads." The hint is clear: Henri IV ought to show the same consideration. Montaigne also took umbrage at the offer of money.

> I have never received any gift whatsoever from the liberality of kings, any more than I have asked it or deserved it; and I have received no payment for the steps I have taken in their service, of which Your Majesty has had partial knowledge. What I have done for your predecessors I will do still more willingly for you. I am, Sire, as rich as I wish to be. When I have exhausted my purse with Your Majesty in Paris, I will make bold to tell you so.

This seems an astonishingly assertive way to talk to a king—but Montaigne was aging and ill (he had a fever at the time), and he had been close to the king for long enough to speak openly. In the *Essays*, he wrote: "I look upon our kings simply with a loyal and civic affection, which is neither moved nor removed by private interest . . . This is what makes me walk everywhere head high, face and heart open." His letter to Henri IV shows that he was as good as his word. Indeed, he comes across in both letters exactly as he does in the *Essays*: blunt, unimpressed by power, and determined to preserve his freedom.

Montaigne may have detected the first signs of what was to become a feature of Henri IV's reign: the king's tendency to make a cult of himself.

He was strong, which was what the country needed after its series of feeble and self-indulgent kings, but he was not subtle. Short speeches and quick, decisive action were his style. Instead of washing regularly and using forks to eat with, like Henri III, he was filthy, the way a real man should be, and reportedly stank like rotting meat. He had charisma. Montaigne liked the idea of a strong king, but he had no love for mystique. In the *Essays*, he wrote of Henri IV with judicious approval rather than mindless devotion; similar reservations come across in his letters. And he won this particular battle, for he never did travel to join Henri IV.

In early 1595, too late for Montaigne to know about it, Henri IV successfully managed to start a war against an external enemy, Spain, and thus begin to drain off the energies of the civil wars, which ended at last in 1598. France started to build up a real collective identity, though still a fragile one, mostly centered on the person of Henri himself. Many were passionately loyal to him, but others hated him just as passionately. He too was eventually assassinated, stabbed to death by the fanatical Catholic François Ravaillac in 1610.

Among his contributions to history was the Edict of Nantes, proclaimed on April 13, 1598, which guaranteed freedom of conscience and some freedom of worship to both sides of the religious divide. Unlike earlier conciliatory treaties, this one succeeded, for a while. From being the land worst afflicted by religious differences, France became the first Western European country formally to recognize two different forms of Christianity. In a speech to *parlement* on February 7, 1599, Henri made it clear that the edict was not based on a weak desire to please, as previous ones had been, and should not be taken as a license to cause trouble. "I shall nip in the bud all factions and all seditious preaching; and I shall behead all those who encourage it."

Imposed so forcefully, with the kind of forthright confidence Montaigne would have appreciated, the Edict of Nantes endured for almost a century, until 1685, when its revocation sent a wave of Huguenot refugees to England and other places. Among these were many Montaigne readers, including Pierre Coste, the man whose samizdat edition of the *Essays* would eventually sneak back home across the Channel and promote a revolutionary new Montaigne to his troubled countrymen.

16. Q. How to live? A. Philosophize only by accident

FIFTEEN ENGLISHMEN AND AN IRISHMAN

STRANGELY, THROUGHOUT THE century leading up to Montaigne's rebranding by Coste in 1724—a period in which the *Essays* had a hard time in France—the English never ceased to admire him. They were the first outside France to adopt Montaigne, and they came to consider him almost one of their own. Something in the English mentality put them instantly on the same wavelength; forever more they continued to chime harmoniously on that wavelength in apparent indifference to intellectual changes going on elsewhere.

It seems worth pausing the story of Montaigne's "afterlife" for a moment (running alongside the main life story, and currently suspended in the mid-nineteenth century, a chapter ago) to take a quick tour through several hundred years of his fortunes on the other side of the Channel—a place to which he seems never to have thought of traveling, and where he would have been most surprised to find himself taken in as a refugee, especially since it was a Protestant country.

Religion was one of the reasons why many English readers, from the late seventeenth century on, felt so free to enjoy Montaigne. It was of no concern to English Protestants when the Church put his book on the *Index*. It even allowed them to enjoy the pleasant feeling of getting one up on Catholics and, more gratifyingly still, on the French. The latter could be portrayed as a people unable to recognize their own best writers, especially after the French Académie began imposing rigorous standards of classical elegance on all its literature. A "free and unruly" writer (as Montaigne described himself) had no place in the new French aesthetics, but the English language welcomed him like a prodigal son. As the exuberant and anarchic home of Chaucer and Shakespeare, English seemed the right language for such an author. Lord Halifax, a dedicatee of one seventeenth-century edition, observed that to translate Montaigne "is not only a valuable acquisition to us, but a just censure of the critical impertinence of those French scribblers who have taken pains to make little cavils and exceptions to lessen the reputation of this great man, whom nature hath made too big to confine himself to the exactness of a studied style." And the essayist William Hazlitt managed to squeeze Montaigne, as well as Rabelais, into a piece called "On Old English Writers and Speakers." He justified their inclusion thus: "But these we consider as in a great measure English, or as what the old French character inclined to, before it was corrupted by courts and academies of criticism."

If they liked the *Essays'* style, English readers were even more charmed by its content. Montaigne's preference for details over abstractions appealed to them; so did his distrust of scholars, his preference for moderation and comfort, and his desire for privacy—the "room behind the shop." On the other hand, the English also had a taste for travel and exoticism, as did Montaigne. He could show unexpected bursts of radicalism in the very midst of quiet conservatism: so could they. Much of the time he was happier watching his cat play by the fireside—and so were the English.

Then there was his philosophy, if you could call it that. The English were not born philosophers; they did not like to speculate about being, truth, and the cosmos. When they picked up a book they wanted anecdotes, odd characters, witty sallies, and a touch of fantasy. As Virginia Woolf said *à propos* Sir Thomas Browne, one of many English authors who wrote in a Montaignean vein, "The English mind is naturally prone to take its ease and pleasure in the loosest whimsies and humors." This is why William Hazlitt praised Montaigne in terms guaranteed to appeal to an unphilosophical nation:

> In taking up his pen he did not set up for a philosopher, wit, orator, or moralist, but he became all these by merely daring to tell us whatever passed through his mind, in its naked simplicity and force.

On one of the rare occasions when Montaigne referred to himself as a philosopher at all, it was to say that it happened only by chance: he was an "unpremeditated and accidental philosopher." He spent so many pages rambling through his thoughts that he was bound to blunder into some great classical theory here and there. The practical philosophy of how to live interested him, but that was different. All this, on the whole, applied equally to the English.

Much of his success there, however, may have been a matter of happy chance rather than deep affinity, as befits an accidental man. The *Essays* happened to find an excellent English translator from the beginning, in a man named John Florio. This made all the difference.

The fact that Florio should have been the first to bring out the hidden Englishman in Montaigne is all the more remarkable because he himself was a multicultural wanderer of a most un-English sensibility. He is usually described as an Italian, although his mother was English and he was born in London in 1553, so he was English more than anything else. But he had an Italian father, Michele Agnolo Florio, a language tutor and author who had come to England as a Protestant refugee many years earlier. When the Catholic Mary Tudor came to the throne, the Florio family found themselves in exile again, and drifted around Europe, which is how the young John picked up so many languages. Once more in England as an adult, he made his name by teaching French and Italian, and by publishing a series of conversational primers as well as a successful English–Italian dictionary.

He translated the *Essays* on the urging of a rich patron, the Countess of Bedford, who also supplied him with a horde of friends and collaborators to help with tracing quotations and promoting the book. Florio repaid the help with ornate dedications, in some cases so elaborate that the dedicatees could hardly have made head or tail of them. A sentence from his epistle to the Countess of Bedford reads:

> So do hir attributes accord to your demerites; whereof to runne a long-breathed careere, both so faire and large a field might envite mee, and my in-burning spirits would encite mee, if I were not held-in by your sweete reining hand (*who have ever helde this desire, sooner to exceede what you are thought, then be thought what you are not*) or should I not prejudice by premonstration your assured advantage, *When your value shall come to the weighing.*

This was typical of what happened when Florio was left to run on unchecked. Like Montaigne, he wrote by exuding ever more complex

thoughts as a spider exudes silk. But while Montaigne always moves forward, Florio winds back on himself and scrunches his sentences into ever tighter baroque spirals until their meaning disappears in a puff of syntax. The real magic happens when the two writers meet. Montaigne's earthiness holds Florio's convolutions in check, while Florio gives Montaigne an Elizabethan English quality, as well as a lot of sheer fun. Where Montaigne writes, "Our Germans, drowned in wine" (*nos Allemans, noyez dan le vin*), Florio has "our carowsing tospot German souldiers, when they are most plunged in their cups, and as drunke as Rats." A phrase which the modern translator Donald Frame renders calmly as "werewolves, goblins, and chimeras" emerges from Floriation as "Larves, Hobgoblins, Robbin-good-fellowes, and other such Bug-beares and Chimeraes"—a piece of pure *Midsummer Night's Dream*.

Shakespeare and Florio did know one another, and Shakespeare was among the first readers of the *Essays* translation. He may even have read parts in manuscript before it went to press; signs of Montaigne seem faintly discernible in *Hamlet*, which predates Florio's edition. A much later play, *The Tempest*, contains one passage so close to Florio that there can be no doubt of his having read it. Eulogizing his vision of a perfect society in the state of nature, Shakespeare's Gonzalo says:

> I'th' commonwealth I would by contraries
> Execute all things, for no kind of traffic
> Would I admit; no name of magistrate;
> Letters should not be known; riches, poverty,
> And use of service, none; contract, succession,
> Bourn, bound of land, tilth, vineyard, none;
> No use of metal, corn, or wine, or oil;
> No occupation, all men idle, all.

Which is remarkably like what Montaigne says about the Tupinambá, in Florio's translation:

> It is a nation . . . that hath no kind of traffike, no knowledge of Letters, no intelligence of numbers, no name of magistrate, nor of politike superioritie; no use of service, of riches, or of povertie; no contracts, no successions, no partitions, no occupation but idle; no respect of kindred, but common, no apparell but naturall, no manuring of lands, no use of wine, corn, or mettle.

Ever since this obvious parallel was spotted by Edward Capell in the late eighteenth century, it has become a popular sport to hunt out signs of influence in other Shakespeare plays. The most promising is certainly *Hamlet*, for its hero often sounds like a Montaigne given a dramatic dilemma to solve and set upon a stage. When Montaigne writes, "We are, I know not how, double within ourselves," or describes himself with the incoherent torrent of adjectives "bashful, insolent; chaste, lascivious; talkative, taciturn; tough, delicate; clever, stupid; surly, affable; lying, truthful; learned, ignorant, liberal, miserly, and prodigal," he could be voicing a monologue from the play. He also observes that anyone who thinks too much about all the circumstances and consequences of an action makes it impossible to do anything at all—a neat summary of Hamlet's main problem in life.

The similarities may just be because both writers were attuned to the atmosphere of their shared late-Renaissance world, with all its confusion and irresolution. Montaigne and Shakespeare have each been held up as the first truly *modern* writers, capturing that distinctive modern sense of being unsure where you belong, who you are, and what you are expected to do. The Shakespearean scholar J. M. Robertson believed that all literature since these two authors could be interpreted as an elaboration of their joint theme: the discovery of self-divided consciousness.

The parallels cannot be taken too far. For one thing, Shakespeare was a dramatist rather than an essayist. He can divide his contradictions between characters and put them into conflict on stage; Montaigne must contain all contradictions within himself. Another difference is that Montaigne does not sit all alone on top of the canon in his native land as Shakespeare does in England. He has therefore attracted less jealousy, and no iconoclasts have come to push him off his pedestal by claiming that he did not write his own *Essays*, as has so often happened with Shakespeare.

Or almost no one. Among the few exceptions is one of the major nineteenth-century "anti-Stratfordians," or Shakespeare-doubters: Ignatius Donnelly. At the end of a large opus arguing that Francis Bacon wrote Shakespeare's plays, Donnelly adds extra chapters proving that Bacon also wrote Montaigne's *Essays*, as well as Robert Burton's *Anatomy of Melancholy* and all of Christopher Marlowe's work. He finds clues planted throughout the *Essays*, such as a passage in which Montaigne writes, "Whoever shall cure a child of an obstinate aversion to bread, *bacon,* or garlic, will cure him of all kind of delicacy." The name Francis occurs several times in the text, admittedly always in the French form François and generally denoting the French king François I. No matter; this too is a clue. To clinch matters, Donnelly cites a discovery made by a Mrs. Pott, who alerted him to the frequent mention, in Shakespeare's plays, of mountains, or *Mountaines*. Since Bacon wrote Shakespeare, any reference to Montaigne in the plays must suggest that he wrote the *Essays* too. "Can anyone believe that all this is the result of accident?" asks Donnelly.

He confesses himself baffled by some sections of the *Essays* that seem pregnant with clues, but which are harder to interpret, notably the story of a young woman who beat her white breasts after her brother was slain. Donnelly gives up:

Who is the young lady? There is nothing more about her in the text. And is it the white breasts that have slain her brother? . . . And where did the bullet come from? Was it from the white breasts? It is all nonsense . . . And there are hundreds of such passages.

The *Essays'* being in French might seem to pose a problem—but not for Donnelly. His explanation is that Bacon wanted to publish a book of skeptical, religiously unorthodox opinions, yet dared not do so in England, so he arranged for it to appear in the guise of a translation. As luck would have it, Francis Bacon's brother Anthony was in France at the time and knew Montaigne. He persuaded Montaigne to lend his name to the ruse, while someone else persuaded Florio to play the part of translator. Thus, Bacon wrote it; Montaigne signed it; Florio, presumably, actually translated it—but from English to French. "Montaigne" was indeed an Englishman, in a more literal way than Lord Halifax or William Hazlitt ever dreamed of.

One aspect of the story has some basis in fact: Anthony Bacon did know Montaigne, and visited him twice, once in the early 1580s and again in 1590. He could easily have brought a copy of the *Essays* back for his brother, which means that Francis could have read it (in French) before publishing his own collection of *Essays* in 1597. That would explain something that has often puzzled people: how did Bacon and Montaigne come up with the same book title within a few years of each other?

It must be said, however, that the title is almost the only point of similarity. All the qualities that suggest "Englishness" in Montaigne are resoundingly absent from his English counterpart. Bacon wrote with more intellectual rigor than Montaigne. He was more incisive, more philosophical, and a lot more boring. When he tackled subjects like reading or traveling, he issued orders. *This* is what you should read, and *that* is what you must visit on a journey. If ever a subject allowed of division into subtopics, he would so divide it, and he would announce each subdivision in advance before marching through them till he got to the end. One thing you can be sure of with Montaigne is that he will never do this to you.

Once the ice had been broken by Florio and Bacon, innumerable English books appeared with the word *Essays* in their title. Some were overtly inspired by Florio's Montaigne, others by Bacon, but in almost every case it was from Montaigne that they took their style of writing and thinking. Very few English essays after the early seventeenth century were philosophically rigorous stabs of thought on important topics; almost all were delightful rambles about nothing in particular. Typical were the works of William Cornwallis, who read Florio in an early manuscript draft and published sequences of *Essayes* in 1600, 1601, 1616 and 1617, exploring such topics as "Of Sleepe," "Of Discontentments," "Of Fantasticknesse," "Of Alehouses," and "Of the Observation, and Use of Things."

Even those who did not use the title often wrote in a recognizably digressive, personal way. While French literature became ever more poised and formal, England produced a series of oddballs such as Robert Burton, who described his way of writing, in his vast treatise *The Anatomy of Melancholy*, as coursing "like a ranging spaniel, that barks at every bird he sees." Even stranger was Sir Thomas Browne, who produced essayistic investigations into medicine, gardens, burial methods, imaginary libraries, and much more in a convoluted baroque style so unlike anyone else's (even Florio's) that any Browne sentence is instantly recognizable as his.

At the height of this high-quirkiness phase of Montaigne's English reception, a new translator came along to straighten things out a little: Charles Cotton, whose new version appeared in 1685 and 1686, not long after the *Essays* went on the *Index* in France. Cotton was more accurate than Florio, and he brought a new generation of English readers to the *Essays*. Surprisingly, the author of this more restrained translation was personally a more wayward and dilettantish character than Florio. Cotton's main claim to fame in his own day was his scatological burlesque poems. He once described himself as a "Northern clod" whose favorite occupation was drinking ale in the pub all evening before retiring to his library to

> Write lewd epistles, and sometimes translate
> Old Tales of Tubs, of Guyen[n]e, and Provence,
> And keep a clutter with th'old Blades of France.

After his death, Charles Cotton's posthumous reputation went through transformations as strange as those of Montaigne or Shakespeare, though on a smaller scale. The nineteenth century considered his comic verse

obnoxious, and admired him instead for lyrical nature poetry which his own contemporaries had ignored. Later, this too slipped into obscurity. People celebrated him rather for a chapter on trout-tickling which he had contributed to Isaac Walton's *The Compleat Angler*—a highly Montaignean work in itself. Today this relic of Cotton is forgotten in most quarters—though not among trout-ticklers—and he is remembered as much for his Montaigne work as anything.

Cotton's remained the standard translation of the *Essays* for over two centuries, and it brought Montaigne to a new breed of less baroque writers, more interested in capturing the psychological realities of everyday life than spinning webs of fantasy. The poet Alexander Pope noted in his copy of Cotton, "This is (in my Opinion) the very best Book for Information of Manners, that has been writ; This Author says nothing but what every one feels att the Heart." A piece in the literary magazine the *Spectator* praised Montaigne's habit of weaving personal experiences and qualities into his book, a practice that might be self-indulgent but was entertaining. As the French critic Charles Dédéyan remarked, the English were happy to let a writer go on about himself, so long as he did it agreeably.

From now on, there would be no shortage of English personal essayists doing just that. They were all of what the critic Walter Pater called "the true family of Montaigne": they showed "that intimacy, that modern subjectivity, which may be called the *Montaignesque* element in literature." Among them was the popular essayist Leigh Hunt, who filled his copy of the *Essays* with underlinings and marginal comments—often rather fatuous. When Montaigne tells a story about seeing a boy lacking hands who wielded a heavy sword and cracked a whip as well as any cart-driver in France, Hunt carefully writes in the margin: "With his arms, of course. Still it is very surprising."

An intellectually sharper admirer was William Hazlitt: he who praised Montaigne for not setting up for a philosopher. Hazlitt's assessment of what makes a good essayist exemplifies what the English now tended to look for in Montaigne. Such writers, says Hazlitt, collect curiosities of human life just as natural history enthusiasts collect shells, fossils, or beetles as they stroll along a forest path or seashore. They capture things as they really are rather than as they should be. Montaigne was the finest of them all because he allowed everything to be what it was, including himself, and he knew how to *look* at things. For Hazlitt, an ideal essay

takes minutes of our dress, air, looks, words, thoughts, and actions; shews us what we are, and what we are not; plays the whole game of human life over before us, and by making us enlightened spectators of its many-colored scenes, enables us (if possible) to become tolerably reasonable agents in the one in which we have to perform a part.

In other words, the essay is the genre that—more than any novel or biography—helps us to learn how to live.

Hazlitt's son, also called William Hazlitt, would edit Cotton's translation together with copies of Montaigne's letters, his Italian travel journal, and a brief biography, to produce a *Complete Works* in 1842. This became the standard edition in Britain over the coming years; it was revised yet again by *his* son in 1877—producing Hazlitt's Hazlitt's Cotton's Montaigne. Between them, the Hazlitts defined the English Montaigne even more lastingly than Florio. This new Montaigne was loved, above all, for those Hazlittesque virtues: his alertness to everyday life as it really was, and his ability to write pleasingly about it without formal literary constraints.

This tradition has continued, from the nineteenth century through the twentieth, and it looks set to carry on into the twenty-first. Every era has produced fresh English Montaigneans; the tradition continues today through the countless ephemeral essayists and weekend newspaper columnists who, knowingly or not, keep the "Montaignesque element in literature" alive.

Of all Montaigne's cross-Channel heirs, the one who deserves the last word is an Anglo-Irishman: Laurence Sterne, eighteenth-century author of *Tristram Shandy.* His great novel, if it can be so classified, is an exaggerated Montaignesque ramble, containing several explicit nods to its French predecessor, and filled with games, paradoxes, and digressions. Dedications and prologues, which ought to be at the beginning, appear all over the place in the wrong order. "The Author's Preface" turns up in volume 3, chapter 20. At one point, a blank page is supplied, so readers can contribute a picture of a character according to their own imagination. Another page presents a series of line diagrams purporting to summarize the pattern of the book's digressions so far.

The book teeters constantly on the edge of dissolution. Whatever plot

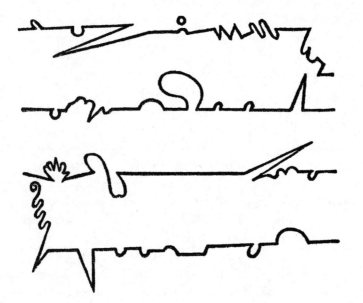

had appeared to be promised at the outset evaporates; the breaks and detours in the narrative take over entirely. "Have I not promised the world a chapter of knots?" Sterne reflects at one point. "Two chapters upon the right and the wrong end of a woman? a chapter upon whiskers? a chapter upon wishes?—a chapter of noses?—No, I have done that:—a chapter upon my uncle Toby's modesty: to say nothing of a chapter upon chapters, which I will finish before I sleep." It is like Montaigne on speed.

But of course, says Sterne, no story that really pays attention to the world as it is could be otherwise. It cannot go straight from its starting point to its destination. Life is complicated; there is no one track to follow.

> Could a historiographer drive on his history, as a muleteer drives on his mule,—straight forward;—for instance, from Rome all the way to Loretto, without ever once turning his head aside either to the right hand or to the left,—he might venture to foretell you to an hour when he should get to his journey's end;—but the thing is, morally speaking, impossible: For, if he is a man of the least spirit he will have fifty deviations from a straight line to make.

Like Montaigne on his Italian trip, Sterne cannot be accused of straying from his path, for his path *is* the digressions. His route lies, by definition, in whichever direction he happens to stray.

Tristram Shandy started an Irish tradition that would reach its most extreme point with James Joyce's *Finnegans Wake*, a novel which divides into offshoots and streams of association over hundreds of pages until, at the end, it loops around on itself: the last half-sentence hooks on to the half-sentence with which the book began. This is much too tidy for Sterne, or for Montaigne, who avoided neat wrap-ups. For both of them, writing and life should be allowed just to flow on, even if that means branching further and further into digressions without ever coming to any resolution. Sterne and Montaigne both engage constantly with a world which always generates more things to write about—so why stop? This makes them both accidental philosophers: naturalists on a field trip into the human soul, without maps or plans, and having no idea where they will end up, or what they will do when they get there.

17. Q. How to live? A. Reflect on everything; regret nothing

SOME WRITERS JUST *write* their books. Others knead them like clay, or construct them by accumulation. James Joyce was among the latter: his *Finnegans Wake* evolved through a series of drafts and published editions, until the fairly normal sentences of the first version—

Who was the first that ever burst?

became weird mutants—

Waiwhou was the first thurever burst?

Montaigne did not smear his words around like Joyce, but he did work by revisiting, elaborating, and accreting. Although he returned to his work constantly, he hardly ever seemed to get the urge to cross things out, only to keep adding more. The spirit of repentance was alien to him in writing, just as it was in life, where he remained firmly wedded to *amor fati*: the cheerful acceptance of whatever happens.

This was at odds with the doctrines of Christianity, which insisted that you must constantly repent of your past misdeeds, in order to keep wiping clean the slate and giving yourself fresh beginnings. Montaigne knew that some of the things he had done in the past no longer made sense to him, but he was content to presume that he must have been a different person at the time, and leave it at that. His past selves were as diverse as a group of people at a party. Just as he would not think of passing judgment on a roomful of acquaintances, all of whom had their own reasons and points of view to explain what they had done, so he would not think of judging previous versions of Montaigne. "We are all patchwork," he wrote, "and so shapeless and diverse in composition that each bit, each moment, plays its own game." No overall point of view existed from which he could look back and construct the one consistent Montaigne that he would have liked to be. Since he did not try to airbrush his previous selves out of life, there was no reason for him to do it in his book either. The *Essays* had grown alongside him for twenty years; they were what they were, and he was happy to let them be.

His refusal to repent did not stop him rereading his book, however, and frequently adding to it. He never reached the point where he could lay down his pen and announce, "Now, I, Montaigne, have said everything I wanted to say. I have preserved myself on paper." As long as he lived, he had to keep writing. The process could have gone on forever:

> Who does not see that I have taken a road along which I shall go, without stopping and without effort, as long as there is ink and paper in the world?

The only thing that stopped him at last was his death. As Virginia Woolf wrote, the *Essays* came to a halt because they reached "not their end, but their suspension in full career."

Some of this continuing labor may have been in response to encouragement by publishers. The early editions had sold so well that the market for new, bigger, and better ones was obvious. And Montaigne had plenty to add in 1588, after his Grand Tour and his experiences as mayor. He wrote even more in the years after that, when new thoughts must have come to mind following his disturbing experiences at the court of the refugee king: not necessarily thoughts to do with French current affairs, but to do with moderation, good judgment, worldly imperfections, and many of his other favorite themes.

The title page of the 1588 edition, which was published by the prestigious Paris firm of Abel L'Angelier rather than his earlier Bordeaux publisher, presented the work as "enlarged by a third book and by six hundred additions to the first two." This is about right, but it underplays the real extent of the increase: the 1588 *Essays* was almost twice as long as the 1580 version. Book III added thirteen long chapters, and, of the existing essays in the first two books, hardly any remained untouched.

The new Montaigne of 1588, which hit the world as the real Montaigne was trailing around after Henri III and planning his recuperation with his new friend Marie de Gournay in Picardy, showed a startling new degree of confidence. As befitted someone who rejected the notion of undoing his sins, he was unrepentant about the digressive and personal nature of the book. Nor did he hesitate to make demands on anyone who entered his world. "It is the inattentive reader who loses my subject, not I," he wrote now, of his tendency to ramble. The pretense of writing for family and friends alone disappeared; he knew what he had, and scorned any notion of diluting it, hiding it, or streamlining it to fit convention.

A more private kind of writerly self-doubt sometimes afflicted him, all the same. He could not pick the book up without being thrown into creative confusion. "For my part, I do not judge the value of any other work less clearly than my own; and I place the *Essays* now low, now high, very inconsistently and uncertainly." Each time he read his own words, this mixture of feelings would assail him—and further thoughts would well up, so out would come his pen again.

As the publisher must have expected, the 1588 *Essays* found an eager market, although some of the readers who had devoured the 1580 edition as a compendium of Stoic wisdom were taken aback by what they found now. Voices of dissent began to be heard. Was Montaigne, perhaps, getting a little *too* digressive; a little too personal? Was he telling us too much about his daily habits? Was there any relation at all between the titles of his chapters and the material contained within them? Were his revelations about his sex life really necessary? And, as his friend Pasquier suggested when they were together in Blois, might he have lost his grasp of the language itself? Did he realize that his writing was full of odd words, neologisms and colloquial Gasconisms?

Whatever uncertainties Montaigne harbored, none of this touched him greatly. If such criticisms led him to revise anything, it was usually to make it more digressive, more personal, and more stylistically exuberant. During the four years of life that remained to him after the publication of the 1588 *Essays*, he continued like this, adding fold upon fold, crag upon crag.

Having given himself a free rein with his 1588 edition, he now galloped away completely. He added no more chapters, but he did insert about a

ESSAIS DE M. DE MONTA.

sent. A tant dire, il faut qu'ils dient, & la verité & le mensonge ne les estime de rien mieux, pour les voir tôber en quelque rencontre. Ce seroit plus de certitude s'il y avoit regle &
verité à mentir tousiours. I'ay veu par fois à leur dômage, au-
cunes de noz ames principesques s'arrester à ces vanitez. Le
demon de Socrates estoit à mon advis certaine impulsion de
volôté, qui se presentoit à luy, sans le Conseil de son discours.
En vne ame bien espuree, côme la sienne, & preparee par cô-
tinuel exercice de sagesse & de vertu, il est vray semblable
que ces inclinations, quoy que fortuites, estoyent tousiours
bonnes & dignes d'estre suyuies. Chacun a en soy, quelque
image de telles agitations. I'en ay eu ausquelles ie me laissay
emporter si vtilement & heureusement, qu'elles pourroyent
estre iugées, auec quelque chose d'inspiration diuine.

De la Constance. CHAP. XII.

LA Loy de la resolution & de la côstance, ne porte pas
que nous ne nous deuions couurir, autant qu'il est en
noftre puissance, des maux & inconueniens qui nous
menassent; ny par consequét d'auoir peur qu'ils nous surpreig-
nent. Au rebours, tous moyens honnestes de se garentir des
maux, sont non seulement permis, mais loüables. Et le ieu de
la constance se ioüe principalement à porter patiemment, &
de pié ferme, les inconueniens, où il n'y à point de remede. De
maniere qu'il n'y à souplesse de corps, n'y mouuemét aux ar-
mes de main, que nous trouuions mauuais, s'il sert à nous ga-
rantir du coup qu'on nous rue. Toutes-fois aux canonades,
depuis qu'on leur est planté en bute, comme les occasions de
la guerre portent souuent, il est messeant de s'esbráler pour la
menasse du coup; d'autant que pour sa violéce & vitesse nous
le tenons ineuitable, & en y à meint vn, qui pour auoir ou
haussé la main, ou baissé la teste, en a pour le moins apprefté à.

thousand new passages, some of which are long enough to have made a whole essay in the first edition. The book, already nearly twice its original size, now grew by another third. Even now, Montaigne felt that he could only hint at many things, having neither time nor inclination to be thorough. "In order to get more in, I pile up only the headings of subjects. Were I to add on their consequences, I would multiply this volume many times over." As he had said of Plutarch, "He merely points out with his finger where we are to go, if we like." Freedom is the only rule, and digression is the only path.

On the title page of one of the copies he worked on, Montaigne wrote the Latin words *viresque acquirit eundo,* from Virgil: "It gathers force as it proceeds." This might have referred to how well his book had been doing commercially; more likely, it described the way it had collected material by rolling like a snowball down a hill. Even Montaigne apparently feared that he was losing control of it. When he gave his friend Antoine Loisel a copy of the 1588 edition, his inscription asked Loisel to tell him what he thought of it—"for I fear I am getting worse as I go on."

It is true that the *Essays* was beginning to strain at the limits of comprehension. One can sometimes make out the skeleton of the first edition through the tangle, especially in those modern editions which supply small letters to mark out the three stages: A for the 1580 edition, B for 1588, and C for everything after that. The effect can be that of glimpsing the outlines of a Khmer stone temple through a mass of tropical foliage. One can only wonder what a "D" layer might have been like. Had Montaigne lived another thirty years, would he have gone on adding to it until it became truly unreadable, like the artist in Balzac's "Unknown Masterpiece" who works his painting into a meaningless black mess? Or would he have known exactly when to stop?

There is no way of answering this, but it seems that, at the time of his death, he did not think he had reached that limit yet. His last years of work resulted in at least one heavily annotated copy, which—once it had passed into the hands of his posthumous editor—became the foundation of almost all later Montaigne *Essays.* This editor was none other than that unusual young woman who had entered his life in Paris just as he was finishing his 1588 edition: Marie de Gournay.

18. Q. How to live? A. Give up control

DAUGHTER AND DISCIPLE

MARIE LE JARS DE Gournay, Montaigne's first great editor and publicist—a St. Paul to his Jesus, a Lenin to his Marx—was a woman of extreme enthusiasm and emotion, all of which she uninhibitedly threw at Montaigne on their first meeting in Paris. She became by far the most important woman in his life, more important even than his wife, mother, and daughter, that formidable triad in the Montaigne household. Like all of them, she would outlive him: not surprising, in her case, since she was thirty-two years his junior. They met when Montaigne was fifty-five, and she was twenty-three.

Marie de Gournay's life started, in 1565, with many similarities to Montaigne's and two crucial differences: she was a woman, and she had less money. Her family, minor provincial nobles, lived partly in Paris and partly at the Picardy château and estate of Gournay-sur-Aronde, which her father bought in 1568. In adulthood, Marie took her last name from this estate. Such a right was normally reserved for sons, but it was typical of her to ignore this rule. She was always determined to claim more from life than her sex and status should have allowed.

In 1577, her father died. This was a personal blow for her and a disaster for the family. Without his income and management, their lives fell to pieces. Existence in Paris was even more expensive than in Picardy, so they gave up the city life almost entirely. By 1580, Marie was confined to a provincial world. It did not suit her much, but—now a stubborn teenager—she did what she could to educate herself using the books in the family library. By reading Latin works alongside their French translations, she gave herself the best classical grounding she could. The result was a patchy knowledge, unsystematic but deeply motivated.

Montaigne might have approved of such an anarchic education—in theory. In practice, one cannot imagine him being content with what Marie de Gournay had, and it would have left him with less confidence in himself.

Montaigne could afford to be offhand about learning and wry about his father's awe of books. Gournay took pride in her attainments because she had had to fight for them, and it was always easy to put her on the defensive. She often felt she was being laughed at. Yes, she said, of course people thought it funny to meet

> a woman pretending to learning without formal schooling, because she instructed herself in Latin by rote, aided by setting the translations side by side with the originals, and who therefore would not dare to speak the language for fear of making a false step—a learned woman who cannot unequivocally guarantee the meter of a Latin verse; a learned woman without Greek, without Hebrew, without aptitude for providing scholarly commentary on authors.

Gournay's tone remained angry and troubled all her life. In her *Peincture de moeurs*, a self-portrait in verse, she described herself as a tangle of intellect and emotion, unable to hide her feelings; her writing bears this out.

The same mixture emerges in what she tells us of her first encounters with Montaigne, first on the page and then in person. Sometime in her late teens, apparently by chance, she came across an edition of the *Essays*. The experience was so shattering that her mother thought she had gone mad: she was on the point of giving the girl hellebore, a traditional treatment for insanity—or so Gournay herself says, perhaps exaggerating for effect. Gournay felt she had found her other self in Montaigne, the one person with whom she had a true affinity, and the only one to understand her. It was the experience so many of his readers have had over the years:

How did he know all that about me? (Bernard Levin)

It seems he is my very self. (André Gide)

Here is a "you" in which my "I" is reflected; here is where all distance is abolished. (Stefan Zweig)

Gournay longed to meet Montaigne in person, but when she made inquiries, the rumor came back that he was dead. Then, when she was in Paris with her mother some years later, in 1588, she heard that he was alive after all. Not only that, but everyone was talking about him, for this was the time of his secret mission between Navarre and the king. At the height of this drama, Marie de Gournay boldly sent Montaigne an invitation to call on her family: an unorthodox thing for a young woman of her position to do, to a man of superior class and age who was currently the talk of the town. Evidently charmed by her chutzpah, and never the man to resist flattery from a young woman, Montaigne accepted the invitation and called on her the next day.

According to Marie de Gournay's account, this meeting must have been emotionally intimate, though probably not physically so, for at the end of it he chastely invited her to become an adoptive daughter to him—an offer she leaped at. She says no more, so one can only imagine the conversation that led up to this. Did she rave at him about her feeling of "affinity"? Did she tell him the hellebore story? It would be in character for her to spill

everything out in an incoherent torrent. In a late addition to the *Essays*,
Montaigne describes an odd episode which apparently occurred at one of
their later meetings. He saw a girl—and added remarks make it clear that it
was Gournay—

> to show the ardor of her promises, and also her constancy, strike
> herself, with the bodkin she wore in her hair, four or five lusty stabs
> in the arm, which broke the skin and made her bleed in good earnest.

Whether or not such self-mutilating intensity characterized their first
meeting, one at least suspects that Marie de Gournay did most of the
talking. The father–daughter idea was probably more hers than his. Perhaps
he even attempted to take sexual advantage of her enthusiasm, and was
persuaded to accept the adoptive relationship instead. From the first
moment of reading the *Essays*, Gournay had felt that they were spiritually of
the same family; now it became official. Montaigne would replace her lost
father, and she would be welcomed into his own small entourage of women
whom he did not quite understand.

Even if he agreed to play her *père d'alliance* mainly to humor her, he did
not then brush her off. Marie's invitation to stay with her mother and
herself in the Picardy countryside gave him a welcome opportunity to

recuperate from his illness, well away from Parisian political demands and any likelihood of being arrested again. It also gave him an opportunity to work. He and his new daughter settled down almost immediately to the job of adding revisions to the 1588 *Essays*. This must have thrilled her; her fantasy was never one of wrapping Montaigne in a shawl and nursing him peacefully into old age. She wanted him to write, so that she could be his apprentice. Her presence probably helped make this happen; having someone so enthusiastic at his side would have encouraged Montaigne to get back to the *Essays* almost immediately after publication, and to keep at it even after leaving Picardy. It set the tone for his last few years of writing.

In return, Marie de Gournay could never be accused of underplaying her *alliance*. When she came to write the preface to his posthumous *Essays*, she signed herself as Montaigne's adoptive daughter, and described him as the man "whom I am so honored in calling Father." She added: "I cannot, Reader, use another name for him, for I am not myself except insofar as I am his daughter." In another work of her own she wrote:

In truth, if someone is surprised that, although we are not father and

daughter except in title, the good will that allies us nevertheless surpasses that of real fathers and children—the first and closest of all the natural ties—let that person try one day to lodge virtue within himself and to meet with it in another; then he will scarcely marvel that it has had more strength and power to harmonize souls than nature has.

What Montaigne's real daughter Léonor thought of this claim to surpass biological family bonds is anyone's guess. One could not blame her if she felt put out, but it seems she did not. She and Marie de Gournay became good friends in later years, with Gournay calling her "sister," as was only logical if they had the same father. When Marie de Gournay wrote of "surpassing," she was probably thinking of the intensity of her own communion with Montaigne rather than of snubbing a rival. The one person she does seem to have felt in competition with was the long-dead La Boétie, with whom she did not hesitate to compare herself. Her dedication finished with a quotation from La Boétie's verse: "Nor is there any fear that our descendants will grudge to enroll our name among those renowned for friendship, if only the fates are willing." And in the *Essays'* preface, she wrote, "He was mine for only four years, no longer than La Boétie was his."

The same passage also contains a strange, and perhaps revealing, remark about Montaigne: "When he praised me, I possessed him." And evidently he did praise her. Her edition of the *Essays* includes some lines in which Montaigne speaks of her as a beloved *fille d'alliance* whom he loves with more than a fatherly love (whatever that means), and cherishes in his retirement as part of his own being. He goes on:

> She is the only person I still think about in the world. If youthful promise means anything, her soul will some day be capable of the finest things, among others of perfection in that most sacred kind of friendship which, so we read, her sex has not yet been able to attain. The sincerity and firmness of her character are already sufficient, her affection for me more than superabundant, and such, in short, that it leaves nothing to be desired, unless that her apprehension about my

end, in view of my fifty-five years when I met her, would not torment her so cruelly.

Finally, he speaks warmly of her sound judgment of the *Essays*—"she a woman, and in this age, and so young, and alone in her district"—and of "the remarkable eagerness with which she loved me and wanted my friendship."

These sentences have fallen under suspicion over the years, since they appear only in Gournay's edition and not in the alternative, personally annotated version of his final *Essays* known as the "Bordeaux Copy." It is only natural to wonder whether she made them up. The tone seems more Gournay than Montaigne and, intriguingly, she herself deleted sections of this passage in a later edition. On the other hand, the Bordeaux Copy contains traces of adhesive in the place where these lines occur, together with a little cross in Montaigne's hand—his usual symbol to indicate an insertion. A pasted-in slip could have fallen out on one of the occasions when the copy was rebound in the seventeenth and eighteenth centuries. Whether the passage is genuine or not, there seems no reason to doubt the affection Montaigne felt for his disciple, bodkins, hellebore, and all.

After that first year, however, with the burst of work in Picardy, he and Gournay kept in touch only by letter. In April 1593, Gournay told another of her literary friends, Justus Lipsius, that she had not met Montaigne for almost five years. Yet they did correspond regularly, for by the time of her letter to Lipsius she was concerned because Montaigne had not written for six months. She was right to worry. Montaigne had died during that time, and a final message sent to her via one of his brothers had not arrived. Lipsius had to break the news to her in his reply. He did it gently, adding, "since he whom you called father is no longer of this world, accept me as your brother." She replied in shock: "Sir, as others fail to recognize my face today, I fear that you will not recognize my style, so utterly has the loss of my father changed me. I was his daughter, I am his tomb; I was his second being, I am his ashes."

By now, she was going through difficult times in other ways too. Her mother died in 1591 and Marie inherited major family debts as well as responsibility for her younger siblings. Determined not to enter a loveless marriage for money, she set out to live purely by writing—a tough path, almost unprecedented for a woman. For the rest of her life, she wrote about any subject she thought might sell—analyses of poetry and style, feminism, religious controversy, the story of her own life—and used all the literary connections she could find. Justus Lipsius was one of the writers she sought out to help her promote her work. But none was more important than the mentor with whom her name would always remain linked: Montaigne.

Skillful use of his reputation brought about her first big breakthrough when, in 1594, she published a novel entitled *Le Proumenoir de Monsieur de Montaigne* (The Promenade of Monsieur de Montaigne). The contents had nothing to do with him at all, apart from the fact that—as she wrote in the dedicatory epistle—it had been inspired by a story she had told him one day as they strolled in her family's garden. In fact the *Proumenoir*'s exotic romp of a narrative was stolen almost entirely from a book by another author. It did extremely well, and paved the way for the book which really began Gournay's career: her great definitive edition of the *Essays*, published in 1595.

The idea of her becoming Montaigne's editor and literary executor apparently arose only after his death, when his widow and daughter found one of his annotated copies of the 1588 edition among his papers. They sent it to Gournay in Paris, so that she might publish it. Perhaps they only wanted her to deliver it to a suitable printer, but she interpreted it as a major editorial commission and set to work. It proved a huge task, one so difficult that it still overwhelms editors more experienced and well equipped than she. To this day, no one can agree about it, so many are the variants, so complex the text, and so great the work of identifying all Montaigne's references and allusions. Yet Gournay did the job brilliantly. Perhaps she yielded to temptation in adding those suspicious lines about herself, or perhaps they were genuine, but on the whole she was more meticulous about accuracy than most editors of her time. Surviving copies of the book's first printing show that she continued to make last-minute ink corrections even while sheets were coming off the press, as well as after publication—a sign of how much she cared about getting everything right.

From now on, she would be less a daughter to Montaigne than an adoptive mother to his *Essays*. "Having lost their father," she wrote, "the *Essais* are in need of a protector." She put the book together, but she also

championed it, defended it, promoted it, and—in this first edition—
equipped it with a long, combative preface which set out to defeat any hint
of criticism in advance. Most of her arguments were rational and tightly
constructed, but she seasoned them with plenty of emotion. Against those
who considered his style vulgar or impure, she wrote, "When I defend him
against such charges, I am full of scorn." And, concerning the allegation that
he wrote in a disorganized manner: "One cannot deal with great affairs
according to small intelligences . . . Here is not the elementary knowledge
of an apprentice but the Koran of the masters, the quintessence of
philosophy."

Nor was she satisfied if people praised the *Essays* faintly. "Whoever says
of Scipio that he is a noble captain and of Socrates that he is a wise man does
them more wrong than one who does not speak of them at all." You cannot
write in measured tones about Montaigne: "Excellence exceeds all limits."
(So much for Montaigne's idea of moderation.) You must be "ravished," as
she had been. On the other hand, you should be able to say *why* you have been
ravished: to compare him point by point to the ancients and show exactly
where he is their equal, and where their superior. The *Essays* always seemed
to Gournay the perfect intelligence test. Having asked people what they
thought of the book, she deduced what she should think of them. Diderot
would make almost the same observation of Montaigne in a later century:
"His book is the touchstone of a sound mind. If a man dislikes it, you may
be sure that he has some defect of the heart or understanding."

But Marie de Gournay had the right to expect a great deal from her
readers, for she was an excellent reader of Montaigne herself. For all her
excesses, she had an astute grasp of why the *Essays* were fit to place among
the classics. At a time when many persisted in seeing the book mainly as a
collection of Stoic sayings—a valid interpretation so far as it went—she
admired it for less usual things: its style, its rambling structure, its
willingness to reveal all. It was partly Gournay's feeling that everyone
around her was missing the point that created the long-lasting myth of a
Montaigne somehow born out of his time, a writer who had to wait to find
readers able to recognize his value. Out of an author who had made himself
very popular while barely seeming to exert himself, she made Montaigne
into a misunderstood genius.

Gournay was happy to acknowledge that she remained in Montaigne's shadow: "I cannot take a step, whether in writing or speaking, without finding myself in his footsteps." In reality her own personality comes through loud and clear, often in ways that are at odds with his. When she extols Montaignean virtues such as moderation, she does it in her crashingly immoderate way. Advocating the arts of Stoic detachment and of slipping quietly through life, she does it emotionally and abrasively. This makes her edition a fascinating wrestling match between two writers, just as happens with Montaigne and Florio, or even Montaigne and La Boétie, in the first stirrings of the conversation that became the *Essays*.

In many ways, this was a literary partnership of the same sort, but very much complicated by the fact of Marie de Gournay's being a woman. It annoyed her that it was never taken as seriously as other such relationships—and neither was she. Ridicule followed her through life; she never found a way of shrugging it off. Instead, she raged. Some of this rage finds its way into the *Essays'* preface: the writer sometimes seems to reach right through the page to grab male readers by the lapels and berate them. "Blessed indeed are you, Reader, if you are not of a sex that has been forbidden all possessions, is forbidden liberty, has even been forbidden all the virtues." The most fatuous men are listened to with respect, by virtue of their beards, yet when she ventures a contribution everyone smiles condescendingly, as if to say, "It's a woman speaking." Had Montaigne been subjected to such treatment, he might have responded with a smile too, but Gournay did not have this gift. The more she let her anger show, the more people laughed. Yet this sense of strain and anguish makes her a compelling writer. The preface is not just the earliest published introduction to Montaigne's canonical work; it is also one of the world's first and most eloquent feminist tracts.

This may seem odd for a text introducing Montaigne, who was not obviously a great feminist himself. But Gournay's feminism remained closely tied to her "Montaignism." Her belief that men and women were equal—neither being superior to the other, though different in experience and situation—was in tune with his relativism. She took inspiration from his insistence on questioning received social assumptions, and his willingness to leap between different people's points of view. For Gournay, if men could exert their imagination to see the world as a woman sees it, even for a few minutes, they would learn enough to change their behavior forever. Yet this leap of perspective was just what they never seemed to manage.

Shortly after publication, alas, Gournay had second thoughts about her blistering preface. By this time she was staying on the Montaigne estate, as a guest of Montaigne's widow, mother, and daughter, who had apparently taken her in out of friendship, loyalty, or sympathy. From their home, she wrote to Justus Lipsius on May 2, 1596, saying that she had written the preface only because she was overwhelmed by grief at Montaigne's death, and that she wished to withdraw it. Its excessive tone, she now said, was the result of "a violent fever of the soul." Shortly after this, sending copies to publishers in Basel, Strasbourg, and Antwerp, she axed the preface and replaced it with a brief, dull note just ten lines long. The original stayed in Gournay's bottom drawer, and parts of it resurfaced in a different form in a 1599 edition of the *Proumenoir*. Later still, she repented of her repentance altogether, perhaps coming to a late Montaignean sense of defiance. The last editions of the *Essays* in her lifetime restored the preface in all its excess and glory.

All these successive *Essays* editions, together with a sequence of lesser and often more contentious works, kept Gournay going through her advancing years. Somehow, she did what she had set out to do: she lived by her pen. By now she had returned to Paris, and there occupied a garret with a single faithful servant, Nicole Jamyn. She ran an occasional salon, and threw herself into friendships with some of the most interesting men of her day, including *libertins* such as François le Poulchre de la Motte-Messemé and François de La Mothe le Vayer. Many people suspected her of being a *libertine* and religious freethinker herself. She did write, in her auto-biographical *Peincture de moeurs*, that she lacked the deep piety she would have liked to have, perhaps a hint that she was an out-and-out unbeliever.

Gournay's books sold, but the publicity that made it happen often took the form of scandal or public mockery. This never focused on the *Essays*, at least not in her lifetime, nor even on her various feminist writings. Mostly, she was ridiculed for her own unorthodox lifestyle or her lesser polemical works. At times, she gained a grudging respect. In 1634 she became one of the founders of the influential Académie française, but two great ironies hover over this achievement. One is that, as a woman, she was never admitted to any of that organization's meetings. The other is that the Académie associated itself for centuries with exactly the arid, perfectionist style of writing that Gournay herself detested. It lent no support either to her own views on literary language or to her beloved Montaigne.

Gournay died on July 13, 1645, just before her eightieth birthday. Her graven epitaph described her just as she would have liked: as an independent writer, and as Montaigne's daughter. Like his, her posthumous reputation was destined to be twisted into bizarre shapes by changing fashions. The exuberant writing style she preferred remained out of favor for a long time. One eighteenth-century commentator wrote: "Nothing can equal the praise she received in her lifetime: but we can no longer give her such eulogy, and whatever merit she may have had as a person, her works are no longer read by anyone and have slipped into an oblivion from which they will never emerge."

The one thing that continued to sell was her edition of Montaigne. But this in turn attracted jealousy, and the eighteenth and nineteenth centuries started to see her as a leech on Montaigne's back. This interpretation had some truth in it, since she did use Montaigne to survive, but it ignored the extent to which she promoted and defended him as well. The sheer intensity of this devotion could attract suspicion. In the twentieth century, she was still being described by one Montaigne editor, Maurice Rat, as "a white-haired old maid . . . who made the mistake of living too long" and whose "aggressive or grumpy attitude" did more harm than good. Even the judicious scholar Pierre Villey, who generally took her side, could not resist poking fun sometimes, and he resented her attempt to set her friendship with Montaigne alongside La Boétie's. In general, the Gournay/Montaigne friendship continued to be judged by different criteria from the Montaigne/La Boétie one. The latter is lauded, deconstructed, theorized, analyzed, eroticized, and psychoanalyzed to within an inch of its life. Gournay's "adoption" has long passed with little more than one of those patronizing smiles that used to annoy her so.

In recent years much has changed, mainly because of the rise of feminism, which recognizes her as a pioneer. Her first great modern champion was a man, Mario Schiff, who wrote a full biographical study in 1910 and published new editions of her feminist works. Since then the journey has been ever upwards. Marjorie Henry Ilsley ended her 1963 biography, *A Daughter of the Renaissance*, with a chapter entitled "Marie de Gournay's Ascending Fortune"; since then, she has climbed even higher, with fresh biographies and scholarly editions of her works coming out regularly, as well as novelizations of her life.

More recently still, there has been a shift in attitudes to her 1595 edition of the *Essays*—which fell into disuse for a hundred years or so, following its first three centuries of unquestioned dominance. Having sunk to the deepest sea bed in the twentieth century, remembered only in a few footnotes, it is now bobbing up again. It seems to have all the formidable resilience of Marie de Gournay herself.

THE EDITING WARS

The rejection of Gournay's edition became most severe at the very moment that her general reputation began to revive. This strange fact has a simple explanation. Before that, her text had no rival; it was immaterial what readers thought of her personality. But in the late eighteenth century a different text did turn up in the archives of Bordeaux: a copy of the 1588 edition, closely annotated in Montaigne's own hand as well as those of secretaries and assistants, including Marie de Gournay herself.

This "Bordeaux Copy," as it became known, still did not attract much attention until the late nineteenth century, when scholars developed a taste for poring over the minutiae of such texts. It now emerged that the Bordeaux Copy and Gournay's 1595 edition were similar in soft focus, but not in detail. Several thousand differences existed, scattered like grit through the book. Of these about a hundred were significant enough to change the meaning, while a few were very major, including the section praising Marie de Gournay herself. Actually all the differences were equally important, for they implied that Gournay had not been a careful editor after all. She had been incompetent at best, and fraudulent at worst. This conclusion sparked an anti-Gournay backlash, followed by a series of

editing wars which ran through the early twentieth century, and which
(after a lull) are raging again today.

The battle followed the rules of classical warfare, focusing on sieges of
key strongholds and access to supplies. Armies of rival transcribers and
editors attacked the Bordeaux Copy, working at roughly the same time,
looking over each other's shoulders, and doing all they could to block each
other's path to the precious object. Each contrived his own technique for
reading the faded ink, and for representing the various levels of addition
and augmentation, as well as different hands. Some got so bogged down in
methodology that they made no further progress. One early transcriber,
Albert Caignieul, wrote to his employers at the Bordeaux Library explaining
why it was taking him so long to produce anything:

> The separation of the various stages was effected by observation and
> analysis of clear material facts . . . We considered that this separation
> was duly effected when these two conditions were fulfilled: 1. to take
> into account all the elements furnished by the analysis. 2. to take only
> these elements into account. The results have demonstrated the
> effectiveness of the method . . .

When, a few years later, he was challenged again—there being still no sign
of any completed transcription—he tried a different tack:

> Everything which remains to be done has been prepared for the most
> part and could be finished in a relatively brief period of time which
> would be, however, difficult to ascertain because of special problems
> which arise suddenly and frequently.

Nothing ever came of Caignieul's project, but others achieved better
results. By the early 1900s, three different versions were in production, one
an "Edition Phototypique," which merely reproduced the volumes in facsimile. The other two were the Edition Municipale, directed by bumptious
scholar Fortunat Strowski, and the Edition Typographique, directed by the
equally opinionated and difficult Arthur-Antoine Armaingaud. They took it
in turns to overtake each other, like two very slow racehorses on a long

course. Strowski won the first lap, bringing out his first two volumes in 1906 and 1909. He then boasted that no other edition would ever be necessary, and persuaded the Bordeaux repository to impose tough new working conditions on Armaingaud, including finger-numbingly low ambient temperatures and the requirement that all pages be read through thick panes of green or red glass to protect them from light. Armaingaud struggled on; his first volume appeared in 1912—though he gave it the false date 1906 to make it look to posterity as though it had appeared at the same time as Strowski's.

The game continued. For a while, Armaingaud edged ahead, but his subsequent volumes got stuck in the pipeline. He also isolated himself with his tendency to promote unusual opinions about Montaigne, notably the idea that he was the true author of *On Voluntary Servitude*. Not unlike Marie de Gournay before him, and many literary theorists after, Armaingaud liked to think of Montaigne as having secret levels of meaning which only he could decipher. As one of his enemies sarcastically put it: "He alone knows him in depth, he alone knows his secrets, he alone can speak of him, in his name, interpret his thought." At least Armaingaud kept up a trickle of output, but Strowski now became distracted by other projects and failed to finish the last volume of his edition. The Bordeaux authorities funding him eventually passed the work to someone else, François Gébelin, who produced the final volume in 1919—fifty years after the idea had first been proposed. Volumes of commentary and concordance followed in 1921 and 1933, produced by the astute Montaignist who now took over the project, Pierre Villey, a man whose achievement was the more noteworthy because he had been blind since the age of three. He finished his work in time for Bordeaux's celebrations of Montaigne's four hundredth birthday in 1933—only to have the organizers of the festivities forget to invite him. Meanwhile, Armaingaud also finished his version, so the world was, at last, presented with two fine transcriptions of the *Essays*. Both books had a key feature in common: having worked so hard to get access to the physical Bordeaux Copy, their editors were determined to stick to it, and to ignore Marie de Gournay's readily available published version almost entirely. They also shared a highly un-Montaignesque tendency to consider themselves the source of the final, unchallengeable word on all matters of *Essays* textual scholarship.

These two editions set the tone for the rest of the century. From now on, the 1595 version would be used only as a source of occasional variant wordings, to be flagged in footnotes. Even this was done only where the difference seemed significant. Otherwise, small variations were taken as a sign of Marie de Gournay's poor editing, and of the 1595 text's corrupt state. Gournay was assumed to have done just what they did—transcribe the Bordeaux Copy—but to have made a hash of it.

As long ago as 1866, however, an alternative explanation had already been put forward, by Reinhold Dezeimeris. Gournay could have done an excellent editing job, he suggested, but on a different copy. It took a while before this idea sank in. Once it did, it won increasing numbers of followers, some of whom worked out in detail how the switching of copies could have happened.

If this theory is true, the story probably began with Montaigne working on the Bordeaux Copy for several years, as its supporters always thought. At a certain point, however, it became so overloaded with notes that it was barely usable. Frustrated with its messiness, Montaigne had a clean copy made—no longer extant, but now dubbed the "Exemplar" for convenience. He carried on making additions to this, mostly minor, for he was almost at the end of his working life by now. When he died, the Exemplar—*not* the Bordeaux Copy—was sent to Marie de Gournay for her to edit and publish. This would explain why it does not survive: authors' manuscripts or marked-up earlier editions were normally destroyed as part of the printing process. Meanwhile, the unused Bordeaux Copy remained intact, like the skin-shell left hooked on a tree when a cicada outgrows it and moves on.

The hypothesis is neat; it accounts for both the survival of the Bordeaux Copy and its textual divergences. It accords with what is known of Marie de Gournay's editorial practice; it would have been odd for her to pay minute attention to last-minute corrections, as she did, if she was so careless with her work in the first place. If accepted, the consequences are dramatic. It means that her 1595 publication, rather than the Bordeaux Copy, is the closest approximation to a final version of the *Essays* as Montaigne would have wanted it to be, and thus that most twentieth-century editing is a misguided blip in history.

Naturally, this debate has thrown the Montaigne world into turmoil, and has sparked a conflict every bit as heated as those of a hundred years ago. Some editors have now dramatically reversed the hierarchy by consigning Bordeaux Copy variants to the humble spot in the footnotes which Gournay occupied for so long, notably the Pléiade edition of 2007 edited by Jean Balsamo, Michel Magnien, and Catherine Magnien-Simonin. Other scholars still support the Bordeaux Copy. It thrives particularly in a 1998 edition by André Tournon, which surpasses earlier editions in its devotion to the microscopic detail of that text. It incorporates Montaigne's own punctuation choices and marks, previously glossed over or modernized—as if to emphasize its physical proximity to Montaigne's hand and to his intentions. It is as if he is still holding the pen, dripping ink.

When the dust settles—assuming it does—a standard will be established for the coming century. There will be several consequences for all Montaigne readers. New editions are likely to foreground one text or the other rather than amalgamating them, since the importance of the variations is now so well appreciated. If Gournay wins, a page of Montaigne may also come to look simpler, for it could reduce the desire for the visually disruptive sprinkling of "A," "B," and "C" letters signifying different layers of composition. They would still be of interest, but they were first put in by editors working from the Bordeaux Copy whose motivation was partly to make their hard work fully visible. Gournay herself never thought of doing such a thing; nor did Montaigne. There would also be consequences for Montaigne readers in languages other than French. A new English translation would be urgently needed, since the two otherwise excellent ones that dominate the market now, by Donald Frame and M. A. Screech, are firmly of the Bordeaux Copy era. We would go back predominantly to the source text used by John Florio, Charles Cotton, and the Hazlitt dynasty.

Whatever happens, this is unlikely to be the end of the story. Disputes will continue, perhaps only about the placement of commas. It would be hard, now, to maintain the hubristic Strowskian belief that a perfect final edition can ever be created. In fact, the *Essays* can never truly be said to be finished. Montaigne the man may have hung up his boots and abandoned his quill, but, so long as readers and editors disagree about the results, Montaigne the author has never quite put that final ink mark on the page.

Montaigne knew very well that, the minute you publish a book, you lose control of it. Other people can do what they like: they can edit it into strange forms, or impose interpretations upon it that you would never have dreamed of. Even an unpublished manuscript can get out of hand, as happened with La Boétie's *On Voluntary Servitude*.

In Montaigne's and La Boétie's time, the absence of copyright law and the admiration of copying as a literary technique allowed even more freedom than would be expected today. Anyone who took a fancy to certain bits of the *Essays* could publish them separately; they could abridge or enlarge the whole, strip out sections they didn't like, rearrange the order, or publish it under a different name. A dozen or so chapters could be extracted and turned into a slim, manageable volume, providing a valuable service to readers whose biceps would not support the full tome. A decluttering service could be offered: confronted with a twenty-page Montaigne ramble, a bold redactor such as "Honoria" could cut it down to two pages which—un-Montaignean notion!—seemed to address the point announced in the title.

Some editors have been even more interventionist than this. Instead of slicing off choice cuts here and there, they have rolled up their sleeves and plunged their hands right into the *Essays* to dismember it like a chicken and make an entirely new creature of it. The outstanding representative of these is also the earliest and most famous: Montaigne's friend and near-contemporary Pierre Charron, who produced a seventeenth-century best seller called *La Sagesse* (Wisdom). Montaigne would barely have recognized himself in it, but it is essentially the *Essays* by another name and in a different format. It has been called a "remake"; one could also call it a "remix," but neither term captures quite how far it departs in spirit from the original. Charron created a Montaigne devoid of idiosyncratic details, of quotations or digressions, of rough edges, and of personal revelations of any kind. He gave readers something they could argue with, or agree with if they wished: a set of statements that no longer slithered away from interpretation or evaporated like a fog. From Montaigne's rambling thoughts on a topic such as the relation of humans to animals, he put together the following neat structure:

1. Features common to animals and humans
2. Features not common to humans and animals
   1. Features advantageous to human beings
   2. Features advantageous to animals
      1. General
      2. Particular
   3. Features of disputable advantage

It is impressive, and dull—so dull that *La Sagesse* met with immense success. Encouraged by this, Charron compressed it even further to produce an abridged *Petit traité de la sagesse*. This sold well too: both went into numerous editions. As the seventeenth century went on, more and more readers encountered their Montaigne in a Charronized form, which was partly why they were able to understand and tackle his Pyrrhonian Skepticism so analytically. (If Pascal still found him infuriatingly elusive, it was because he actually read the original.) Marie de Gournay, however, did not approve of Charron. In the preface to her 1635 edition of the *Essays* she dismissed him as a "bad copyist," and remarked that the only good thing to be said for reading him was that he reminded you of the genius of the real Montaigne.

    Charron's successors in the seventeenth and eighteenth centuries remixed Montaigne even further, and sometimes they remixed Charron too. While the *Essays* remained on the *Index*, remixes and remakes were the only form in

which the book could be published in France. The market was therefore
flooded with slim, uncredited Montaignes, or with works whose titles
evoked purified essences: *L'Esprit des Essais de Montaigne* (The Spirit of the
Essays of Montaigne), or *Pensées de Montaigne* (Thoughts of Montaigne). This
last purged him so thoroughly that the book runs only to 214 small pages,
introduced by the remark, "There are few books so bad that nothing good
can be found in them, and few so good that they contain nothing bad."

Authors have always undergone abridgement. Reductions of great works
still thrive in the publishing industry today, often under titles such as
"Compact Editions." A spokesman for one such recent British series was
quoted as saying, "*Moby-Dick* must have been difficult in 1850—in 2007 it's
nigh-on impossible to make your way through it." Yet the danger in cutting
too much blubber out of *Moby-Dick* is that of being left with no whale.
Similarly, Montaigne's "spirit" resides in the very bits editors are most eager
to lose: his swerves, his asides, his changes of mind, and his restless
movement from one idea to another. No wonder he himself was driven to
say that "every abridgment of a good book is a stupid abridgment."

Yet he also knew that reading always involved some process of selection.
He did it himself whenever he picked up a book, and he did it even more
decidedly if he then flung it aside in boredom. Montaigne read only what

interested him; his readers and editors do the same to him. All readings of the book eventually become an *Esprit des Essais de Montaigne*, even the most scholarly ones.

Indeed, perhaps these are more prone to it than any other kind. To a striking extent, modern critics seem to remix and remake a Montaigne who resembles themselves, not only individually but as a species. Just as Romantics found a Romantic Montaigne, Victorian moralists found a moralist one, and the English in general found an English Montaigne, so the "deconstructionist" or "postmodernist" critics who flourished throughout the late twentieth century (and just into the twenty-first) fall with delight upon the very thing they are predisposed to see: a deconstructionist and postmodernist Montaigne. This kind of Montaigne has become so familiar to the contemporary critical eye that it takes considerable effort to lean back far enough to see it for what it is: an artifact, or at least a creative remix.

Postmodernists consider the world as an endlessly shifting system of meanings, so they concentrate upon a Montaigne who speaks of the world as a dancing *branloire*, or who says that human beings are "diverse and undulating," and "double within ourselves." They think objective knowledge is impossible, and are therefore drawn to Montaigne's writings on perspective and doubt. (This book is as prone to such temptations as any other, being a product of its time.) It is beguiling; it is flattering. One looks into one's copy of the *Essays* like the Queen in *Snow White* looking into her mirror. Before there is even time to ask the fairy-tale question, the mirror croons back, "*You're* the fairest of them all."

One feature of recent critical theory makes it more than usually prone to this magic-mirror effect: its habit of talking about the text rather than the author. Instead of wondering what Montaigne "really" meant to say, or investigating historical contexts, critics have looked primarily to the independent network of associations and meanings on the page—a network which can be cast like a great fishing net to capture almost anything. This is not only a feature of strict postmodernism. Recent psychoanalytical critics also apply their analysis to the *Essays* itself rather than to Montaigne the man. Some treat the book as an entity with its own subconscious. Just as an analyst can read a patient's dreams to get to what lurks beneath, so a critic can probe the text's etymologies, sounds, accidental slips, and even printing errors in order to discover hidden levels of meaning. It is acknowledged that Montaigne had no intention of putting them there, but that does not matter, since the text has its own intentions.

Out of this train of thought have come readings which, in their way, are as baroque and beautiful as Montaigne's own writing. To choose one of the most appealing examples, Tom Conley's "A Suckling of Cities: Montaigne in Paris and Rome" picks up on a simple remark in Montaigne's "Of Vanity": that he knew about Rome before he knew of the Louvre in Paris. "Louvre," the French royal palace at the time, resembles the French word *louve* or "female wolf." For Conley, this reveals the text's subconscious link to the female wolf who suckled Rome's founding twins Romulus and Remus. Their mouths opened up as they sucked; in the same way, we open up our perspective on cities such as Rome or Paris by thinking about how they have survived through the centuries. The mouth opens up this perspective; it *opens it*, which is *l'ouvre* in French. Therefore, when Montaigne mentions the Louvre in the same breath as Rome, his text reveals a hidden image in which "the essayist's lips seal themselves around a royal teat."

The suckling image leads us to breasts, which are multiplied all over Rome in the form of the city's numerous domes and belvederes. "Erogenous tips that rise on the horizon of the city-view are assimilated into a multiplicity of points of nourishment." The vision of Montaigne's lips becomes even stranger:

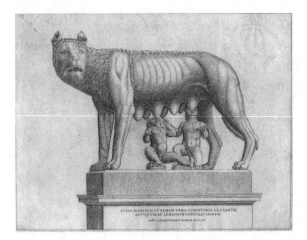

Montaigne sucks the erect tip of the temple of Jupiter Optimus Maximus on the Saturnian Hill of Rome from above as he puckers his lips about the nipples of the founding she-wolf from below.

This can all be found in Montaigne's note about the Louvre—but more follows. In the same essay, Montaigne goes on: "I have had the abilities and fortunes of Lucullus, Metellus, and Scipio more in my head [*plus en teste*] than those of any of our men." Insignificant though this line may seem, *tester* or *teter*, in French, means "suckle." These three classical heroes can be visualized as portraits, perhaps embossed on coins, which Montaigne puts in his mouth: "qu'il *teste*." A great "suction and flow of space and time" therefore flows through these few pages.

And still there is more. Montaigne writes in this essay of his being "embabooned" by Roman history—*embabouyné*, which means "enchanted" or "bewitched," but can also mean "suckled." The French word becomes even more suggestive if one reads it as "*en bas bou(e) y n(ais)*," meaning, "down in the mud I am born." This refers, again, to the two infants and the she-wolf, for they had to bend down low in the Tiber mud to suckle from beneath her. Since mud is squishy and brown, the embabooned Montaigne can now be seen as descending into "a presymbolic world of aroma and excrement."

Conley's essay is itself bewitching, or embabooning—and he is not merely playing with words like Romulus and Remus flinging handfuls of Tiber mud around. Nor is he proposing that Montaigne "really" had nipples on the brain when he wrote about Rome. The purpose is to pick out a network of associations: to find in a few apparently straightforward words of text a meaning as atmospheric and revealing as a dream. The result has a dreamlike beauty of its own, and there is no reason to become annoyed because it shows little apparent relation to Montaigne. As Montaigne said about Plutarch, every line of a rich text like the *Essays* is filled with pointers indicating "where we are to go, if we like." Modern critics have taken this very much to heart.

And all the time, the real patient on the analyst's couch—the one whose dreams cry out for interpretation—is not the *Essays* text, nor the person of Montaigne, but the critic. By treating Montaigne's text as a treasure-house of clues to something unknown, and at the same time separating these clues from their original context, such literary detectives are subjecting themselves to a well-established trick for opening up the subconscious. It is precisely the technique that a fortune teller uses when laying out tea leaves from a cup, or a psychologist when applying a Rorschach test. One sets out a random field of clues, separated from their conventional context, then watches to see what emerges from the observer's mind. The answer, inevitably, will be something at least as rarefied and whimsical as *L'Esprit des Essais de Montaigne.*

Regrettably to anyone with a taste for such things, this trend in modern critical theory—the last of the lily pads on this wayward frog-leap tour through the history of Montaigne-reading—seems to be passing into history already. Recent years have seen a reaction against it: a slow change of weather. More and more literary scholars are returning to history. Once again, they soberly study the sixteenth-century meanings of Montaigne's language and try to fathom his intentions and motivations. It looks like the end of an era—and the beginning of another.

What would Montaigne have made of it all? He enjoyed following pointing fingers around a page of Plutarch, yet he claimed to be exasperated by much literary interpretation. The more a critic works on a text, he said, the less anyone understands it. "The hundredth commentator hands it on to his successor thornier and rougher than the first one had found it." Any text can be turned into a jumble of contradictions:

> See how Plato is moved and tossed about. Every man, glorying in applying him to himself, sets him on the side he wants. They trot him out and insert him into all the new opinions that the world accepts.

Would a time ever come, Montaigne wondered, when the interpreters would get together and agree of a particular work: "There has been enough about this book; henceforth there is nothing more to say about it"? Of course not; and Montaigne knew that his own work must keep going through the same mill for as long as it had readers. People would always find things in him that he never intended to say. In doing so, they would actually create those things. "An able reader often discovers in other men's writings perfections beyond those that the author put in or perceived, and lends them richer meanings and aspects."

> I have read in Livy a hundred things that another man has not read in him. Plutarch has read in him a hundred besides the ones I could read, and perhaps besides what the author had put in.

Over the centuries, this interpretation and reinterpretation creates a long chain connecting a writer to all future readers—who frequently read each other as well as the original. Virginia Woolf had a beautiful vision of generations interlinked in this way: of how "minds are threaded together— how any live mind is of the very same stuff as Plato's & Euripides . . . It is this common mind that binds the whole world together; & all the world is mind." This capacity for living on through readers' inner worlds over long periods of history is what makes a book like the *Essays* a true classic. As it is reborn differently in each mind, it also brings those minds together.

There can be no really ambitious writing without an acceptance that other people will do what they like with your work, and change it almost beyond recognition. Montaigne accepted this principle in art, as he did in life. He even enjoyed it. People form strange ideas of you; they adapt you to their own purposes. By going with the flow and relinquishing control of the process, you gain all the benefits of the old Hellenistic trick of *amor fati*: the cheerful acceptance of whatever happens. In Montaigne's case, *amor fati* was one of the answers to the general question of how to live, and as it happened it also opened the way to his literary immortality. What he left behind was all the better for being imperfect, ambiguous, inadequate, and vulnerable to distortion. "Oh Lord," one might imagine Montaigne exclaiming, "by all means let me be misunderstood."

19. Q. How to live? A. Be ordinary and imperfect

BE ORDINARY

THIS BOOK HAS been, in part, the story of how Montaigne has flowed through time via a sort of canal system of minds. Samples have been taken at each lock: from

—Montaigne's first enthusiastic readers, who praised his Stoic wisdom and his skill in collecting fine thoughts from the ancients;

—the likes of Descartes and Pascal, who found him distasteful and fascinating in equal measure for his Skepticism and his blurring of the boundary between humans and other animals;

—the *libertins* of the seventeenth century, who loved him as a daring freethinker;

—Enlightenment philosophers of the eighteenth century, who were drawn again to his Skepticism and his liking for New World cultures;

—Romantics, who hailed a "natural" Montaigne while wishing he would warm up;

—readers whose own lives were disrupted by war and political turmoil, and who made Montaigne a hero and companion;

—late nineteenth-century moralists who blushed at his bawdiness and deplored his lack of ethical fiber, but managed to reinvent him as a respectable gentleman like themselves;

—some four hundred years of Montaigne-reading English essayists and accidental philosophers;

—a not-so-accidental philosopher, Friedrich Nietzsche, who admired Montaigne's lightness of spirit and reimagined his Stoic and Epicurean tricks of living for a new era;

—modernists like Virginia Woolf, who tried to capture the feeling of being alive and conscious;

—editors, transcribers, and remixers, who molded Montaigne into different shapes;

—late twentieth-century interpreters who built extraordinary structures out of a handful of Montaigne's words.

All along the way, there have been those who thought he wrote too much about his urinary system, those who thought he needed help with his writing style, and those who found him too cozy; as well as those who found a sage in him, or a second self so close that they were unsure whether they were reading the *Essays* or writing it themselves.

Many of these disparate readings have been transformations of the three great Hellenistic traditions, as transmitted—and altered—by Montaigne. This is natural, since those traditions were the foundation of his thought, and their lines of influence run through the whole of European culture. They can hardly be separated from each other even in their earliest origins; in Montaigne's modernized version they became more entangled than ever. They are held together above all by their shared pursuit of *eudaimonia* or human flourishing, and by their belief that the best way of attaining it is through equanimity or balance: *ataraxia*. These principles bind them to Montaigne, and through him to all the later readers who come to the *Essays* looking for companionship, or for a practical, everyday wisdom they can *use*.

Modern readers who approach Montaigne asking what he can do for them are asking the same question he himself asked of Seneca, Sextus, and Lucretius—and the same question they asked of *their* predecessors. This is what Virginia Woolf's chain of minds really means: not a scholarly tradition, but a series of self-interested individuals puzzling over their own lives, yet doing it cooperatively. All share a quality that can simply be thought of as "humanity": the experience of being a thinking, feeling being who must get on with an ordinary human life—though Montaigne willingly extended the union of minds to embrace other species too.

This is why, for Montaigne, even the most ordinary existence tells us all we need to know:

I set forth a humble and inglorious life; that does not matter. You can tie up all moral philosophy with a common and private life just as well as with a life of richer stuff.

Indeed, that is just what a common and private life is: a life of the richest stuff imaginable.

BE IMPERFECT

Montaigne was so often in poor health in his last few years that he seemed to pass half his time in the borderlands between life and death—that zone he had briefly visited in his prime, after his riding accident. He was not yet old, being only in his late fifties, but he knew that his kidney-stone attacks could kill him at any time, and sometimes he longed for it, so great was the agony. But these days the stone did not grab him by the ruff like a bullying strongman and pull him up close to death's tyrannical face. It enticed him "artfully and gently," leaving him plenty of time to think between attacks. Death looked friendly, just as the Stoics said it should be.

> I have at least this profit from the stone, that it will complete what I have still not been able to accomplish in myself and reconcile and familiarize me completely with death.

What he had first realized after his fall into unconsciousness was now amply confirmed: nature does everything for you, and there is no need to trouble your head about anything. It leads us by the hand, he wrote, as if "down a gentle and virtually imperceptible slope, bit by bit." We hardly need to look where we are going. By making him ill, nature gave him what he had sought for so long: *ataraxia*, and thus *eudaimonia*. The greatest moments of well-being he had known in life came immediately after an attack, when the stone passed through. There was physical relief, but also a liberating spiritual lightness.

Is there anything so sweet as that sudden change, when from extreme

pain, by the voiding of my stone, I come to recover as if by lightning
the beautiful light of health, so free and so full . . . ?

He even came to find a similar pleasure in the midst of the attacks
themselves. They were still painful, but he learned to delight in their few
compensations, including the glow of satisfaction he felt on seeing
admiration in other people's eyes:

> There is pleasure in hearing people say about you: There indeed is
> strength, there indeed is fortitude! They see you sweat in agony, turn
> pale, turn red, tremble, vomit your very blood, suffer strange
> contractions and convulsions, sometimes shed great tears from your
> eyes, discharge thick, black, and frightful urine, or have it stopped up
> by some sharp rough stone that cruelly pricks and flays the neck of
> your penis; meanwhile keeping up conversation with your company
> with a normal countenance, jesting in the intervals with your servants.

Only he knew the truth: that it was easier to joke and keep up conversations
in the grip of pain than an observer could ever guess. As his earlier near-
death experience had intimated, one's outward appearance might bear no
relation to what was going on in one's inner world. This time he really was
in agony, unlike the moments when he had been ripping at his doublet. Yet
he still felt the same insouciance of soul. The experience seemed to touch
him lightly.

> I am already growing reconciled to this colicky life: I find in it food
> for consolation and hope.

He drew a similar lesson from the fact of aging in general. It was not that
age automatically conferred wisdom. On the contrary, he thought the old
were more given to vanities and imperfections than the young. They were
inclined to "a silly and decrepit pride, a tedious prattle, prickly and
unsociable humors, superstition, and a ridiculous concern for riches." But
this was the twist, for it was in the adjustment to such flaws that the value
of aging lay. Old age provides an opportunity to recognize one's fallibility

in a way youth usually finds difficult. Seeing one's decline written on body and mind, one accepts that one is limited and human. By understanding that age does *not* make one wise, one attains a kind of wisdom after all.

Learning to live, in the end, is learning to live with imperfection in this way, and even to embrace it.

> Our being is cemented with sickly qualities . . . Whoever should remove the seeds of these qualities from man would destroy the fundamental conditions of our life.

Even philosophy needs to be "thickened and obscured" before it can be applied to real life. "There is no need to light up affairs so deeply and so subtly." Nothing is to be gained from living like Tasso, blinding oneself with one's own brilliance. It is better to be moderate, modest, and a little vague. Nature will take care of the rest.

All through these last years, mellower than ever, Montaigne continued to work on the *Essays*. He remained at home, but still wrote letters, including several to Henri IV. And he saw friends, writers, and former colleagues from Bordeaux and elsewhere, among them Francis Bacon's brother Anthony. His daughter, Léonor, now grown up, married François de la Tour on May 27, 1590, in a ceremony at the Montaigne estate. The following year, Montaigne became a grandfather, when Léonor gave birth to a daughter named Françoise on March 31, 1591. Still he kept writing, adding his last fancies and anecdotes, including his final thoughts on the art of living in harmony with ordinariness and imperfection. He looked more and more like a man who had learned how to live; or perhaps it was just his usual nonchalance, developed to a more masterly degree than ever.

20. *Q. How to live? A. Let life be its own answer*

NOT THE END

AN ATTACK OF the stone assailed Montaigne in early September of 1592. He had been through this many times before, and probably took it in his stride at first. But this time, as he had always known might happen, severe complications ensued. Instead of the stone passing through and giving him that rush of relief and joy, it stayed where it was. Then an infection set in.

His whole body began to swell. Before long, the inflammation spread to his throat. This produced a condition known as "cynanche," taking its name from the Greek for a leash or noose used to strangle a dog or other animal—a name that gives a vivid sense of how unpleasant it was. As it grew, Montaigne's throat closed ever more tightly, until he had to struggle for every breath.

The cynanche in turn led to a quinsy, a serious throat infection, still considered potentially fatal today if left untreated. It would have needed a course of antibiotics, but no such thing was available for Montaigne. From now on, with his throat swollen, he could not speak, but he remained fully conscious and was able to communicate his wishes to those around him by writing notes.

Three days went by after the quinsy set in. Montaigne sat propped in his bed, while his family and servants gathered to watch and wait. The room became the setting for the kind of overcrowded deathbed scene he had always hoped to avoid. Such rituals made death worse than it needed to be; they did nothing but terrify the dying man and everyone around him. The doctors and preachers bending over the bed; the grief-stricken visitors; the "pale and weeping servants; a darkened room; lighted candles; . . . in short, everything horror and fright around us"—it was all very remote from the simple, even absent-minded death he would have preferred. Yet, now that it came to it, he did not attempt to make the crowd go away.

Once it became obvious that no hope of recovery remained, he wrote his

last testament and final wishes. One local writer, Bernard Automne, asserted that during these last days Montaigne "got up out of bed in his nightshirt," and had his valets and other minor beneficiaries of his will called in, so he could pay them their bequests in person. Maybe this is true, although it does not fit well with the descriptions of him lying paralyzed. No account of his last hours is completely reliable; all are secondhand. But one, at least, should be fairly accurate: it was written by Montaigne's old friend Étienne Pasquier based on what he heard from Françoise, who remained at her husband's side throughout. Unlike La Boétie all those years ago, Montaigne did not send his wife away from his deathbed.

With the will arranged, Montaigne had a last mass said in his room. He could now barely breathe. According to Pasquier, he rose up in bed while the priest was speaking, "with a desperate effort, hands clasped," to commend his own spirit to God. It was a final act of Catholic convention: a brief acknowledgment to God in the life of this joyfully secular man.

Shortly afterwards, the last small channel of air in his throat closed. A stroke may have carried him off, or he may simply have suffocated. Surrounded by family, friends, and servants, Michel Eyquem de Montaigne died on September 13, 1592, at the age of fifty-nine.

Montaigne's death must have been distressing to watch—the struggle for air, the desperate effort, the hideous swelling—and he seemed to be fully aware of what was going on, another thing he had hoped to avoid. But perhaps it did not feel so distressing to him. On the day of his riding accident, he had thrashed around vomiting blood while his soul floated in pleasure; the same thing could have happened at the end too. He may have felt only the sensation of his life being gently detached from his lips: that slender thread being cut at last.

Étienne Pasquier and another friend, Pierre de Brach, composed their hearsay accounts of the scene for their contemporaries, making Montaigne's death an exemplary Stoic one. They performed the same service for his memory as he had done for La Boétie's. Montaigne had lived happily, wrote Pierre de Brach in a letter to Justus Lipsius; now, he had died happily, and well. The only ones to feel pain would be his survivors, who would be for ever deprived of his agreeable company.

The first job those survivors had to handle was the funeral ceremony, along with a rather gruesome dismantling of Montaigne's body. As a note in the family's Beuther *Ephemeris* recorded:

> His heart was placed in the church of Saint Michel, and Françoise de la Chassaigne madame de Montaigne, his widow, had his body taken to Bordeaux and interred in the church of the Feuillants, where she had a raised tomb built for him, and bought the rights for this from the church.

It was not unusual to separate out the body parts for burial, though it does seem a strange choice to put only the heart, rather than the whole body, in the little twelfth-century church on the estate. That would have made a peaceful resting place: he could have lain alongside his own father as well as the tiny skeletons of so many of his own children.

Instead, the remains of his remains went to the church of the Feuillant

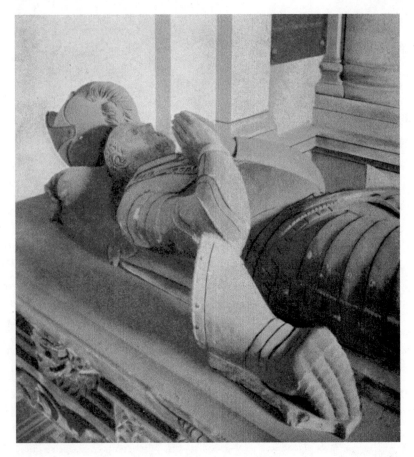

Order, an odd decision, again, and apparently not the original one. The first plan had been to bury him in the cathedral of Saint-André in Bordeaux; its canons authorized this on December 15, 1592. That would have placed him among members of Françoise's family, rather than his own. But she changed her mind, either because she herself was a devotee of the Feuillants, or because he was: he had expressed admiration for them in the *Essays*. The decision was certainly good for the monks. In return for housing Montaigne's body and saying regular masses for his soul, they received a generous rent which they used to fund a paint job on the building's interior. They gave him a magnificent tomb, which survives; it shows him lying in full knight's armor with his hands drawn out of his gauntlets and joined in prayer. Epitaphs in Greek and Latin cover the sides of the tomb, praising his Christian Pyrrhonism, his adherence to the laws and religion of his ancestors, his "gentle ways," his judgment, his honesty, and his bravery. The Latin text ends, movingly:

> Françoise de la Chassaigne, left a prey, alas, to perpetual mourning, has erected this monument to the memory of this husband whom rightly she regrets. He had no other wife; she will have had no other husband.

His body, minus the heart, was laid in this tomb at last on May 1, 1594, a year and a half after his death. He had already had to wait a long time for his eternal rest—and it was not to be eternal at all. About a decade later, work began on enlargements to the church and alterations to its layout. This would have left Montaigne's tomb stranded a long way from the new altar, in breach of the agreement with Françoise. She sued the Feuillants, and won. They were obliged to move the tomb, in 1614, to a prime position in the new chapel.

There he lay, and the decades went by peacefully until the French Revolution came along some nine generations later. The new secular state abolished the Feuillants along with other religious orders, and confiscated their property, including the church and everything in it. This was during a time when Montaigne was being held up as a hero of the Enlightenment— a freethinking *philosophe*, someone worthy of honor by the revolutionary regime. It seemed wrong to leave him where he was. So it was ordered in 1800 that he be disinterred and reburied in the hall of monuments in Bordeaux's great new secular temple: the Académie des sciences, belles-lettres et arts. The precious remains were extracted and conveyed with portentous solemnity to the new location, accompanied by cavalry in procession and saluted all the way with brass fanfares.

Two and a half years later, an antiquary working through records at the same Bordeaux Académie made an embarrassing discovery. The body that had been moved was not Montaigne's. It was that of his nephew's wife, a woman named Marie de Brian who had been buried in the same tomb along with other members of the family. Quietly, with no brass or cavalry this time, she was retrieved from the hall of monuments and returned to her original place. Montaigne remained where he had been all the time, untouched, in the original tomb. The man who so disliked building work, idealistic "innovation," and unnecessary upheavals had, after all, remained undisturbed by the Revolution, which had swept over his head like a wave over a deep sea bed.

Then, in May 1871, a fire destroyed the church. The tomb remained mostly undamaged, but it now sat unprotected amid the church's gaping ruins for almost a decade. In December 1880, officials opened it to assess the state of the revered relic, and found that the lead shell around Montaigne's remains had crumbled to bits. They sorted out the fragments, and made a new oak coffin for him. The restored tomb then spent five years in temporary quarters in the Depository of the Charterhouse, before being installed on March 11, 1886 in the entrance hall of a new building at the University of Bordeaux, containing the faculties of theology, science, and literature. Today, it is at the Musée d'Aquitaine in Bordeaux, where it can be seen on proud display.

There could hardly have been a more appropriate set of posthumous adventures for someone so attuned to the flux of the world, and so aware of how all human endeavors become muddled by error. Even after he died, something seemed to keep pulling Montaigne back into the stream of life rather than leaving him frozen in perfect remembrance. And his real legacy has nothing to do with his tomb at all. It is found in the turbulent fortunes of the *Essays*, his endlessly evolving second self. They remained alive, and, for Montaigne, it was always life that mattered. Virginia Woolf was especially fond of quoting this thought from his last essay: it was as close as Montaigne ever came to a final or best answer to the question of how to live.

Life should be an aim unto itself, a purpose unto itself.

Either this is not an answer at all, or it is the only possible answer. It has the same quality as the answer given by the Zen master who, when asked, "What is enlightenment?" whacked the questioner on the head with a stick.

Enlightenment is something learned on your own body: it takes the form of things happening to you. This is why the Stoics, Epicureans, and Skeptics taught tricks rather than precepts. All philosophers can offer is that blow on the head: a useful technique, a thought experiment, or an experience— in Montaigne's case, the experience of reading the *Essays*. The subject he teaches is simply himself, an ordinary example of a living being.

Although the *Essays* present a different facet to every eye, everything in them is united in that one figure: Montaigne. This is why readers return to him in a way they do to few others of his century, or indeed to most writers of any epoch. The *Essays* are *his* essays. They test and sample a mind that is an "I" to itself, as all minds are.

Some might question whether there is still any need for an essayist such as Montaigne. Twenty-first-century people, in the developed world, are already individualistic to excess, as well as entwined with one another to a degree beyond the wildest dreams of a sixteenth-century winegrower. His sense of the "I" in all things may seem a case of preaching to the converted, or even feeding drugs to the addicted. But Montaigne offers more than an incitement to self-indulgence. The twenty-first century has everything to gain from a Montaignean sense of life, and, in its most troubled moments so far, it has been sorely in need of a Montaignean politics. It could use his sense of moderation, his love of sociability and courtesy, his suspension of judgment, and his subtle understanding of the psychological mechanisms involved in confrontation and conflict. It needs his conviction that no vision of heaven, no imagined Apocalypse, and no perfectionist fantasy can ever outweigh the tiniest of selves in the real world. It is unthinkable to Montaigne that one could ever "gratify heaven and nature by committing massacre and homicide, a belief universally embraced in all religions." To believe that life could demand any such thing is to forget what day-to-day existence actually is. It entails forgetting that, when you look at a puppy held over a bucket of water, or even at a cat in the mood for play, you are looking at a creature who looks back at you. No abstract principles are involved; there are only two individuals, face to face, hoping for the best from one another.

Perhaps some of the credit for Montaigne's last answer should therefore go to his cat—a specific sixteenth-century individual, who had a rather pleasant life on a country estate with a doting master and not too much competition for his attention. She was the one who, by wanting to play with Montaigne at an inconvenient moment, reminded him what it was to be alive. They looked at each other, and, just for a moment, he leaped across the gap in order to see himself through her eyes. Out of that moment—and countless others like it—came his whole philosophy.

There they are, then, in Montaigne's library. The cat is attracted by the scratching of his pen; she dabs an experimental paw at the moving quill. He looks at her, perhaps momentarily irritated by the interruption. Then he smiles, tilts the pen, and draws the feather-end across the paper for her to chase. She pounces. The pads of her paws smudge the ink on the last few words; some sheets of paper slide to the floor. The two of them can be left there, suspended in the midst of their lives with the *Essays* not yet fully written, while we go and get on with ours—with the *Essays* not yet fully read.

ACKNOWLEDGMENTS

My five years of "voluntary servitude" to Montaigne have been an extraordinary half-decade, during which I have learned a lot—not least about the kindness of the friends, scholars, and colleagues who have helped me in so many ways.

In particular, I wish to thank Warren Boutcher, Emily Butterworth, Philippe Desan, George Hoffmann, Peter Mack, and John O'Brien, for the warmth of their encouragement, the generosity of their assistance, and their willingness to share their time, knowledge, and experience.

My gratitude goes to Elizabeth Jones for supplying me with fascinating material from her documentary, *The Man Who Ate His Archbishop's Liver*, as well as to Francis Couturas at the Musée d'art et d'archéologie du Périgord in Périgueux, Anne-Laure Ranoux at the Musée du Louvre, Anne-Sophie Marchetto of *Sud-Ouest*, and to Michel Iturria for permission to use his cartoon "Enfin! Une groupie!" I am also extremely grateful to John Stafford for allowing me to use his photographs.

I relied a great deal on libraries including the Bibliothèque nationale de France, the Bibliothèque municipale de Bordeaux, the British Library, and the London Library, and I thank the staff of all these for their expertise. Stanford University Press's generosity in so readily granting permission to quote from Donald Frame's translation is very much appreciated.

The book was completed with the help of an Authors' Foundation grant from the Society of Authors, and a London Library Carlyle Membership; I am most grateful for both.

As always, many thanks go to my agent Zoë Waldie at Rogers, Coleridge & White, and to my editor, Jenny Uglow, as well as Alison Samuel, Parisa Ebrahimi, Beth Humphries, Sue Amaradivakara, and everyone else at Chatto & Windus who believed in the book and helped bring it to life.

For reading the manuscript in various stages of disarray, advising me wisely, and reassuring me that everything was going according to plan, however unlikely this looked, I thank Tündi Haulik, Julie Wheelwright, Jane and Ray Bakewell, and Simonetta Ficai-Veltroni—who lived with Montaigne for so long and never lost faith in him (or me).

I first met Montaigne when, some twenty years ago in Budapest, I was so desperate for something to read on a train that I took a chance on a cheap *Essays* translation in a secondhand shop. It was the only English-language book on the shelf; I very much doubted that I would enjoy it. There is no one in particular I can thank for this turn of events: only Fortune, and the Montaignean truth that the best things in life happen when you don't get what you think you want.

CHRONOLOGY

1533 (Feb. 28)	Montaigne is born.
1539?–48	He goes to school at the Collège de Guyenne, Bordeaux.
1548 (Aug.)	Salt-tax riots in Bordeaux; Montaigne witnesses the mob killing of Moneins.
1548–54	He studies: probably law, probably in Paris and/or Toulouse.
1554	He begins work at the Cour des Aides in Périgueux.
1557	All Périgueux men are transferred to the Bordeaux *parlement.*
1558–59	Montaigne becomes friends with Estienne de La Boétie.
1559	Treaty of Câteau Cambrésis ends France's foreign wars, with disastrous consequences.
1562	Massacre of Vassy: beginning of the civil wars. In Rouen with Charles IX, Montaigne meets three Tupinambá Brazilians.
1563 (Aug. 18)	La Boétie dies, Montaigne at his bedside.
1565 (Sept. 23)	Montaigne marries Françoise de La Chassaigne.
1568 (June 18)	Pierre Eyquem dies, and Montaigne inherits the estate.
1569	Montaigne publishes his translation of Sebond's *Natural Theology.* Montaigne's brother Arnaud dies in a tennis accident.
1569 or early 1570	Montaigne himself almost dies in a riding accident.
1570	Montaigne retires from the Bordeaux *parlement.* His first baby is born, and dies after two months. He edits the works of La Boétie.
1571 (Feb.)	Montaigne makes his birthday inscription in his library.
(Sept. 9)	His only surviving child, Léonor, is born.

1572	Montaigne probably begins work on the *Essays*.
(Aug.)	St. Bartholomew's massacres.
1574	Death of Charles IX; Henri III becomes king.
1576	Montaigne has his medal struck, with scales and the motto *epekho*.
1578	He suffers his first kidney-stone attacks.
1580	*Essais*: 1st edition.
(June)–1581 (Nov.)	Montaigne travels in Switzerland, Germany, and Italy.
1581 (Aug.)	He is elected mayor of Bordeaux.
1582	*Essais*: 2nd edition.
1583 (Aug.)	He is reelected mayor of Bordeaux.
1584 (Dec.)	Henri de Navarre stays at Montaigne estate.
1585	Plague on the estate; Montaigne flees.
1587	*Essais*: 3rd edition.
(Oct.)	Henri de Navarre again calls at Montaigne estate.
1588	Montaigne in Paris on secret mission, then follows court of Henri III. He meets Marie de Gournay.
(May)	Day of the Barricades; Henri III flees Paris.
(June)	*Essais*: the much enlarged 5th edition (the 4th, if it existed, has never been traced).
(10 July)	Montaigne imprisoned in the Bastille, and released.
(Autumn)	He recuperates in Picardy with Marie de Gournay.
(Dec.)	Henri III has the duc de Guise assassinated.
1588–92	Montaigne works on final additions to the *Essays*.
1589 (Aug.)	Henri III is assassinated; Henri IV succeeds to the throne, though his claim is disputed.
1592 (Sept. 13)	Montaigne dies of a quinsy.
1595	Marie de Gournay's edition of the *Essais*, which will dominate Montaigne-reading for three centuries.
1601	Death of Montaigne's mother Antoinette de Louppes de Villeneuve.
	Pierre Charron's "remix," *La Sagesse*.
1603	*Essayes*: first English translation by John Florio.
1616	Death of Montaigne's daughter, Léonor.

1627	Death of Montaigne's widow Françoise de La Chassaigne.
1637	Descartes's *Discours de la méthode.*
1645	Death of Marie de Gournay.
1662	Blaise Pascal dies, leaving the notes published as the *Pensées.*
1676	*Essais* placed on *Index of Prohibited Books.*
1685–86	*Essays* translated into English by Charles Cotton.
1724	French *Essais* published in London by refugee Pierre Coste.
1772	Discovery of Montaigne's travel journal in an old trunk.
	Annotated "Bordeaux Copy" of *Essais* unearthed from archives and used to authenticate the journal.
1789	French Revolution.
1800	Revolutionary authorities decide to re-bury Montaigne as a secular hero in the Bordeaux Académie, but the plan goes awry.
1850	Montaigne's "plague" letters published, causing consternation.
1854	*Essais* removed from the *Index of Prohibited Books.*
1880–86	Montaigne's tomb renovated and moved to University of Bordeaux.
1906	First volume of Strowski's edition published, based primarily on "Bordeaux Copy."
1912	First volume of Armaingaud's edition published, based primarily on "Bordeaux Copy."
2007	New Pléiade edition published, based primarily on Gournay's 1595 edition.

NOTES

Unless otherwise specified, Montaigne references are to Donald Frame's translation of the *Essays*: Montaigne, *The Complete Works*, tr. and ed. D. Frame (London: Everyman, 2005). In each case the standard volume and chapter citation is followed by the Frame page number.

Full details of works listed here by author only or with brief titles can be found in *Sources*, pp. 365–70 below.

Q. How to live?

1   The Oxford Muse: http://www.oxfordmuse.com.

5   Melon: III:13 1031. Sex: III:13 1012. Singing: II:17 591. Repartee: II:17 587; III:8 871. Being alive: III:13 1036.

5   Levin: *The Times* (Dec. 2, 1991), p. 14. Pascal: Pascal, *Pensées* no. 568, p. 131.

6   "There is always a crowd": Woolf, V., "Montaigne," 71. "As we face each other": "The Mark on the Wall," in Woolf, V., *A Haunted House: The Complete Shorter Fiction* (London: Vintage, 2003), 79–80.

6   Tabourot et al.: Étienne Tabourot, sieur des Accords, *Quatrième et cinquième livre des touches* (Paris: J. Richer, 1588), V: f. 65v. Cited Boase, *Fortunes* 7–8 and Millet 62–3. Emerson 92. Gide, A., *Montaigne* (London & New York: Blackamore Press, 1929), 77–8. Zweig, "Montaigne" 17.

7   Amazon readers: http://www.amazon.com/Michel-Montaigne-Complete-Penguin-Classics/dp/0140446044. Comments from tepi, Grant, Klumz, diastole1 and lexo-2x.

7   "Do I contradict myself?": Whitman, W., "Song of Myself," in *Leaves of Grass* (Brooklyn, 1855), 55.

7   "I cannot keep my subject still": III:2 740.

8   Firing a pistol: Saint-Sernin, J. de, *Essais et observations sur les Essais du seigneur de Montaigne* (London: E. Allde, 1626), f. A6r.

9   "It is the only book in the world": II:8 338.

10   Our own bum: III:13 1044.

10   Flaubert: Gustave Flaubert to Mlle Leroyer de Chantepie, June 16, 1857, cited Frame, *Montaigne in France* 61.

1. *Q. How to live? A. Don't worry about death*

12   Young man who died of fever: I:20 73.

13   "To philosophize is to learn how to die": Cicero, *Tusculan Disputations* I: XXX, 74. Cicero took the idea from Plato's *Phaedo* (67 e). Montaigne used it for the title of his essay: I:20.

13   Death of Arnaud, and "With such frequent and ordinary examples": I:20 71.

14   "At every moment": I:20 72.

14   Montaigne imagining his deathbed scene: III:4 771.

14   Death a few bad moments: III:12 980.

15   Riding: we do not know exactly when this incident occurred, but Montaigne says it was during the second or third civil wars, which puts it between autumn 1568 and early 1570: II:6 326.

Montaigne's feeling of escape: III:5 811. On Montaigne and riding, see Balsamo, J., "Cheval," in Desan, *Dictionnaire* 162–4.

15   Far-flung vineyards: Marcetteau-Paul 137–41.

16   Montaigne's speculations: Marrow: II:12 507. Remora: II:12 417. Cat: I:21 90–1.

17   Montaigne's description of the accident and its after-effects: II:6 326–30. All quotations in the next few pages are from this description, unless otherwise specified.

20   "Enfeeblement and stupor": III:9 914. Petronius and Tigillinus: III:9 915. Both from Tacitus: Petronius from *Annals* XIV:19; Tigillinus from *Histories* I:72. Marcellinus: II:13 561–2. Source is Seneca, *Letters to Lucilius*, Letter 77. Loeb edn II:171–3.

21   "I never saw one of my peasant neighbors": III:12 980.

21   "If you don't know how to die": III:12 979.

21   "Battered and bruised," "I still feel the effect," and return of his memory: II:6 330.

22   "Bad spots": III:10 934.

2. Q. How to live? A. Pay attention

23   Montaigne's retirement: it was made official on July 23, 1570, but the transfer to his successor was signed in April 1570, so he must have made the decision earlier. See Frame, *Montaigne* 114–15. On his rejected application: ibid., 57–8.

24   Retirement inscription: as translated in Frame, *Montaigne* 115.

24   Montaigne's mid-life crisis compared to Don Quixote and Dante: Auerbach, E., *Mimesis*, tr. W. A. Trask (Princeton, NJ: Princeton University Press, 2003), 348–9.

26   On the Montaigne château and tower, see Gardeau and Feytaud; Willett; Hoffmann 8–38; Legros 103–26; and Legros, A., "Tour de Montaigne," in Desan, *Dictionnaire* 984–7. "Very big bell": I:23 94.

27   Shelves: III:3 763. Inheritance from La Boétie: III:12 984.

28   "I keep their handwriting": II:18 612. South American collection: I:31 187.

28   Private library trend: Hale 397. "Room behind the shop" and "Sorry the man": III:3 763.

28   Murals in side-chamber: Willett 219; Gardeau and Feytaud 47–8. Roof-beam quotations: Legros. On other similar inscriptions: Frame, *Montaigne* 9.

29   On the fashion for retirement: Burke 5. "Let us cut loose": I:39 214.

29   Seneca's warnings: Seneca, "On Tranquillity of Mind," in *Dialogues and Letters* 34, 45.

30   A "melancholy humor": II:8 337–8. Runaway horse, water reflections and other images: I:8 24–5.

31   On reverie: Morrissey, R. J., *La Rêverie jusqu'à Rousseau: recherches sur un topos littéraire* (Lexington, KY: French Forum, 1984), esp. 37–43.

31   The reverie of writing: II:8 337–8. "Chimeras and fantastic monsters": I:8 25.

31   Salvation lies in paying full attention: Seneca, *Letters to Lucilius*, Letter 78, Loeb edn II:199.

31   Writing for family and friends: "To the reader," *Essays* I p. 2. On commonplace books, see Moss, A., *Printed Commonplace-Books and the Structuring of Renaissance Thought* (Oxford: Clarendon, 1996). I am indebted to Peter Mack for the suggestion that Montaigne was partly inspired to write the *Essays* by reading Amyot's translation of Plutarch.

32   The dates of his writing are derived from Villey's study in *Les Sources*: see Frame, *Montaigne* 156. There has since been some disagreement about the dating.

32   "Each man is a good education to himself": II:6 331. Source is Pliny, *Natural History* XXII: 24.

33   "It is a thorny undertaking": II:6 331.

33   "I meditate on any satisfaction," and having himself woken from sleep: III:13 1040.

33   Heraclitus, Fragment 50. Heraclitus, *The Art and Thought of Heraclitus*, tr. and ed. C. H. Kahn (Cambridge: Cambridge University Press, 1979), 53. Stream of consciousness: James, W., *The Principles of Psychology* (New York: Henry Holt, 1890), I:239.

33   Montaigne quotes Heraclitus: II:12 554. "Now gently, now violently": II:1 291. Sand dunes: I:31 183. "A perpetual multiplication and vicissitude of forms": III:6 841. *Branloire*: III:2 740. See Rigolot 203. On general sixteenth-century fascination with flux and metamorphosis: Jeanneret, *Perpetuum mobile*.

35   Theories of sex with lame women: III:11 963. Source for Aristotle is *Problemata* X: 24, 893b. See Screech 156–7.

35   "That our happiness must not be judged until after our death": I:19 64–6. Sources for Solon are Herodotus, *Histories* I: 86, and Plutarch's "Life of Solon," in *Lives*, LVIII.

36   "If my mind could gain a firm footing": III:2 740.

36   "I do not portray being": III:2 740.

37   "Observe, observe perpetually": Woolf, V., "Montaigne," 78.

37   Mynah birds: Huxley, A., *Island* (London: Chatto & Windus, 1962), 15.

37   "It will cause no commotion" and "You must drink quickly": Seneca, "On the Shortness of Life," in *Dialogues and Letters* 68–9.

37   "A consciousness astonished at itself": Merleau-Ponty 322. Astonishment and fluidity: Burrow, C., "Frisks, skips and jumps" (a review of Ann Hartle's *Michel de Montaigne*), *London Review of Books* Nov. 6, 2003.

37   "I try to increase it in weight": III:13 1040.

38   "When I walk alone" and "When I dance, I dance": III:13 1036.

3. *Q. How to live? A. Be born*

39   His birth: I:20 69, and Montaigne, *Le Livre de raison*, entry for Feb. 28. On his nickname of Micheau: Frame, *Montaigne* 38. Eleven months: II:12 507–8. "Does this sound strange?": *Gargantua*, I:3, in Rabelais, *The Complete Works* 12–14.

39   Honesty: II:11 377. Kidney stones: II:37 701.

40   "Most" of his ancestors: III:9 901.

40   Family and nobility: Frame, *Montaigne* 7–8, Lazard 26–9; Supple 28–9. On Eyquem family: Cocula, A.-M., "Eyquem de Montaigne (famille)," and Balsamo, J., "Eyquem de Montaigne (généalogie ascendante)," in Desan, *Dictionnaire* 381–3. On the wine-growing business: Marcetteau-Paul.

41   Nobility of the sword: Supple 27–8.

41   Born "in confiniis Burdigalensium et Petragorensium": Montaigne, *Le Livre de raison*, entry for Feb. 28.

42   Bordeaux background: Lazard 12; Frame, *Montaigne* 5–6. The English wine fleet: Knecht, *Rise and Fall* 8.

42   Pierre's way of signing documents: see e.g. the entry on Montaigne's birth in the family record book: Montaigne, *Le Livre de raison*, entry for Feb. 28. See Lacouture 32.

43   "If others examined themselves attentively": III:9 931.

43   Jewish ancestry: most biographers have surmised that his mother's family was Jewish, with the
      main exception of Roger Trinquet (Trinquet, *La Jeunesse de Montaigne*). See Lazard 41 and Frame,
      Montaigne 17–20. Montaigne on Jews: I:14 42–3, I:56 282, II:3 311.

44   Montaigne's parents' marriage, and his mother's age: Frame, *Montaigne* 29.

44   Antoinette's legal documents, and Pierre's wills: Lazard 45, and Frame, *Montaigne* 24–5.

44   She stayed until about 1587: this is based on the fact that, when she wrote her own will on April
      19, 1597, she had apparently lived away from the castle for about ten years. Document of Aug.
      31, 1568, and Antoinette's will: both translated in Frame, *Montaigne* 24–7.

45   Montaigne's indolence, and his father's home improvements: III:9 882–4. Also see II:17 601–2.

45   Montaigne's father: Balsamo, J., "Eyquem de Montaigne, Pierre," in Desan, *Dictionnaire* 383–6.

45   Brantôme: P. de Bourdeilles, seigneur de Brantôme, *Oeuvres completes*, ed. L. Lalanne (Paris,
      1864–82), V: 92–3. Cited in Desan, P., "Ordre de Saint-Michel," in Desan, *Dictionnaire* 734, and
      Supple 39.

46   Pierre's stories: I:14 14.

46   The effect of Italy on French soldiers: Lazard 32, 14; Frame, *Montaigne* 10.

47   Montaigne's description of his father: II:12 300–1.

48   Stress of Pierre's mayoralty: III:10 935.

48   "I want to sell some pearls": I:35 200.

48   The neglected notebook and the Beuther *Ephemeris* are both in the Bibliothèque municipale de
      Bordeaux. "I think I am a fool to have neglected it": I:35 201. A facsimile edition of the Beuther,
      with transcriptions, was published as Montaigne, *Le Livre de raison*. See Desan, P., "Beuther," in
      Desan, *Dictionnaire* 100–5, which also discusses the neglected notebook. Montaigne's dating and
      numbering errors include the age of his brother Arnaud when he died from the tennis accident
      (I:20 71; Frame, *Montaigne* 33), his own age when he married, (II:8 342), the date of his arrest in
      Paris in 1588, which he later corrected (Montaigne, *Le Livre de raison*, entries for July 10 and July
      20), and the age of his first daughter when she died (Montaigne's dedication to La Boétie's
      translation of Plutarch's *Lettre de consolation*, 1570).

49   Half-finished jobs: III:9 882. Montaigne's affectation of indifference: III:10 935.

49   Pierre's kidney-stone attacks: II:37 701; III:2 746.

49   Pierre's wills: Frame, *Montaigne* 14.

50   "Completing some old bit of wall": III:9 882. "One should not try to surpass one's father":
      Nietzsche, *The Gay Science* 142 (s. 210).

50   Holy persons and oracles: II:12 387.

51   Eyquems famous for their harmony: I:28 166. "Out of respect for the good reputation": this is
      quoted by Montaigne in his letter to his father, published in his edition of La Boétie, *La
      Mesnagerie* [etc.], and in Montaigne, *The Complete Works*, tr. D. Frame, 1285.

52   Montaigne's siblings: Balsamo, J., 'Frères et soeurs de Montaigne', in Desan, *Dictionnaire*
      419–21.

52   Montaigne sent out to peasant family: III:13 1028; Montaigne's ordinariness made him
      extraordinary: II:17 584.

53   Let your children "be formed by fortune": III:13 1028.

53   Horst: Banderier, G., "Précepteur de Montaigne," in Desan, *Dictionnaire* 813.

53   "My father and mother," "without artificial means," and compliments from teachers: I:26 156–7.

54   Moderns inferior because they learned Latin artificially: I:26 156.

55   "We volleyed our conjugations," but little later knowledge of Greek: I:26 157. See also II:4 318.

55   Woken by musical instrument: I:26 157. Only twice struck with rod, and "wisdom and tact": II:8 341.

55   Erasmus: Erasmus, D., *De pueris statim ac liberaliter instituendis declamatio* (Basel: H. Froben, 1529). "All the inquiries a man can make": I:26 156–7.

56   Decline through lack of practice: II:17 588; Latin exclamation: III:2 746.

57   Ephemeral quality of French gave him freedom: III:9 913.

57   Latin commune: Étienne Tabourot, sieur des Accords, *Les Bigarrures* (Rouen: J. Bauchu, 1591), Book IV, ff. 14r–v. Experiments were also tried by Robert Estienne and François de La Trémouïlle. See Lazard 57–8.

57   Montaigne's advice on education: I:26 135–50.

58   "There is no one who": III:2 746.

58   Montaigne blames his father for changing his mind: I:26 157. On other possibilities: Lacouture 19–21.

60   Bordeaux in Montaigne's time: Cocula, A.-M., "Bordeaux," in Desan, *Dictionnaire* 123–5.

60   Collège de Guyenne: Hoffmann, G., "Étude & éducation de Montaigne," in Desan, *Dictionnaire* 357–9. Curriculum from Elie Vinet, *Schola aquitanica* (1583). On the school regime: Lazard 62–3; Trinquet; Porteau, P., *Montaigne et la vie pédagogique de son temps* (Paris: Droz, 1935). Montaigne says he lost his Latin at school: I:26 158.

61   Montaigne's acting: I:26 159.

61   Gouvéa: Gorris Camos, R., "Gouvéa, André," in Desan, *Dictionnaire* 438–40.

61   The salt-tax uprising: Knecht, *Rise and Fall* 210–11, 246. Closing of the Collège: Nakam, *Montaigne et son temps* 85.

61   Killing of Moneins: I:24 115–16.

62   On Montmorency, the "pacification," and Bordeaux's loss of privileges: Knecht, *Rise and Fall* 246–7, Nakam, *Montaigne et son temps* 81–2.

4. *Q. How to live? A. Read a lot, forget most of what you read, and be slow-witted*

64   Montaigne's reading, and not being discouraged by the tutor: I:26 158. For hypotheses on who this tutor was, see Hoffmann, G., "Étude & éducation de Montaigne," in Desan, *Dictionnaire* 357–9.

64   Montaigne's discovery of Ovid: I:26 158. On Ovid and Montaigne, see Rigolot, and McKinley, M., "Ovide," in Desan, *Dictionnaire* 744–5.

64   Montaigne's early discoveries, and "but, for all that, it was still school": I:26 158.

66   Thrill of Ovid wore off: II:10 361. But still emulated style: II:35 688–9. Villey found 72 references to Ovid in the *Essays*: Villey, *Les Sources* I:205–6. See Rigolot 224–6. Virgil could be brushed up a little: II:10 362.

66   The "diversity and truth" of man, and "the variety of the ways he is put together": II:10 367. Tacitus: III:8 873–4.

66   Montaigne on Plutarch: "He is so universal": III:5 809. He is "full of *things*": II:10 364. "Not so bad after all!" and flies on mirrors: Plutarch, "On Tranquillity of Mind," *Moralia* VI, 467C and 473E, Loeb edn VI: 183, 219. Plutarch points where we are to go if we like: I:26 140. "I think I know him even into his soul": II:31 657. It does not matter how long a person one loves has been

dead: III:9 927. Montaigne admired the two celebrated French translations of Plutarch by Jacques Amyot: Plutarch, *Vies des hommes illustres* (Paris: M. de Vascosan, 1559), and *Oeuvres morales* (Paris: M. de Vascosan, 1572), both tr. J. Amyot. See Guerrier, O., "Amyot, Jacques," in Desan, *Dictionnaire* 33–4.

67   On Montaigne's library: Sayce 25–6. The collection was dispersed after his death; attempts have since been made to reconstruct a list. See Villey, *Les Sources* I:273–83; Desan, P., "Bibliothèque," in Desan, *Dictionnaire* 108–11.

67   Petrarch, Erasmus and Machiavelli: Friedrich 42. Machiavelli's letter is cited in Hale 190. Cicero: II:10 365; Virgil: II:10 362.

68   "I leaf through now one book" and "Actually I use them": III:3 761–2. "We who have little contact": III:8 873. "If I encounter difficulties": II:10 361.

68   Lucretius: Screech, M.A., *Montaigne's Annotated Copy of Lucretius* (Geneva: Droz, 1998).

69   "Gentleness and freedom": I:26 157.

69   "Memory is a wonderfully useful tool": II:17 598. "There is no man": I:9 25.

69   Wishing he could remember ideas and dreams: III:5 811. "I'm full of cracks": II:17 600. Source is Terence, *The Eunuch*, I:105.

69   Lyncestes: III:9 893. Source is Quintius Curtius Rufus, *History of Alexander the Great* VII:1. 8–9.

70   Montaigne on public speaking: III:9 893–4.

70   Tupinambá: I:31 193. La Boétie's death: Montaigne's letter to his father, in his edition of La Boétie's works: La Boétie, *La Mesnagerie* [etc.], and in Montaigne, *The Complete Works*, tr. D. Frame, 1276–7.

70   Irritation that people did not believe him: I:9 25. On his ability to remember quotations, see Friedrich 31, 338. Baudier: from a prose commentary attached to his Latin verses, "To the noble heroine Marie de Gournay," Baudier, D., *Poemata* (Leyden, 1607), 359–65. Cited Millet 151–8, and Villey, *Montaigne devant la postérité* 84–5. Malebranche: Malebranche 187–8.

71   A bad memory implies honesty: I:9 26–7; II:17 598. It keeps anecdotes brief: I:9 26. It makes for good judgment: I:9 25. It prevents petty resentments: I:9 27.

71   Stewart: Stewart, D., *Elements of the Philosophy of the Human Mind*, in *Collected Works*, ed. W. Hamilton (Edinburgh: T. Constable, 1854–60), II:370–1.

72   "I have to solicit it nonchalantly": II:17 598. The effort to remember makes one forget: III:5 811. The effort to forget makes one remember: II:12 443.

72   "What I do easily and naturally": II:17 599. "So sluggish, lax, and drowsy": I:26 157.

72   "There is no subtlety so empty": II:17 600–1. "Tardy understanding": I:26 157.

72   What he grasped he grasped firmly: II:17 600. "What I saw, I saw well.": II:10 31. "Bold ideas": I:26 157.

72   Nadolny, S., *Die Entdeckung der Langsamkeit* (München: Piper, 1983), translated by R. Freedman as *The Discovery of Slowness* (New York: Viking, 1987). On the Slow Movement, see http://www.slowmovement.com/. See also Honoré, C., *In Praise of Slow* (London: Orion, 2005). There is a World Institute of Slowness: http://www.theworldinstituteofslowness.com/.

73   "I am nearly always in place": III:2 746. "Incapable of submitting": I:26 159.

73   "I know not which of the two": III:13 1034.

73   "I remember that from my tenderest childhood": II:17 582. Only "sprinkled": II:17 584.

74   "Where smallness dwells" and "Where is the master?": III:17 590. Lack of respect because of height: II:17 589–90. Horseback ploy: III:13 1025.

74 Strong, solid build: II:17 590. Leaning on stick: II:25 633. Dressing in black and white: I:36 204. Cloak: I:26 155.

75 La Boétie's poem: this is the second of two poems to Montaigne included in Montaigne's edition of La Boétie's works: La Boétie, *La Mesnagerie* [etc.], ff. 102r–103r ("Ad Belotium et Montanum") and 103v–105r ("Ad Michaëlem Montanum"). They have been published in *Montaigne Studies* 3, no. 1, (1991) with an English translation by R. D. Cottrell (16–47).

75 Toulouse: Montaigne says he met the physician Simon Thomas there (I:21 82) and mentions its Martin Guerre trial, though he does not say that he attended it in person: III:11 959. Paris: III:9 903.

76 Montaigne's magistracy: see Almqvist, K., "Magistrature," in Desan, *Dictionnaire* 619–22. On early years in Périgueux and the transfer to Bordeaux: Frame, *Montaigne* 46–51, including Frame's translation of the report of Montaigne's speech.

77 Montaigne's job: five of Montaigne's interpretations have survived. See Lazard 89.

77 "It is more of a job": III:13 996. Judge Bridlegoose: *Tiers livre*, chaps 39–44, in Rabelais, *The Complete Works*. Tossing dice: 457.

78 Cases of injustice: III:13 998. Montaigne on the law: see Tournon, A., "Justice and the Law," in Langer (ed.), *Cambridge Companion* 96–117, and "Droit," in Desan, *Dictionnaire* 284–6. On other contemporary critics of the law, see Sutcliffe, F., "Montaigne and the European legal system," in Cameron (ed.), *Montaigne and his Age* 39–47.

78 Fallibility of judges: II:12 514. Fallibility of laws: III:13 1000.

79 Trips to Paris: Montaigne is known to have made several between 1559 and 1561. See Lazard 91, 107.

79 Henri II "could never call by his right name": I:46 244.

79 On the French political and religious background in the 1550s and 1560s: see Holt; Knecht, *Rise and Fall* and *The French Civil Wars*; Nakam, *Montaigne et son temps*.

82 "It is folly": Michel de L'Hôpital cited in Knecht, *Rise and Fall* 338. "Everyone considers his own God" and "*Un roi, une foi, une loi*": Elliott, J. H., *Europe Divided 1559–1598* (London: Fontana, 1968), 93–4, the former a quotation from Pedro Cornejo's *Compenio y breve relación de la Liga* (Brussels, 1591), f. 6.

82 "A great fear": Knecht, *Rise and Fall* 349. Vassy and the outbreak of war: ibid., 352–5.

83 Pasquier to M. de Fonssomme, Spring 1562: Pasquier, E., *Lettres historiques* 98–100. Cited Holt 50.

84 "I do not believe that God": II:23 628–9.

85 Monluc's stories: Monluc 246–72. More wheels and stakes ordered: Nakam, *Montaigne et son temps* 144.

87 Montaigne on Monluc: II:8 348.

87 The d'Escars plot and Montaigne's response: see Frame, *Montaigne* 53–5; which also translates the report of Montaigne's speech, from Payen, J.-F., *Recherches sur Montaigne. Documents inédits*, no. 4 (Techener, 1856), 20. Montaigne's admiration for the Lagebâton faction: II:17 609.

88 "By my nature I am subject to sudden outbursts": III:5 824. The response is discussed in Frame, *Montaigne* 52–5.

5. *Q. How to live? A. Survive love and loss*

90 La Boétie: see Cocula; and Magnien, M., *Montaigne Studies* 11 (1999) is mostly devoted to La Boétie.

90 "So entire and so perfect": I:28 165. "So taken with each other": I:28 169.

92 La Boétie's poem was included in Montaigne's edition of La Boétie's works: La Boétie, *La Mesnagerie* [etc.], ff. 103v–105r ("Ad Michaëlem Montanum"). It has been published in *Montaigne Studies* 3, no. 1, (1991), with an English translation by Robert D. Cottrell (16–47), and is also translated in Frame, *Montaigne* 75.

92 Wills plunging and losing themselves: I:28 170. On the question of love and friendship, see Schachter, M. D., "'That friendship which possesses the soul': Montaigne loves La Boétie," *Journal of Homosexuality* no. 41 3–4 (2001) 5–21, and Beck, W.J., "Montaigne face à la homosexualité," *BSAM* 6e sér. 9–10 (jan–juin 1982), 41–50.

92 Ugliness: III:12 986. See Desan, P., "Laid-Laideur" in Desan, *Dictionnaire* 561. Socrates and Alcibiades: Plato, *Symposium* 102 (216a–b).

93 "Our souls mingle," "If you press me," and "Our friendship has no other model": I:28 169. "Many a time I should be glad": Plato, *Symposium* 102 (216a–b).

94 Montaigne on the *Voluntary Servitude*: I:28 175. The original manuscript has never been located, and is known only through copies made of it, of which that by Henri de Mesmes is thought most reliable. It is the basis for most modern editions, including the English translation used here, by D. L. Schaefer: La Boétie, "Of Voluntary Servitude" (see "Sources"). Rimbaud of political sociology: Lacouture 86. See Magnien, M., "Discours de la servitude volontaire," in Desan, *Dictionnaire* 272–6.

95 Nero and Julius Caesar: La Boétie, "Of Voluntary Servitude," 210–11. Tyranny as mysterious as love: ibid. 194. "A million men serving miserably": ibid. 192.

95 "You see, love": Colonel Abdullah Nasur, interviewed for *The Man Who Ate His Archbishop's Liver*, Channel 4 (UK), March 12, 2004. Thanks to Elizabeth C. Jones for this quotation.

96 "A deep forgetfulness of freedom," and power of habit: La Boétie, "Of Voluntary Servitude", 201.

96 A few freed by study of history: La Boétie, "Of Voluntary Servitude," 205–6.

96 Aims of La Boétie: see Smith, 53.

96 "Contr'un," in *Reveille-matin des François* (1574) and Goulart, S., *Mémoires de l'estat de France sous Charles IX* (1577, and 2nd edn 1579). It would also be included in a work called *Vive description de la tyrannie*. See Magnien, M., "Discours de la servitude volontaire," in Desan, *Dictionnaire* 273–4, and Smith, M., introduction to his edition of La Boétie, *De la Servitude volontaire* (1987), 24–6.

97 *Anti-Dictator*: La Boétie, *Anti-Dictator*, tr. H. Kurz (New York: Columbia University Press, 1942). Later such editions include a publication of the Kurz translation as *The Politics of Obedience: The Discourse of Voluntary Servitude* (New York: Free Life Editions, 1975), with an introduction by libertarian Murray Rothbard, reissued as *The Politics of Obedience and Étienne de la Boétie* (Montreal, New York & London: Black Rose Books, 2007); and *The Will to Bondage*, ed. W. Flygare, with an introduction by James J. Martin (Colorado Springs: Ralph Myles, 1974), which combines the Protestant French edition of 1577 with an anonymous English translation of 1735.

97 "Anonymous, low-visibility, one-man revolution": Martin, James J., introduction to La Boétie, *The Will to Bondage*, ed. W. Flygare (Colorado Springs: Ralph Myles, 1974), ix.

97 Opposing female suffrage: Spooner, L., "Against woman suffrage," *New Age*, Feb. 24, 1877. This

and other texts are available on http://www.voluntaryist.com/. The idea that one can bring about a revolution by not voting has inspired a novel by the Portuguese writer José Saramago, *Seeing*, tr. M. Jull Costa (London: Vintage, 2007).

97   "It seemed to me": Emerson, 92.

98   All Montaigne's remarks on the *Voluntary Servitude*: I:28 175–6.

98   Montaigne's revelation of its authorship: see Magnien, M., "Discours de la servitude volontaire," in Desan, *Dictionnaire* 274–5.

98   "In exchange for this serious work": I:28 176. "These verses may be seen elsewhere": I:29 177. The 29 sonnets, translated into English by R. P. Runyon, can be seen in Schaefer (ed.), *Freedom over Servitude* 223–35.

99   Pléiade poets: La Boétie, "Of Voluntary Servitude," 214. "But to return to our purpose": ibid. 208. "But to return from where": ibid. 215.

100   Attribution to Montaigne: Armaingaud, A., "Montaigne et La Boétie," *Revue politique et parlementaire* 13 (mars 1906), 499–522 and (mai 1906), 322–48, later developed in his *Montaigne pamphlétaire: l'enigme du "Contr'Un"* (Paris: Hachette, 1910). Schaefer, D. L., "Montaigne and La Boétie" in Schaefer (ed.), *Freedom over Servitude* 1–30, esp. 9–11; and his *Political Philosophy of Montaigne*. On Schaefer, see Supple, J., "Davis Lewis Schaefer: Armaingaud rides again," in Cameron and Willett (eds), *Le Visage changeant* (259–75). Martin, D., "Montaigne, author of *On Voluntary Servitude*," in Schaefer (ed.), *Freedom over Servitude* 127–88 (flute: 137).

100   Impotence trick: I:21 83–4. Montaigne's honesty: I:9 25–30. His dull-wittedness in games: II:17 600–1.

101   Montaigne on La Boétie: Travel Journal, in *The Complete Works*, tr. D. Frame, 1207.

102   Montaigne's letter to his father was published in his edition of La Boétie's works: La Boétie, *La Mesnagerie* [etc.]; also in *The Complete Works*, tr. D. Frame, 1276–88, from which all following quotations are taken.

104   "His mind was modeled": I:28 176.

106   Montaigne and La Boétie's disagreement about the experience of dying: II:6 327.

106   "Nothing but dark and dreary night": I:28 174. "I was overcome": "Travel Journal," in *The Complete Works*, tr. D. Frame, 1207 (entry for May 11, 1581). "I have missed such a man extremely" and "No pleasure has any savor": III:9 917.

107   Seneca on replacing friends: Seneca, *Letters to Lucilius*, Letter 9. Loeb edn I:45. "Some worthy man": III:9 911. "Is it not a stupid humor": III:3 755.

107   "Joined and glued": I:39 216.

107   Inscription to La Boétie: a conjectural reconstruction was included in the Thibaudet edition of Montaigne's works (Montaigne, *Oeuvres completes*, Paris: Pléiade, 1962). English versions are found in Starobinski, *Montaigne in Motion* tr. Goldhammer 311 (n.32) (used here) and Frame, *Montaigne* 80.

108   Find an admirable man: Seneca, *Letters to Lucilius*, Letter 12. Loeb edn I:63. Live for others, and for a friend: ibid. Letter 48, I:315.

108   "He is still lodged in me": Montaigne, dedicatory epistle (to Henri de Mesmes) in his edition of La Boétie's works, La Boétie, *La Mesnagerie* [etc.], in *The Complete Works*, tr. D. Frame, 1291.

6. *Q. How to live? A. Use little tricks*

109   On the combination of the Hellenistic philosophies in Montaigne and in general, see Hadot.

109   Translations of *eudaimonia* and *ataraxia*: Nussbaum 15, except *ataraxia* as "freedom from disturbance and anxiety," which comes from Popkin xv.

110   Pacuvius: Seneca, *Letters to Lucilius*, Letter 12. Loeb edn I:71. Lucretius's two possibilities, cited by Montaigne: I:20 78. Source is Lucretius, *De rerum natura* III: 938–42.

111   Pretend you never had it: Plutarch, "In consolation to his wife," *Moralia.* Loeb edn VII:610. Pretend you have lost it: Plutarch, "On Tranquillity of Mind," *Moralia.* Loeb edn VI: 469–70.

111   Seeing the world as it is: Seneca, *Letters to Lucilius*, Letter 78. Loeb edn II:199.

112   Questions asked all of a sudden: Epictetus, *Discourses* II:16 2–3 and III:8 1–5, cited Hadot 85. Living "appropriately": III:13 1037.

112   "How good it is": Marcus Aurelius, *Meditations*, tr. M. Hammond (Harmondsworth: Penguin, 2006), 47 (VI:13). Flying up to the heavens: ibid. 120 (XII:24).

112   "Place before your mind's eye": Seneca, *Letters to Lucilius*, Letter 99. Loeb edn III: 135.

112   Eternal recurrence: This idea found in Nemesius *De natura hominis* XXXVII: 147–8, Plato, *Timaeus* 39d, and Cicero, *De natura deorum* II:20. See White, Michael J., "Stoic natural philosophy (physics and cosmology)," in Inwood, B. (ed.), *Cambridge Companion to the Stoics* (Cambridge: Cambridge University Press, 2003), 124–52, and Barnes, J., "La Doctrine du retour éternel," in *Les Stoïciens et leur logique. Actes du colloque de Chantilly 18–22 septembre 1976* (Paris, 1978), 3–20. The idea was developed further by Friedrich Nietzsche: see e.g. Nietzsche, *The Gay Science*, s. 341, and Stambaugh, J., *Nietzsche's Thought of Eternal Return* (Washington, DC: Center for Advanced Research in Phenomenology & University Press of America, 1988).

113   "Do not seek": Epictetus, *Manual* VIII: as cited and translated in Hadot 136.

113   "If I had to live over again": III:2 751–2.

114   Seneca's asthma attacks: Seneca, *Letters to Lucilius*, Letter 54. Loeb edn I:363–5.

115   Lycas and Thrasylaus: II:12 444. Lycas story from Erasmus, *Adages* no. 1981: "In nihil sapiendo iucundissima vita." Thrasylaus story from Aelian, *Various Histories* IV: 25.

115   "A painful notion": III:4 770.

115   Consoling the widow: III:4 765.

116   "I was once afflicted": III:4 769.

116   "I let the passion alone": III:4 769.

116   "Gently sidestep": III:5 775.

116   Zaleucus: I:43 239. Source is Diodorus Siculus, *Bibliotheca historica* XII: V: 21.

117   "Don't bother your head": III:12 979. "Our thoughts are always elsewhere" and "barely brushing the crust": III:4 768.

117   Pasquier to A. M. de Pelgé, 1619, in Pasquier, *Choix de lettres* 45–6, as translated in Frame, *Montaigne* 283. Raemond, *Erreur populaire* 159. Expilly, C., sonnet in Goulart edition of Montaigne's *Essais* (1595), and in *Poèmes* (Paris: A. L'Angelier, 1596), cited in Boase, *Fortunes* 10.

118   "We are, I know not how, double within ourselves": II:16 570. The idea of an internalized La Boétie was first explored by Michel Butor in *Essais sur les Essais* (1968).

118   Montaigne might have published letters instead: I:40 225. Master/slave relationship: Wilden, A., "Par divers Moyens on arrive à pareille fin: a reading of Montaigne," *Modern Language Notes* 83 (1968), 577–97, esp. 590.

119 "Assiduously collected": Montaigne's dedicatory epistle to La Boétie's "Vers françois" in his
edition of La Boétie's works: La Boétie, *La Mesnagerie* [etc]. The epistle is in *The Complete Works*,
tr. D. Frame, 1298.

120 Sebond translation: II:12 387–8. The original was Sebond, R. de, *Theologia naturalis, sive liber
creaturarum* (Deventer: R. Pafraet, 1484); translated by Montaigne as Sebond, *Théologie naturelle*
(Paris: G. Chaudière, 1569). On Sebond, see Habert, M., "Sebond, Raimond," in Desan,
Dictionnaire 898–900.

121 "Being by chance at leisure": II:12 388. On the time he took, see Montaigne's dedicatory epistle
to his father, in *The Complete Works*, tr. D. Frame, 1289.

121 "Apology for Raymond Sebond": II:12 386–556. Marguerite de Valois apparently asked
Montaigne to write it some time around 1578–79, after reading his translation. See E. Naya,
"Apologie de Raimond Sebond," in Desan, *Dictionnaire* 50–4, esp. 51. On this work in general,
see Blum, C. (ed.), *Montaigne: Apologie de Raymond Sebond: de la "Theologia" à la "Théologie"* (Paris: H.
Champion, 1990).

121 "As the rope": Cons, L., *Anthologie littéraire de la Renaissance française* (New York: Holt, 1931), 143, as
translated in Frame, *Montaigne* 170.

7. *Q. How to live? A. Question everything*

123 Estienne: he tells this story in the introduction to his edition of Sextus Empiricus, *Sexti Philosophi
Pyrrhoniarum Hypotyposeon libri III*, ed. H. Estienne. ([Geneva]: H. Stephanus, 1562), 4–5. Hervet's
encounter is related in Popkin 33–4.

124 "I hold back": II:12 454. On Pyrrhonian Skepticism as transmitted to and by Montaigne, see
Bailey; Popkin; and Nussbaum.

124 Grains of sand: Bailey 21–2.

125 Three statements of the *epekho*: Sextus Empiricus, *Outlines of Skepticism* 49–51 (Book I: 196, 197, and
202 respectively).

126 "If you postulate": II:12 452.

126 Moore, T., *Poetical Works*, ed. A. D. Godley (London: H. Frowde, Oxford University Press,
1910), 278.

126 Stories about Pyrrho: II:29 647–8. Source for all these stories, both of his indifference and of
his failure to maintain it, is Diogenes Laertius, *Lives and Opinions of Eminent Philosophers* X:52–4.

127 "He did not want to make himself a stump," and "regimenting, arranging, and fixing truth":
II:12 454.

127 Montaigne's medals or *jetons*: one copy survives in a private collection. His own description of
it: II:12 477. See Demonet, M.-L., *A Plaisir: sémiotique et skepticisme chez Montaigne* (Orléans: Editions
Paradigme, 2002), esp. 35–77.

128 "Soften and moderate": III:11 959. The puniness of knowledge and the astoundingness of the
world: III:6 841. "Unassumingness" and "Deep need to be surprised": Friedrich 132, 130.

129 "My footing is so unsteady": II:12 516–17. On his changing opinions: II:12 514.

129 Effects of fever, medicine, or a cold: II:12 515–16. Socrates raving: II:2 302 and II:12 500. "All
philosophy . . . raving mad" and "The philosophers, it seems to me": II:12 501.

129 Animals see colors differently: II:12 550. We may need eight or ten senses: II:12 541–2. We may
be cut off by our nature from seeing things as they are: II:12 553.

130 "We, and our judgment": II:12 553.

130 "Become wise at our own expense": II:12 514.

130 "We must really strain our soul": III:13 1034. Taking pleasure in memory lapses: III:13 1002.

130 On the Church's approval of Pyrrhonian Skepticism: Popkin 3–6, 34.

131 "An extraordinary infusion": II:12 390. Church had the right to police his thoughts: I:56 278.

131 "Otherwise I could not keep myself": II:12 521.

131 Cats hypnotizing birds: in Montaigne's time, an interest in such powers of the "imagination" often coincided with disbelief in witches and demons, for it provided an alternative explanation for strange phenomena. "I plunge head down": III:9 902. This passage was criticized in Arnauld, A. and Nicole, P., *La Logique ou l'art de penser* (Paris: C. Savreux, 1662). See Friedrich 287. "Don't crucify people": Quint 74.

132 Inquisition: "Travel Journal," in *The Complete Works*, tr. D. Frame, 1166. On providence, see Poppi, A., "Fate, fortune, providence, and human freedom," in Schmitt, C. et al. (eds), *The Cambridge History of Renaissance Philosophy* (Cambridge: Cambridge University Press, 1988), 641–67.

133 Fortification against heresy: Raemond, *Erreur populaire* 159–60. "Beautiful Apology" and "Strange things of which we do not know the reason": Raemond, *L'Antichrist* 20–1. On Raemond, see Magnien-Simonin, C., "Raemond, Florimond de," in Desan, *Dictionnaire* 849–50.

134 The parrotfish and other examples of cooperation: II:12 427–8. Mathematical tuna fish: II:12 428. Repentant elephant: II:12 429. The halcyon: II:12 429–30. Octopuses and chameleons: II:12 418.

135 "A hare without fur or bones": II:12 430–1.

135 Bossuet, J.-B., *Troisième Sermon pour la fête de tous les saints* (1668), cited in Boase, *Fortunes* 414.

136 Descartes on animals: Discourse 5 of his *Discourse on Method* (1637) is devoted to this subject. See Gontier, T., *De l'Homme à l'animal: Montaigne et Descartes ou les paradoxes de la philosophie moderne sur la nature des animaux* (Paris: Vrin, 1998), and his "D'un Paradoxe à l'autre: l'intelligence des bêtes chez Montaigne et les animaux-machines chez Descartes," in Faye, E. (ed.), *Descartes et la Renaissance* (Paris: H. Champion, 1999) 87–101.

136 "When I play with my cat": II:12 401. "We entertain each other with reciprocal monkey tricks": II:12 401n. This passage appeared in the posthumous 1595 edition and is excluded from some modern editions (see Chapter 18 above).

136 "All of Montaigne": Lüthy 28. The article: Michel, P., "La Chatte de Montaigne, parmi les chats du XVIe siècle," *Bulletin de la Société des Amis de Montaigne* 29 (1964), 14–18. The dictionary entry: Shannon, L., "Chatte de Montaigne," in Desan, *Dictionnaire* 162.

137 "The defect" and "We have some mediocre understanding": II:12 402.

138 Descartes's crisis by the stove: Descartes, *Discourse on Method* 35–9 (Discourse 2).

139 Descartes's argument is put forward in his *Discourse on Method* and *Meditations*. "Everything I perceive clearly and distinctly cannot fail to be true": *Meditations* 148–9 (Meditation 5).

139 "The Meditation of yesterday": Descartes, *Meditations* 102 (Meditation 2).

140 The evil demon: Descartes, *Meditations* 100 (Meditation 1). Demons in clouds, and altering threads of brain: Clark 163. God as deceiver: Descartes, *Meditations* 98 (Meditation 1). See Popkin 187.

141 "We are, I know not how": II:16 570. "We have no communication with being": II:12 553.

142 Pascal's "FIRE" notes, dated 1654: cited Coleman, F. X. J., *Neither Angel nor Beast* (New York & London: Routledge & Kegan Paul, 1986), 59–60.

142 "Spirit of geometry": Pascal, B., *De l'Esprit géométrique* [etc.] (Paris: Flammarion, 1999).

142 "The great adversary": Eliot 157.

143 Futility of fighting Pyrrhonism: Pascal, *Pensées* no. 164, p. 41.

143 "He puts everything into a universal doubt" and "so advantageously positioned": Pascal, "Discussion with M. de Sacy," in *Pensées* 183–5.

144 "Of all authors": Eliot 157.

144 "It is not in Montaigne": Pascal: *Pensées* no. 568, p. 131.

144 *Montaigne:* "How we cry and laugh": I:38 208. *Pascal:* "Hence we cry and laugh": Pascal, *Pensées* no. 87, p. 22. *Montaigne:* "They want to get out of themselves": III:13 1044. *Pascal:* "Man is neither angel nor beast": Pascal, *Pensées* no. 557, p. 128. *Montaigne:* "Put a philosopher in a cage": II:12 546. *Pascal:* "If you put the world's greatest philosopher on a plank": Pascal, *Pensées* no. 78, p. 17.

145 "A bad case of indigestion": Bloom, H., *The Western Canon* (London: Papermac, 1996), 150. Borges, J. L., "Pierre Menard, author of the *Quixote*," in *Fictions* (Harmondsworth: Penguin, 1999), 33–43.

145 "We have such a high idea": Pascal, *Pensées* no. 30, p. 9. "It seems to me": I:50 268.

146 "Whoever looks at himself": Pascal, *Pensées* no. 230, pp. 66–7. "On contemplating our blindness": ibid. no. 229, p. 65.

146 "What does the world think about?": Pascal, *Pensées* no. 513, p. 123. "Human sensitivity to little things": ibid. no. 525, p. 124.

147 Voltaire: "On the *Pensées* of Pascal," in his *Letters on England*, tr. L. Tancock (Harmondsworth: Penguin, 1980), Letter 25, 120–45. "I venture to champion humanity," ibid. 120. "When I look at Paris," ibid. 125. "What a delightful design": ibid. 139.

147 "I accept with all my heart": III:13 1042.

148 We cannot rise above humanity: II:12 556. "It is an absolute perfection . . .": III:13 1044.

148 "Convenience and calm," and moral danger: Pascal, "Discussion with M. de Sacy," in *Pensées* 188 and 191.

148 Malebranche: Malebranche 184–90. "His ideas are false but beautiful": ibid. 190. "The mind cannot be pleased": 184.

149 Montaigne the "seducer": Guizot, *Montaigne: études et fragments*, cited Tilley 275. The "prodigious seduction machine": Mathieu-Castellani, G., *Montaigne: l'écriture de l'essai* 255.

149 "Thoughts which come naturally": La Bruyère, J. de, *Characters*, tr. J. Stewart (Harmondsworth: Penguin, 1970), Book I, no. 44, p. 34 (translation of *Caractères*, 1688).

149 On the *libertins*, see Pessel, A., "Libertins—libertinage," in Desan, *Dictionnaire* 588–9, and *Montaigne Studies* 19 (2007), which is devoted to the topic. On Marie de Gournay, see Dotoli, G., "Montaigne et les libertins via Mlle de Gournay," in Tetel (ed.), *Montaigne et Marie de Gournay* 105–41, esp. 128–9. On La Fontaine, see Boase, *Fortunes* 396–406.

150 La Rochefoucauld: La Rochefoucauld, F. de, *Maxims*, tr. L. Tancock (Harmondsworth: Penguin, 1959). "At times we are as different": ibid. no. 135, p. 51. "The surest way to be taken in": ibid. no. 127, p. 50. "Chance and caprice": ibid. no. 435, p. 88. "We often irritate others": ibid. no. 242, p. 66.

150 *Bel esprit:* "gay, lively, full of fire" is the definition given in Bohours, *Entretiens d'Ariste et d'Eugène* (1671), 194, cited in Pessel, A., "Libertins—libertinage," in Desan, *Dictionnaire* 589. *Honnêteté:* Académie definition as cited in Villey, *Montaigne devant la postérité* 339. See Magendie, M., *La Politesse mondaine et les théories de l'honnêteté, en France, au XVII siècle* (Paris: Alcan, 1925).

151 "A witty coquetry": Nietzsche, *Human, All Too Human*, Aphorism 37, p. 41.

151 "Freest and mightiest" and "That such a man wrote": Nietzsche, "Schopenhauer as Educator," in *Untimely Meditations* 135. "If I had to live over again": III:2 751–2. On Nietzsche and Montaigne, see Donellan, B., "Nietzsche and Montaigne," *Colloquia Germanica* 19 (1986), 1–20; Williams, W.D., *Nietzsche and the French: A Study of the Influence of Nietzsche's French Reading on His Thought and Writing* (Oxford: Blackwell, 1952); Molner, David, "The influence of Montaigne on Nietzsche: a *raison d'être* in the sun," *Nietzsche Studien* 22 (1993), 80–93; Panichi, Nicola, *Picta historia: lettura di Montaigne e Nietzsche* (Urbino: Quattro Venti, 1995).

151 Arnauld and Nicole's attack: Arnauld, A. and Nicole, P., *La Logique ou l'art de penser* (Paris: C. Savreux, 1662), and 2nd edn (Paris: C. Savreux, 1664). See Boase, *Fortunes* 410–11.

152 Suppressed books are more marketable: III:5 781.

152 "It is not in Montaigne": Pascal, *Pensées* no. 568, p. 131.

8 Q. How to live? A . Keep a private room behind the shop

154 "I have never yet seen": III:5 830. "I make advances": III:3 755.

154 Depressing to be accepted out of pity: III:5 828–9. Dislikes being troublesome: III:5 800. "I abhor the idea," and the story of the frantic Egyptian: III:5 816. "In truth, in this delight": III:5 828.

155 "Only one buttock" and "sauce of a more agreeable imagination": III:5 817.

155 "In place of the real parts" and "What mischief": III:5 791. "Even the matrons": III:5 822. Source for latter is *Diversorum veterum poetarum in Priapum lusus* (Venice: Aldus, 1517), no. 72(1), f. 15v. and no. 7(4–5), f. 4v., adapted by Montaigne.

155 "Our life is part folly," and the Bèze and Saint-Gelais quotes: III:5 822–3. Bèze, T. de, *Poemata* (Paris: C. Badius, 1548), f. 54v. Saint-Gelais, "Rondeau sur la dispute des vits par quatre dames," in *Oeuvres poétiques françaises*, ed. D. H. Stone (Paris: STFM, 1993), I:276–7.

156 Françoise de La Chassaigne and her family: Balsamo, J., "La Chassaigne (famille de)" and "La Chassaigne, Françoise de," in Desan, *Dictionnaire* 566–8. On Françoise and the marriage: Insdorf, 47–58. Montaigne on Aristotle's ideal age: II:8 342. Source is Aristotle, *Politics* VII:16 1335a. Montaigne recorded Françoise's birth date in his Beuther *Ephemeris* diary, as well as their marriage: entries for Dec. 13 and Sept. 23, respectively.

156 "Wives always have a proclivity": II:8 347.

156 "I admonish . . . my family": II:31 660.

157 Socrates and the water-wheel: III:13 1010. Source is Diogenes Laertius, *Lives and Opinions of Eminent Philosophers*, II:36. Socrates's use of his wife's temper as philosophical practice: II:11 373.

157 Description by Gamaches: Gamaches, C., *Le Sensé raisonnant sur les passages de l'Escriture Saincte contre les pretendus réformez* (1623), cited Frame, *Montaigne* 87. Her correspondence with Dom Marc-Antoine de Saint-Bernard: Frame, *Montaigne* 87–8.

157 Françoise's tower: Gardeau and Feytaud 21.

158 "My thoughts fall asleep": III:3 763.

158 "The husband and wife must have separate bedrooms": Alberti, L. B., *On the Art of Building*, tr. J. Rykwert, N. Leach and R. Tavernor (Boston, MA, 1988), 149, cited Hale 266.

158 "Whoever supposes": I:38 210. On differing opinions of the marriage, see Lazard 146.

159 "Let us let them talk" and "I have, so I believe": Montaigne's epistle to his wife for La Boétie's translation of Plutarch's *Lettre de consolation*, in La Boétie, *La Mesnagerie* [etc.] and in *The Complete Works*, tr. D. Frame, 1300.

159 Montaigne's remarks on his marriage: III:5 783–6.

159 "I have often heard the author say": F. de Raemond's marginalia in his copy of the *Essays*, cited in Boase, "Montaigne annoté par Florimond de Raemond," 239, and in Frame, *Montaigne* 93, from which this translation is taken.

160 "A man . . . should touch his wife prudently," and curdling sperm: III:5 783. Kings of Persia: I:30 179. On such theories, see Kelso, R., *Doctrine for the Lady of the Renaissance* (Urbana: University of Illinois Press, 1956), 87–9.

160 Better for a wife to pick up licentiousness from someone else: I:30 178. Women prefer that anyway: III:5 787.

160 Ideal marriage similar to ideal friendship: III:5 785. But not freely chosen, and women not "firm": I:28 167.

160 "Wounded to the heart": Sand, G., *Histoire de ma vie* (Paris: M. Lévy, 1856), VIII: 231. On women's education, and Louise Labé: Davis, N.Z., "City women and religious change," in Davis, *Society and Culture* 72–4. It has been suggested that Labé was a pseudonym for a group of male poets: Huchon, M., *Louise Labé: une créature de papier* (Geneva: Droz, 2006).

161 "Women are not wrong": III:5 787–8. "Males and females are cast": III:5 831. The double standard: III:5 789. "We are in almost all things unjust": III:5 819.

162 "We should have wife, children, goods": I:39 215.

162 Entries on the deaths of children: from Montaigne, *Le Livre de raison*, entries for Feb. 21, May 16, June 28, July 5, Sept. 9, and Dec. 27.

163 Montaigne on the loss of his children: I:14 50. The dating of his riding accident: II:6 326. "In the second year": Montaigne's dedicatory epistle to his wife for La Boétie's translation of Plutarch's *Lettre de consolation* in La Boétie, *La Mesnagerie* [etc], and in *The Complete Works*, tr. D. Frame, 1300–1.

164 "I see enough other common occasions for affliction": I:14 50.

164 Essay on sadness: I:2 6–9. Date of 1572–74 given by Donald Frame in his edition of *The Complete Works*, p.vii. Niobe: I:2 7. The story comes from Ovid, *Metamorphoses* VI: 304.

164 Léonor: see Balsamo, J., "Léonor de Montaigne," in Desan, *Dictionnaire* 575–6.

165 "The government of women," the *fouteau* story, and Léonor's "backward constitution": III:5 790. Punishment by gentle stern words: II:8 341.

165 "I handle the cards": I:23 95. The game of meeting at extremes: I:54 274.

166 "It is pitiful": III:9 882. "There is always something": III:9 880. "Fermenting wine": II:17 601. On bad harvests, plague, and his using influence to sell wine: Hoffmann 9–10.

166 "I stand up well": II:17 591. Never studied a title deed: III:9 884.

167 "I cannot reckon": II:17 601.

167 Negative catechism: cf. I:31 186.

167 Admiring practical and specific knowledge: III:9 882–3. "Having had neither governor nor master" and "Extremely idle, extremely independent": II:17 592. "Freedom and laziness": III:9 923.

167 Better to lose money than track every penny: II:17 592. Misers often swindled too: III:9 884. The marquis du Trans story: II:8 346. Montaigne does not name him; he was identified as such by Raemond in a marginal note. See Boase, "Montaigne annoté par Florimond de Raemond."

168 "Nothing costs me dear," and wanting a son-in-law: III:9 883–4. "I avoid subjecting myself": III:9 897. "I try to have no express need": III:9 899. "I have conceived a mortal hatred": III:9 900.

168 Hippias of Elis: III:9 899. The story comes from Plato, *Hippias minor* 368 b–d, and Cicero, *De oratore* III:32 127.

169 Nietzsche's "free-spirited people": Nietzsche, *Human, All Too Human*, Aphorism 291, 173–4.

9. Q. How to live? A. Be convivial: live with others

170 "There are private, retiring, and inward natures" and "My essential pattern": III:3 758.

170 Conversation better than books: I:17 59. "The sharp, abrupt repartee": III:8 871. "Wonderful brilliance": I:26 140.

170 "No propositions astonish me": III:8 855. He likes being contradicted: III:8 856–7. Sweet conversation: Raemond, *Erreur populaire* 159. No "waiting on people": III:3 758.

171 Small talk bores him: II:17 587. His attention wanders: III:3 754. But he sees its value: I:13 39.

171 Affability an art for living well: III:13 1037. "Gay and sociable wisdom": III:5 778.

171 Goodwill: Nietzsche, *Human, All Too Human*, Aphorism 49, p. 48.

172 Foix family: see Balsamo, J., "Foix (famille de)," in Desan, *Dictionnaire* 405–8. The man who threw too many parties: II:8 344. The man who blew his nose: I:23 96. Montaigne's contemporary Florimond de Raemond identified them as Jean de Lusignan and François de La Rochefoucauld, respectively: see Boase, "Montaigne annoté par Florimond de Raemond." Female dedicatees: Diane de Foix, comtesse de Gurson (I:26), Marguerite de Gramond (I:29), and Mme d'Estissac (II:8).

172 He organized a deer hunt for Henri of Navarre in 1584: see Montaigne, *Le Livre de raison*, entry for Dec. 19. On jousting: III:8 871. On indoor amusements: I:54 273. The puzzles were probably similar to those described in his near-contemporary Tabourot des Accords's collection *Bigarrures*: Étienne Tabourot, sieur des Accords, *Les Bigarrures* (Rouen: J. Bauchu, 1591), [Book 1].

172 Millet-tosser: I:54 274. Child born with part of another child attached: II:30 653–4. Hermaphroditic shepherd: II:30 654. Man without arms: I:23 95. "Monsters" contrary to habit, not nature: II:30 654.

173 "I have seen no more evident monstrosity": III:11 958.

173 Business of the estate: see Hoffmann 14–15.

173 Not knowing whether he would be murdered in his sleep: III:9 901.

174 Botero: Botero, G., *The Reason of State and the Greatest of Cities*, tr. R. Peterson and P. J. and D. P. Waley (London, 1956), 279, cited Hale 426. "A porter of ancient custom": II:15 567.

174 Guarded houses suffered more attacks, with explanation from Seneca: II:15 567–8. Source is Seneca, *Letters to Lucilius*, Letter 68. Loeb edn II:47. No glory in robbing an open household: II:15 567. "Your valet may be of the party": II:15 568.

174 Soldiers disarmed by Montaigne's open face: III:12 988–90.

174 The attack in the forest: III:12 990–1. This is different from the hold-up in 1588 on his way to Paris, which is also related in the *Essays*.

175 Stories of confrontation and submission: I:1 1–5.

176 The stag: II:11 383. One critic, David Quint, sees this stag story as a primal scene replayed throughout the *Essays* but never finally resolved. Quint 63.

177 Seeking and granting mercy without cringing: I:5 20. "Pure and clean confidence": I:24 115.

178 "When weapons flash": III:1 739. Source is Lucan VII:320–2.

178 Epaminondas: II:36 694–6, I:42 229, II:12 415, and (for "in command of war itself") III:1 738.

See Vieillard-Baron, J.-L., "Épaminondas," in Desan, *Dictionnaire* 330.

178 "Let us take away": III:1 739.

178 Cruelly hating cruelty: II:11 379. Hatred of hunting: II:11 383. Chicken or hare: II:11 379. On Montaigne and cruelty, see Brahami, F., "Cruauté," in Desan, *Dictionnaire* 236–8, and Hallie, P. P., "The ethics of Montaigne's 'De la cruauté,'" in La Charité, R. C. (ed.), *O un amy! Essays on Montaigne in Honor of Donald M. Frame* (Lexington, KY: French Forum, 1977), 156–71.

178 "Even the executions of the law": II:11 380–1. "I am so squeamish": III:12 992.

179 Frenchmen and their other halves: I:31 193. "It is one and the same nature": II:12 416.

179 "There is a certain respect" and "I am not afraid to admit": II:11 385.

179 Pascal mocked Montaigne: Pascal, "Discussion with M. de Sacy," in *Pensées* 188.

180 Leonard Woolf on Montaigne and cruelty, and the drowning of the puppies: Woolf, L., 17–21.

180 William James: James, W., "On a certain blindness in human beings," from *Talks to Teachers on Psychology* (New York: Henry Holt, 1912), in *The Writings of William James*, ed. J. J. McDermott (Chicago: University of Chicago Press, 1977), 629–45. "Zest and tingle": 629–31. Forgetting this is the worst error: 644–5.

10. Q. How to live? A. Wake from the sleep of habit

182 "I remember lying": Woolf, V., *Diary* I:190 (entry for Sept. 8, 1918).

182 Examples of divergent customs: I:23 98–9; I:49 263–5; II:12 431–2.

183 "This great world": I:26 141.

183 Potatoes from the Americas: Hale 173.

183 France's colonial prospects and adventures: Knecht, *Rise and Fall* 287, 297–300 (Brazil), 392–4 (Florida).

184 Montaigne's conversation with the Tupinambá: I:31 193. His collection of Americana: I:31 187. The servant who knew Brazil, and others to whom he introduced Montaigne: I:31 182–4.

184 Montaigne's reading: López de Gómara, *Historia de las Indias*, translated into French by Martin Fumée in 1568 as *Histoire generalle des Indes*. Bartolomé de Las Casas, *Brevisima relación de la destruccion de las Indias*, translated into French as *Tyrannies et cruautés des Espagnols . . .* (1579). Thevet, A., *Les Singularitez*, and Léry, J. de, *Histoire d'un voyage fait en la terre du Brésil* (La Rochelle: A. Chuppin, 1578). Anecdotes from Léry here taken from modern English translation: Léry, *History of a Voyage*. Elderly people without white hair: ibid. 56–7. Fighting for honor: ibid. 112–21. Cannibal feasts: ibid. 122–33. The human foot: ibid. 163–4. Léry felt safer: ibid. 169. Cannibalism in Sancerre: Léry, J. de, *Histoire mémorable de la ville de Sancerre* ([La Rochelle], 1574). On Léry, see Lestringant, F., *Jean de Léry ou l'invention du sauvage*, 2nd edn (Paris: H. Champion, 2005).

186 Incas and Aztecs: III:6 842.

186 "This is a nation": I:31 186.

186 "Once upon a time, there was no snake": Kramer, S. N., *History Begins at Sumer* (New York, 1959), 222, cited Levin 10.

186 Typee: Melville, H., *Typee*, cited Levin 68–9.

186 Stoics: Seneca, *Letters to Lucilius*, Letter 90. Loeb edn II: 395–431. On Stoics and primitivism, see Lovejoy, A. O. and Boas, G., *A Documentary History of Primitivism and Related Ideas*, Vol. 1 (Baltimore: Johns Hopkins Press, 1934), 106–7.

187 Wild fruit: I:31 185. The two cannibal songs: I:31 191–2. "Purely natural poetry": I:54 276.

187   Afterlife of cannibal love song: Chateaubriand, *Mémoires d'outre-tombe*, ed. M. Levaillant and G. Moulinier (Paris: Gallimard, 1964), 247–8 (Book VII, chap. 9), cited Lestringant 189. Kleist, Herder and Goethe: see Langer, U., "Montaigne's 'coulevre': notes on the reception of the *Essais* in 18th-century Germany," *Montaigne Studies* 7 (1995), 191–202, and Bouillier, *La Renommée de Montaigne en Allemagne* 30–1. On Goethe, see Bouillier, V., "Montaigne et Goethe," *Revue de littérature comparée* 5 (1925), 572–93. On German stoves: Moureau, F., "Le Manuscrit du *Journal de Voyage*: découverte, édition et copies," in Michel et al. (eds), *Montaigne et les Essais 1580–1980*, 289–99, this 297.

189   "They burn the victims alive": I:30 181.

189   "I am not sorry": I:31 189.

189   Coste: Montaigne, *Essais*, ed. P. Coste (London, 1724, and La Haye, 1727). On Coste, see Rumbold, M.E., *Traducteur Huguenot: Pierre Coste* (New York: P. Lang, 1991). Marveling that he had to wait so long: e.g. Nicolas Bricaire de la Dixmerie, *Eloge analytique et historique de Michel Montagne* (Amsterdam & Paris: Valleyre l'aîne, 1781), 2. See Moureau, F., "Réception de Montaigne (XVIIIe siècle)," in Desan, *Dictionnaire* 859.

190   Diderot, D., *Supplément au voyage de Bougainville* (1796). English translation by J. Hope Mason and R. Wokler in Diderot, *Political Writings* (Cambridge: Cambridge University Press, 1992), 31–75. Follow nature to be happy: 52–3. On Diderot, see Schwartz, J., *Diderot and Montaigne: the Essais and the Shaping of Diderot's Humanism* (Genèva: Droz, 1966).

191   On Rousseau and Montaigne: see Fleuret, and Dréano. Rousseau's copy of the *Essais* is now in the University of Cambridge Library.

191   Rousseau, *Discourse on the Origin of Inequality*. "I see an animal": 26. Harsh conditions make him strong: ibid. 27. Civilization makes him "sociable and a slave": ibid. 31. Savages do not kill themselves: ibid. 43. Murder under a philosopher's window: ibid. 47.

192   Rousseau, *Émile*. See Fleuret 83–121.

193   "I place Montaigne foremost": this preface appears in the Neuchâtel edition but not in modern ones based on the Paris manuscript. It is included as an appendix to Angela Scholar's translation: Rousseau, *Confessions*, 643–9, this 644. "This is the only portrait of a man": preface to Paris version, Rousseau, *Confessions* 3.

193   "I know men": Rousseau, *Confessions* 5.

193   Montaigne "bears the entire form of the human condition": III:2 740.

193   Contemporary accusations: Cajot, J., *Plagiats de M. J. J. R[ousseau], de Genève, sur l'éducation* (La Haye, 1766), 125–6. Bricaire de la Dixmerie, N., *Eloge analytique et historique de Michel Montagne* (Amsterdam & Paris: Valleyre l'aîne, 1781), 209–76, this 259.

11. Q. How to live? A. Live temperately

195   On early nineteenth-century responses, especially to Montaigne's friendship with La Boétie, see Frame, *Montaigne in France* 17–23. Sand: Sand, G., *Histoire de ma vie* (Paris: M. Lévy, 1856), VIII: 230–1. Lamartine: "All that I admire in him," "because it is you," and "friend Montaigne": Lamartine to Aymon de Virieu, May 21 [1811], July 26, 1810, and Nov. 9, 1809, respectively, in Lamartine I:290, I:235, I:178.

196   On visits to the tower, see Legros. On the state of the château before nineteenth century: Willett 221.

197   Compan and Gaillon: cited Legros 65–75.

197 "I have no great experience": II:12 520. "I like temperate and moderate natures": I:30 177. "My excesses do not carry me very far away": III:2 746. "The most beautiful lives": III:13 1044.

198 Lamartine turns against Montaigne: Lamartine to Aymon de Virieu, 21 May [1811], in Lamartine I:290. Sand "not Montaigne's disciple": George Sand to Guillaume Guizot, July 12, 1868, in Sand, G., *Correspondance* (Paris: Garnier, 1964–69), V: 268–9.

198 On Tasso: II:12 441. Poetry requires "frenzy": II:2 304. But "The archer who overshoots the target": I:30 178.

199 "No poet": Chasles, P., *Etudes sur le XVIe siècle en France* (Paris: Amyot, 1848), xlix. "Stoic indifference": Lefèvre-Deumier, J., *Critique littéraire* (Paris: Firmin-Didot, 1825–45), 344. On both, see Frame, *Montaigne in France* 15–16. "Moderation sees itself as beautiful": Nietzsche, *Daybreak* 167 (Book IV, s. 361).

200 On Renaissance ecstasy, see Screech 10.

200 "Transcendental humors frighten me": III:13 1044.

200 Mediocrity: III:2 745. Human and subhuman: III:13 1044.

201 Living appropriately: III:13 1037. "There is nothing so beautiful": III:13 1039.

201 West, R., *Black Lamb and Gray Falcon* (London: Macmillan, 1941), II:496–7.

12. Q. How to live? A. Guard your humanity

203 On the question of who was behind the attack on Coligny, see Holt 83–5. On the St. Bartholomew's massacres in general, see Diefendorf, and Sutherland, N. M., *The Massacre of Saint Bartholomew and the European Conflict 1559–72* (London: Macmillan, 1972). Montaigne says nothing about the massacres in the *Essays*, but he may have written about them in his diary, the Beuther *Ephemeris*—pages are missing for August 24 and October 3, the dates of massacres in Paris and Bordeaux, respectively. Perhaps he regretted what he had written and removed the pages, or perhaps his descendants did. See Nakam, *Montaigne et son temps* 192.

205 The story of the Lussaults is quoted in Diefendorf 100–2. On purification by fire and water: Davies, N.Z., "The rites of violence," in her *Society and Culture* 152–87, esp. 187.

205 On the death toll, see Holt 94 and Langer, U., "Montaigne's political and religious context," in Langer (ed.), *Cambridge Companion* 14.

205 The Bordeaux massacres: Holt 92–4. Singing and lutes in Orléans: Holt 93. Interpretation of children's involvement, superhuman scale of events, and Roman medal: Crouzet II: 95–8. Charles IX's medals: Crouzet II: 122–3.

207 Jean La Rouvière: cited in Salmon, J. H. M., "Peasant revolt in Vivarais, 1575–1580," in *Renaissance and Revolt* (Cambridge: Cambridge University Press, 1987), 221–2. See Holt 112–14.

207 Imminent Apocalypse: see Cunningham and Grell 19–91, which also analyzes each "horseman" in turn. Werewolf, twins, and nova: Crouzet II: 88–91. "Final ruin": Gournay, *Apology for the Woman Writing* [etc.] 138. Postel: Crouzet II: 335.

209 The Devil's last great effort: see Clark 321–6. Wier: Wier, J., *De praestigis daemonum* (Basel: J. Oporinus, 1564), cited in Delumeau, 251. Bodin and witches: Bodin, J., *On the Demon-Mania of Witches*, tr. R. A. Scott (Toronto: Centre for Reformation and Renaissance Studies, 1995), a translation of *De la Démonomanie des sorciers* (Paris: I. Du Puys, 1580), 200 ("legal tidiness") and 198 (public rumor "almost infallible"). On revival of medieval techniques such as swimming and searing: Clark 590–1. The witch panic would remain at its height until around 1640, peaking at

different times in different parts of Europe, and resulting in tens of thousands of deaths. Torture is useless: II:5 322–3. "Putting a very high price": III:11 961.

210   Antichrist: Africa/Babylon story reported in Jean de Nury's *Nouvelles admirables d'un enfant monstre* (1587), cited Crouzet II:370. Raemond: Raemond, *L'Antichrist.* See Magnien-Simonin, C., "Raemond, Florimond de," in Desan, *Dictionnaire* 849–50.

210   Zeal: Crouzet II: 439–44.

210   Radical Protestant publications of this period include François Hotman's *Francogallia* (mostly written earlier, but published 1573 and very popular in the wake of the massacre), Theodore de Bèze's *Du Droit des magistrats sur leurs subiets* (1574) and the *Vindiciae contra tyrannos* of 1579, by Hubert Languet, though some attribute it to Philippe Duplessis-Mornay. See Holt 100–1.

211   Stories of Henri III's sartorial and behavioral excesses are mostly based on Pierre de L'Estoile, an intermittently reliable Protestant memoirist. L'Estoile, P. de, *The Paris of Henry of Navarre as seen by Pierre de l'Estoile,* ed. N. Lyman Roelker (Cambridge, MA: Harvard University Press, 1958). Eating with forks, wearing nightclothes, washing hair: Knecht, *Rise and Fall* 489.

212   Montaigne on penitential processions: I:26 140. On the vagueness of predictions: I:11 34–5. Witchcraft as imagination: III:11 960–1.

212   Dangers of imagination: Del Rio, M., *Disquisitionum magicarum libri sex* (1599) and Lancre, P. 212 *De l'Incrédulité et mescreance du sortilège* (1622), both cited in Villey, *Montaigne devant la postérité* 360, 367–71. See Courcelles, D. de, "Martin Del Rio," and Legros, A., "Lancre, Pierre Rostegui de," both in Desan, *Dictionnaire* 243–4, 561–2.

213   *Politiques:* Crouzet II:250–2. "He wears the skin of a lamb": Dieudonné, R. de, *La Vie et condition des politiques et athéistes de ce temps* (Paris: R. Le Fizelier, 1589), 17.

213   *Politiques'* accusations against Leaguists: see e.g. *Lettre missive aux Parisiens d'un Gentilhomme serviteur du Roy . . .* (1591), 4–5, cited in Crouzet II:561. Montaigne: "Our zeal does wonders" and "There is no hostility": II:12 393–4.

214   *Politiques* thought everything would calm down: see e.g. Loys Le Caron's *De la Tranquillité de l'esprit* (1588), Saint-Germain d'Apchon's *L'Irenophile discours de la paix* (1594), and Guillaume du Vair's *La Constance et consolation ès calamitez publiques* (1594–95). Crouzet II: 555–7.

214   Foremost among critics who consider Montaigne's experience as dominated by war is Frieda Brown: see Brown, F., *Religious and Political Conservatism in the* Essais *of Montaigne* (Geneva: Droz, 1963). On this issue, see Coleman, J., "Montaigne and the Wars of Religion," in Cameron (ed.), *Montaigne and his Age* 107. Montaigne: "I am amazed to see" and "Whoever considers": I:26 141. "It will be a lot": II:16 577. "I do not despair about it": III:9 892.

216   Lipsius letters: Justus Lipsius to Montaigne, Aug. 30, 1588, and Sept. 18, 1589, cited Morford, M. P. O., *Stoics and Neostoics: Rubens and the Circle of Lipsius* (Princeton, NJ: Princeton University Press, 1991), 160.

216   Zweig unimpressed by *Essays* at first: all these remarks from Zweig, "Montaigne" 8–9.

217   Zweig's exile: Zweig, *World of Yesterday* 430–2. "I belong nowhere": ibid. xviii.

218   "The similarity of his epoch": Zweig to Jules Romains, Jan. 22, 1942, cited Bravo Unda, G., "Analogies de la pensée entre Montaigne et Stefan Zweig," *Bulletin de la Société des Amis de Montaigne* 11, no.2 (1988), 95–106. "In this brothership": Zweig, "Montaigne" 10.

219   The question for a person of integrity: Zweig, "Montaigne" 14. "He has none of the rolling tirades": ibid. 15. Montaigne's use of his failings: ibid. 76.

219   Rules extracted by Zweig: Zweig, "Montaigne" 55–8.

219 Suicide note: reproduced in appendix to Zweig, *World of Yesterday* 437.

220 Nothing left but one's naked existence: Zweig, "Montaigne" 10. "Only a person": ibid. 7. Leonard Woolf: Woolf, L. 18–19.

220 Macé-Scaron: Macé-Scaron 76.

221 Flaubert: Gustave Flaubert to Mlle Leroyer de Chantepie, June 16, 1857, cited Frame, *Montaigne in France* 61.

13. *Q. How to live? A. Do something no one has done before*

222 Details of all early *Essays* editions in "Sources"; also see Sayce and Maskell. Millanges: see Hoffmann 66–83. On both Millanges editions (1580 and 1582), see Blum, C., "Dans l'Atelier de Millanges," in Blum & Tournon (eds), *Editer les* Essais *de Montaigne* (79–97). On the first edition's print run: Desan, P., "Édition de 1580," in Desan, *Dictionnaire* 297–300, this 300.

223 La Croix du Maine: La Croix du Maine 329. The *Essays* also featured in Antoine Du Verdier's similar bibliography, *La Bibliothèque d'Antoine Du Verdier, seigneur de Vauprivas* (Lyon, 1585), entry on "Michel de Montaigne," 872–81. The *Essays* did better than Montaigne expected: III:9 895. "A public article of furniture": III:5 781.

223 "Sir, then Your Majesty must like me": La Croix du Maine 329. Cf. Montaigne's description of his book as "consubstantial with its author": II:18 612.

223 Red wine: Scaliger and Dupuy both cited in Villey, *Montaigne devant la postérité* 73. From red to white to red: III:13 1031. "Effrontery": Malebranche, *La recherche de la vérité* (1674), 369, cited Marchi 48. Pascal: Pascal, *Pensées* no. 534, p. 127.

223 Pattison: Pattison, M., review article in *Quarterly Review* 198 (Sept. 1856), 396–415, this 396. "Twaddling": St John, B., *Montaigne the Essayist* (London: Chapman & Hall, 1858), I: 316–17. "The very man," "the kernel": Sterling 323–4.

224 "I turn my gaze inward": II:17 606. On this passage, see Starobinski 225–6. Also see Coleman 114–15, disputing this translation. On the *Essays* as a Baroque or Mannerist work, see: Buffum; Butor; Sayce, R.A., "Baroque elements in Montaigne," *French Studies* 8 (1954), 1–15; Nakam, G., "Montaigne manieriste," in her *Le dernier Montaigne* 195–228; Rigolot, F., "Montaigne's anti-Mannerist Mannerism," in Cameron and Willett (eds), *Le Visage changeant de Montaigne* 207–30. Montaigne: "Grotesques" and "Monstrous bodies": I:28 164. Horace on poetry: Horace, *Ars poetica* 1–23.

225 Writing with rhythm of conversation: II:17 587. He speaks of his *"langage coupé"* in his instructions to the printer in the Bordeaux copy: see Sayce 283.

225 "Of a hundred members and faces": I:50 266.

225 "Of Coaches": III:6 831–49. On the title of this essay: see Tournon, A., "Fonction et sens d'un titre énigmatique," *Bulletin de la Société des Amis de Montaigne* 19–20 (1984), 59–68, and his entry "Coches," in Desan, *Dictionnaire* 175–6. "Of Physiognomy": III:12 964–92.

226 Thackeray: see Dédéyan I:288. "Often they only denote it by some sign" and "words . . . in a corner": III:9 925. See McKinley, M. B., *Words in a Corner: Studies in Montaigne's Latin Quotations* (Lexington, KY: French Forum, 1981).

14. Q. How to live? A. See the world

227   "Perpetual variety of the forms of our nature": III:9 904. "Honest curiosity": I:26 139. Feeling presence of his classical heroes: III:9 928. "Rub and polish": I:26 136.

228   Sluicing out stones: Travel Journal, in *The Complete Works*, tr. D. Frame, 1243. His father, grandfather, and great-grandfather: II:37 702. Venetian turpentine: Travel Journal 1143. The goat: II:37 718–19. On spas: II:37 715–16.

229   On his route and dates of travel, see the Travel Journal, in *The Complete Works*, tr. D. Frame.

230   Mattecoulon took part in two killings, while acting as second in someone else's duel. He was saved from prison only by the French king's direct intervention. All this, as Montaigne commented, in obedience to a code of honor that made no sense. II:27 639; Travel Journal 1257. On another young man who left in Padua, M. de Cazalis, see Travel Journal 1123.

230   On traveling conditions: Heath, M., "Montaigne and travel," in Cameron (ed.), *Montaigne and His Age* 121–32; Hale 145–8. Montaigne's change of route: Travel Journal 1130.

231   Montaigne's preference for riding: III:6 833–4. On river travel: III:6 834, Travel Journal, 1092 and 1116. On seasickness: Travel Journal, 1123. Riding more comfortable during a kidney-stone attack: III:6 833–4, III:5 811.

231   Going with the flow: III:9 904–5. "If it looks ugly on the right": III:9 916. On Virginia Woolf: Woolf, L., *Downhill All the Way* (London: Hogarth, 1968), 178–9. "Roll relaxedly": II:17 605.

234   No path: Travel Journal, 1115.

234   Late starts: III:9 905; III:13 1024. Eats local food in local style, and wishes he had his cook: Travel Journal 1077, 1086–7.

234   Other travelers closed up in themselves: III:9 916–17. "In truth there entered": Travel Journal 1087.

234   Keeping the journal in Italian: III:5 807. His Italian was good, though not flawless, and early published editions of the Journal tidied it up somewhat. See Garavini, F., "Montaigne: écrivain italien?" in Blum and Moreau (eds), *Études montaignistes* 117–29, and Cavallini, C., "Italianismes," in Desan, *Dictionnaire* 515–16. Handkerchief in Augsburg: Travel Journal 1096–7.

235   Christening: Travel Journal, 1094–5. Synagogue: ibid. 1119. Circumcision: ibid. 1152–4.

235   White beard and eyebrow: Travel Journal 1063. Cross-dressing and sex changes: ibid. 1059–60.

235   Swiss table manners and bedrooms: Travel Journal 1072, 1077.

236   Birdcage: Travel Journal 1085. Ostriches: ibid. 1098–9. Hair-duster: ibid. 1096. Remote-control gates: ibid. 1099–100.

236   Fugger gardens: Travel Journal 1097–8.

236   Michelangelo: Travel Journal 1133.

236   The Travel Journal: after being found and published, it was deposited in the royal library and should now be in the Bibliothèque nationale, but at some point it went missing. We now have only the 1774 published version, plus a handwritten copy with a different text. See Moureau, F., "La Copie Leydet du *Journal de Voyage*," in Moureau, F. and Bernouilli, R. (eds.), *Autour du Journal de voyage de Montaigne* (Geneva & Paris: Slatkine, 1982), 107–85; and his "Le manuscrit du *Journal de Voyage*: découverte, édition et copies," in Michel et al. (eds), *Montaigne et les Essais 1580–1980* 289–99; and Rigolot, F., "*Journal de voyage*," in Desan, *Dictionnaire* 533–7. "Three stools": Travel Journal 1077. "In front and behind": ibid. 1078. "As big and long as a pine nut": ibid. 1243. Swiss stoves: ibid. 1078.

237   On the secretary: see Brush, C. B., "The secretary, again," *Montaigne Studies* 5 (1993), 113–38, esp. 136–8.

The secretary probably came from Montaigne's own household: he shows familiarity with local towns around the estate: Travel Journal 1089, 1105. Long speeches: Travel Journal 1068–9, 1081.

238 Poland or Greece, and "I never saw him less tired": Travel Journal 1115.

238 Venice: Travel Journal 1121–2. On Franco, see Rigolot, F., "Franco, Veronica," in Desan, *Dictionnaire* 418.

238 Ferrara: Travel Journal 1128–9. Meeting Tasso: II:12 441. Fencing in Bologna: Travel Journal 1129–30. Trick gardens: ibid. 1132, 1135–6.

238 Entering Rome: Travel Journal ibid. 1141–3.

239 Inquisition officials: Travel Journal 1166. "It seemed to me": 1178.

239 Rome intolerant but cosmopolitan: Travel Journal 1142, 1173. Roman citizenship: *Essays* II:9 930; Travel Journal 1174.

239 Sermons, disputations, and prostitutes: Travel Journal, 1172. Vatican library: ibid. 1158–60. Circumcision: ibid. 1152–4.

240 Audience with Pope: Travel Journal 1144–6.

240 Penitential procession: Travel Journal 1170–1.

241 Exorcism: Travel Journal 1156. Execution of Catena: ibid. 1148–9; cf. II:11 382 on violence to dead bodies.

242 Tops of walls: Travel Journal 1142. Tops of columns: ibid. 1152.

242 Spoils of Seneca and Plutarch: II:32 661. Mental exertion required: Travel Journal 1150–1.

243 Goethe: Goethe, J. W., *Italian Journey*, tr. W. H. Auden and E. Mayer (Harmondsworth: Penguin, 1970; repr. 1982): "All the dreams": 129 (entry for Nov. 1, 1786); "I am now in a state of clarity": ibid. 136 (entry for 10 Nov. 1786). Freud: Freud, S., "A disturbance of memory on the Acropolis," in *Works*, tr. and ed. J. Strachey (London: Hogarth, 1953–74), 22 (1964), 239–48, this 241. "The Rome and Paris that I have in my soul": II:12 430. "I enjoyed a tranquil mind": Travel Journal 1239.

244 Loreto: Travel Journal 1184–5. La Villa: ibid. 1210, 1240–6.

15. Q. How to live? A. Do a good job, but not too good a job

245 The jurats' two letters and his journey to Rome: Travel Journal 1246–55.

245 "I excused myself": III:10 934. The king's letter: translated in Frame, *Montaigne* 224.

246 Arrival home: Travel Journal 1270, and Montaigne, *Le Livre de raison*, entry for Nov. 30.

246 On his tasks as mayor, and the difficulties of the time: Lazard 282–3; Lacouture 227–8; Cocula, A.-M., *Montaigne, maire de Bordeaux* (Bordeaux: Horizon chimérique, 1992). Ears to everyone and judgment to no one: III:8 855.

247 On Matignon, see Cooper, R., "Montaigne dans l'entourage du maréchal de Matignon," *Montaigne Studies* 13 (2001), 99–140; and his "Matignon, Maréchal de" in Desan, *Dictionnaire* 640–4.

248 On Pierre's exhaustion by travel: III:10 935. Montaigne's travels as mayor: Frame, *Montaigne* 230. His work at the château: Nakam, *Montaigne et son temps* 311.

248 "This was done in my case": III:10 934. On his reelection, against opposition: Frame, *Montaigne* 230.

248 Montaigne as go-between: Frame, *Montaigne* 232–4.

249 Vaillac rebellion and exile from Bordeaux: Frame, *Montaigne* 238–40. Letters from Montaigne to Matignon, May 22 and 27, 1585, in *The Complete Works*, tr. D. Frame, 1323–7.

249 Contemporary admiration: Thou, J.-A. de, *Mémoires* (1714), and Duplessis-Mornay to Montaigne, Nov. 25, 1583, translated in Frame, *Montaigne*, 229, 233.

250 "Order" and "gentle and mute tranquillity": III:10 953.

250 "A languishing zeal" and "That's a good one!": III:10 950. Keeping a city uneventful during "innovation": III:10 953. True motives for apparent commitment: III:10 951.

251 What duty commanded: III:10 954.

251 Shakespeare, W., *King Lear* (written c. 1603–6). "I mortally hate to seem a flatterer": I:40 225–6.

251 "I frankly tell them my limits": III:1 731. Openness draws people out, and not difficult to get on between two parties: III:1 730.

252 Not everyone understood: III:1 731. "When all is said and done": III:8 854.

253 Matignon to Henri III, June 30, 1585, and to Montaigne, July 30, 1585, both translated in Frame, *Montaigne* 240.

253 Montaigne's letters to the jurats of Bordeaux, July 30 and 31, 1585, in *The Complete Works*, tr. D. Frame, 1328–9.

253 Order forbidding entry to the city: see Bonnet, P., "Montaigne et la peste de Bordeaux," in Blum and Moreau (eds), *Études montaignistes* 59–67, this 64.

254 Criticism of Montaigne's decision: Detcheverry, Grün, Feugère, and Lecomte, all cited in Bonnet, P., "Montaigne et la peste de Bordeaux," in Blum and Moreau (eds), *Études montaignistes* 59–67, this 59–62. The letters were first published in Detcheverry, A., *Histoire des Israélites de Bordeaux* (Bordeaux: Balzac jeune, 1850).

255 "I hold back": II:12 454.

255 On nihilism in this period, see Gillespie, M. A., *Nihilism before Nietzsche* (Chicago: University of Chicago Press, 1995).

255 Faguet: his writings are collected with a preface by A. Compagnon as Faguet, *Autour de Montaigne*. Champion: Champion, E., *Introduction aux Essais de Montaigne* (Paris, 1900): see Compagnon, A., Preface to Faguet 16.

255 Guizot: Guizot, G., *Montaigne: études et fragments*. "He will not make us into the kind of men our times require": ibid. 269. Guizot worked for 25 years to produce an edition of the *Essays* and a study of Montaigne's life, and completed neither, but his friends assembled this collection of fragments after his death.

256 Michelet: Michelet, *Histoire de France* (1861) VIII: 429 ("Feeble and negative" idea) and X: 397–8 ("watch himself dream"). Both as cited in Frame, *Montaigne in France* 42–3.

256 Church, R. W., "The Essays of Montaigne," in *Oxford Essays Contributed by Members of the University. 1857* (London: John Parker, 1857), 239–82. "The nothingness of man . . . the idea of duty": ibid. 265. "Indolence and want of moral tone": ibid. 280. On Church, see Dédéyan I: 295–308.

256 Halifax's remarks are reproduced in Hazlitt's 1842 edition of Montaigne, *The Complete Works* xxxv.

257 Honoria's edition: Montaigne, *Essays*, ed. Honoria (1800) (see "Sources"). It was a project along the lines of Henrietta Maria Bowdler's *The Family Shakespeare* (1807), which gave the word "bowdlerize" to the English language. "If, by separating the pure ore" and "He is also so often unconnected": Honoria's introduction, xix. Montaigne rebuked for not mentioning the St. Bartholomew's massacre: Honoria's edition, 104n. Do not try waking children with music: ibid. 157n. Montaigne's regulation of his life, his conformism, and his "many excellent religious sentiments": Honoria's introduction, xviii.

258 "I doubt if I can decently admit": III:12 975.

258 The succession question, and the preference of the *politiques*: Nakam, *Montaigne et son temps* 329–32.

259 Visit of Navarre, including the stag hunt: Montaigne, *Le Livre de raison*, entry for Dec. 19, as translated in Frame, *Montaigne* 235.

260 Still working on task: Montaigne to Matignon, Jan. 18, 1585, in *The Complete Works*, tr. D. Frame, 1314–15.

261 "Guelph to the Ghibellines": III:12 972. "There were no formal accusations": III:12 972. Siege of Castillon: Frame, *Montaigne* 256.

261 "A mighty load of our disturbances": III:12 969. Plague: III:12 976.

261 Watching people dig their own graves: III:12 979.

262 "I, who am so hospitable": III:12 976. On Montaigne's political work during and after his refugee wanderings: Frame, *Montaigne* 247.

262 The invitation to Montaigne and his wife, and the allowance, are alluded to in a letter from Catherine de' Medici to a treasurer on Dec. 31, 1586: see Frame, *Montaigne* 267.

263 Montaigne working with Corisande: Frame, *Montaigne* 269–70.

263 Montaigne's mission, and letters mentioning it: Frame, *Montaigne* 270–3. English anxieties: ibid. 276.

264 Attack in the forest: Montaigne to Matignon, Feb. 16 [1588?], in *The Complete Works*, tr. D. Frame, 1330–1.

265 Henri III and Guise in Paris, and the Day of the Barricades: see Knecht, *Rise and Fall* 523–4. The Pope's comment: cited Neale, J. E., *The Age of Catherine de Medici*, new edn (London: Jonathan Cape, 1957), 96.

265 "I have never seen": Pasquier to Sainte-Marthe, May 1588, in Pasquier, *Lettres historiques* 286–97.

266 Montaigne's arrest and release: Montaigne, *Le Livre de raison*, entries for July 10 and 20; latter as translated in Frame, *Montaigne* 281. As usual Montaigne mixed up his dates: he wrote the entry first on the page for July 20, then realized his mistake and rewrote it on the page for July 10. The second version is briefer; either he found it tedious to write it out twice, or revision made him more concise. "No prison has received me": III:13 999–1000.

267 Brach: Pierre de Brach to Justus Lipsius, Feb. 4, 1593, translated in Frame, *Montaigne* 282. On Brach, see Magnien, M., "Brache, Pierre de," in Desan, *Dictionnaire* 126–8.

268 On Marie de Gournay, see Chapter 18 above.

269 Pasquier's advice on style, and Montaigne's ignoring of it: Pasquier to A. M. de Pelgé, 1619, in Pasquier, *Choix de lettres* 45–6, as translated in Frame, *Montaigne* 283. "Oh, miserable spectacle!": Pasquier, *Lettres historiques* 286–97. On Étienne Pasquier, see Magnien, C., "Estienne Pasquier 'familiar' de Montaigne?" *Montaigne Studies* 13 (2001), 277–313.

269 Preachers urging killing of king: e.g. Boucher, J., *De justa Henrici tertii abdicatione* (Aug. 1589). See Holt 132.

269 A city gone mad: L'Estoile and Thou, both cited in Nakam, *Montaigne et son temps* 341–2.

270 "This proposition, so solemn": II:12 392.

270 "The most express ways that we have": III:12 971.

271 Montaigne's letters to Henri IV: Montaigne to Henri IV, Jan. 18 [1590?] and Sept. 2 [1590?], in *The Complete Works*, , tr. D. Frame, 1332–6.

272 "I look upon our kings": III:1 728.

273 On Henri IV's manly habits: Knecht, *Rise and Fall* 559–61.

273 Henri IV's speech of 1599: cited Knecht, *Rise and Fall* 545–7.

16. Q. How to live? A.Philosophize only by accident

274 "Free and unruly": II:17 587. Halifax: letter included in original edition of Cotton's translation (1685–86), and reproduced in Hazlitt's 1842 edition, unnumbered prelim. leaf. Hazlitt: Hazlitt, W., "On old English writers and speakers," Essay X in *The Plain Speaker* (London: H. Colburn, 1826), II: 277–307, this 305.

275 "The English mind": Woolf, V., "Reading," in *Essays*, ed. A. McNeillie (London: Hogarth, 1986–), III:141–61, this 154. "In taking up his pen": Hazlitt 180.

275 "Unpremeditated and accidental philosopher," and explanation of what he means by this: II:12 496–7.

276 On Florio: Yates, *John Florio*; Pfister, M., "Inglese italianato—Italiano anglizzato: John Florio," in Höfele, A. and Koppenfels, W. von (eds), *Renaissance Go-Betweens: Cultural Exchange in Early Modern Europe* (Berlin & New York: Walter de Gruyter, 2005), 31–54. His conversational primers and dictionary: Florio, J., *Firste Fruites* (London: T. Woodcock, [1578]), *Second Frutes* (London: T. Woodcock, 1591), and *A Worlde of Wordes* (London: E. Blount, 1598). His translation of the *Essays*: Montaigne, *Essayes* (1603): see "Sources" for full details.

276 "So do hir attributes": Montaigne, *Essayes* (1915–21), I: 2.

277 "Our Germans, drowned in wine": II:2 298. "Our carowsing tospot German souldiers": Montaigne, *Essayes* (1915–21), II:2 17. "Werewolves, goblins, and chimeras": I:18 62. "Larves, Hobgoblins, Robbin-good-fellowes": Montaigne, *Essayes* (1915–21), I:17 67. The chapter number differs in Florio because it is based on a different text, that of Marie de Gournay's 1595 edition. On this issue, see Chapter 18 above.

278 Gonzalo's speech: *The Tempest* II. i.145–52. The similarity is to a passage from Montaigne's "Of Cannibals": Montaigne, *Essayes* (1915–21), I:30 220. Again, chapter numbering differs because the editions are based on different texts. "Traffic" means commerce; "letters," literature; "use of service," keeping servants; "succession," inheritance; "bourn," land boundaries; and "tilth," tilling land, i.e. agriculture. The similarity was first noticed by Edward Capell, in his *Notes and Various Readings to Shakespeare* (London: H. Hughs, [1775]), II:63.

278 Comparison with *Hamlet*: "We are, I know not how, double within ourselves": II:16 570. "Bashful, insolent; chaste": II:1 294. Too much thinking makes action impossible: II:20 622. On this question, see Boutcher, W., "Marginal commentaries: the cultural transmission of Montaigne's *Essais* in Shakespeare's England," in Kapitaniak and Maguin (eds), *Shakespeare et Montaigne*, 13–27, and his "'Learning mingled with Nobilitie': directions for reading Montaigne's *Essais* in their institutional context," in Cameron and Willett (eds), *Le Visage changeant de Montaigne*, 337–62, esp. 337–9; and Peter Mack's forthcoming *Shakespeare, Montaigne, and Renaissance Ethical Reading*. Much work has been done recently on the dating of *Hamlet*; it is now thought to date from late 1599 or early 1600, which creates a problem if Shakespeare is thought to have read Florio's translation. But we know that manuscript copies of the latter were in circulation well before the publication date: Shakespeare's contemporary William Cornwallis mentioned their "going from hand to hand" in 1599.

279 Shared theme: Robertson, J. M., *Montaigne and Shakespeare* (London: The University Press, 1891), cited in Marchi 193. Shared atmosphere also discussed in Sterling 321–2.

279 Bacon wrote Montaigne: Donnelly, I., *The Great Cryptogram: Francis Bacon's Cipher in the So-called Shakespeare Plays* (London: Sampson, Low, Marston, Searle & Rivington, 1888), II: 955–65, 971–4. "Bacon" and "white breasts": Donnelly II: 971. "Mountaines": II: 972–3. "Can anyone believe

that all this is the result of accident?" II: 974. Role of Anthony Bacon: II:955.

280 On the Bacon brothers: See Banderier, G., "Bacon, Anthony," and Gontier, T., "Bacon, Francis," in Desan, *Dictionnaire* 89–90. Francis Bacon does mention Montaigne in his *Essays*, but not in its first edition.

281 Cornwallis: Cornwallis, W., *Essayes*, ed. D. C. Allen (Baltimore: Johns Hopkins University Press, 1946).

281 Burton: Burton, R., *The Anatomy of Melancholy* (New York: NYRB Classics, 2001), I: 17.

281 Browne: Browne, Thomas, *The Major Works* (Harmondsworth: Penguin, 1977). See Texte, J., "La Descendance de Montaigne: Sir Thomas Browne," in his *Etudes de littérature européenne* (Paris: A. Colin, 1898), 51–93.

281 Cotton: Montaigne, *Essays*, tr. Cotton (1685–86): see "Sources" for full details. On Cotton, see Nelson, N., "Montaigne with a Restoration voice: Charles Cotton's translation of the *Essais*," *Language and Style* 24, no. 2 (1991), 131–44; and Hartle, P., "Cotton, Charles," in *Oxford Dictionary of National Biography* (http://dx.doi.org/10.1093/ref:odnb/6410), from which the poem is also taken.

282 Pope: cited Coleman 167.

282 *Spectator*: *Spectator* no. 562 (July 2, 1714), cited Dédéyan I: 28. Doing it agreeably: Dédéyan I: 29.

283 The Montaignesque element: Pater, W., "Charles Lamb," in *Appreciations* (London: Macmillan, 1890), 105–23, this 116–17.

283 Leigh Hunt's comment: Montaigne, *Complete Works* (1842), 41, British Library's copy (C.61.h.5). This passage is I:22 95 in Frame's edition.

283 Hazlitt on essay-writing: Hazlitt 178–80.

283 Hazlitt's Cotton's Montaigne: Montaigne, *Complete Works* (1842). Hazlitt's Hazlitt's Cotton's Montaigne: Montaigne, *Essays*, tr. C. Cotton, ed. W. Hazlitt and W. C. Hazlitt (London: Reeves & Turner, 1877). On the Hazlitt family business, see Dédéyan I: 257–8.

284 Sterne: Sterne, L., *Tristram Shandy*, ed. I. Campbell Ross (Oxford: Oxford Paperbacks, 1998). References to Montaigne: 38, 174, 289–90 (Vol. 1 chap. 4, Vol. 2 chap. 4, Vol. 4 chap. 15). The line diagrams: 453–4 (Vol. 6, chap. 40). Promised chapters: 281 (Vol. 4, chap. 9). "Could a historiographer": 64–5 (Vol. 1, chap. 14).

17. *Q. How to live? A. Reflect on everything; regret nothing*

286 Joyce, J. *Finnegans Wake*: these examples given in Burgess, A., *Here Comes Everybody*, rev. edn (London: Arena, 1987), 189–90.

286 Montaigne was a different person in the past: III:2 748–9. "We are all patchwork": II:1 296.

287 "Who does not see . . . ?" III:9 876.

287 "Not their end": Woolf, V., "Montaigne," 77.

287 1588 edition: Montaigne, *Essais*, "5th edn" (1588): see "Sources."

288 "It is the inattentive reader": III:9 925.

288 "For my part": III:8 872.

290 "In order to get more in": I:40 224. Plutarch's pointing finger: I:26 140.

290 "It gathers force": this is written on the title page of the "Bordeaux Copy": *Montaigne: Essais. Reproduction en fac-similé.* Source is Virgil, *Aeneid*, 4: 169–77.

290 "I fear I am getting worse": Montaigne to A. Loisel, inscription on a copy of the 1588 *Essais*, in *The Complete Works*, tr. D. Frame, 1332.

18. *Q. How to live? A. Give up control*

291   On Marie de Gournay: Fogel; Ilsley; Tetel (ed.), *Montaigne et Marie de Gournay*; Nakam, G., "Marie le Jars de Gournay, 'fille d'alliance' de Montaigne (1565–1645)," in Arnould (ed.), *Marie de Gournay et l'édition de 1595 des Essais de Montaigne*, 11–21. Her collected works are available as Gournay, *Oeuvres complètes* (2002).

292   "A woman pretending to learning": Gournay, *Apology for the Woman Writing* (1641 version), as translated by Hillman and Quesnel in their edition of Gournay, *Apology for the Woman Writing and Other Works*, 107–54, this 126.

292   Tangle of intellect and emotion: Gournay, *Peincture des moeurs*, in *L'Ombre de la demoiselle de Gournay* (1626), as cited in Ilsley 129.

293   Hellebore: Gournay, *Preface* (1998) 27.

293   "How did he know all that about me?" Levin: *The Times* (Dec. 2, 1991), p. 14. "It seems he is my very self": Gide, A., *Montaigne* (London & New York: Blackamore Press, 1929), 77–8. "Here is a 'you'": Zweig, "Montaigne" 17.

293   Meeting: Gournay, *Preface* (1998) 27.

294   Bodkin: I:14 49. In the Bordeaux Copy, he only says "a girl," but Gournay's own edition specifies "a girl in Picardy" whom he saw just before his trip to Blois.

295   Working together in Picardy: in fact, only three of the new additions are in her handwriting. *Montaigne: Essais. Reproduction en fac-similé*, ff. 42v., 47r. and 290v. See Hoffmann, G. and Legros, A., "Secrétaires," in Desan, *Dictionnaire* 901–4, this 901.

295   "The man whom I am so honored in calling father" and "I cannot, Reader": Gournay, *Preface* (1998) 27, 29. "In truth, if someone is surprised": Gournay, *The Promenade of Monsieur de Montaigne*, in Gournay, *Apology for the Woman Writing* [etc.], 21–67, this 29.

296   Léonor as Gournay's sister: Ilsley 34.

296   "Nor is there any fear": Gournay, *The Promenade of Monsieur de Montaigne*, in Gournay, *Apology for the Woman Writing* [etc.] 21–67, this 32. "He was mine for only four years" and "When he praised me": Gournay, *Preface to the* Essays 99.

296   "She is the only person I still think about." II:17 610. Suspicions about this passage date back to Arthur-Antoine Armaingaud, who queried it in a speech published in the first *Bulletin of the Société des Amis de Montaigne* in 1913. See Keffer 129. She deleted it from her 1635 edition of the *Essais*. On slips falling out: see e.g. I:18 63n. and I:21 624n. in D. Frame's edition of the *Complete Works*. On the rebinding of the Bordeaux Copy, see Desan, P., "Exemplaire de Bordeaux," in Desan, *Dictionnaire* 363–8, this 366.

297   Letters to Lipsius: Gournay to Lipsius April 25, 1593 and May 2, 1596, as translated in Ilsley 40–1 and 79–80; Lipsius to Gournay, May 24, 1593, published in Lipsius, J., *Epistolarum selectarum centuria prima ad Belgas* (Antwerp: Moret, 1602), I:15, and here as translated in Ilsley 42.

298   The *Proumenoir*: Gournay, M. de, *Le Proumenoir de Monsieur de Montaigne* (Paris: A. l'Angelier, 1594), translated in Gournay, *Apology for the Woman Writing* [etc.] 21–67. Its origins explained in the epistle: 25.

298   Gournay's edition: Montaigne, *Essais* (1595): see "Sources."

298   On her last-minute corrections: Sayce and Maskell 28 (entry 7A); and Céard, J., "Montaigne et ses lecteurs: l'édition de 1595," a paper given in a debate about the 1595 edition at the Bibliothèque nationale in 2002, 1–2, http://www.amisdemontaigne.net/ceard1595.pdf .

298 Gournay as protector: Gournay, *Preface to the* Essays: "Having lost their father": 101. "When I defend him": 43. "One cannot deal with great affairs": 53. "Whoever says of Scipio": 79. "Excellence exceeds all limits": and "ravished": 81. Judging people by what they think of the *Essays*: 31. Diderot: article "Pyrrhonienne," in the *Encyclopédie*, cited in Tilley 269.

300 "I cannot take a step": Gournay, *Preface to the* Essays 85. On the contradictions between her personality and Montaigne's: Bauschatz, C. M., "Imitation, writing, and self-study in Marie de Gournay's 1595 'Préface' to Montaigne's *Essais*," in Logan, M. R. and Rudnytsky, P. L. (eds), *Contending Kingdoms* (Detroit: Wayne State University Press, 1991), 346–64, this 346.

300 "Blessed indeed": Gournay, *Preface to the* Essays 35.

301 Change of mind about the Preface: Gournay to Lipsius, May 2, 1596, cited McKinley, M., "An editorial revival: Gournay's 1617 Preface to the *Essais*," *Montaigne Studies* 7 (1996), 193. The ten-line preface was used in all seventeenth-century editions up to 1617, when the longer one returned in a revised form: Montaigne: *Essais*, ed. Gournay (Paris: J. Petit-pas, 1617). A different version had meanwhile appeared in Gournay, *Le Proumenoir* (1599).

301 Lacking piety: Gournay, *Peincture des moeurs*, in *L'Ombre* (1626). See Ilsley 129. On Gournay as a secret *libertine*: Dotoli, G., "Montaigne et les libertins via Mlle de Gournay," in Tetel (ed.), *Montaigne et Marie de Gournay* 105–41.

302 On the Académie: Ilsley 217–42. Gournay's views on style: Ilsley 200–16, and Holmes, P. P., "Mlle de Gournay's defense of Baroque imagery," *French Studies* 8 (1954), 122–31, this 122–9.

302 Gournay's epitaph: cited Ilsley 262. On her changing reputation after death: Ilsley 266–77. "Nothing can equal": Niceron, J.-P., *Mémoires pour servir à l'histoire des hommes illustres dans la République des lettres* (Paris, 1727–45), XVI:231 (1733), cited Ilsley 270.

302 Gournay as leech: this accusation was most notably made by Chapelain, who was connected with a planned rival Elzevir edition: see Boase, *Fortunes* 54, and Ilsley 255.

302 "White-haired old maid": Rat, M., introduction to Montaigne, *Oeuvres complètes* (Paris: Gallimard, 1962), as translated by R. Hillman in Gournay, *Apology for the Woman Writing* 18. Villey: Villey, *Montaigne devant la postérité* 44.

302 Reviving reputation: Schiff, M., *La Fille d'alliance de Montaigne, Marie de Gournay* (Paris: H. Champion, 1910). Novels based on her life: Mairal, M., *L'Obèle* (Paris: Flammarion, 2003), and Diski, J., *Apology for the Woman Writing* (London: Virago, 2008). New scholarly editions include that of her complete works: Gournay, *Oeuvres complètes* (2002).

304 The editing wars: see Keffer, including his translation of the letters of Cagnieul: 62–3; and Desan, P., "Cinq siècles de politiques éditoriales des Essais," in Desan, *Montaigne dans tous ses états* (121–91).

305 On Strowski's boasting: Compagnon, A., "Les Repentirs de Fortunat Strowski," in Tetel (ed.), *Montaigne et Marie de Gournay* 53–77, this 69. On Armaingaud's dating: Keffer 18–19. His attribution of the *Servitude volontaire*: Armaingaud, A., *Montaigne pamphlétaire* (Paris: Hachette, 1910). "He alone knows him": Perceval, E. de, article in the *Bulletin de la Société des Bibliophiles de Guyenne* (1936), translated in Keffer 163. On Villey: Defaux, G., "Villey, Pierre," in Desan, *Dictionnaire* 1023–4. On his blindness: Villey, P., "Le Travail intellectuel des aveugles," *Revue des deux mondes* (1 mars 1909), 420–43. On not being invited in 1933: Keffer 21.

306 Among later twentieth-century editions to prioritize the Bordeaux Copy were the Pléiade edition by A. Thibaudet and M. Rat: Montaigne, *Oeuvres complètes* (Paris: Gallimard, 1962), used by D. Frame for his translation, and the revised version of Villey's edition: Montaigne, *Les Essais,*

ed. P. Villey and V.-L. Saulnier (Paris: PUF, 1965).

306 Dezeimeris hypothesis: Dezeimeris, R., *Recherche sur la recension du texte posthume des Essais de Montaigne* (Bordeaux: Gounouihou, 1866). Working out the logistics, and on this theory in general: Maskell, D., "Quel est le dernier état authentique des Essais de Montaigne?" *Bibliothèque d'humanisme et Renaissance* 40 (1978), 85–103, and his "The evolution of the *Essais*," in McFarlane and Maclean (eds), *Montaigne: Essays in Memory of Richard Sayce* 13–34; Desan, P., "*L'Exemplar* et L'Exemplaire de Bordeaux," in Desan, *Montaigne dans tous ses états* 69–120; Balsamo, J. and Blum, C., "Édition de 1595," in Desan, *Dictionnaire* 306–12; Arnould, J-C. (ed.), *Marie de Gournay et l'édition de 1595 des* Essais *de Montaigne;* O'Brien.

307 The new Pléiade edition and the Tournon edition: see "Sources" for full details. A. Tournon and J. Céard, representing the two positions, took part in a debate at the Bibliothèque nationale on Feb. 9, 2002, "Les deux visages des *Essais*" (The Two Faces of the *Essays*): see their two papers at http://www.amisdemontaigne.net/visagesessais.htm.

308 De-cluttering: Montaigne, *Essays*, ed. Honoria (1800).

308 Charron: Charron, *De la Sagesse*. Relations of humans to animals: 72–86. On Charron, see Gontier, E., "Charron, Pierre," in Desan, *Dictionnaire* 155–9. "Remake": Bellenger 188. Charron, *Petit traité de la sagesse* (Paris, 1625).

309 Bad copyist: Montaigne, *Les Essais*, ed. Gournay (Paris: Jean Camusat, 1635), Preface, cited Villey, *Montaigne devant la postérité* 162.

310 Purified essences: *L'Esprit des Essais de Montaigne* (Paris: C. de Sercy, 1677). *Pensées de Montaigne, propres à former l'esprit et les moeurs* (Paris: Anisson, 1700), which includes "There are few books so bad": 5.

310 "*Moby-Dick* must have been difficult": Ben Hoyle, "Publisher makes lite work of the classics," *The Times* (April 14, 2007). "Every abridgment of a good book is a stupid abridgment": III:8 872.

311 "Diverse and undulating": I:15. "Double within ourselves": II:16 570.

312 The subconscious, and Conley's example: Conley. Montaigne's remark that he knew of Rome before he knew of the Louvre: III:9 927. "Embabooned": III:9 928. Conley refers to Cotgrave, R., *A Dictionarie of the French and English Tongues* (London: A. Islip, 1611): *embabouyner* meant "to deceive, gull, ride, bring into a fools Paradise; to give sucke unto; to use like a child."

313 "Where we are to go, if we like": I:26 140.

314 "The hundredth commentator": III:13 995. "See how Plato is moved": II:12 538.

314 "There has been enough about this book": III:13 995. "An able reader": I:24 112. "I have read in Livy": I:26 140.

315 "Minds are threaded together": Woolf, V., *A Passionate Apprentice: The Early Journals*, ed. M. A. Leaska (London: Hogarth, 1990), 178–9. Cited in Lee, H., *Virginia Woolf* (London: Vintage, 1997), 171.

19. Q. How to live? A. Be ordinary and imperfect

317 "I set forth a humble and inglorious life": III:2 740.

318 "I have at least this profit": II:37 698. Also, on becoming habituated to the kidney-stone attacks and to his proximity to death: III:13 1019.

318 "Down a gentle and virtually imperceptible slope": I:20 76. See also III:13 1020, III:13 1030. "Is there anything so sweet": III:13 1021.

318 Finding pleasure in the midst of the attacks: III:5 775. "There is pleasure": III:13 1019.

319   "I am already growing reconciled": II:37 697.

319   "A silly and decrepit pride": III:2 752.

320   "Our being is cemented": III:1 726–7.

320   "Thickened and obscured" and "There is no need": II:20 621–2.

320   Montaigne's letters to Henri IV are included in Montaigne, *The Complete Works*, tr. D. Frame, 1332–6. On his visitors: Frame, *Montaigne* 303–4.

320   Léonor and her children: this daughter Françoise died in early adulthood, but another daughter of Léonor's by a second marriage, Marie de Gamaches, grew up to inherit the Montaigne estate and to pass it on through the family for centuries. Frame: *Montaigne* 303–4. On the Gamaches family: Legros, A., "Gamaches (famille de)," Desan, *Dictionnaire* 425–6.

20. Q. How to live? A. Let life be its own answer

321   This account of Montaigne's death is based mainly on Pasquier's: Pasquier, *Choix de lettres* 48–9, cited Frame, *Montaigne* 304–6. "Pale and weeping servants": I:20 81–2. Bernard Automne: Automne, B., *Commentaire sur les coustumes générales de la ville de Bourdeaux* (Bordeaux: Millanges, 1621), cited Frame, *Montaigne* 305. A discussion of the precise causes of Montaigne's death, hosted by the Société des Amis de Montaigne in 1996, concluded that a stroke may have finished him off: Eyquem, A. (et al)., "La Mort de Montaigne: ses causes rediscutées par la consultation posthume de médecins spécialistes de notre temps," *Bulletin de la Société des Amis de Montaigne*, series 8, no. 4 (juillet–déc. 1996), 7–16.

323   Brach's account: Pierre de Brach to Justus Lipsius, Feb. 4, 1593, cited Villey, *Montaigne devant la postérité* 350–1, and Millet 64–6.

323   "His heart was placed": Montaigne, *Le Livre de raison*, entry for Sept. 13. On his burial in the church, see Legros, A., "Montaigne, Saint Michel de," and Balsamo, J., "Tombeau de Montaigne," in Desan, *Dictionnaire* 683–4 and 983–4 respectively.

323   The Feuillants: Balsamo, J., "Tombeau de Montaigne," in Desan, *Dictionnaire* 983–4. Montaigne on the Feuillants: I:37 205.

325   Inscriptions on tomb: cited Millet 192–3; translated in Frame, *Montaigne* 307–8.

325   Posthumous adventures of Montaigne's remains: Frame, *Montaigne* 306–7, and Balsamo, J., "Tombeau de Montaigne," in Desan, *Dictionnaire* 983–4. Revolutionary reburial: Nicolaï, A., "L'Odyssée des cendres de Montaigne," *Bulletin de la Société des Amis de Montaigne*, series 2, no. 15 (1949–52), 31–45.

326   "Life should be an aim unto itself": III:12 980. Virginia Woolf: in her diary, she wrote, "More & more do I repeat my own version of Montaigne 'It's life that matters.'" Woolf, V., *Diary* III:8 (entry for April 8, 1925). She said much the same in two other entries: II:301 (May 5, 1924) and IV:176 (Sept. 2, 1933), and in her essay on Montaigne: Woolf, V., "Montaigne," in *Essays* IV: 71–81.

327   No longer any need for Montaigne? For an early postwar discussion of this possibility, see Spencer, T., "Montaigne in America," *The Atlantic* 177, no. 3 (March 1946), 91–7. We cannot gratify heaven or earth by committing murder: I:30 181.

SOURCES

Works written, translated, or edited by Montaigne

La Boétie, E. de, *La Mesnagerie de Xenophon, Les regles de mariage de Plutarque, Lettre de consolation de Plutarque à sa femme.* Ed. M. de Montaigne (Paris: F. Morel, 1572 [i.e. 1570]).

Montaigne, M. de, *Oeuvres complètes.* Ed. A. Thibaudet and M. Rat (Paris: Gallimard, 1962). (Old Pléaide edition)

——*The Complete Works.* Tr. C. Cotton, ed. W. Hazlitt (London: J. Templeman, 1842).

——*The Complete Works.* Tr. and ed. D. Frame (London: Everyman, 2005). (Originally published Palo Alto: Stanford University Press, 1943)

——*Le Livre de raison de Montaigne sur l'*Ephemeris historica *de Beuther.* Ed. J. Marchand (Paris: Compagnie Française des Arts Graphiques, 1948). (A facsimile edition of Montaigne's family diary)

——*Essais* (Bordeaux: S. Millanges, 1580).

    2nd edn (Bordeaux: S. Millanges, 1582).

    3rd edn (Paris: J. Richer, 1587).

    "5th edn" (Paris: A. L'Angelier, 1588).

    A facsimile edition of the annotated "Bordeaux" copy of this edition was published as *Montaigne: Essais. Reproduction en fac-similé de l'exemplaire de Bordeaux de 1588.* Ed. R. Bernouilli (Geneve: Slatkine, 1987).

    Ed. M. de Gournay (Paris: A. L'Angelier, 1595).

    Ed. P. Coste (London: J. Tonson & J. W. Watts, 1724).

    Ed. P. Coste (La Haye: P. Gosse & J. Nealme, 1727).

    Ed. P. Villey and V.-L. Saulnier (Paris: PUF, 1965).

    Ed. A. Tournon (Paris: Imprimerie nationale, 1988).

    Ed. J. Balsamo, M. Magnien, and C. Magnien-Simonin (Paris: Gallimard, 2007) (Pléiade).

——*Essayes.* Tr. J. Florio (London: V. Sims for E. Blount, 1603).

    Tr. J. Florio (London: Everyman, 1915–21).

——*Essays.* Tr. C. Cotton (London: T. Basset, M. Gilliflower, W. Hensman, 1685–86).

    Tr. C. Cotton, ed. W. Hazlitt and W. C. Hazlitt (London: Reeves & Turner, 1877).

——*Essays, Selected from Montaigne with a Sketch of the Life of the Author.* Ed. Honoria (London: T. Cadell, W. Davies & E. Harding, 1800).

——*The Complete Essays.* Tr. M.A. Screech (London: Penguin, 2004). (Originally published London: Allen Lane, 1991).

——*Journal de voyage.* Ed. M. de Querlon (Rome & Paris: Le Jay, 1774).

    Ed. F. Garavini (Paris: Gallimard, 1983).

    Ed. F. Rigolot (Paris: PUF, 1992).

——"Travel Journal," in *The Complete Works* (ed. D. Frame), 1047–1270.

Sebond, R. de, *Théologie naturelle.* Tr. M. de Montaigne (Paris: G. Chaudière, 1569).

Other works

Arnould, J.-C. (ed.), *Marie de Gournay et l'édition de 1595 des Essais de Montaigne. Actes du colloque (1995)* (Paris: H. Champion, 1996).

Bailey, A., *Sextus Empiricus and Pyrrhonian Skepticism* (Oxford: Clarendon Press, 2002).

Bellenger, Y., *Montaigne: une fête pour l'esprit* (Paris: Balland, 1987).

Blum, C. and Moreau, F. (eds), *Études montaignistes en hommage à Pierre Michel* (Paris: Champion, 1984).

Blum, C. and Tournon, A. (eds), *Editer les* Essais *de Montaigne. Actes du colloque tenu à l'Université Paris IV-Sorbonne les 27 et 28 janvier 1995* (Paris: H. Champion, 1997).

Boase, A. M., "Montaigne annoté par Florimond de Raemond," *Revue du XVIe siècle*, 15 (1928), 237–278.

——*The Fortunes of Montaigne: A History of the Essays in France, 1580–1669.* (London: Methuen, 1935).

Bouillier, V., *La Renommée de Montaigne en Allemagne* (Paris: Champion, 1921).

Brunschvigg, L., *Descartes et Pascal, lecteurs de Montaigne* (Neuchâtel: La Baconnière, 1942).

Buffum, I., *Studies in the Baroque from Montaigne to Rotrou* (New Haven: Yale University Press, 1957).

Bulletin de la Société des Amis de Montaigne.

Burke, P., *Montaigne* (Oxford: Oxford Paperbacks, 1981).

Butor, M., *Essais sur les* Essais (Paris: Gallimard, 1968).

Cameron, K. (ed.), *Montaigne and His Age* (Exeter: University of Exeter Press, 1981).

Cameron, K. and Willett, L. (eds), *Le visage changeant de Montaigne/The Changing Face of Montaigne* (Paris: H. Champion, 2003).

Charron, P., *De la Sagesse livres trois* (Bordeaux: S. Millanges, 1601).

——*Of Wisdome: Three Bookes*, tr. S. Lennard (London: E. Blount & W. Aspley [n.d.—before 1612]). (Also in facsimile: Amsterdam: Theatrum Orbis Terrarum; New York: Da Capo, 1971)

Clark, S. *Thinking with Demons: The Idea of Witchcraft in Early Modern Europe.* New edn (Oxford: Oxford University Press, 1999).

Cocula, A.-M., *Étienne de La Boétie* (Bordeaux: Sud-Ouest, 1995).

Coleman, D. G., *Montaigne's* Essais (London: Allen & Unwin, 1987).

Compagnon, A., "Montaigne chez les post-modernes," *Critique*, 433–4 (juin-juillet 1983), 522–534.

Conley, T., "A suckling of cities: Montaigne in Paris and Rome," *Montaigne Studies*, 9 (1997), 167–186.

Crouzet, D., *Les Guerriers de Dieu* (Seyssel: Champ Vallon, 1990).

Cunningham, A. and Grell, O. P., *The Four Horsemen of the Apocalypse* (Cambridge: Cambridge University Press, 2000).

Davis, N. Z., *Society and Culture in Early Modern France* (London: Duckworth, 1975).

——"A Renaissance text to the historian's eye: the gifts of Montaigne," *Journal of Medieval and Renaissance Studies*, 15 (1985), 47–56.

Dédéyan, C., *Montaigne chez les amis anglo-saxons* (Paris: Boivin, 1946).

Delumeau, J., *La Peur en Occident, XIVe–XVIIIe siècles* (Paris: Fayard 1978).

Desan, P., "Montaigne en lopins ou les *Essais* à pièce décousues," *Modern Philology*, 88, no. 4 (1991), 278–291.

——*Montaigne dans tous ses états* (Fassano: Schema, 2001).

——*Portraits à l'essai: iconographie de Montaigne* (Paris: H. Champion, 2007).

——(ed.), *Dictionnaire de Montaigne* (Paris: H. Champion, 2004); new edn 2007.

Descartes, R., *Discourse on Method and the Meditations*, tr. F. E. Sutcliffe (Harmondsworth: Penguin, 1998). (Translation of *Discours de la méthode*, 1637 and *Meditationes de prima philosophia*, 1641)

Diefendorf, B., *Beneath the Cross* (Oxford: Oxford University Press, 1991).

Dréano, M., *La Renommée de Montaigne en France au XVIIIe siècle* (Bordeaux: Editions de l'Ouest, 1952).

Eliot, T. S., "The *Pensées* of Pascal," in his *Selected Prose* (London: Faber, 1975).

Emerson, R. W., "Montaigne; or, the Skeptic," from *Representative Men* (1850), in *Collected Works*, ed.

W. E. Williams and D. E. Wilson, Vol. IV (Cambridge, MA & London: Belknap Press of Harvard University Press, 1987), 83–105.

Faguet, E., *Autour de Montaigne* (Paris: H. Champion 1999).

Fleuret, C., *Rousseau et Montaigne* (Paris: A.-G. Nizet, 1980).

Fogel, M., *Marie de Gournay: itinéraires d'une femme savante* (Paris: Fayard, 2004).

Frame, D., *Montaigne in France, 1812–1852* (New York: Columbia University Press, 1940).

——*Montaigne's Discovery of Man* (New York: Columbia University Press, 1955).

——*Montaigne: A Biography* (London: H. Hamilton, 1965).

Friedrich, H., *Montaigne*, tr. D. Eng, ed. P. Desan (Berkeley: University of California Press, 1991). (Translation from the German: *Montaigne*, 1947)

Gardeau, L. and Feytaud, J. de, *Le Château de Montaigne* (Paris: Société des Amis de Montaigne, 1984).

Gournay, M. de, *Oeuvres completes*, ed. J.-C. Arnould, É. Berriot, C. Blum et al. (Paris: H. Champion, 2002).

——*Apology for the Woman Writing and Other Works*, ed. and tr. R. Hillman and C. Quesnel (Chicago & London: Chicago University Press, 2002).

——*Le Proumenoir de Monsieur de Montaigne* (Paris: A. L'Angelier, 1594).

——"Préface" (1595 version), in her edition of Montaigne, *Essais* (Paris: A. L'Angelier, 1595).

——*Preface to the* Essays *of Michel de Montaigne. By his adoptive daughter, Marie Le Jars de Gournay*, tr. and ed. R. Hillman and C. Quesnel, based on the edition by F. Rigolot (Tempe, Arizona: Medieval & Renaissance Texts & Studies, 1998).

——*Égalité des hommes et des femmes* (Paris, 1622).

——*Apologie pour celle qui escrit* (1626 version), and *Peincture des moeurs*, in *L'Ombre de la demoiselle de Gournay* (Paris: J. Libert, 1626).

——*Apologie* (1641 version), in *Les advis ou Les présens de la demoiselle de Gournay*, 3rd edn (Paris: T. du Bray, 1641).

Gray, F., *Le Style de Montaigne* (Paris: Nizet, 1958).

Greengrass, M., *Governing Passions: Peace and Reform in the French Kingdom, 1576–1585* (Oxford: Oxford University Press, 2007).

Guizot, G., *Montaigne: études et fragments*, ed. M. A. Salles (Paris: Hachette, 1899).

Hadot, P., *Philosophy as a Way of Life*, ed. Arnold I. Davidson, tr. M. Chase (Oxford: Blackwell, 1995).

Hale, J., *The Civilization of Europe in the Renaissance* (London: HarperCollins, 1993).

Hartle, A., *Michel de Montaigne: Accidental Philosopher* (Cambridge: Cambridge University Press, 2003).

Haydn, H., *The Counter Renaissance* (New York: Scribner, 1950).

Hazlitt, W., "On the periodical essayists." Lecture V in *Lectures on the Comic Writers* (London: Taylor & Hessey, 1819), 177–208.

Hoffmann, G., *Montaigne's Career* (Oxford: Clarendon Press, 1998).

Holt, Mack P., *The French Wars of Religion*, 2nd edn (Cambridge: Cambridge University Press, 1995).

Horowitz, M. C., "Marie de Gournay, editor of the *Essais* of Michel de Montaigne: a case-study in mentor–protégée friendship," *Sixteenth Century Journal*, 17 (1986), 271–284.

Ilsley, M. H., *A Daughter of the Renaissance: Marie le Jars de Gournay, Her Life and Works* (The Hague: Mouton, 1963).

Insdorf, C., *Montaigne and Feminism* (Chapel Hill, NC: University of North Carolina Press, 1977).

Jeanneret, M., *Perpetuum mobile* (Paris: Argô, 2000).

——*Perpetual Motion: Transforming Shapes in the Renaissance from da Vinci to Montaigne*, tr. N. Pollet (Baltimore & London: Johns Hopkins University Press, 2001).

Kapitaniak P. and Maguin, J.-M. (eds), *Shakespeare et Montaigne: vers un nouvel humanisme* (Montpellier: Société française Shakespeare, 2004).

Keffer, K., *A Publication History of the Rival Transcriptions of Montaigne's Essays* (Lewiston, NY: E. Mellen, 2001).

Knecht, R. J., *The French Civil Wars, 1562–1598* (Harlow: Longman, 2000).

——*The Rise and Fall of Renaissance France* (London: Fontana, 1996); new edn: Oxford: Blackwell, 2001.

La Boétie, E. de, *Mémoire sur la pacification des troubles*, ed. M. Smith (Geneva: Droz, 1983).

——*De la Servitude volontaire, ou, Contr'un*, ed. M. Smith (Geneva: Droz, 1987).

——*Slaves by Choice*, tr. M. Smith (Egham, Surrey: Runnymede Books, 1988).

——"Of Voluntary Servitude," tr. D. L. Schaefer, in Schaefer (ed.), *Freedom Over Servitude: Montaigne, La Boétie, and* On Voluntary Servitude (Westport, CT: Greenwood Press, 1998), 189–222.

Lacouture, J., *Montaigne à cheval* (Paris: Seuil, 1996).

La Croix du Maine, François Grudé, seigneur de, "Messire Michel de Montagne," in *Premier volume de la Bibliothèque du sieur de la Croix-dumaine* (Paris: Abel L'Angelier, 1584), 328–330.

Lamartine, A., *Correspondance*, 2e série (1807–29) ed. C. Croisille and M.-R. Morin (Paris: H. Champion, 2004).

Langer, U. (ed.), *The Cambridge Companion to Montaigne* (Cambridge: Cambridge University Press, 2005).

Lazard, M., *Michel de Montaigne* (Paris: Fayard, 1992).

Legros, A., *Essais sur poutres. Peintures et inscriptions chez Montaigne* (Paris: Klincksieck, 2000).

Léry, J. de, *History of a Voyage to the Land of Brazil*, tr. J. Whatley (Berkeley: University of California Press, 1990). (Translation of *Histoire d'un voyage fait en la terre du Brésil*, 1578).

Lestringant, F., *Cannibals: The Discovery and Representation of the Cannibal from Columbus to Jules Verne*, tr. R. Morris (Cambridge: Polity Press, 1997). (Translation of *Le cannibale*, 1994)

Levin, H., *The Myth of the Golden Age in the Renaissance* (London: Faber, 1970).

Lüthy, Herbert, "Montaigne, or The Art of Being Truthful," in H. Bloom (ed.), *Michel de Montaigne* (New York: Chelsea House, 1987), 11–28. (Originally published in *Encounter*, Nov. 1953, 33–44)

Macé-Scaron, J., *Montaigne: notre nouveau philosophe* (Paris: Plon, 2002).

Magnien, M., *Etienne de la Boétie* (Paris: Memini Paris, CNRS Éditions, 1997).

Magnien-Simonin, C., *Une Vie de Montaigne, ou Le sommaire discours sur la vie de Michel Seigneur de Montaigne* (Paris: H. Champion, 1992).

Malebranche, N., *The Search After Truth*, tr. and ed. T. M. Lennon and P. J. Olscamp (Cambridge: Cambridge University Press, 1997). (Translation of *La Recherche de la verité*, 1674)

Marcetteau-Paul, A., *Montaigne propriétaire foncier: inventaire raisonné du* Terrier de Montaigne *conservé à la Bibliothèque municipale de Bordeaux* (Paris: H. Champion, 1995).

Marchi, D., *Montaigne among the Moderns* (Providence, RI & Oxford: Berghahn Books, 1994).

Maskell, D., "Quel est le dernier état authentique des Essais de Montaigne?" in *Bibliothèque d'humanisme et Renaissance*, 40 (1978), 85–103.

Mathieu-Castellani, G., *Montaigne: l'écriture de l'essai* (Paris: PUF, 1988).

——*Montaigne ou la vérité du mensonge* (Geneva: Droz, 2000).

McFarlane, I. D. and Maclean, Ian (eds), *Montaigne: Essays in Memory of Richard Sayce* (Oxford: Clarendon Press, 1982).

McGowan, M., *Montaigne's Deceits: The Art of Persuasion in the* Essais (London: University of London Press, 1974).

Merleau-Ponty, M., "Lecture de Montaigne," in *Éloge de la philosophie et autres essais* (Paris: Gallimard, 1960), 321–347.

Michel, P. et al. (eds), *Montaigne et les Essais 1580–1980: Actes du Congrès de Bordeaux* (Paris: H. Champion; Geneva: Slatkine, 1983).

Millet, O., *La Première Réception des* Essais *de Montaigne (1580–1640)* (Paris: H. Champion, 1995).

Monluc, B. de, *The Commentaries of Messire Blaize de Montluc* (London: A. Clark for H. Brome, 1674). (Translation of *Commentaires*, 1592)

Montaigne Studies

Nakam, G., *Montaigne et son temps: les événements et les* Essais (Paris: Nizet, 1982).

——*Les* Essais *de Montaigne: mirroir et procès de leur temps* (Paris: Nizet, 1984).

——*Le dernier Montaigne* (Paris: H. Champion, 2002).

Nietzsche, F., *Untimely Meditations*, tr. R. J. Hollingdale (Cambridge: Cambridge University Press, 1983). (Translation of *Unzeitgemässe Betrachtungen*, 1876)

——*Human, All Too Human*, tr. M. Faber and S. Lehmann (London: Penguin, 1994). (Translation of *Menschliches, allzu menschliches*, 1878)

——*Daybreak*, tr. R. J. Hollingdale (Cambridge: Cambridge University Press, 1982). (Translation of *Morgenröte*, 1881)

——*The Gay Science*, tr. W. Kaufman (New York: Random House, 1991). Translation of *Die fröhliche Wissenschaft*, 1882)

Nussbaum, M. C., *The Therapy of Desire* (Princeton: Princeton University Press, 1994).

O'Brien, J., "Are we reading what Montaigne wrote?" *French Studies*, 58 (2004), 527–532.

Pascal, B., *Pensées and Other Writings*, tr. A. and H. Levi (Oxford: Oxford World's Classics, 1999).

Pasquier, E., *Choix de lettres*, ed. D. Thickett (Geneva: Droz, 1956).

——*Lettres historiques pour les années 1556–1594*, ed. D. Thickett (Geneva: Droz, 1966).

Plato, *Symposium*, tr. W. Hamilton (Harmondsworth: Penguin, 1951).

Plutarch, *Moralia*, tr. W. C. Helmbold. Loeb edn (London: W. Heinemann; Cambridge, MA: Harvard University Press, 1936–57).

Popkin, R., *The History of Skepticism from Erasmus to Spinoza* (Berkeley: University of California Press, 1979).

Pouilloux, J-Y., *Lire les* Essais *de Montaigne* (Paris: Maspero, 1970).

Quint, D., *Montaigne and the Quality of Mercy: Ethical and Political Themes in the* Essais (Princeton: Princeton University Press, 1998).

Rabelais, F., *The Complete Works*, tr. J. Le Clerc (New York: The Modern Library, 1944).

Raemond, F. de, *Erreur populaire de la papesse Jane*, 2nd edn (Bordeaux: S. Millanges, 1594).

——*L'Antichrist* (Lyon: Jean Pillehotte, 1597).

Rigolot, F. *Les Métamorphoses de Montaigne* (Paris: PUF, 1988).

Rousseau, J-J., *Discourse on the Origin of Inequality*, tr. F. Philip, ed. P. Coleman (Oxford: Oxford University Press, 1994). (Translation of *Discours sur l'origin et les fondaments de l'inégalité parmi les hommes*, 1755)

——*Émile*, tr. Allan Bloom (London: Penguin, 1991). (Translation of *Émile*, 1762)

——*Confessions*, tr. A. Scholar (Oxford: Oxford University Press, 2000). (Translation of *Les Confessions*, 1782)

Sayce, R. A., *The Essays of Montaigne: A Critical Exploration* (London: Weidenfeld & Nicolson, 1972).

Sayce, R. A. and Maskell, D., *A Descriptive Bibliography of Montaigne's Essais 1580–1700*. (London: Bibliographical Society & Modern Humanities Research Association, 1983).

Schaefer, D. L., *The Political Philosophy of Montaigne* (Ithaca & London: Cornell University Press, 1990).

——(ed.), *Freedom Over Servitude: Montaigne, La Boétie, and On Voluntary Servitude* (Westport, CT: Greenwood Press, 1998).

Screech, M. A., *Montaigne and Melancholy* (Harmondsworth: Penguin, 1991).

Seneca, *Ad Lucilium epistulae morales [Letters to Lucilius]*, tr. Richard M. Gummere. Loeb edn (Cambridge, MA: Harvard University Press; London: W. Heinemann, 1917–25).

——*Dialogues and Letters* (Harmondsworth: Penguin, 2005).

Sextus Empiricus, *Outlines of Skepticism*, ed. J. Annas and J. Barnes (Cambridge: Cambridge University Press, 2000).

Smith, M. C., *Montaigne and Religious Freedom: The Dawn of Pluralism* (Geneva: Droz, 1991).

Starobinski, J., *Montaigne in Motion*, tr. A. Goldhammer (Chicago: Chicago University Press, 1985). (Translation of *Montaigne en mouvement*, 1982)

Sterling, J., "Montaigne and his Essays," *London and Westminster Review*, 29 (1838), 321–352.

Supple, J. J., *Arms versus Letters: The Military and Literary Ideals in the* Essays *of Montaigne* (Oxford: Clarendon Press, 1984).

Tetel, A. (ed.), *Montaigne et Marie de Gournay: actes du colloque international de Duke* (Paris: H. Champion, 1997).

Thevet, A., *Les Singularitez de la France antarctique* (Paris: Les heretiers de Maurice de la Porte, 1557).

Tilley, A., "Montaigne's interpreters," in his *Studies in the French Renaissance* (Cambridge: Cambridge University Press, 1922), 259–293.

Trinquet, R., *La Jeunesse de Montaigne* (Paris: Nizet, 1972).

Villey, P., *Les Sources et l'évolution des* Essais *de Montaigne* (Paris: Hachette, 1933).

——*Montaigne devant la postérité* (Paris: Boivin, 1935).

Willett, L., "Romantic Renaissance in Montaigne's chapel," in Yannick Portebois and Nicholas Terpstra (eds), *The Renaissance in the Nineteenth Century—Le XIXe Siècle renaissant* (Toronto: Center for Reformation and Renaissance Studies, 2003), 217–240.

Woolf, L., *The Journey Not the Arrival Matters* (London: Hogarth, 1969).

Woolf, V., *The Diary of Virginia Woolf*, ed. A. Oliver Bell (London: Penguin, 1980–85).

——"Montaigne," in *Essays*, ed. A. McNeillie (London: Hogarth, 1986–), IV: 71–81.

Yates, F.A., *John Florio: The Life of an Italian in Shakespeare's England* (Cambridge: Cambridge University Press, 1934).

Zweig, S., *The World of Yesterday* (Lincoln, NE: University of Nebraska Press, 1943).

—— "Montaigne," in *Europäisches Erbe*, ed. R. Friedenthal (Frankfurt am Main: S. Fischer, 1960), 7–81.

LIST OF ILLUSTRATIONS

INDEX

⊞ OTHER PRESS

You might also enjoy these titles from our list:

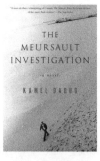

THE MEURSAULT INVESTIGATION
by Kamel Daoud

He was the brother of "the Arab" killed by the infamous Meursault, the antihero of Camus's classic novel. Harun gives his brother a story and a name — Musa — and describes the events that led to Musa's casual murder on a dazzlingly sunny beach.

"A tour-de-force reimagining of Camus's *The Stranger*, from the point of view of the mute Arab victims."
—*The New Yorker*

THE GLASS ROOM by Simon Mawer
A FINALIST FOR THE MAN BOOKER PRIZE

A stunning portrait of a family trying to impose order and beauty on a world on the brink of chaos at the outbreak of World War II

"Achieves what all great novels must: the creation of an utterly absorbing world the reader can scarcely bear to leave. Exciting, profoundly affecting, and altogether wonderful." —*Daily Mail*

KATHERINE CARLYLE by Rupert Thomson

Unmoored by her mother's death, Katherine Carlyle abandons the set course of her life and starts out on a mysterious journey to the ends of the world.

"*Katherine Carlyle* left me stunned and amazed. It's a masterpiece."
—PHILIP PULLMAN, author of the best-selling His Dark Materials trilogy

Also recommended:

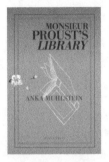

MONSIEUR PROUST'S LIBRARY
by Anka Muhlstein

A witty and erudite account of French history through
the eyes of Marcel Proust

"Looks at *In Search of Lost Time* by way of the
books that Proust himself read and the way they
influenced both the book and its characters...
A marvelous book." —*Publishing Perspectives*

THE IMPOSSIBLE EXILE:
STEFAN ZWEIG AT THE END OF THE WORLD
by George Prochnik

An original study of exile, told through the biography
of Austrian writer Stefan Zweig

"Subtle, prodigiously researched, and enduringly
human throughout, *The Impossible Exile* is a
portrait of a man and of his endless flight."
—*The Economist*

ALL DAYS ARE NIGHT by Peter Stamm

A novel about survival, self-reliance, and art,
by Peter Stamm, finalist for the 2013 Man Booker
International Prize

"A postmodern riff on *The Magic Mountain*...
a page-turner." —*The Atlantic*

"Air[s] the psychological implications of our beauty
obsession and the insidious ways in which it can
obscure selfhood." —*New Republic*

█ OTHER PRESS

www.otherpress.com